CONTENTS

SECTION 1: STARTING POINTS

SECTION 2: PSYCHOLOGY TOPICS

STARTING POINTS

In this section:

HOW TO USE THIS BOOK

STRUCTURE OF THE BOOK

The key aim of this book is to guide you in studying and revising A level Psychology. It is not intended to be a complete guide to the subject, but should be used as a companion to your textbooks, which it is designed to complement rather than duplicate.

We have divided the book into three sections. **Section One: Starting Points** contains syllabus information and study tips – all the information to get you started on your A level study, plus advice on organising your coursework, planning your revision and tips on how to tackle the examination itself. Use the **Syllabus Checklists** to find out exactly where you can find the study units relevant to your particular syllabus.

Section Two: Psychology Topics, the main body of the text, contains the core of A level Psychology. It has been devised to make study easy, and enjoyable, and has been divided into chapters to cover the themes you encounter in your syllabus. The chapters are divided into sections and units, each covering a topic of study. The **Chapter Roundup** at the end of each chapter provides a brief summary of each unit. To reinforce what you have read and learned, there is an **Illustrative Question** at the end of each chapter. All questions are taken from papers recently set by the examination boards. The tutorial notes and suggested answers give you practical guidance on how to answer A level questions, and provide additional information relevant to that topic. There is also a **Question Bank**, with further examples of A level exam questions for you to attempt, and notes highlighting important points and pitfalls.

Section Three: Test Run focuses on the end of your course. First, you can assess your progress using the **Test Your Knowledge Quiz** and analysis chart. Then, as a final test, you should attempt the **Mock Exam**, under timed conditions. This will give you invaluable examination practice and, together with the notes specially written by the author, will help you judge how close you are to achieving your A level pass.

USING YOUR SYLLABUS CHECKLIST

You will find it useful to use our checklist to record what you have covered, and how far you still have to go.

The checklist for each examination is in two parts. First, there is the outline of the syllabus, followed by a list of where you will find these topics covered in this book. Although the checklists are detailed, it is not possible to print entire syllabuses. **You are therefore strongly recommended to obtain an official copy of the syllabus for your examination and consult it when the need arises**. The examination board addresses are given after the syllabus checklists. When you have revised a topic, make a note of the date in the column provided, and if you have attempted relevant questions, note these as well.

Second, there is a Paper Analysis which gives you useful details of the examination such as the time allocated for each paper and the number of questions which have to be answered. The different types of question which may be set are explained in detail later in the section on 'The Examination'.

SYLLABUS CHECKLISTS AND PAPER ANALYSIS

ASSOCIATED EXAMINING BOARD (AEB)
A level (0675) and AS level (0975), modular and terminal routes.

Section Syllabus topic	Covered in Unit No.	Completed on (date)	Questions attempted
1 Social psychology			
1.1 Social cognition	1.1		
1.2 Social relationships	1.2		
1.3 Social influence	1.3		
1.4 Pro- and antisocial behaviour	1.4		
2 Comparative psychology			
2.1 Evolutionary determinants of behaviour	2.1		
2.2 Reproductive strategies	2.2		
2.3 Kinship and social behaviour	2.3		
2.4 Behaviour analysis	2.4		
3 Bio-psychology			
3.1 Basic neural and hormonal processes and their influence on behaviour	3.1		
3.2 Cortical functions	3.2		
3.3 Awareness	3.3		
3.4 Motivation, emotion and stress	3.4		
4 Atypical development and abnormal behaviour			
4.1 Atypical development	4.1		
4.2 Conceptions and models of abnormality	4.2		
4.3 Psychopathology	4.3		
4.4 Therapeutic approaches	4.4		
5 Cognitive psychology			
5.1 Perceptual processes	5.1		
5.2 Attention and performance limitations	5.2		
5.3 Memory	5.3		
5.4 Language and thought	5.4		
6 Development psychology			
6.1 Early socialisation	6.1		
6.2 Cognitive development	6.2		
6.3 Social behaviour and diversity in development	6.3		
6.4 Adolescence, adulthood and old age	6.4		
7 Perspectives in psychology			
7.1 Approaches to psychology	7.1		
7.2 Controversies in psychology	7.2		
7.3 Ethical issues in psychology	7.3		
8 Research methods in psychology			
8.1 The nature of psychological enquiry	8.1		
8.2 The design and implementation of investigations	8.2		
8.3 Data analysis	8.3		

Paper analysis

Terminal route, A level There will be an end-of-year examination in the Summer only.

Paper 1 *Coursework* 20% of total mark   two investigations
The investigation should be between 1,200 and 2,000 words.
It must be related to the syllabus.
The investigations must include one experimental and one non-experimental method and must be drawn from a different syllabus section.

Paper 2 *3 hours* 40% of total mark
Answer four questions from at least three sections (sections 1, 2, 3 and 4). Each section contains four questions, one from each subsection.

Paper 3 *3 hours* 40% of total mark

Answer one question from sections 5, 6 and 7. Each section contains four questions, one from each unit of that section.
Answer all questions from section 8.

Modular route, A level There will be modular examinations in Spring and Summer each year.

	Coursework	20% of total mark	Two investigations as above
Module 4	*1½ hours*	20% of total mark	Sections 1 and 2, answer one question from each section.
Module 5	*1½ hours*	20% of total mark	Sections 3 and 4, answer one question from each section.
Module 6	*1½ hours*	20% of total mark	Sections 5 and 6, answer one question from each section.
Module 7	*1½ hours*	20% of total mark	Answer+ one question from section 7 and all questions from section 8.

Each section contains four questions, one from each unit of that section.

Terminal and modular route, AS level

	Coursework	20% of total mark	One investigation.
Modules 4–6	*1½ hours*	40% of total mark	Select any one module from A level.
Module 7	*1½ hours*	40% of total mark	As module 7 for A level above.

Notes

- Quality of language will be assessed in all written papers and coursework.
- The same questions will be used in the terminal and modular Summer exams.

4

NORTHERN EXAMINATIONS AND ASSESSMENT BOARD (NEAB)
A level end–of–course (4476), A level modular (4477)
AS level end–of–course (3476), AS level modular (3477)

Section	Syllabus topic	Covered in Unit No.	Completed on (date)	Questions attempted
PS1	Perspectives in psychology			
	The study of psychology	7.1.1, 7.2.2		
	The biological approach	2.1.1, 3.1.1, 3.2.2, 4.3.1		
	Behaviourist and cognitive approaches	2.4.1, 7.1.1, 5.2.1		
	Person-centred approaches	3.4.1, 4.2.2, 6.3.1, 6.4.2, 7.1.1		
	Methods and debate in psychology	7.1.1, 7.1.2, 8.1.1, 8.1.2		
PS2	Research methods and data analysis			
	Methods	7.2.1, 8.1.1, 8.1.2, 8.2		
	Issues	8.1.1, 8.1.2, 8.3.2		
	Data analysis	8.3.1		
	Drawing conclusions/representing data	8.3.1		
PS3	Issues in psychology			
	Human relationships	1.2.1, 1.2.2, 6.1.1		
	Human ageing	6.4.3		
	Psychology amd work	1.3.3, 9.2.1, 9.2.2		
	Substance abuse	9.1.1		
	Paranormal phenomena	9.1.2		
PS4	Atypical psychology			
	Definition and classification	4.2.1, 4.2.2, 4.4.2		
	Treatment	4.4.1, 4.4.2		
	Emotional disorders	4.3.1, 4.3.2, 4.3.3		
	Research in atypical psychology	4.4.1, 8.1.1, 8.1.2		
PS5	Social psychology			
	Attitudes	1.1.3		
	Social influence	1.3.1, 1.3.3		
	Groups	1.3.2, 1.3.3		
	Social cognition	1.1.1, 1.1.2		
	Applied social psychology	1.1.1, 1.3.3, 5.3.5		
PS6	Child development			
	Issues	2.3.3		
	Cognitive	5.4.1, 6.2.1		
	Social	6.1.1, 6.3.2, 6.3.3		
	Moral development	6.3.1		
PS7	Cognitive psychology			
	Perception	5.1.1, 5.2.1		
	Remembering and forgetting	5.3.1, 5.3.3, 5.3.4		
	Language	2.4.3, 5.4.1, 5.4.4		
	Thinking and problem-solving	5.4.3		
	Artificial intelligence	5.4.3		
PS8	Health psychology			
	Health and illness	9.3.1		
	Psychology aspects of illness	9.3.2, 9.3.3		
	Lifestyles and health	4.3.4, 9.3.4		
	Stress and illness	3.4.3		
	Coping and stress management	3.4.4		

Section	Syllabus topic	Covered in Unit No.	Completed on (date)	Questions attempted
PS9 Psychology in education				
	Learning and its assessment	6.2.2, 7.2.1, 9.4.1		
	Reading	5.4.2, 9.2.1, 9.4.2		
	Social dynamics in the classroom	3.4.1, 3.4.3, 4.1.1, 6.3.1, 9.4.1		
	Assessment and modification of behaviour	4.4.1, 9.4.3		
	Special needs	4.1.1, 4.1.2, 4.1.3		

Paper analysis

A level end-of-course scheme (4476)

Paper 1   *3 hours*   41% of total mark   Section A (PS01), section B (PS02) and section C (PS05). Answer four questions, at least one from each section.
PS02 contains two pieces of stimulus material on research methods with short-answer questions.
PS01 and PS05 contain five questions each.

Paper 2   *3 hours*   41% of total mark
Section A (PS06), section B (PS07) and section C (PS03, PS04, PS08, PS09). Answer four questions, at least one from each section.
Each section contains four or five questions.

Practical skills   18% of total mark, see below.

A level modular scheme (4477)

Five *compulsory* modules

  Module   PS02   *1½ hours*   13⅔% of total mark
          Answer both questions (two pieces of stimulus material on research methods with short-answer questions).

  Modules   PS01, PS05, PS06 and PS07   Each paper   *1½ hours*   13⅔% of total mark
          Answer all questions from section A (short answer questions), in 30 minutes.
          Answer two (out of five) questions from section B (essays) in 1 hour.

One *optional* module, choose from modules PS03, PS04, PS08 and PS09   Paper same as above.

Practical skills   3% from each module, contributes 18% to total mark.

AS level end-of-course scheme (3476)

Paper 1   *3 hours*   82% of total mark   This will be the same paper as for the A level.
Practical skills   18% of total mark, see below.

AS level modular scheme (3477)

3 *compulsory* modules

  Module   PS02   *1½ hours*   27⅓% of total mark   As for A level, module PS02.
  Modules   PS01 and PS05   Each paper   *1½ hours*   27⅓% of total mark
          As for A level, modular papers.

Practical skills   6% from each module, contributes 18% to total mark.

Practical skills assessment
- Modular route, one assessment for each skill in each module.
- A level end-of-course scheme, two assessments per skill; AS level, one assessment per skill.
- There are 4 skills: designing, implementing, interpreting and communicating.
- There is no specification about the type or length of each activity.

Notes
- A level candidates may take one optional module from a related science syllabus.
- Quality of language will be assessed in section B of the module tests or the whole of end-of-course paper.
- The questions in the end-of-course and modular Summer exams are similar, but the modular ones are shorter (20 marks rather than 30 marks).

OXFORD & CAMBRIDGE EXAMINATIONS & ASSESSMENT COUNCIL (OCEAC)
Modular A level (9674) and AS level (8501) [NB these codes may change]

Section	Syllabus topic	Covered in Unit No.	Completed on (date)	Questions attempted
Themes				
	Methodology	7.2.1, 8.1.1, 8.1.2, 8.2.1		
	Perspectives	7.1.1, 7.1.2		
	Ethics	7.3.1, 7.3.2, 7.3.3		
Core studies Consult the syllabus for a list of 24 named studies				
	Cognitive psychology	4.1.3, 5.3.1, 5.3.2, 5.3.3, 5.3.4, 5.3.5		
	Social interaction	1.2. 1, 1.2.2, 1.2.3, 1.3.1, 1.4.1, 6.3.3		
	Developmental psychology	1.4.2, 6.1.1, 6.1.2, 6.2.1, 6.2.3		
	Social cognition	1.1.2, 1.1.3, 7.2.1, 8.1.1, 9.3.3		
	Abnormal psychology	4.2.1, 4.2.2, 4.2.3, 4.3.1, 4.3.2, 4.3.3, 4.4.1		
	Physiological psychology	3.1.1, 3.1.2, 3.1.3, 3.3.3, 3.4.2		
	Comparative psychology	2.1.1, 2.1.3, 2.2.1, 2.3.3, 2.4.3, 2.4.4, 7.3.2		
	Culture and identity	1.4.4, 5.1.4, 6.1.3, 6.2.3, 6.3.2, 7.2.1, 7.2.3		
Specialist choices				
	Psychology and education	4.1.1, 4.1.3, 7.1.1, 7.2.1, 9.4.1, 9.4.3		
	Psychology and health	3.4.3, 3.4.4, 9.1.1, 9.3.2, 9.3.3, 9.3.4		
	Psychology and the environment	1.4.1, 2.4.1, 9.5.1		
	Psychology and organisations	1.3.2, 1.3.3, 3.4.1, 9.2.1, 9.2.3		
	Psychology and sport	1.3.2, 1.3.3, 1.4.2, 2.4.1, 3.4.1, 6.3.3		

Paper analysis

A level modular syllabus (9674)

Paper 1   Core studies   *3 hours*   40% of total mark

Section A: twenty compulsory short–answer questions on core studies.

Section B: one stimulus question (out of three) requiring an extended answer.

Section C: one stimulus question (out of three) requiring an extended answer.

Sections B and C relate the core studies to research issues.

Paper 2   Coursework folder 1   10% of total mark, 5% each

One piece of practical work, about 1–1,500 words in length.

One assignment, about 1,000 words in length, covering psychological assumptions, evidence, and applications.

NB any work that is excessively long will incur a mark penalty.

Paper 3   Coursework folder 2   10% of total mark

One piece of practical work.

One assignment.

Paper 4   Research methods   *1½ hours*   10% of total mark

Candidates are given source material one week before the examination. There is a choice of two sources and a list of tasks.

Paper 5   Specialist choices   *3 hours*   30% of total mark

Answer any three stimulus–response structured essays out of eight, two questions will be set on each specialist choice.

Candidates may take:

Module 1 (papers 1 and 2) in the first year.

Module 2 (papers 3, 4, and 5) at any time up to four years later.

Or take modules 1 and 2 at the end of the course.

AS level modular syllabus (8501)

Paper 1	*3 hours*	80% of total mark	As for A level.
Paper 2	Coursework folder	20% of total mark	As for A level.

EXAMINATION BOARD ADDRESSES

AEB   The Associated Examining Board
Stag Hill House, Guildford, Surrey GU2 5XJ
Tel: 01483 506506

NEAB   Northern Examinations and Assessment Board
12 Harter Street, Manchester M1 6HL
Tel: 0161 953 1180

OCEAC   Oxford and Cambridge Examinations and Assessment Council
Purbeck House, Purbeck Road, Cambridge CB2 2PU
Tel: 01223 411211

1 Hills Road, Cambridge CB1 2EU
Tel. 01223 553311

STUDYING AND REVISING PSYCHOLOGY

THE DIFFERENCE BETWEEN GCSE AND A/AS LEVEL

Psychology as a subject is probably new to you, unlike some of the other A levels you may have chosen to study.

There is a quantitative difference between A levels and GCSE, generally speaking A levels involve more hours in the classroom, more work at home, longer essays, longer examinations, and there may be more examinations.

There is also a qualitative difference. A levels require a thoughtful and critical approach rather than simply churning out a previously learned set of facts. The emphasis is on understanding and applying a body of knowledge (facts) to novel situations, organising material into a coherent whole, using empirical data, being able to evaluate all research and make comparisons. The words which are used in A level questions indicate the kind of thinking expected, for example: assess, discuss, justify, analyse, consider, contrast. This approach is also reflected in the kinds of question which are set; the examiner aims to prevent the use of prepared essays which only demonstrate a candidate's ability to learn. It is also reflected in the fact that there are no right answers, there are only legitimate answers which must be supported by psychologically informed argument and research.

Opinions are a feature of A level study. You must learn to form your own which are based on empirical evidence. Reading psychological material will help you form opinions; arguments and discussions with classmates and teachers will help too, as will writing essays. Psychological journals are a good source of recent empirical data, and some are specifically written with students in mind.

AS levels

AS levels offer an alternative to A level. They enable students to study more subjects while maintaining the depth of study. This means that less time is spent studying the subject, the examination is shorter and the coursework less, but the syllabus remains as deep and the questions are as difficult. The latest syllabus revisions mean that AS levels are a subset of the full A level syllabus so that you can do an AS level and then decide to turn this into an A level after a further year's study.

STUDY STRATEGIES AND TECHNIQUES

Many of the ideas discussed below are drawn directly from psychology, since psychology is the study of behaviour.

1. *Enjoy it.* You do best at things you enjoy (and vice versa).

2. *Organisation.* The key to both understanding and remembering the material is a logical framework for organising the facts. Ausubel called this 'advance organisers', Bruner talked of categories and coding systems. Sensible organisation serves to make the material more meaningful, which is also linked with making it more memorable.

3. *Writing notes.* The purpose of notes is to record highly condensed material from which you can revise later. Organising material also makes it more meaningful and helps memory.
   - Use abbreviations, your own or standard ones (Ψ stands for 'psychology').
   - Highlight keywords.
   - Record information in diagrammatic summaries. Visual information is memorable.
   - Write numbered lists.
   - Flexibility helps for reorganising: use a loose-leaf file, a card index, or word processor.

④ *Class notes*. Many students start the year with the intention of copying up their class notes after each lesson. This is probably a waste of time, unrealistic and usually not done. A more pragmatic solution might be to read the notes after each lesson, writing in additional comments or side headings and using a highlighter to mark key words. This helps to consolidate the day's learning and to make the notes more useful later.

⑤ *Book notes*. Brevity is difficult. Either make notes as you read and then do the same as with class notes, or force yourself only to write after each section of the book using the PQRST method (below).

⑥ *Cross-syllabus notes*. Essays often require material from several areas of the syllabus, therefore it helps to 'limber up' by making notes that connect different topics across the syllabus. It also makes you organise the material differently, thus improving your memory.

⑦ *Personal glossary*. Keep a list of key words and empirical data, for later revision.

⑧ *Speed reading*. Learn to skim through long texts and select relevant data. Some books give key words in bold, italic, or underlined text which helps speed reading. There are also methods for reading which improve recall (variously called the SQ3R or PQRST methods):

• Survey or preview the chapter.	S	P 1
• List questions to actively involve yourself.	Q	Q 1
• Read the text.	R	R 1
• Recall or self-recite.	R	S 1
• Review or test yourself.	R	T E

⑨ *Handwriting and expressive skills*. If you know that these are likely to cause problems for you, practise them.

⑩ *Targets and work plans*. Success is related to motivation. Find ways to increase yours. It helps to have:
  • Realistic targets so that you can have a sense of achievement, otherwise you end up feeling the work is a never-ending task.
  • Rewards which are task- or time-related, such as 'After each hour I can have a snack'.
  • A study timetable with a record of how much you did and a list of things to do.
  • A pleasant place to study. You can then associate studying with a sense of relaxation.

⑪ *Wider reading*. It is important to go beyond your teachers' notes and to use more than one book, as each person and book are inevitably biased. Be sure to include recent material; psychological journals are useful.

⑫ *Revision techniques* are closely related to study skills. In the act of studying you are also learning and revising. The notes you make during study will later be used for revision. See 'Revision Techniques', below.

⑬ *Individual differences*. Different people find different strategies more effective. Therefore part of what you are learning is to select your best techniques.

WRITING ESSAYS

① *Essay plans*. This is an important skill for writing timed essays. Practising the skill under non-stressful conditions helps reduce stress in exams.
  • 'Free associate' to every significant word of the question; this helps to understand the question.
  • Brainstorming: write down everything you can think about in the broad area.
  • Go through each topic area in the psychology syllabus (e.g. section headings in this book) to see if there is anything relevant to the question.
  • Reread your notes, cross out anything which is irrelevant to the question.
  • Organise and place what's left in a logical order; you now have a structure for your essay.

② *Description and evaluation*. The AEB divides knowledge into two skill clusters. Your answers should always contain material from both areas:

- *Description* (Skill A): knowledge and understanding of psychological concepts, theories, evidence and applications. The Skill A cluster can also be demonstrated through the accuracy, detail and coherence of your answer.
- *Analysis and evaluation* (Skill B): critical awareness of your knowledge. This can be demonstrated by noting positive and negative features of the concepts, theories, evidence and applications you mention. You might comment on methodology and usefulness. The Skill B cluster can also be demonstrated by drawing on material from across the syllabus (eclecticism) and commenting on individual, social and cultural diversity, as well as through selectivity and coherent elaboration.

③ *Criticism*

- Theories can be criticised in terms of their quality, coherence, comprehensiveness (in terms of known evidence), alternatives, falsifiability, ability to generate empirical research, and cultural specificity.
- Empirical evidence can be criticised in terms of its purpose, type of subjects used, any special apparatus, nature of experimental (or other) procedure, findings, conclusions.
- Criticism can be both positive and negative. A good essay should present a balanced view.

④ *Depth and breadth*. You can present a few studies/theories but in considerable detail (depth) or you can present a number of studies/theories but, because of time constraints, this will have to be somewhat superficial (breadth). Both can gain high marks since markers are aware of the trade-off between the two.

⑤ *Avoid*

- Common-sense or anecdotal material. Psychology aims to be an objective, empirical science and you must convince the examiner that your answer is drawn from what you have learned rather than being based on casual knowledge.
- The 'machine gun' approach. This is unlikely to do well because of a lack of selectivity.
- Waffle. The person marking the essay easily recognises such material.

COURSEWORK

Coursework is stressful in a different way to exams. Because you have a large amount of time you may feel pressured to go to extraordinary lengths to produce a brilliant piece of work. This is not necessary. Your aim should be maximum gains for minimum effort.

Maximum gains

- It's the report that gets the marks.
- Experimental research and design is a compulsory question on the written papers, conducting your research will help with answering this question.
- Writing the introduction and discussion part of the report leads to a greater understanding of that part of the syllabus.
- All results, significant or not, lead to worthwhile discussions.

Minimum efforts

- The best design is a simple one: one hypothesis, one group of participants.
- Don't reinvent the wheel: there are marks for good design or for minimal teacher guidance, but not for originality of design or materials. Replicate past research, use existing questionnaires.
- Data collection can also be very time consuming so select a design which minimises this. You could test a group of people rather than individuals, or use data which has already been collected, such as exam results (but you must respect confidentiality).
- Enjoy it. Choose topics of interest to you, but be guided by the advice of your teacher about what is suitable or permissible.

Ethics and public relations

Ethical considerations are paramount to any research. You should be familiar with ethical guidelines (see units 7.3.1 and 7.3.2). In particular do not use any drugs or alcohol, do not use any restricted psychological tests and only use children or animals under close supervision. You are in a position of responsibility when acting as a researcher. Do not treat your subjects trivially even if they are friends or family. Remember, for many people you may be their first and last close encounter with psychology. Do nothing which will bring psychology into disrepute.

Writing the report

Your report should look like a journal article. The AEB recommends that the total length of the report should be between 1,200 and 2,000 words, excluding tables, figures and appendices. You can use the following divisions:

1 *Title*. Should give the reader a good idea what the study is about, not too long or vague.

2 *Table of contents* (optional).

3 *Abstract* (summary, about 150 words). This gives the reader a chance to find out the bare essentials without going any further. Be concise.
   - *One sentence summary* giving, for example, the topic(s) to be studied, the hypothesis, some brief theoretical background, similar research findings.
   - *Participants* and *setting*: who, when, where, how many, what groups.
   - *Method*: what design, experimental treatment, questionnaires, tests.
   - *Major findings*, statistics, significance levels.
   - *What does it mean?* Mention the implications of your findings and future suggestions.

4 *Introduction* (about 600 words). This should not be a general essay.
   - *Introductory paragraphs*: outline the general theoretical background.
   - *Specific and directly relevant* psychological studies, one or two are sufficient.

5 *Aims*. Explain what you plan to investigate and why. Justify the direction of the hypotheses.

6 *Hypotheses*, unambiguous alternative and null hypotheses, one- or two-tailed.

7 *Method* (about 600 words). Provide sufficient details for precise replication:
   - *Design*: describe any design decisions including variables and ethical considerations.
   - *Participants* and *researchers*, including sampling methods and how participants were assigned to conditions.
   - *Apparatus/materials*. The exact details should be placed in the appendices, include mark schemes for any tests or questionnaires.
   - *Standardised procedures* may also be placed in an appendix and referred to here.
   - *Controls* such as counterbalancing, single- or double-blind, standardised procedures.

8 *Results*
   - *Actual results*. Include all raw data in an appendix, in a readable form. You do not need to include details such as names or all actual answer sheets, one example will suffice.
   - *Descriptive statistics*. Numerical and graphical presentation help provide a 'feel' for the data. One or two graphs are sufficient. Take special care that all graphs and tables have clear titles, all graphical axes are labelled, and all graphs drawn on graph paper.
   - *Inferential statistics*. Justify the choice of test. In the main text, state the observed and critical values of the test, degrees of freedom, significance level and whether the test was one- or two-tailed. State your conclusion in terms of the hypothesis. Present the mathematical calculations in an appendix. If you use a computer or calculator program you still must present all data except the mathematical workings.

9 *Discussion* (about 600 words).
   - *Explanation of findings*. State the outcome of your study in psychological rather than statistical terms. Mention any additional observations.

- *Relationship to background research*. Use new material to discuss the outcome in terms of relevant background literature/research.
- *Limitations and modifications regarding*, for example, experimental treatments, measurement scales, sampling, lack of controls, procedures, and/or statistical treatments. Consider both your design (what you intended to do) and what you actually did.
- *Implications and suggestions for further research*. Record one or two ideas about any wider implications, applications or ideas for follow-up research.
- *Conclusion*. State your findings and the key points of the discussion.

10 *References*. This is not a bibliography. Make sure all key references are included, given in the correct form and in alphabetical order.

11 *Appendices*. Some details are better in an appendix so that they do not interrupt the flow of text.

12 *Report style and quality of language*. A good report style requires conciseness, you will lose marks for lengthy reports which do not follow the proscribed scientific style. You must express your ideas well, and use specialist terms, and good spelling, punctuation and grammar.

Copying

If a textbook says exactly what you want to say, copy it but use quotation marks and state the source. Never risk copying someone else's project, it may mean disqualification for both of you.

Common faults with the report

- The introduction is too long. Remember it is not an essay.
- The method is not sufficiently explained for replication, usually because the student hasn't designed the research themselves and doesn't understand the design.
- The results are presented unimaginatively and unclearly, a mass of bar charts or lists of numbers don't help the reader see what you've found out.
- The statistical presentation indicates little understanding.
- The discussion is too brief, and doesn't offer insightful understanding of the results. Alternatively, the discussion is too long, and will lose marks for conciseness.

REVISION TECHNIQUES

1 *Mnemonic techniques*. Memory research (see unit 5.3.5) suggests the following techniques should improve memory:
- *Repetition*.
- *Organisation*: gives meaning to the material, for example reorder your notes.
- *Category headings and numbered lists*: provide a framework to jog your memory and help chunk the data. They provide cues to aid retrieval.
- *Visual images:* help condense, connect and/or organise information.
- *Acoustic images*: memorising out loud, as in learning lines for a play.
- *Elaboration*: discussions with friends or writing essays.
- *Meaningful connections*: acronyms, acrostics, rhymes.
- *Avoid forgetting*: rest periods help to consolidate learning.

2 *Set a revision timetable*, with realistic goals and, very importantly, small rewards for reaching them. See 'Targets and work plans' in the section on study skills.

3 *Work for short spells* with adequate breaks. You may not feel tired but a change of activity will make you much more effective.

4 *Key notes*. Make up your own pass cards, based on summaries of key topic areas.

5 *Revise with friends* (as long as you can stay on the task), for example, criticise each other's essays. Stress is reduced by the presence of others.

⑥ *Study past papers*, not for question-spotting, but to see how the questions relate to the syllabus, and to write essay plans. This is a kind of mental 'limbering up' by tackling novel questions. Read the chief examiner's reports to see how previous candidates fared.

THE EXAMINATION

QUESTION STYLES

❶ *Short answers*. OCEAC and NEAB use short-answer questions, for example:

> Give a psychological definition of obedience. (2 marks)

Remember that the number of marks gives some indication of the expected length of answer. You do not have to read through the whole paper before you begin because all the questions are compulsory. Write some answer for each question.

❷ *Stimulus question format*. The question starts with a paragraph or more for you to read (the stimulus). This is followed by a set of compulsory, related questions. Be sure to read all of the stimulus thoroughly before attempting any of the questions. Examples in chapter 9.

❸ *Differentiated questions*. The question is broken down into parts, each given an individual mark. For example:

> (a) Critically consider how gender roles are acquired. (14 marks)
> (b) Using research examples show how gender roles affect our behaviour and our perception of others' behaviour. (10 marks)

Sometimes the question isn't divided into parts, but aspects of the question have been differentiated. For example:

> Describe and assess evidence from psychological research into the effects of media violence on children. (24 marks)

❹ *Essay questions*. A question which is undifferentiated, for example:

> Discuss the importance of attachment. (24 marks)

It may help you, when answering such a question, to make up your own differentiated sections and answer the question according to this plan.

❺ *Open book*. The research question for the OCEAC examination is given to students a week before they are required to write their answer.

EXAMINATION TECHNIQUES

❶ *Overall strategy*. You should decide how much time to allocate to planning each essay, and to reading everything through at the end. You can then work out how much time you have to write each essay. You might prefer to do your best question first, or leave it until the end because you can reel it off. You do not have to answer the questions in the order they are set. Be sure to put some answer down for all the questions: every mark counts.

❷ *Select the questions to answer*. You might cross out everything you can't answer, and then assess which of the rest you can do best. Do not answer more questions than required. Your time would be better spent rereading what you've written. Do not answer too few.

❸ *Write an essay plan before answering*. Identify the key words of the question so you are sure what has to be answered. Ideally your answer should be a structured argument rather than a shopping list of loosely related facts. This needs a plan. See 'Essay plans', above.

④ *Organise your answer*. See 'Writing essays', above.
- Introductions are not necessary in an examination but they can be a useful way of setting out your essay plan. This is especially important when a quotation has been used in the question, marks are lost if the quotation is not addressed.
- You can enumerate the arguments you present (first, second, third and so on).
- It helps to flag important points, for example underlining key words and names. This can be done at the end, which has the added advantage of making you rercad the essay.
- A conclusion can be a useful means of referring back to the original question. Don't waste time with a trite conclusion.

⑤ *Question strategies*
- Answer the question, if you are going to use a prepared answer at least shape it to the actual question. If the question seems ambiguous, state your understanding of it.
- Don't ignore features of the question, for example when the question says 'or' make sure you only select one of the alternatives. When the question says 'human' do not present non-human animal evidence.
- When a question is split into parts, use the marks for each part to give you an idea of how much to write.
- Use specific references where possible. If you know the author's name and date, use them. These strengthen the answer but arguments are more important and an examiner will be able to identify standard pieces of research without the specific reference.

⑥ *Reread your essays*. This always jogs the memory and helps pick up thoughtless oversights.

Coping with stress

In unit 3.4.4 techniques for reducing stress are listed, for example:

❶ *Increase your sense of control*. Positive thinking, for example 'It's too late to worry now, just get on with it'.

❷ *Writing essay plans*. This frees available cognitive resources for constructing the essay rather than trying to recall everything which might be relevant.

❸ *Avoiding ego defence mechanisms* such as denial; recognise the feeling of stress and intellectualise your problem.

❹ *Relaxation and rest*. Have a break and think pleasant thoughts unrelated to the exam, use self-hypnosis.

❺ *Social support*. Think about comforting people or things.

❻ *Physical exercise and emotional discharge*. Go for a run before the exam, stretch your legs, find some means of discharging tension during the exam (which doesn't disturb others).

Final preparation
- Check the time, date and place for the examination.
- Check you have the necessary equipment.
- Take some physical exercise before the exam to relieve tension and clear the mind.
- Arrive in good time.
- Practice relaxation techniques while waiting for the exam to start.
- Look forward to the conclusion of your studies.

PSYCHOLOGY TOPICS

In this section:

Each chapter features:

■ *Units in this chapter:* a list of the main topic heads to follow.

■ *Chapter overview:* key ideas which are covered in the chapter are introduced.

■ *The main text:* this is divided into numbered topic units for ease of reference.

■ *Chapter roundup:* a summary of the units in the chapter.

■ *Illustrative questions:* typical exam questions, with tutorial notes
and our suggested answers.

■ *Question bank:* further questions, with comments on the pitfalls to avoid and points to include in framing your own answers.

SOCIAL PSYCHOLOGY

Units in this chapter

Chapter overview

Social psychology is concerned with those aspects of human behaviour which involve people and their relationships with other people, groups, institutions and society as a whole. It is distinct from sociology, which is less concerned with the individual as a separate entity and more with the structure and functioning of reference groups such as the family and social classes.

1.1 SOCIAL COGNITION

1.1.1 SOCIAL AND CULTURAL INFLUENCES ON PERCEPTION

Many of the processes involved in physical perception are also involved in social perception – sensory data is modified by learned expectations or schema to help us understand the social world.

- *Impression formation* consists of taking a limited amount of information and producing a global perception of another individual.
- This perception can then be used to make inferences about an individual.

Empirical studies of social perception

1 *Lists of adjectives*, as in the classic studies by **Asch** (1946). Participants were shown a list of adjectives describing an individual, and asked to rate that individual on a number of personality characteristics. The lists generated a stereotype (schema) which generated further expectations.

2 *Fuller descriptions* were given by **Luchins** (1957). Participants read two paragraphs about 'Jim' and were asked to give descriptions of Jim's other characteristics and make

predictions about what he would do in certain situations. Interestingly, no one said, 'How am I to know?'

③ *Real-life encounters* as arranged by **Kelley** (1950). Students were given a description of a substitute lecturer and, after the lecture asked to assess the lecturer's performance and his personality. These were positive if the word 'warm' had been included in the original description, or negative if the word 'cold' was used. Limited information generated expectations. Was this simply due to demand characteristics?

Sources of bias in social perception

① *Centrality.* Asch (1946), like Kelley, showed that adjectives such as warm/cold, murderous, or intelligent have greater weight than others such as polite and blunt. These are 'central traits'.

② *Primacy/recency.* Luchins (1957) varied the order of negative and positive paragraphs about Jim and found a primacy effect; first impressions were more important. However, if a time interval was allowed between paragraphs, a recency effect was shown.

③ *Non-verbal cues* are given greater weight than verbal ones. **Argyle** *et al.* (1972) played a videotape of three messages (friendly, neutral and hostile) spoken in three different styles (friendly, neutral and hostile). Participants were more influenced by style than message in their interpretations of the meaning of the message.

④ *Inconsistent data.* **Haire and Grunes** (1950) found that participants ignored or adjusted the meaning of the word 'intelligent' when it was included in the description of a factory worker.

⑤ *Individual differences exist.* Women tend to use different cues from men. Your own personality influences the way you perceive or weight the same or different characteristics in others.

Models of social perception

① *Stereotypes and schema theory.* A stereotype is a schema, a structured cluster of concepts. Schema are built from past experience or cultural views. They provide a means of organising information and generating future expectations which *filter* out other information and simplify our social perceptions. External filters or *gatekeepers* (such as the media) control the flow of information and bias our social perceptions.

Psychologists develop explicit personality theories which embody expectations about clusters of associated traits. Each individual has an *implicit personality theory*, equivalent to their schema about how people behave. The *halo effect* is an example of this: it predicts that a person who is seen as physically attractive, will be assumed to possess other desirable traits

(Stereotypes are discussed later in this unit, and schema theory appears in unit 5.3.2.)

② *Social identity theory (SIT).* A person's self-image has two components: personal identity and social identity. Social identity is determined by the various social groups to which you belong, such as your football club or gender. *Tajfel* (1982) developed this theory in relation to prejudiced behaviour but it can also be used to understand social perception:

• *Ingroup favouritism* and *outgroup bias* enhance social and personal esteem, and lead to biased perceptions of in- and outgroup members.
• *Illusion of outgroup homogeneity*: members of an outgroup are perceived as less diverse than are members of the ingroup, thus confirming existing stereotypes. **Linville** *et al.* (1989) asked elderly people and college students to rate their own group and the other group in terms of traits such as friendliness. Both tended to perceive the ingroup as more differentiated (e.g. there were both friendly and unfriendly group members) and the outgroup as more homogenous (all group members were much the same).

③ *Social representations theory.* Biased social perceptions serve an important function in maintaining the stability of our social representations. **Moscovici** (1981) described a social representation as a shared belief within a social group used to explain social events.

Such explanations evolve through conversation and media reports, eventually becoming regarded as 'facts' which are not necessarily static. Social representations are more than schema because the concept includes social dynamics.

Echabe and Rovira (1989) tested recall of AIDS-related information by individuals who had different beliefs about AIDS (conservative or liberal). These social representations of AIDS resulted in distorted recall of information about AIDS, biased in a direction which confirmed pre-existing beliefs.

1.1.2 ATTRIBUTION THEORY

We do not observe traits, we observe behaviours and *infer* personal attributes which may have *caused* the behaviour.

Theories of attribution

① *Loci of causality*. **Heider** (1958) proposed two sources (loci) of causality:

- The *person*: internal or dispositional factors, such as a person's beliefs, attitudes and personality.
- The *situation*: external or situational factors, such as money, social norms or luck.

We prefer to make dispositional attributions; this is called the *fundamental attribution error*. **Heider and Simmel** (1944) found that participants described objects (e.g. triangles and circles) shown in a film in anthropomorphic terms, indicating our tendency to infer 'personalities' even when no causation could possibly be involved.

② *The correspondent inference theory*. **Jones and Davis** (1965) suggested that we observe behaviour and infer a corresponding attitude, as when we assume that film stars have similar personalities to the roles they play. An observer (the one making attributions) is likely to make dispositional rather than situational attributions about an actor (the one who is observed) when the behaviour is:

- *Intentional*: the actor performed the action deliberately and voluntarily.
- *Uncommon* or unusual.
- *Low in social desirability*: non-conformist or untypical.
- *Hedonic relevance*: the action will affect the observer rather than be irrelevant.

Empirical evidence from **Jones and Harris** (1967) showed that participants judged an essay writer's opinion to be the same as that expressed in their essay (pro- or anti-Castro) even when the raters knew that the essay was written under no-choice conditions. Only when they were told that the essay had been copied was the bias overcome.

Attribution may be more complex in real life. **Jones and Nisbett** (1971) gave additional information about the essayists' political persuasions (essays were either pro- or anti-marijuana). In the free-choice condition, a moderate essay was seen as conforming to the author's opinion. The same essay was seen as moderately unfavourable if the author was supposedly asked to write a strongly favourable essay.

③ *Covariation rule or cube theory*. **Kelley** (1967) proposed that attributions are based on our observation of covariations: the tendency for two things to occur at the same time, such as drinking and hangovers. Covariance is determined by three (cubed) axes:

- *Consistency*: covariation over time.
- *Distinctiveness*: the co-occurrence and co-absence of two things leads us to suppose that one causes the other.
- *Consensus*: our observations are shared by others.

The theory predicts that external attributions will be made when there is sufficient evidence of all three, whereas internal attributions occur when distinctiveness and consensus are low and consistency is high. **McArthur** (1972) gave participants 12 event-depicting sentences which contained information (high or low) about consistency, distinctiveness and consensus, for example: 'John laughs at almost all comedians' (low distinctiveness) or 'Almost everyone who hears the comedian laughs' (high consensus). Participants attributed external or internal causes as the model predicted.

④ *Causal schemata.* **Kelley** (1971) found that his original model, when tested empirically, was found to be unsatisfactory. For example, he found that the three axes were not used to the same extent, people did use other sources of information, and that he had overestimated people's ability to assess covariation. Therefore, he developed a new model. Observers rely on *causal schemata* (general ideas about how causes interact to produce specific behaviours) to provide rapid interpretation of often ambiguous and complex social perceptions. The two main kinds of causal schemata are:

* *Multiple necessary causes*: a group of behaviours are jointly necessary for a particular cause to be attributed.
* *Multiple sufficient causes*: any one of several behaviours is sufficient to arouse an attribution. The *discounting principle* is an example of this, suggesting that we reject the more common, dispositional explanation for a behaviour when the situational explanation is more reasonable – a film star advertising soap powder is more likely to be acting for the money (external) than because he or she really likes it (internal).

⑤ *Three-dimensional model.* **Weiner** (1980) proposed three dimensions of attribution:

* *Locus*: external or internal (E or I).
* *Stability*: stable or unstable (S or U).
* *Controllability*: controllable or uncontrollable (C or U).

A person might explain their lateness to school 'It always takes me a long time to walk to school' (locus: E, stability: S, controllability: C) or 'I'm just a born latecomer' (locus: I, stability: S, controllability: U).

⑥ *Self-perception theory.* **Bem** (1972) noted that the same processes of attribution are used to infer our own motives as well as those of others. For example, you jump when you hear a firework and infer that you are a jumpy sort of person.

⑦ *Locus of control.* **Rotter** (1966) described an important individual difference. Some people believe that behaviour, both theirs and others, is largely under external control, whereas others see themselves as 'in control'.

Attributional bias

A bias is a prejudice, a systematic factor which produces mistakes. People behave in a predictably biased manner when making attributions:

① *Fundamental attribution error.* The overemphasis on dispositional rather than situational factors. *Ross et al.* (1977) asked observers to rate the general knowledge of questioners (participants who made up the questions) and answerers. The former were rated as superior, a biased judgement overlooking their situational advantage.

② *Self-serving bias.* We tend to take credit for our successes, identify an internal cause, and disassociate from our failures, blaming external factors. This serves to protect self-esteem, and to give us a sense of control. **Jones** *et al.* (1968) asked participants to teach arithmetic to two pupils. When the pupils were tested pupil 1 reportedly did well and pupil 2 did poorly. After further instruction and another test, participants were told that pupil 2 had either done badly again or improved. The 'teacher' attributed improved performance to themselves but blamed the pupil if the pupil had continued to do poorly.

③ *Ingroup bias.* Attributions tend to enhance the status of the ingroup as a part of in- and outgroup processes. **Duncan** (1976) showed White participants a video of a White or Black person violently pushing another during a heated conversation. Participants made internal attributions ('violent personality') when the pusher was Black and external ones for the White aggressor ('he was provoked').

④ *Actor/observer divergence.* The 'actor' tends to attribute cause to situational factors, whereas observers attribute the same actions to disposition. This can be understood in terms of the self-serving bias and the fundamental attribution error. **Nisbett** *et al.* (1973) asked participants to explain, for themselves and a friend, the reasons for selecting a particular course of study. Their self-attributions included factors such as what the course has to offer (situational explanation), whereas attributions about others was related to personality factors (dispositional explanation).

⑤ *Defensive attribution.* The greater the consequences of an action, the more that attributions will be dispositional rather than situational. The end result is that we feel safer because things only go wrong when it is someone's fault. **Walster** (1966) described a car accident and asked participants to rate the car owner's responsibility. The more serious the consequences of the accident, the more responsibility the owner was assigned. **Lerner**'s (1980) *just-world-hypothesis* explains our defensive response to disasters as a means of reducing our own anxieties.

⑥ *Perceptual salience.* **Quattrone** (1982) gave participants material about experimenter bias and, later, asked them to what extent they thought situational factors might have influenced opinions expressed in a set of free-choice essays for or against nuclear power. The outcome was that the fundamental attribution bias was reversed because participants were led to believe that the experimenter might have influenced the essayists (experimenter bias); participants preferred the situational explanation because the situation had been made more salient.

Applications of attribution theory

Attribution retraining involves teaching people to make more appropriate attributions and change their 'attributional style', especially to emphasise internal control.

① *Failure.* **Dweck** (1975) retrained 12 children who were experiencing difficulty with failure. One group were told they were taking too long and should try harder, while a second group were given only positive feedback. The first group showed greater persistence and attributed any failures to lack of effort, the second group were more likely to give up, probably continuing to attribute failure to lack of ability.

② *Depression.* **Seligman** reformulated his theory of learned helplessness to incorporate attribution theory, proposing that the key factor in learned helplessness and in depression is that the person attributes failure to themselves (internal) rather than to external factors, and they see these attributions as unchanging (stable) and as global rather than specific. A depressive attributional style can be overcome through retraining.

③ *Addiction.* Addicts typically see their behaviour as being governed by physical craving and beyond their voluntary control. However, if they can blame situational factors they may overcome their addiction. **Robins** *et al.* (1974) reported that many US servicemen who had taken opium when in Vietnam were able to give it up spontaneously when they returned home. It is possible that their addiction was associated with environmental cues (external attributions) and, having left these behind, they were able to give up. Studies which show high relapse rates for alcoholics and smokers treated in clinics would support such a view.

1.1.3 ORIGINS OF PREJUDICE AND DISCRIMINATION

Social and cultural stereotypes

A stereotype is a social perception of an individual in terms of group membership or physical attributes rather than actual personal attributes. They may be either positive or negative in what they denote and connote.

① *Why do we have stereotypes?* They are an example of human cognitive processes: categorising, making generalisations and generating expectations. Stereotypes are cognitive schema which summarise large amounts of information and provide an instant picture from meagre data.

② *How do stereotypes develop?*

  • Indirectly from *gatekeepers* (*a priori* knowledge): the media, parents and other members of our culture.

- Directly through *conditioning*. **Staats and Staats** (1958) told participants to learn word pairs: a nationality name paired with another word. In one group, Dutch was always paired with a favourable word, and Swedish with an unfavourable word. This was reversed with the other group. When participants were asked to rate national groups this was related to the learned pairings.

③ *Why are stereotypes resistant to change?*

- *Confirmatory bias*: we seek out information which confirms rather than challenges our beliefs. **Cohen** (1981) described a woman in a videotape as either a waitress or a librarian, and showed her doing a variety of things. When participants were later asked a series of questions, such as 'What was she drinking?' they tended to remember those features which were consistent with their stereotypes.
- *Self-fulfilling prophecy*: our beliefs generate expectations which affect perception and behaviour.
- *Anchorage in personality*: any change may involve changes in personal and/or social identity, stereotypes are part of who you are.
- *Kernel of truth*: stereotypes are often valid, at least in part.

④ *Disadvantage of stereotypes*. They are at least partly inaccurate because they do not allow for exceptions and are based on superficial characteristics. They tend to be irrational, resistant to change and to lead to prejudice and discrimination.

⑤ *Factors which arouse stereotypes*. Physical features stand out most in initial or superficial encounters, therefore most stereotypes are based on such characteristics.

Prejudice

Prejudice is literally the act of pre-judgement, an *attitude* held prior to direct experience about a group of people. Prejudices are generally regarded as negative or hostile, but there are positive prejudices, such as ingroup favouritism. Prejudices are often held towards minority groups, groups which have less power but are not necessarily fewer in number.

Causes of prejudice

Explanations of prejudiced behaviour can be grouped in terms of theoretical approaches:

- *Psychodynamic*. Frustrations are projected on outgroups and expressed as hostility.
- *Social learning*. Prejudices are learned through conditioning and imitation.
- *Cognitive-informational*. Prejudices arise from cognitive schemas (stereotypes).
- *The individual* approach emphasises individual personality or emotional state.
- *The interpersonal* approach emphasises what goes on within a social group.
- *The intergroup* approach emphasises the relationships between groups of people.

① *The prejudiced personality* (an individual, psychodynamic approach). **Adorno** *et al.* (1950) developed a set of scales for testing prejudice or *authoritarianism*, such as the potentiality for Fascism (F) scale. They tested about 2,000 White, middle-class Americans, finding a prejudiced-type personality with the following traits:

- *Self-concept*: had a more favourable impression of themselves, and of their parents.
- *Cognitive style*: tended to be rigid and found ambiguity harder to cope with.
- *Moral view*: favoured law and order.
- *Values*: more concerned with status, success, and traditional customs.
- *Personal style*: avoided psychological interpretations and repressed feelings.

Adorno *et al.* collected information about the person's upbringing, finding that prejudiced-type people tended to have parents who gave conditional love, strict discipline, expected unquestioning loyalty and were insensitive to the child's needs.

Such experiences create an insecure adult who respects authority and power, conforms more readily to group norms (see below, conformity) and may increase their self-esteem through ingroup favouritism (see below, social identity). In addition, people who find ambiguity hard to cope with search for simplistic interpretations of reality and deny negative feelings in order to maintain consistency. A person with repressed feelings will project these onto scapegoats (see below). This accounts for both the existence of prejudices and the hostility element which is often present.

Evaluation: the sample was biased, some data was retrospective, there may have been a response set on the F-scale (agreement leads to authoritarian-type answers), authoritarianism of the left was overlooked and the study was correlational.

❷ *Frustration: the scapegoat theory* (an individual, psychodynamic approach). Frustration arises from many situations, including economic ones or overcrowding. This may lead to aggression (the *frustration-aggression hypothesis*, unit 1.4.2) which may be projected onto other, less powerful, people or objects. This *scapegoat* is usually a socially determined group. **Freud** explained this in terms of 'displacement' – when direct action against a frustrator is not possible, it is redirected through the outgroup. **Weatherly** (1961) insulted participants while they completed a questionnaire, and later asked them to describe a series of pictures some of which contained Jewish cues. Those who had shown strong anti-Semitic tendencies in the questionnaire now demonstrated exaggerated prejudices.

❸ *Conformity* (an interpersonal and individual, social learning approach). People conform to group norms. If one of those norms is that prejudiced behaviour towards certain groups is acceptable, then people will behave in that way. **Pettigrew** (1959) tested conformity and prejudice in a group of White Americans; northerners who were most conformist were *least* prejudiced whereas least conformist southerners were *most* prejudiced. The same personality type behaves differently depending on the attitude of their culture towards Blacks. **Rogers and Frantz** (1962) found White immigrants to former Rhodesia became more racially prejudiced the longer they stayed there. Presumably they were progressively conforming to the dominant cultural norms.

❹ *Stereotypes* (an interpersonal, cognitive-informational approach). The simple fact of having stereotypes leads to the formation of prejudices, but this would only account for different treatment, not the hatred that is found with some prejudiced behaviour.

❺ *Social identity theory (SIT)* (an intergroup, cognitive-informational approach, see unit 1.1.1). Prejudiced and *ethnocentric* behaviour is rooted in the basic human tendency to categorise things (cognitive), form groups (social) and then favour one's own group over all others (personal). This account does not fully explain the violence of feeling associated with some prejudices.

The **Robbers Cave Experiment** (**Sherif** *et al.*, 1961) is the classic study of how prejudice forms through the effects of in- and outgroup behaviour. Twenty-two White, well-adjusted, 11-year-old boys were selected to go on a summer camp for three weeks. In stage 1 the ingroup was developed. The boys were divided into two groups, they were given lots of co-operative activities and a sense of group identity (a name, hats and t-shirts). In stage 2 the groups became aware of each other and a tournament was organised (competition). There was aggression and fights after every match. In stage 3 the researchers resolved the conflict through co-operative activity involving superordinate goals, such as repairing a failed water supply. By the time they went home all traces of in- and outgroup prejudice had disappeared. Three factors led to the prejudiced behaviour: ethnocentrism (in- and outgroups), competition and stereotypes.

Tajfel *et al.* (1971) showed that ingroup favouritism could be created with *no* competition and with *minimal group* membership. Schoolboys, who had been randomly classed as over- or underestimators after an initial task, were favourably biased when judging other members of their group (either over- or underestimators). **Billig and Tajfel** (1973) *told* their participants that group membership was determined randomly but participants still showed ingroup favouritism. The results may be due to demand characteristics, but in real life we sometimes have little other basis for determining our behaviour.

❻ *Realistic conflict theory* (an intergroup, psychodynamic explanation). Prejudice stems from direct competition between social groups over scarce and valued resources, such as unequal distribution of wealth, unemployment or disputes over territory. In- and outgroup attitudes are turned into hostility because the outgroup becomes the scapegoat for economic problems. This was the case in **Sherif** *et al.*'s study though a similar study by **Tyerman and Spencer** (1983) did not find that the presence of competition led to intergroup conflict and hostility. *Marxist Exploitation Theory* suggests that the ruling class uses prejudice as a means of maintaining its position and continuing to exploit the under class. **Hovland and Sears** (1940) found a negative correlation between the number of lynchings (mainly Blacks) in the southern US in the years 1882 to 1930 and the economic indices of the time. High aggression (lynchings) towards Blacks is a product of prejudice. The economic index is an indication of frustration, when the price of cotton is low there will be fewer jobs and greater hardship. **Langford and Ponting** (1992) interviewed non-Aboriginal Canadians and concluded that continuing prejudices towards Aboriginals were positively related to perceived conflict. It might help if Aboriginal rights movements dealt directly with feelings of perceived competition.

Prejudice and discrimination

Individuals have prejudices (attitudes with cognitive and affective components), and they may behave differently as a result. Such unequal *treatment* of individuals or groups based on arbitrary characteristics is called discrimination.

The link between attitudes and behaviour is uncertain. For example, **LaPiere** (1934) found that, although hoteliers claimed (in a postal questionnaire) that they did not serve Chinese, almost all of them did when LaPiere arrived at the hotel with a Chinese couple. Critics have suggested that the fact that LaPiere was White and the Chinese couple were 'Americanised' may have affected the hoteliers' reactions. **DeFleur and Westie** (1958) found that 30% of White students behaved the *opposite* to their previously expressed views. They were first asked if they would be photographed with Black colleagues, and then the photograph was taken.

The link between attitudes and behaviour depends on factors such as relevance, situation and individual differences.

Empirical studies of discrimination

1. *Physical attractiveness.* **Stewart** (1980) found that attractive defendants received lighter sentences. **Landy and Sigall** (1974) gave male college students a set of essays, each with a photograph attached. Essays thought to be written by a more attractive woman were rated more highly. However, attractiveness may sometimes call up a less desirable stereotype. **Dermer and Thiel** (1975) found that very attractive women were judged as being egotistic, materialistic and likely to have unsuccessful marriages.

2. *Culture or race.* **Katz and Braly** (1933) asked college students to characterise 12 ethnic groups from a list of traits. There was considerable agreement though this may be because of demand characteristics. **Gilbert** (1951) repeated the study and found that students showed an increased awareness of the undesirability of such statements; some refused point blank to participate and others commented on the inaccurate nature of such statements, whilst they still produced stereotypical views. **Karlins** *et al.* (1969) concluded that the content had changed since 1933 but students still held consistent prejudices.

3. *Gender.* **Condry and Condry** (1976) showed films of a baby, labelled alternatively as a boy or girl, and asked participants to rate emotional responses; presumed sex led to different interpretations of the same behaviour. **Fidell** (1970) sent personnel profiles about a man or woman (e.g. Patrick or Patricia Clavel) to over 200 psychology professors – people who might have been expected to know better. They rated the man more highly. **Mischel** (1974) used the essay-assessment technique to show how gender affected rating of academic abilities, again favouring men (John was better than Joan) but only if the essay was on masculine topics such as law or city planning; women did better on essays related to dietetics or primary education (gender roles are also discussed in unit 6.3.2).

4. *Ageism.* Negative age bias applies to all age stereotypes – those of adolescents as well as individuals in late adulthood. Such stereotypes may be held by people of all ages, including peers.

1.1.4 REDUCTION OF PREJUDICE AND DISCRIMINATION

❶ *Enforced contact.* **Deutsch and Collins** (1951) found that prejudice possibly increased when Black and White residents lived in separate buildings, whereas it decreased when they were randomly assigned apartments in the same buildings irrespective of race. However, attempts to desegregate US schools did little to change attitudes and in some cases aggravated racial tension.

❷ *Equal status.* When the US Supreme Court declared segregation unconstitutional in 1954, they sought the advice of social psychologists who argued that equal status would be necessary to eliminate false stereotypes. **Minard** (1952) found that Black and White miners were not prejudiced when they worked together below ground; above ground, when their positions were unequal their attitudes changed.

❸ *Co-operation.* **Sherif**'s study found that co-operation and superordinate goals overcame prejudice. **Aronson** *et al.* (1978) developed the jigsaw method to foster mutual interdependence. Schoolchildren worked in groups where each member had a piece of work to prepare and teach to other group members for an end-of-project test. There was some attitude change but it was limited, probably because time spent in the classroom is limited compared with home and cultural influences.

❹ *Challenging stereotypes* through the use of advertising and propaganda. Phrases like 'Black is beautiful' try to create a positive bias. Direct campaigns about the danger of stereotyping have been mounted in America, using the caption 'We shouldn't infect children with poisonous stereotypes'.

❺ *Direct instruction.* **Elliott** (1977) gave a lesson in discrimination by telling her brown-eyed pupils that they were more intelligent and treating them more favourably. The blue-eyed children became the underdogs until she reversed her treatment. Years later the children said that this taught them to be more careful about discrimination.

Why have such attempts failed?

❶ *Prejudice is inevitable*
- Stereotype formation and social identity are processes *basic to human nature*.
- The hostility factor is due to intergroup conflicts which may also be inevitable and would require *massive political and social changes*, which are at best slow.

❷ *Holding prejudices has benefits related to social norms*
- Positive discrimination for the ingroup *increases self-esteem*.
- Prejudices provide a means of *displacing aggression*.
- Stereotypes and prejudices *make the world more manageable*.

❸ *Resistance to attitude change* is like resistance to changing stereotypes (see unit 1.1.3).

❹ *Generalising from the particular.* It is quite common for people to like *individual* members of an outgroup, but still feel prejudiced towards the *group* as a whole. For example, **Stouffer** *et al.* (1949) found that racial prejudice among soldiers diminished in battle but did not extend to relations back at base. See also **Minard**, above.

❺ *Increased contact increases conflict.* Forced desegregation may even have an effect opposite to that intended, increasing aggression through resentment. For the minority group, integration may lead to lowered self-esteem because it emphasises their inferior position, thus creating stronger hostilities.

❻ *The 'dollar gap'.* **Abeles** (1976) suggested that even though conditions are improving for Blacks, the gap between the rich and the poor remains. A survey of Black people living in poor areas of America showed that they have rising expectations which leads to a sense of dissatisfaction and militancy.

❼ *It doesn't always fail.* See **Sherif** *et al.*, above.

1.2 SOCIAL RELATIONSHIPS

1.2.1 THEORIES OF INTERPERSONAL RELATIONSHIPS

❶ *Social exchange theory*. **Thibaut and Kelley** (1959) described relationships as an exchange of costs and rewards, an 'economic theory'. Satisfaction (profit) in a relationship is determined by rewards and costs, the *comparison level* (CL – the ratio between actual rewards and expected rewards), and the comparison level for alternatives (CLalt – a relationship will end or diminish if a better alternative exists).

Relationships develop through key stages:

* *Sampling*: explore rewards and costs directly or indirectly (observing others).
* *Bargaining*: prospective partners establish sources of profit and loss.
* *Commitment*: routines are established.
* *Institutionalisation*: norms and mutual expectations are established.

Evaluation. The theory is an interesting if mechanistic attempt to quantify attraction. In reality it is difficult to define rewards or costs precisely and attraction is determined by more than personal satisfaction.

❷ *Equity theory*. This is a development of social exchange theory. **Walster** *et al.* (1978) suggested balance is achieved more through perceived fairness than objective economics. A stable or equitable relationship is one where each partner feels that he/she is rewarded in equal measure. Inequity results in striving to restore balance or dissolution. The *matching hypothesis* is an example of this (see unit 1.2.2). Empirical studies have yielded mixed support at best. It may be that physical attractiveness is not matched but that balance is maintained by other positive aspects of a person's character, such as money or status.

❸ *Reinforcement-affect model*. **Clore and Byrne** (1974) proposed a theory based on conditioning theory: we learn to associate positive feelings (affect) with people or situations which reward us (reinforcement). The *MUM effect* describes our reluctance to transmit bad news. **Veitch and Griffitt** (1976) placed participants in a waiting room where they listened to either good or bad news with a stranger present. When they were asked to rate the stranger the degree of liking was related to the kind of news they had been listening to. **Rabbie and Horwitz** (1960) found that strangers expressed greater liking for each other when they were successful in a game-like task than when they were unsuccessful.

Duck (1992) criticises such bogus stranger methods for being laboratory-based. **Byrne** (1971) gives examples of real-world evidence for similarity and liking, for example, jurors being more lenient with defendants with similar attitudes.

❹ *Need satisfaction*. **Argyle** (1994) has listed seven basic motives or needs, each of which can be satisfied at least in part by interpersonal relationships:

* *Biological*: eating and drinking together, hunting together.
* *Dependency*: being comforted or nurtured.
* *Affiliation*: seeking the company of others.
* *Dominance*: establishing social order.
* *Sex*: reproduction.
* *Aggression*: interpersonal hostility.
* *Self-esteem*: being valued by others.

Evaluation. This model presents a one-sided picture, omitting the behaviour of other people.

❺ *Sociobiological theories*. Sociobiologists such as **Wilson** (1986) proposed that we can understand interpersonal relationships in terms of adaptiveness; only those behaviours which increase an individual's reproductive success are naturally selected (see unit 2.2). This theory would predict, for example, that women can increase their reproductive success by choosing high-status males who can control sufficient resources to provide for the offspring. Men use physical characteristics, such as youth and symmetry

(= 'attractiveness') as a guide to reproductive ability. **Darwin** suggested that the preferences of one sex are reflected in the behaviour of another. **Dunbar** (1995) found that 'lonely hearts' ads supported this: women seek resources and offer attractiveness whereas the reverse is true for males.

Evaluation. This approach is directed at reproductive relationships only, is deterministic and based on animal behaviour.

1.2.2 FORMATION, MAINTENANCE AND DISSOLUTION OF INTERPERSONAL RELATIONSHIPS

Factors which affect liking

Kerckhoff and Davis (1962) used the term *filter* to describe how superficial traits are used in initial selection of friends or partners.

1. *Physical attractiveness.* Many studies show that people who are physical attractive tend to be treated better (see unit 1.1.3). The *matching hypothesis* predicts that people select partners of comparable attractiveness. This may be to maintain balance (*Equity Theory*), or a fear of rejection, or because the *halo effect* makes the other appear to possess a cluster of positive characteristics (see unit 1.1.1). Support for this comes from **Murstein** (1972) who asked dating couples to rate themselves in terms of physical attractiveness, and asked independent judges to rate them. He found that real pairs were more similar than random pairs.

   Silverman (1971) confirmed these findings in a field study, noting that the greater the degree of physical attractiveness, the more physical intimacy was displayed.

   The computer dance experiment (**Walster** *et al.*, 1966) did not find support for the matching hypothesis. Nearly 400 male and female students were randomly paired at a dance, and later asked to rate their date. Physical attractiveness (which was independently assessed) proved to be the most important factor in liking, above such qualities as intelligence and personality. It was also the best predictor of the likelihood that they would see each other again.

2. *Propinquity or proximity.* Physical closeness increases the probability of interaction and acquaintance. **Festinger** *et al.* (1950) found that people who lived in the end apartments in a U-shaped housing block had most passive contact with other residents, and had developed the greatest number of friendships with other residents. **Clarke** (1952) found that 50% of the people living in Columbus, Ohio married people who lived within walking distance of their house. **Segal**'s (1974) study of police cadets seated alphabetically, found that surname (because of the alphabetical seating) was a better predictor of friendship than religion, age, education or hobbies.

   Familiarity is associated with liking. **Saegart** *et al.* (1973) gave participants the task of rating the tastes of various drinks, during which they came into contact with a stranger 1, 2, 5 or 10 times; liking of the stranger was positively related to the frequency of meeting. **Zajonc** (1968) asked participants to read lists of words, some of which were repeated more than others. When they rated the words for pleasantness this was related to frequency of exposure.

3. *Reciprocity.* Knowing that someone likes you enables you to reciprocate such feeling. **Backman and Secord** (1959) arranged group discussions, informing participants beforehand that certain group members would like them very much. During initial meetings this was a good predictor of liking, but after six meetings participants preferred those participants who actually expressed reciprocal feelings. Both are evidence of reciprocity. **Hewitt** (1972) found that we like those who evaluate us positively, but only if it is deserved; otherwise it is seen as unfounded flattery (the *ingratiation effect*) and results in decreased liking. The opposite (the *extra credit effect*) occurs when we receive deserved criticism; people value honesty.

4. *Similarity.* Similarity reinforces and confirms our own attitudes, and thus reduces uncertainty and anxiety. **Newcomb** (1961) offered 17 male students rent-free housing,

58% of those paired with a room-mate with similar attitudes formed friendships as opposed to friendships between 25% of those with dissimilar room-mates. **Hill *et al.*** (1976) studied 231 couples who dated over a two-year period. Those who stayed together (55% of them) tended to be more alike in terms of age, intelligence, education and other career plans; those who separated often explained this in terms of attitude differences. **Byrne and Nelson** (1965) found a significant linear relationship between attraction and similar attitudes when participants rated people on the basis of seeing their responses to an attitude questionnaire.

⑤ *Complementarity.* Do opposites attract each other? Some people seek a partner who fills in the gaps in their own personality or complements their personality, as in the case of dominant and submissive partners. This may be useful in avoiding stormy relationships.

⑥ *Perceived competence.* People who are capable, intelligent and knowledgeable appear more attractive. This may be due to the operation of a *halo effect*, they are endowed with other favourable characteristics. **Aronson *et al.*** (1966) coined the term *pratfall effect* to describe the outcome of their 'College Bowl' quiz. Participants were asked to rate the attractiveness of contestants, the most attractive was the intelligent but clumsy one.

⑦ *Skill at communicating.* **Duck** (1992) points out that people who have difficulty making friends and relationships often have difficulties communicating, particularly the basic skill of striking up a conversation. We like good communicators and people who respond well to our non-verbal signals. **Oden and Asher** (1977) gave children who were rejected by their peers training in social skills, and found that peer ratings quickly improved.

Maintenance

① *Resistance to change.* Liking, like all attitudes, is resistant to change (see unit 1.1.3).

② *Daily routine.* **Duck** (1992) suggested that relationships, once established, are 'buried in daily routines', and offer comfortable predictability. Many relationships are of a perpetual but dormant kind, such as distant friends or parent–child relationships which continue with only occasional contact.

③ *Cognitions.* **Duck and Pond** (*sic*) (1989) noted that the key factor about routines is the way that the partners talk to one another in and about their interactions; relationships are not a string of routines but are the cognitions which surround them.

④ *Self-disclosure.* Relationships acquire depth through progressively sharing more intimate secrets; unless the friend 'matches' such behaviour the disclosure will stop.

⑤ *Maintenance strategies.* **Dindia and Baxter** (1987) interviewed 50 married couples and found that they used either repair strategies, such as issuing ultimatums or preventative (maintenance) strategies, such as spending time together.

The causes of dissolution

This research has practical applications; selecting an appropriate kind of counselling is relative to the cause or stage of dissolution.

① *Personal factors* such as distasteful personal habits, change in interests or attitudes, poor role models (e.g. parents' divorced), dissonance (e.g. partners from different religious backgrounds) or poor social skills.

② *Situational factors* such as deception, boredom, relocation, conflict, or a better alternative.

③ *Fatal attraction theory.* **Felmlee** (1995) proposed that the same characteristic(s) which initially caused attraction, ultimately lead to dissolution. Such characteristics might initially be exciting or different but later appear predictable or strange.

④ *Social exchange theory* predicts that dissolution will occur when rewards and costs are in a state of imbalance.

⑤ *Transactional analysis* (see unit 4.4.1) suggests that crossed transactions leads to relationship breakdown.

⑥ *Stages in dissolution.* **Duck** (1984) has put forward a model of relational dissolution, which includes appropriate strategies of repair:

- *Breakdown*: dissatisfaction leads to breaking point. Repair strategy: correct own behavioural faults.
- *Intra-psychic phase*: brooding focus on the relationship, at first in private but then with confidants preparatory to facing your partner. Repair strategy: re-establish liking for partner.
- *Dyadic phase*: talking with partner, deciding whether to break up or repair the relationship. Repair strategy: express conflict, clear the air and reformulate rules for a future relationship.
- *Social phase*: including others in the debate, enlisting the support for your 'side'. Repair strategy: outsiders may help patch things up or encourage separation.
- *Grave dressing phase*: post-mortem for public consumption and private readjustment. Repair strategy: decide on a mutually acceptable version of events, and/or attempt to salvage friendship out of the break-up.

1.2.3 COMPONENTS OF INTERPERSONAL RELATIONSHIPS

① *Goals and conflicts.* **Argyle** (1983) suggested that one of the reasons for relationship dissolution is that partners had different goals of which they were unaware. **Argyle and Furnham** (1983) found that the main factors relating to satisfaction in relationships were:

- Common interests.
- Social and emotional support.
- Material and instrumental help.

② *Rules.* **Argyle and Henderson** (1984) suggested that informal rules are important in controlling the common sources of conflict or difficulties in a relationship, for regulating rewards and for facilitating the communication of affect (liking). Thus there are rules of 'affect' and rules of 'exchange'. Argyle and Henderson prepared a list of possible relationship rules and found that six emerged as the most critical because they distinguished behaviour between different quality of friendships and were most often cited as contributing to friendship breakdown.

③ *Power and roles.* All social relationships involve a power structure (see social power, unit 1.3.2). Social roles dictate culture-specific behaviours.

Individual, social and cultural variation

The fact that there are variations in relationships poses a problem for all interpersonal relationship theories.

① *Individual differences*
- *Gender differences*: **Argyle and Henderson** (1984) found, for instance, that females were more likely to endorse rules concerning intimate conversation, showing affection, being emotionally supportive and respecting privacy.
- *Age differences*: **Argyle and Henderson** (1984) found that age differences were small though older people tended to be more concerned about privacy. Children under 10 tend to base relationships on rules of exchange, maladjusted children may continue to do this .
- *Kinds of relationships*: **Mills and Clark** (1984) make a distinction between *communal* relationships (family, friends and lovers), which are governed largely by equality of affect, and *exchange* relationships which are based on a balance of rewards. **Argyle and Henderson** (1984) found 'general rules' to distinguish friendship from other relationships and 'quality rules' to distinguish between ordinary and high-quality friendship.
- *Personality differences*: some people are 'joiners' and have a greater *need for affiliation*; others prefer to be alone. **Hill** (1987) developed an interpersonal orientation scale to test the different motives that people have for relationships, namely for social comparison, positive stimulation, social support or attention.

② *Social and cultural factors.* Social norms affect the way individuals conduct their relationships. **Argyle et al.** (1986) compared the friendship rules selected by people from Japan and Hong Kong (collectivistic cultures), and Italy and Britain (individualistic cultures). They found evidence of universal features, for example all respondents distinguished between intimate and non-intimate relationships.

They also found differences, such as the Japanese endorsing more rules for avoiding conflict, the Italians being more concerned with regulating intimacy, and there were more rules for obedience in the East. **Moghaddam** *et al.* (1993) concluded that social relationships tend to be individualistic, voluntary and temporary in Western cultures, whereas elsewhere they are collective, obligatory and permanent.

European psychologists focus on certain kinds of relationship which don't exist elsewhere and tend to ignore other kinds of relationship, such as arranged marriages. **Yelsma and Athappilly** (1988) compared happiness in arranged Indian marriages with both Indian and American love matches, and found satisfaction higher in the former.

Evaluation. Such research is plagued with the difficulties inherent in cross–cultural misunderstanding (see unit 7.2.3).

1.2.4 Effects of interpersonal relationships

1 *Fulfilling basic needs.* Interaction with others is a basic human need, a biological necessity for reproduction. **Schachter** (1959) found that social isolation had similar effects to total sensory isolation. In his study participants were given plenty to do and their senses were not limited, nevertheless most of them lasted less than two days. They were withdrawn, apathetic, showed some schizophrenic reactions and reported that they thought and dreamt about other people.

2 *Self-development*
- *Social comparison*: many self-concepts are comparative terms, such as tall or clever; we need other people to set the standards by which we come to know ourselves.
- *Feedback*: we see ourselves as others see us (**Cooley**'s *looking-glass self*, unit 6.3.3). Interaction with others promotes a sense of self-worth.
- *Learning how to form relationships*: early relationships help children understand the feelings of others (empathy), they act as a model for adult relationships, and provide practice in interpersonal interactions, such as resolving squabbles and forming relationships.

3 *Emotional support.* People are bolder in the presence of friends because this reduces stress. **Kamarck** *et al.* (1990) found a lower cardiovascular response to a psychologically stressful task when participants were with a friend. **Schachter** (1959) found that participants who were expecting to receive a painful rather than painless electric shock preferred to wait with others than on their own.

4 *Emotional outlet.* Friends also act as confidants and therapists.

5 *Happiness.* **Argyle** (1992) distinguished two sources of happiness:
- *Positive emotions*, such as joy and fun, are provided by friends through sharing enjoyable experiences and positive feedback.
- *Positive states of mind*, such as contentment with life, come from social networks and relationships. **Haring-Hidore** *et al.* (1985) did a meta-analysis of a large number of studies and found a positive correlation between subjective well-being and being married. On the other hand, **Harding** (1985) found that women at home with children had negative feelings about marriage.

6 *Mental health.* Since relationships are important for self-development, emotional support and reducing stress, it is not surprising to find that they are positively associated with mental health. **Cowen** *et al.* (1973) found, in a study of 800 schoolchildren, that lack of friendships in childhood was related to later psychiatric treatment. Maladjustment may be a cause or an effect of early peer rejection, but once the cycle is started it is self-fulfilling. **Cochrane** (1988) reported that the mental hospitalisation rate for single persons is three times higher than for married persons, and nearly six times higher for divorced people. There are gender differences: married women are more likely to be hospitalised than men, but divorced and widowed men are more likely to be hospitalised than women. This suggests that relationships offer different kinds of support for men and women.

1.3 SOCIAL INFLUENCE

Social influences are the forces exerted by other people which affect your behaviour. Ancient astrologers believed in an invisible force called *influentia* which flowed down from the heavenly bodies and affected human behaviour.

1.3.1 CONFORMITY, OBEDIENCE AND INDEPENDENT BEHAVIOUR

- *Conformity* = a change in behaviour as a result of real or imagined group pressure or norms. **Kelman** (1958) suggested that a person may comply (public but not private change of opinions), identify (both public and private opinions change) or internalise the new norms (true change).
- *Norms* are the rules established by a group to regulate the behaviour of its members.
- *Obedience* = behaving as instructed but *not necessarily* changing your opinions. Usually in response to *individual* rather than group pressure, though you might obey group norms. Obedience is by *direction* whereas conformity is affected by example.
- *Independent behaviour* = resisting social influences. True independence means following one's conscience rather being disobedient or non-conformist. For example, Galileo's resistance to ideas of his time was healthy non-conformity (independence) whereas going round a roundabout in an anticlockwise direction is foolish. *Apparent non-conformity* occurs when an individual is apparently not conforming to group norms but is in fact conforming to a different set of group norms.

Studies of conformity

1 *Early studies.* **Allport** (1924) and **Jenness** (1932) found that people behaved differently in groups than when they were working alone. Participants shifted their individual judgements (about the pleasantness of odours or number of beans in a bottle) towards group means after having group discussions.

2 *Informational social influence: in an ambiguous situation.* In many situations, especially social ones, there is no 'right' answer and therefore we look to others for information (*informational social influence*). **Sherif** (1936) used the *autokinetic effect* (a point of light moves erratically when viewed in total darkness) to demonstrate group influence. He showed the light to individuals and asked them to estimate how far and in which direction it moved. After about 100 trials they had reached a consistent level of judgements and then viewed the light in groups. They were not asked to arrive at a group estimate but nevertheless, after a few exposures, the judgements of the group tended to converge and persisted when the individuals were tested later. The group performance had created a socially determined standard or *norm* which is necessary in ambiguous situations.

   Pettigrew (1959) has shown how conformity to social norms can explain why some groups are prejudiced (unit 1.1.3). **Stoner's** (1968) classic study of the *risky shift* found that when individuals tended towards a cautious decision, the group was more cautious. If the individual opinion was risky, the group decision was more risky. The shift was always in the direction of greater polarisation, and individual opinion, tested later, changed in the direction of the group.

3 *Informational social influence: in an u*nambiguous *situation.* **Asch** (1952) suggested that Sherif's results had been caused by an ambiguous stimulus. He presented groups with a unambiguous problem: on card 1 there were three lines of varying length, one of which was the same length as the 'standard' (on card 2). There were six confederates who were primed to give wrong answers on certain trials (*informational social influence*), and a true participant who always answered last. Approximately 75% of the participants conformed at least once, 5% conformed all of the time and 24% never conformed; the average rate was 37%.

Later experiments by Asch (1956) showed that:

- A group of three participants was sufficient to create the effect.
- A larger group did not increase conformity. **Venkatesan** (1966) found that mass conformity had the opposite effect, the last participant displayed *reactance* (below).
- A second dissenter cut conformity rates by 25%, even when the dissenter disagreed with the participant.
- Conformity increased if the group members were regarded as of high status.
- Conformity decreased if the participants were not face-to-face.

Crutchfield (1955) used a more efficient method than Asch, testing 600 participants using the *Crutchfield apparatus* (a cubicle with switches and lights). Participants were given a question, they could see the selection made by other (non-existent) participants, and were asked to register their own choice. They were tested on up to 50 different items. When the question was clear-cut, 30% conformed. If the question was an insoluble mathematical one (therefore ambiguous), conformity was 80%. If the question asked for agreement or disagreement with a statement of opinion, 58% conformed.

④ *Normative social influence.* In some situations we are influenced by others because we want approval or because we want to be seen as part of a group. Conformity to social roles is an example of a normative social influence. The **Stanford Prison Study (Zimbardo** *et al.*, 1973) aimed to find out whether alleged brutality by prison guards was an inevitable outcome of the role or due to personal characteristics of prison guards. Twenty-four male volunteers were randomly assigned the role of prisoner or guard in a simulated prison in the Stanford University psychology department. The 'prisoners' were arrested, searched, given ID numbers, issued with a uniform and ankle chain. Guards had uniforms, clubs, handcuffs and reflective sunglasses (deindividuation). Zimbardo intended the study to last two weeks but the increasing malice of the guards and depression levels among the prisoners forced it to be abandoned after six days. The guards woke prisoners in the night, locked them in closets and got them to clean the toilet with their bare hands. The prisoners also changed their behaviour, one went on a hunger strike, and those who broke down asked to be paroled not simply to quit. The study shows the strong pressures which exist to comply with social norms and roles.

Studies of obedience

① *Experimental work.* **Milgram** (1963) questioned whether obedience was a trait of the German nation or a universal aspect of social behaviour. He advertised for volunteers for a study of memory. In each trial, two participants drew lots for their roles, the 'learner' (a confederate) was strapped in a chair in one room, the 'teacher' (true participant) was told to administer increasingly stronger electric shocks as punishment for mistakes. The experimenter used special 'prods' to encourage the 'teacher' to continue, despite hearing the 'learner's' yelps of pain. No one stopped below 300 volts (intense shock), 65% of the participants continued to the highest level of 450 volts, past the level marked 'danger, severe shock'. Later variations (**Milgram**, 1974) included:

- *Proximity of 'learner'*: if the 'teacher' was placed in the same room as the 'learner' and had to press the learner's hand on the shock plate, obedience fell to 30%.
- *Proximity of experimenter*: when instructions were given over the phone the 'teacher' often said they were giving the shocks when they weren't. Overall, 21% of 'teachers' continued to obey.
- *Perceived authority*: when the experiment was conducted in a run-down building rather than a prestigious university setting, obedience fell to 47.5%.
- *Social support*: if the 'teacher' was paired with other two other 'teachers' (confederates) who dissented, only 10% of the real participants continued to 450 volts.
- *Deindividuation*: **Zimbardo** (1969) arranged for the learner to be introduced to the participant and wear a name tag, or to wear a lab coat and hood. The latter condition led to more electric shocks.
- *Responsibility*: if the learner had a heart condition obedience didn't change!
- *Individual differences*: the experiment was repeated with over 1,000 participants from all walks of life. It was found that educated participants were less obedient, and military participants were more obedient. This may be related to their group norms.

- *Cultural differences*: **Smith and Bond** (1993) report a number of cross-cultural replications with different rates of obedience, for example 85% in Germany and 40% for male Australians. It is likely that such studies did not exactly replicate Milgram's study.
- *Gender differences*: Milgram found that female participants were equally obedient but **Kilham and Mann** (1974) found much lower conformity rates in Australian women (12% compared to Australian males at 40%).

There have been many practical and ethical comments made in relation to Milgram's study:

- *Debriefing*: after the experiment all participants were told the real details and had a 'friendly reconciliation' with the 'learner'. Later, Milgram sent out a questionnaire to give further support to participants. Only 1% said they were sorry to have participated. Some felt the experience had been worthwhile, even if only to warn them about blind obedience in the future.
- *Artificiality*: the participants were in an unfamiliar situation, the norms were set by the 'experimenter'.
- *Distress to participants*: **Baumrind** (1964) criticised Milgram for the stress and emotional conflict experienced by participants. Milgram defended himself by saying that he expected very low levels of obedience; before the experiment he had asked psychiatrists, students and ordinary people how participants would behave. They thought that at most only 3% of the participants might go as far as 450 volts.
- *Distasteful conclusions*: **Aronson** (1992) suggested that people are more likely to criticise ethics when the results tell us something distasteful about human nature. It is easier to blame inhuman behaviour on evil personalities than to accept that it may be part of the human psyche and group processes.

   (See also the evaluation of all studies of conformity and obedience, below.)

② *Field studies.* **Hofling** *et al.* (1966) conducted a more realistic experiment where nurses were told to administer a drug to a patient. This instruction was contrary to their rules: nurses were not permitted to accept instructions over the telephone, nor from an unknown doctor, nor for a dose in excess of the safe amount. Nevertheless 21 out of 22 nurses obeyed the order (95%). Nurses defended themselves by saying it often happens, a doctor would be annoyed if they refused. Their behaviour might be interpreted as conforming to expected role behaviour rather than being obedient.

   Langer *et al.* (1978) approached people who were using a photocopier and asked if they could use it first, almost everyone obeyed even when no excuse was offered. This suggests a social norm to agree to 'reasonable' requests and also indicates that people often obey 'mindlessly', most of the time we are 'on auto-pilot' (see unit 5.4.3).

Independent behaviour

In Asch's study the majority did *not* conform, and in Milgram's study 35% *dis*obeyed.

❶ *Rebellion.* The research evidence indicates that individuals obey and conform, but that groups don't because they set their own norms (**Asch**, above). **Gamson** *et al.* (1982) set up a (fictitious) public relations firm, MHRC, who were collecting evidence of community opinions about a Mr C. who was suing an oil company. Groups of nine participants were asked to discuss on videotape their attitudes towards Mr C's lifestyle. The participants soon realised that they were being manipulated to produce a tape of evidence supporting the oil company's position. When the majority opinion was anti-authority, they refused to sign an affidavit giving MHRC permission to use the tape in a trial. But some groups did sign; rebellion occurred only when the group norm was anti-authoritarian. Conformity may lead to disobedience.

❷ *Resisting persuasion. Reactance theory* suggests that, under appropriate circumstances, people will react against attempts to restrict or control personal decisions by selecting an opposing choice. **Venkatesan** (1966) asked groups of students to select one of three identical suits. The true participant (last to register an opinion) conformed to majority opinion except when most of the confederates made statements strongly favouring one suit. When individuals feel forced to conform they may react by asserting their independence.

❸ *Social pressure.* **Milgram** (in Tarvis, 1974) tried this task: to ask a stranger in an underground train if they could have their seat, offering no excuse. He says that he felt overcome with blind panic and couldn't do it, revealing the enormous inhibitory anxiety that ordinarily prevents us from breaching social norms and behaving independently.

❹ *Individual differences.* Some people are more non-conformist. Affiliators need social approval more than others. **Burger and Cooper** (1979) assessed participants' desire for personal control and then asked them to rate a set of cartoons in terms of funniness in the presence of another participant (confederate) who was expressing his own (predetermined) opinions. Participants who were high in their desire for personal control were less influenced by the confederate. **Crutchfield** (1955) found that non-conformists tended to be self-reliant, expressive, unpretentious, and lacked feelings of inferiority. Conformists respect authority, are submissive, inhibited, lacking in insight and overly accepting.

❺ *Gender differences.* **Eagly and Carli** (1981) claimed that women are more easily influenced than men but **Eagly** (1978) suggested that women may be more oriented towards interpersonal goals and thus *appear* more conformist.

❻ *Cultural differences.* Cultural differences can also account for varying rates of independence (see above).

Factors which affect conformity and obedience

- *Uncertainty.* In ambiguous situations we need informational social influence, in new situations we need social norms to guide us (normative social influence).
- *Deindividuation.* Anonymity shifts our sense of responsibility, it increases obedience and decreases conformity.
- *Group behaviour (social pressure).* Groups as small as three create pressure to conform. Too much pressure reduces conformity (reactance). One dissenter reduces conformity and obedience.
- *Individual differences.* Some people are more likely to be conformist or obedient.
- *Gradual changes* mean that a person can be unaware of obedience before it's too late. In **Milgram**'s study the shocks increased by only 15 volts each time, what does one more step matter?
- *Mindlessness.* Most of the time we are on auto-pilot.
- *Social desirability.* There are situations where both conformity and obedience are adaptive features of behaviour, such as doing what your parents tell you. **Kelman and Lawrence** (1972) conducted a national survey after the trial of William Calley for an infamous massacre during the Vietnam War. His defence was that it was his duty as a soldier to obey orders. Half of the respondents said it is 'normal, even desirable' to obey legitimate authority.

Evaluation of empirical studies

❶ *Experimental artefacts*
- *Demand characteristics.* Participants behave in certain ways because features of the experiment 'demand' a typical response.
- *Desire to please the experimenter.* In **Crutchfield**'s experiment, many participants said they didn't want to spoil the results so they had gone along with the others.
- *Anxiety* fosters conformity and obedience.
- *Paid volunteer participants* may feel they have entered into a social contract and therefore should obey norms about behaviour in experiments.
- *Experiments are social situations.* In **Asch**'s study the participants expressed how much of an outsider they felt by dissenting. Belonging to the group is more important than correctness.

❷ *Ecological validity.* What do the results tell us about real life?
- In real life people sometimes have the option simply to *do nothing*, which may not be possible in an experiment.

- Many of the experimental situations were *oversimplified*.
- All of the experiments involved *strangers*. We may behave differently with individuals or groups who know us and we know them.

③ *Child of the times.* Social norms are always changing. **Perrin and Spencer** (1980) replicated Asch's study but did not obtain evidence of conformity, concluding that people might have learned to be more self-reliant. **Doms and Avermaet** (1981) did reproduce the same results as Asch and suggest that Perrin and Spencer's use of science and engineering students could have biased their results.

④ *Ethical issues*
- *Deception.* Many of the experiments required a single blind design which denies participants the right to informed consent.
- *The right to withdraw* and *post hoc debriefing* may overcome some ethical objections.
- *Emotional distress* may be created during the experiment because of social pressure or because of imagined harm to other participants. Participants may feel disturbed after the experiment, when they realise the extent of their conformity/obedience.
- *Means versus ends.* The findings of these studies demonstrate an important aspect of human behaviour and social influence that was not previously expected. This 'end' may be seen to justify the means.

Theoretical accounts

① *Law of social impact.* **Latané** (1981) proposed that the amount of influence that others exert depends on three factors: the strength, number and immediacy of those exerting social pressure. This principle was derived mainly from studies of bystander intervention.

② *Social influence model (SIM).* **Tanford and Penrod** (1984) described the amount of influence in terms of group size and number of target persons. According to this model, as each person is added to the group social influence initially rises rapidly but then tails off, as new group members have less and less overall effect.

③ *Social identity theory (SIT)* can be used to explain social influence in terms of group processes (see unit 1.1.1). Conformity and obedience are necessary components of group processes.

1.3.2 SOCIAL POWER: LEADERSHIP AND FOLLOWERSHIP

Leaders, power and norms are important concepts in explaining the processes of conformity and obedience.
- *Leadership* = any behaviour that moves a group closer to attaining its goals. The question of a *good* leader is related to the particular goals of a group.
- *Social power* = the capacity to produce intended and foreseen effects in others (i.e. influence them) while remaining simultaneously immune to reciprocal influence.
- *Followership* = those who are influenced by a leader are not always passive.

Sources of social power

Collins and Raven (1969) identified different means by which a person or group achieve influence:
- *Reward*: tangible or social rewards, such as money, approval, or group membership.
- *Expert*: when individuals are uncertain they follow the advice of experts.
- *Legitimate*: from an employer or parent, from a sense of duty or loyalty.
- *Referent*: through being liked or respected, and providing reference points.
- *Informational*: based upon information which is independent of the nature of the source, as in information to blackmail someone.

Explanations of leadership: emergence and effectiveness

① *The trait approach.* Leaders are born not made, a view described as *The Great Man (or Woman) Theory* by **Carlyle** (1841). Certain personality traits might be associated with leader success, e.g. height, physical attractiveness, greater sensitivity, dominance, intelligence, or the person who talks most. **Mann** (1959) reviewed the literature from 1900–57, and concluded that there was little evidence to differentiate leaders from non-leaders in terms of personality. On the other hand, **Stogdill** (1974) also did a review of empirical studies and reported some significant traits.

Evaluation. **Lord** (1977) suggested that questionnaires may produce evidence of traits because people present themselves in a desirable way; observational studies show little support for trait theory. There is probably no universal set of characteristics, though flexibility or 'social intelligence' may be significant in predicting leader success (**Riggio**, 1990).

② *The situational approach.* In a study of communication networks **Leavitt** (1951) demonstrated that seating position determined who became the leader. Many leaders arise because they have been appointed. Even when this appointment is random, a group may perceive that person as a leader. **Bell and French** (1950) showed that acting petty officers who were selected randomly were nevertheless kept in that position and regarded as leaders by their subordinates.

Evaluation. The problem with such studies is that they tend to use artificially imposed leaders, limited tasks and unrepresentative group members.

③ *Leadership style.* **Lewin** *et al.* (1939) arranged for groups of children to make soap models under different styles of leadership (the leader rotated):

- *Authoritarian* group: the leader made all decisions without giving reasons, and was remote. The children misbehaved when left alone.
- *Democratic* group: Decisions were made only after consultation, the leader gave reasons for any criticism or praise, offered help if required and joined in with the group. This group had the highest morale and co-operation, and kept working when alone. They made fewer models but these were of better quality than the others.
- *Laissez-faire* group: The leader played a passive role, made no attempt to organise the group, and made no positive or negative evaluations. This group made the fewest models and they misbehaved, but they were friendly towards their leader.

Weiss and Friedrichs (1986) found that basketball coaches who engaged in more frequent rewarding, social support and adopted a democratic style, produced more satisfied and successful athletes. **Bales** (1950), using interaction process analysis, proposed two different leadership styles: *task-* and *socioemotional*-orientation.

④ *Combined approach.* It is clear that certain leaders are effective in certain situations, such as needing an authoritarian leader in a crisis. **Fiedler** (1965) developed a *contingency theory* which suggests that the effectiveness of a particular leadership style is contingent on the favourability of the situation for the leader.

- *Style* is expressed in terms of the leader's relationship with a subordinate – the least preferred co-worker (LPC). Leaders who had a relationship-oriented style would be likely to rate their LPC highly (high LPC score), whereas a task-oriented leader would give a low rating to the hypothetical LPC.
- The situation may be *favourable*: one which the leader finds easy to control, where the leader has the group's loyalty and confidence, and the group has a clearly defined task structure.

LPC scores and the 'favourability' of the situation can be used to predict whether a leader would be effective or not in that situation:

SITUATIONAL FACTORS			
STYLE	Highly favourable	Moderately favourable	Highly unfavourable
High LPC	ineffective	effective	ineffective
Low LPC	effective	ineffective	effective

When conditions are unfavourable, members are willing to overlook interpersonal conflicts in order to get on with the task, therefore a task-oriented (LPC) leader is best. In favourable conditions there is little interpersonal conflict and therefore a task-oriented leader is again best. In a moderately favourable situation, when conflict and tension within a group is highest, one needs a relationship-oriented leader.

Evaluation. Fiedler tested this model with managerial boards, basketball teams and bomber crews, and found support. However, the model has been criticised because one can't be sure that style causes effectiveness, the concept of an LPC score is rather vague, the theory ignores input from group members and overlooks the fact that leadership may change with time.

An alternative approach, *Normative Theory* (**Vroom and Yetton**, 1973) accounted for leader effectiveness in terms of the extent to which followers participate in decision-making. Leaders who permit an optimum level of participation by followers are more effective than leaders who allow too much or too little participation.

Applications of leadership theories

1. *Leadership training programmes* teach specific skills which leaders are lacking, such as how to recognise shortcomings and how to improve interactions with employees. Such programmes are expensive.

2. *Redesign the job to fit the leader.* **Fiedler** recognised that leaders often find it impossible to change, therefore his *Leader Match programme* aimed to train leaders to find a strategy within their range to fit the situation.

3. *Job satisfaction.* The relationship between leaders and workers is important for job satisfaction (see unit 9.2.1).

Followership

1. *Individual differences.* **Adorno** *et al.* (unit 1.1.3) found that authoritarian types were more obedient. **Milgram** (unit 1.3.1) set out to see if certain types of people or cultures were more obedient. There is other evidence that some people are more willing to conform or obey (see unit 1.3.1).

2. *The role of expectations.* Followers' behaviour may be affected by the expectations that their leaders hold, thus fulfilling these expectations (the *self-fulfilling prophecy*). **McGregor** (1960) proposed two kinds of leader: those who agree with Theory X (workers dislike work and need to be coerced) or Theory Y (workers will work harder if they are appreciated). The leaders' views will affect the followers' self-expectations.

1.3.3 COLLECTIVE BEHAVIOUR

Groups

'Group' implies: interaction over time, individual perception of membership, norms, roles, affective relations, and shared goals. Group effects include:

1. *Bystander apathy and deindividuation.* See crowd behaviour, below.

2. *Personal and social identity* ('Social identity theory', unit 1.1.1)

3. *Decision-making*

   - *Group polarisation*: group decisions polarise the opinions of individual group members (see **Stoner** in unit 1.3.1). **Myers and Bishop** (1970) found that when prejudiced persons discuss racial issues with similar others, their attitudes become more prejudiced; whereas if mildly biased people discuss such matters with like-minded people, they become less prejudiced. Groups develop more arguments favouring their initial position, thus polarising it further. Also, members who previously saw themselves as risky or cautious now find, in comparison with others, they aren't so extreme and must change to maintain their self-image.

   - *Groupthink*: a group may be influenced by ingroup pressures to conform and express solidarity rather than to evaluate a decision objectively. **Janis** (1982) coined the term to explain how President Kennedy's advisers made a series of mistaken decisions which led to the Bay of Pigs invasion of Cuba.

   - *Brainstorming*: groups generate more ideas but are inefficient in terms of time.

④ *Social facilitation.* Individual performance is enhanced when working in the presence of other people who are co-acting or in front of an audience (= the *coaction* and *audience effects* respectively). **Triplett** (1897) observed that cyclists performed better when in a race than in practice, and demonstrated the effect when asking people to turn fishing reels alone or in pairs. **Zajonc** *et al.* (1969) demonstrated the effect with cockroaches.

- *Mere presence*: **Schmitt** *et al.* (1986) found that participants' performance on a simple task was slower even if the observer wore a blindfold and earphones.
- *Quality versus quantity*: quantity improves when people are co-acting, quality improves when people are working alone. **Dashiell** (1930) found that participants may be faster at multiplication when coacting but they also made more errors.
- *Dominant and non-dominant responses*: **Zajonc** (1980) suggested that there are different kinds of task: well-learned, instinctive, simple motor tasks (dominant) and novel, complicated, conceptual tasks (non-dominant). Performance on the former is improved by the presence of others but depressed on the latter. **Markus** (1978) asked participants to take off their shoes (dominant response) and put on a lab coat, some large socks and shoes (non-dominant response). This was done either alone, while an observer watched or with the observer's back turned. The simple task was done fastest when being watched, the more difficult task was fastest when alone.
- Why? *Increased arousal* and the desire to present a *favourable image* increases motivation when the task is simple, but when the task is difficult *evaluation apprehension* depresses performance, and the presence of others takes *attention* away from the task causing loss of speed and more errors. The *Yerkes-Dodson effect* predicts that performance is best under conditions of optimum stress.

⑤ *Social inhibition.* The *interaction* of individuals, rather than their mere presence or coaction, may lead to depressed performance. The *Ringlemann effect* describes the fact that individual performance may decrease in proportion to the number of workers on a task, e.g. a tug-of-war team. **Latané** *et al.* (1979) conducted research on sensory feedback in groups and individuals, and suggested that poorer performance is due to:

- *Co-ordination losses*: poorer performance due to lack of co-ordination of effort.
- *Social loafing*: each member is making less effort because they feel their lack of effort will not be detected and others will take up the slack.

⑥ *Juries* are a special and important example of a small group.

Crowd behaviour

A crowd is a large but temporary gathering of persons with a common focus. Crowd behaviour may lack personal control and may be antisocial (see also 'Crowding' unit 9.5.1). Explanations include:

① *Bystander apathy* (unit 1.4.1)

② *Deindividuation.* The presence of a crowd (or group) leads individual members to feel anonymous and act according to a different set of rules than they would normally. **LeBon** (1985) suggested that people behave in an extreme way in crowds because they lose their sense of identity. **Zimbardo** (1969) suggested that:

- *Individuated behaviour*: rational, consistent with personal norms, controlled.
- *Deindividuated behaviour*: unrestrained, acting on primitive impulses, free to commit antisocial acts; caused by being a member of a crowd, or when wearing a uniform (see **Zimbardo** in unit 1.3.1). **Diener** *et al.* (1976) observed the behaviour of over 1,000 children on Hallowe'en, the house owner asked some of the children to give their names. Those who remained anonymous were more likely to steal some money and/or extra chocolate when briefly left alone.

③ *Social contagion.* Once antisocial behaviour has emerged it is catching or contagious. Individuals in the crowd *imitate* the behaviour of others and it becomes a *norm* of the crowd.

④ *Density–intensity hypothesis.* **Freedman** (1973), suggested that the physiological arousal of a crowd heightens the mood you are in. In some situations a crowd may be associated with enjoyment, as in a rock concert, or prosocial behaviour, as at a peace gathering. However, if you are not enjoying yourself you might feel stressed, or behave antisocially.

⑤ *Explanations of uncontrolled crowd or mob behaviour.* There are two views:

- *Unruly*: deindividuation and a focus on external events decrease self awareness. Intense activity and overcrowding lead to arousal. This brings the wild, antisocial behaviour associated with a mob. It can also lead to ecstatic behaviour.
- *Orderly*: the social cognitive view is that crowds are not unruly (without rules). They are obeying a different set of norms appropriate to the situation. **Reicher** (1984) analysed mob behaviour in the race riots in St Paul's, Bristol and observed that the violence was selective and restrained: the riot lasted only a few hours, the damage was almost entirely limited to police vehicles and the rioters warned other people away from the area. He concluded that there were clear rules which controlled crowd behaviour. **Marsh** *et al.* (1978) suggested that football hooliganism can be seen as an example of rules of disorder which prevent violence escalating beyond a certain point.

1.4 PRO- AND ANTISOCIAL BEHAVIOUR

1.4.1 PROSOCIAL BEHAVIOUR

- *Prosocial behaviour* = voluntary behaviour which benefits others (society).
- *Altruism* = putting the interests of others first, possibly with some risk or cost to yourself. The *primary* motive should not be reward.
- *Helping behaviour* = providing assistance to someone in need with no personal sacrifice.

Altruism

❶ *Biological altruism.* The principle of natural selection would seem to predict that individuals should behave selfishly to promote their own survival. However, even though an altruistic act may decrease *individual* survival chances, it increases the survival of the genes; altruism is selfish at the levels of the *genes*. This is called *apparent altruism* and *kin selection* (because one's kin are being favoured). *Reciprocal altruism* describes occasions when an animal behaves altruistically in the expectation of a return 'favour'. These concepts are discussed further in unit 2.3.1.

❷ *Psychological or human altruism.* Altruism in humans is influenced by personal choice, empathy, morals and social norms. The behaviour of the bystander, **Lenny Skutnik**, who drowned while saving passengers from an aircrash in the Potomac River illustrates all of these. There may be some sense of reward for 'doing good' (e.g. when giving blood) but **Lerner and Lichtman** (1968) demonstrated that self-interest (*egotistic altruism*) is not the only factor in human behaviour. Participants were to work in pairs, a random number would be drawn to determine which one should choose the roles: one would be the 'learner' and receive electric shocks, and the other would be a 'control'. Most of the true participants behaved altruistically and took the role of learner even if, for example, were told they had won but that the other participant was scared or said she would leave the experiment unless she was the control.

Helping behaviour

- *Co-operation* = helping behaviour which has mutual benefits. In some situations people don't behave co-operatively, such as when fire breaks out in a cinema. **Deutsch and Krauss** (1960) investigated co-operative and competitive behaviour using the *Trucking Game*. Participants each run a trucking firm, Acme or Bolt, and must co-operate over the use of one-way roads and gates to avoid deadlock and mutual loss. Communication is of great importance and has practical applications in conciliation work.

- *Routine courtesies* = behaviours which smooth the wheels of social interaction, for example, opening the door for someone or making a guest feel comfortable.
- *Assistance in an emergency* which may involve minimal cost to the helper but be vital to the other, as in the tragic death of **Kitty Genovese**. At least 38 people heard her screams at 3.15 a.m., some turned on their lights which frightened the attacker away. He returned twice, finally raping and stabbing her to death. The first and only call to the police was at 3.50 a.m. In the case of **James Bulger**, bystanders observed the young boy being roughly treated yet decided it was not appropriate to interfere. On the other hand, **Lenny Skutnik** (above) did help in an emergency at considerable risk to himself.

The bystander effect

1 *Diffusion of responsibility.* The more people there are, the more help there should be. However, the reverse appears to be true – the presence of others (bystanders) decreases the likelihood that anyone will offer help. Mann (1981) observed that the bystander effect was particularly likely in large crowds of over 300 – more people may mean that each person feels less responsibility. **Darley and Latané** (1968) responded to the Kitty Genovese case by testing their bystander hypothesis. They arranged for a group of students (all confederates bar one) to discuss personal problems over an intercom. During the conversation, one confederate admitted he was prone to seizures and later complained of feeling unwell and begged for help. When participants thought they were the only listener, 85% helped before the confederate lapsed into silence; if there was one bystander 62% helped and with 4 bystanders 31% helped. The average delay was 52, 93 and 166 seconds respectively. The difference may be due to the fact that participants couldn't see if anyone else was helping.

   Latané and Darley (1968) arranged for participants to fill out a bogus questionnaire in a room which filled with smoke. If the participant was alone 75% reported the emergency within six minutes. If two other participants were present this dropped to 12%. However, laboratory studies may not represent real responses.

   Piliavin *et al.* (1969) conducted a field experiment on the New York subway which demonstrated a reversal of the diffusion of responsibility effect. One experimenter would stagger and collapse as the subway train pulled out of the station. The more passengers in the immediate vicinity of the victim, the more likely help would be given. This may be because the costs of helping were low and not helping were high; it was also clearly an emergency (i.e. relatively unambiguous) and less easy to ignore.

2 *Ambiguity: informational influence or pluralistic ignorance.* In ambiguous or novel situations we look to others to tell us what to do. Each non-responding bystander sends the same message to the others, 'It's OK, no action needs to be taken'. **Clark and Word** (1972) arranged for participants to fill out a questionnaire in a lab. A maintenance worker walked through the room with a ladder; next door he could be heard working, then sounds of a crash. Regardless of whether the participant was alone or in a group, 100% helped when the crash was followed by 'Oh my back, I can't move', whereas only 30% helped in the ambiguous situation when nothing was heard after the crash.

3 *Evaluation apprehension.* The bystander fears that he may do something inappropriate or actually wrong, and wants to avoid looking foolish. The larger the audience the more inhibited we feel.

4 *Decision time.* An emergency situation requires a person to take immediate, unplanned action and therefore we use superficial cues and act impulsively. Arousal has a clouding effect on efficient decision-making. Given time to reflect, other moral and social factors might force altruistic action.

5 *Confusion of responsibility.* If you help, other bystanders may mistake your involvement for actually being responsible for the victim's suffering or that you know the victim.

6 *Costs of intervening.* Social exchange theory (unit 1.2.1) predicts that our behaviour will be determined by relative costs and rewards. There may be real costs in terms of physical danger, or long-term matters, such as court appearances, which make people disinclined to get involved.

⑦ *Attention.* A bystander may simply not notice the victim. **Darley and Batson** (1973) arranged a lecture on the Good Samaritan, the students had to pass a man lying in a doorway, moaning, as they went to the appropriate room. Some students thought they had to rush because they were late, 45% of them helped compared with 63% of those who had plenty of time. Some of the 'late' students said they hadn't noticed the man, others thought he might have been drunk.

⑧ *Characteristics of the victim (behaviour or appearance).* We may misattribute what we observe, for example thinking that a fighting couple are having a 'lover's quarrel'. In the study by **Piliavin** *et al.* (above) when the victim carried a white cane 95% of passengers offered help within 10 seconds, if he appeared drunk help came in 50% of the trials. They also found that varying the race (Black or White) of the victim, or his attractiveness (presence of an ugly facial birthmark) would alter the likelihood of helping. **Bickman** (1974) left a dime in a telephone box. If the experimenter was dressed in a suit he got the dime back 77% of the time, if he was wearing unkempt work clothes there was a 38% return rate.

⑨ *Characteristics of the helper.* **Piliavin** *et al.* found that men are more likely to help than women, but this is probably because women feel more open to attack and may have less confidence in their ability to help. **Hartshorne and May** (1928) gave children tasks which assessed their honesty and helpfulness in many different situations and found a correlation of only 0.23 between various types of helping. **Rushton** (1980) found that children who help or share in one situation are more likely to do the same in *similar* situations. This suggests that there is not a consistent trait of 'helpfulness' but there is situational consistency.

    Rosenhan (1970) produced evidence that being helpful or even altruistic is something we learn from our parents. He interviewed people who had been involved in the US civil rights movement of the 1960s, and found that the 'fully committed' had warm relations with their parents and their parents were liberals who expressed outrage about moral issues *and* did something about it. The study was, however, correlational and used retrospective data.

⑩ *Characteristics of the situation.* Ambiguity and crowd size affect the decision to intervene. The location may be important as well. Urban situations are more impersonal and therefore people are less likely to intervene than in rural ones. **Korte and Kerr** (1975) used the lost-letter method and found that 70% of the stamped postcards dropped in small towns around Boston were posted as compared with 61% of those dropped in Boston itself.

⑪ *Making people more helpful.* **Beaman** *et al.* (1978) showed a group of students a film about helpfulness. Two weeks later each was observed in an apparent emergency, 43% offered to help compared with 25% of those who had not seen the film. **Bryan and Test** (1967) noted how many drivers (out of a total 4,000 cars which passed by) stopped to help a stranded woman motorist. In the 'model' condition a man was changing a wheel for a lady driver five minutes down the road and 1.5% of drivers stopped, whereas less than 1% stopped in the no-model condition (see also unit 6.3.1).

    The victim can also help. **Cialdini** (1985) found that everyone was driving past as he lay by the roadside after a car accident, but he knew how to de-victimise himself by pointing to individuals and giving them explicit instructions.

Theories of prosocial behaviour

① *Law of social impact* (unit 1.3.1).

② *The decision model.* **Latané and Darley** (1968) outlined various factors which lead a person to decide whether or not to help in an emergency:

- Notice something is wrong.
- Define it as an emergency.
- Decide whether to take personal responsibility.
- Decide what kind of help to give.
- Implement the decision.

Evaluation. This is a useful model though it doesn't indicate why individuals decide to say 'no' at any particular stage, nor does it indicate why people might be helpful.

❸ *Arousal: cost–reward model.* **Piliavin** *et al.* (1969) suggested that the primary motive is the need to reduce the arousal created by seeing someone in distress. The decision to help is based on a cost-benefit analysis. This model does not explain selfless behaviour.

❹ *The empathy–altruism hypothesis.* **Batson** *et al.* (1981) suggested that people are more motivated to help someone when they feel empathy for a victim than just because they can see that the victim is distressed. Batson claimed that empathy is an innate trait, like altruism, and that people are not always motivated to behave selfishly as suggested by Piliavin's model.

❺ *The negative-state relief model.* **Cialdini** (1987) offered a different source of motivation: the helper's desire to reduce their own negative state of distress which has been created through empathising with the victim. Here again helping behaviour is seen as an ultimately selfish act.

❻ *Normative explanations.* Many social norms direct individuals to behave prosocially, for example norms for social justice and responsibility, and for reciprocity. People who joined the French resistance during the Second World War, took on the altruistic norms of the group.

1.4.2 ANTISOCIAL BEHAVIOUR

- *Antisocial behaviour* = behaviour which is harmful to others.
- *Aggression* = a first act of hostility with the deliberate intention of harming another against their will; this includes self-assertiveness. Anger may be present.
  - *Instrumental* or *hostile* aggression: aggression which is a means to an end (goal-oriented) or appears senseless.
  - *Legitimate* aggression, as in acting in defence or to protect another. An individual may not intend harm but be judged as behaving aggressively.

Social-psychological theories of aggression

1 The social learning approach

We *learn* both aggressiveness and how to express aggression through direct reinforcement (conditioning theory), indirect reinforcement (observational learning), identification (with significant others) and imitation (modelling).

Evidence

❶ *Modelling.* **Bandura** *et al.* (1961, 1963) showed that, if children watched someone else behave aggressively towards Bobo-the-doll (punching it, shouting at it and hitting it with a hammer), they were more likely to be aggressive *and* to imitate specific actions when they were placed on their own with the doll. Other findings and later variations found that imitation was even more likely if:

- The model was *rewarded*.
- The model had high *status*. For example, a favourite hero or heroine on TV.
- The child *identified* with the model, for example same sex.
- The child saw the model live rather than in a film or a *cartoon*.
- The child had low *self-esteem*.

Evaluation. The results may be due to demand characteristics produced by the unfamiliar social situation; the children had to look for cues of what to do with Bobo. Also ethical objections should be considered.

❷ *Media influences.* Watching violence on TV may lead to increased aggression (unit 1.4.3).

❸ *Childrearing practices.* **Patterson** *et al.* (1989) observed 200 families and concluded that *coercive home environments* may create aggressiveness in a number of ways:

- *Control theory*: harsh discipline and lack of supervision results in disrupted bonding between parent and child, and lack of identification.

- Some parental behaviours, such as nagging, *provoke* aggressiveness in the children.
- *Modelling*: parents solve disputes aggressively, children have no alternative models.
- Such children become *resistant* to punishment, and progressively harder to restrain.
- This aggressive behaviour leads them to be *rejected* by their peers and join deviant peer groups.

④ *Cross-cultural studies* show differences in aggression and indicate that social practices must be important (see unit 1.4.4).

Evaluation

- *Oversimplified*. People are *not* consistently rewarded for aggression, often they are punished.
- It *can* account for *cultural and individual* differences between people.
- It explains the fact that people *imitate specific* acts of violence.

2 The motivational perspective

Individuals are driven or motivated to behave in an aggressive manner because of being physiologically aroused and because of the presence of specific cues.

① *The frustration–aggression hypothesis.* **Dollard** *et al.* (1939) suggested that frustration always leads to some form of aggression and aggression is always the result of frustration. Aggression motivates us to do something. It has the properties of basic drives such as hunger, but is triggered by external, social factors rather than internal, biological ones. It is a learned drive. **Geen and Berkowitz** (1967) first frustrated their participants and then showed a film of an aggressive or non-aggressive nature. Aggression was later assessed through the level of electric shocks the participants administered to a learner. If the participant had watched an aggressive film or there was an aggressive trigger present in the room, such as a gun, the number of shocks given was greater.

② *The arousal–aggression hypothesis.* A general state of physiological arousal may be a better explanation for aggression than frustration. Anger, happiness, pain, overcrowding, physical exercise, loud music, stimulating drugs and high temperatures are 'exciting' and increase the likelihood of aggression. **Calhoun** (1962) showed that crowding could produce aggressive behaviour in rats - despite plenty of food, some ate their young (see unit 9.5.1). **Berkowitz** *et al.* (1979) induced pain by placing participants' hands in cold or warm water while they delivered rewards or punishments to a partner (not shocks). The cold water condition led them to cause greater harm to their partner. **Baron and Ransberger** (1978) analysed records of collective violence in the US over a four-year period. They found that aggression increased as temperature rose, but only up to a point. Over 90° F. aggression dropped. (See also the 'density–intensity hypothesis' in unit 1.3.3.)

Evaluation

- Arousal doesn't always lead to aggression.
- Aggression may arise *before arousal*.
- It doesn't explain *instrumental* aggression.
- Arousal is related to the presence of certain *hormones* (a biological explanation).

Other theories of aggression

We can evaluate social-psychological theories by looking at the alternatives.

① *The ethological approach.* **Lorenz** (1966) argued that the same laws applied to all animals because they are governed by the same laws of natural selection. His observations of non-human animal behaviour led him to suggest that aggression is:

- *Innate tendency* which is triggered by environmental signals. **Tinbergen** (1951) demonstrated that the male stickleback will behave aggressively when it sees anything red (even a post office van).
- *Adaptive response*: the strongest, most aggressive animal controls the food, territory and mating, thereby promoting its own survival and that of its gene pool.
- *Not naturally harmful*: a species will eventually become extinct unless it evolves a form of natural regulation such as *ritualised fighting*, *threat displays* and *appeasement*

behaviours. It is possible that violent people are less sensitive to such signals. Species evolve *evolutionarily stable strategies* to maximise aggression and survival (unit 2.1.1).

Evaluation. This approach is deterministic, may not be applicable to human behaviour and does not account for cultural differences.

❷ *The biological approach.* Biological factors may be due to innate differences (genetic) or duc to environmental (possibly social) factors, as in the case of diet or drugs such as alcohol.

- *Hormones. Adrenalin*, for physiological arousal, associated with a fight or flight response to danger; *testosterone*, male hormones associated with states of aggression; and *progesterone*, female hormones present around ovulation and prior to menstruation (pre-menstrual tension) may prepare mothers for parental aggressiveness.
- *Genes.* **Mednick and Hutchings** (1978) found that adopted children with biological fathers who were criminals, were more likely to become criminals themselves. This supports a genetic link. Some personality disorders may have a genetic origin but are also moderated by the effects of experience.
- *Brain differences.* In humans there is some evidence that limbic tumours are associated with aggressive behaviour.
- *Brain chemistry.* **Brown** *et al.* (1979) compared an aggressive group of marines with a control group, and found a significant negative correlation between aggression and levels of *serotonin*, a neurochemical. In high doses it is associated with low arousal and sleep. Some people may be born with lower production of serotonin. **Mawson and Jacobs** (1978) found that murder rates are highest in those countries which eat most corn. Corn contains a substance important in the production of serotonin.

Evaluation. This approach does explain individual but not cultural differences; certain factors, such as hormones, may be a cause *or* an effect of aggression; it is a deterministic and reductionist account. **Siann** (1985) concluded that no physiological system has been found to have an invariant effect on aggressive behaviour, i.e. it is not the sole cause.

❸ *The psychodynamic approach.* **Freud** (1920) argued that aggression is an innate, unconscious drive. Like **Lorenz**, he felt that aggression naturally builds up and then needs to be discharged (*catharsis*), either through destruction or through more socially acceptable forms, such as sport. If the energy remains pent up this will cause psychological disorders, such as depression, suicide or masochism. **Hokanson** (1970) found that blood pressure was lowered as a result of displacing aggressive feelings by administering electric shocks or fantasising about harming the experimenter who had mildly irritated the participant. Other studies have not found catharsis effective.

Evaluation. Sports activity is often associated more with increased rather than decreased aggression, and this account does not explain cultural differences.

Control of aggressive behaviour

Solutions are related to cause
- *Unlearning aggression*: if aggression is learned it can be unlearned. For example, providing non-aggressive models, or models who are negatively reinforced (or punished), or rewarding non-aggressive behaviour or teaching non-aggressive means of resolving disputes.
- *Using non-aggressive means of punishment*: parents can be taught better skills, such as the *time-out* technique which avoids direct confrontation and avoids rewarding aggressive behaviour with attention (see unit 4.4.1).
- *Removing aggressive cues*: reducing violence in the media so that aggressive behaviour is not triggered in individuals with a tendency to be aggressive.
- *Socially acceptable ways of channelling catharsis* (aggression). We can learn to express our aggression verbally, to channel it into other activity such as sport, or fantasise about violent action while never doing anything.
- *Undoing aggressive motives.* A tense situation might be diffused through incompatible responses, such as tickling someone who is angry or offering apologies (a form of submission). **Baron** (1983) annoyed participants and then gave them a chance to vent

their anger. Those participants who had been shown a non-violent cartoon in the interim were less aggressive than those shown neutral pictures.

- *Ritualising aggression.* Encouraging people to express angry feelings in ways which prevent escalation. For example, learning appropriate appeasement gestures or effective threat displays which stop further aggression.
- *Chemical means.* Giving drugs to counteract hormones in cases of excessive aggression, or changing diet to avoid substances which increase aggression.
- *Psychosurgery* (lobotomy) is a controversial method used in the past. Recent use is very rare and not related to aggression.
- *Encouraging prosocial behaviour* discourages and controls antisocial behaviour.

1.4.3 MEDIA INFLUENCES ON PRO- AND ANTISOCIAL BEHAVIOUR

The media includes: television, radio, films, videos, computers, books and magazines.

How media exert both pro- and antisocial influences

❶ *Stereotypes.* All media need to communicate a great deal of information in a relatively short time, so they use standard cultural stereotypes such as foreigners playing 'baddies', overweight people depicted as 'jolly', and wolves as big and bad. Such stereotypes may or may not reflect reality, and may be positive or negative. **Manstead and McCulloch** (1981) found that the majority of advertisements still use gender stereotypes. **Mulac** *et al.* (1985) analysed the content of a number of children's programmes, and found strong gender stereotyping: males were more dynamic and female characters had greater socio-intellectual status and aesthetic quality.

    Williams' (1985) study of Canadians who had their first exposure to TV (the residents of 'Notel') found that children's sex role attitudes became more traditional and sex-stereotyped after they had been exposed to Americanised television culture.

    Gunter (1986) found that people who watch a lot of television hold more stereotyped beliefs, suggesting that the use of stereotypes on television does have an influence. Alternatively, people (e.g. children) who have a more simplistic cognitive style may prefer to watch more television.

❷ *Counter-stereotypes.* The effects of inaccurate or undesirable stereotypes may be overcome by presenting people in atypical roles in an effort to promote social change, such as Black female judges or men sewing curtains. However, stereotypes are resistant to change (unit 1.1.3). The deliberate manipulation of stereotypes, for good or bad, is ethically questionable because it presumes that certain stereotypes are preferable.

    It does appear that changing stereotypes has had positive consequences. **Greenfield** (1984) found that *Sesame Street*'s use of ethnic and disabled minorities helped children from minority groups have a greater sense of cultural pride.

❸ *Norm formation.* The media presents norms of how to behave in social situations, such as the way soap operas present a particular form of conflict-resolution which promotes a confrontational approach. **Gerbner and Gross** (1976) found that people who watch a lot of television rate the outside world as being more dangerous and threatening than it actually is (*deviance amplification* or *moral panic*).

❹ *Displacement effect.* A media bias would be less harmful if it was sufficiently counterbalanced by experience of the real world. However, people who spend a lot of time watching television or reading books have less time for real interactions. **Mutz** *et al.* (1993) found that decreased television watching does not lead to increases in other activities, possibly because television provides instant rewards with little effort and children then find it harder to generate their own activities. **Gunter** (1982) found evidence that 'heavy' television viewing at an early age had a damaging effect on how well children learn to read. **Keith** *et al.* (1986) have also found that children who watch far more television than average perform less well at school.

❺ *Social deprivation.* Watching television may displace social interactions resulting in children who lack social skills, though **Lyle and Hoffman** (1972) found that popular children watch as much television as their less popular peers. Therefore, it may be more of a problem for children who already lack social skills; withdrawn children may find that the TV or computer games offer the kind of company that they otherwise lack. This activity then prevents them from overcoming their social problems.

6 *Stimulation hypothesis.* Television is an ideal medium to present educational information, and is a resource much used by schools. *Sesame Street* provides preschool children with carefully considered material to promote emotional, social and intellectual development. The BBC and ITV have an extensive schools programme, and there is the Open University as well as many adult programmes specifically aimed at education. The value of television and all media is related to *what* you actually watch, read or listen to.

7 *Traditional view.* In the past people complained about children reading 'penny novellas'. The media is a scapegoat for many problems; television, videos and computers are relatively new media which have potential for good and bad.

Does violence on TV lead to increased aggression?

1 *Amount of violence on TV.* **Gunter and Harrison** (1995) reported that violence only takes up 1% of programme time but 33% of all programmes carried some violence, and almost 20% happens in children's programmes.

2 *Link between television violence and aggressive behaviour.* This view was supported by **Comstock** (1991) who reviewed nearly 200 studies. However this does not mean that TV is the *cause*, such *correlations* may be due to the fact that aggressive personalities watch more violence on television. **Wiegman** *et al.* (1992) followed 400 Dutch secondary school pupils over a period of three years, and found that positive correlations between watching television violence and aggressive behaviour disappeared if initial levels of aggression were taken into account. **Parke** *et al.* (1977) looked at the effect of violent and non-violent films on Belgian and American male juvenile delinquents. Aggression increased on some measures in the 'violent-film' group but on other measures increased only in those who were naturally high in aggression.

Certain programmes may function as a trigger for the expression of aggression. **Friedrich and Stein** (1973) showed aggressive cartoons, prosocial, or neutral films to preschool children and then observed them playing. Children who initially were above average in aggression were affected by the violent cartoons, whereas those who were neutral did not react to either type of programme.

3 *Aggressive personalities.* It is clear that not everyone is affected by vicarious violence in the same way, for example you might watch an aggressive film but not imitate the behaviour. However, watching violence probably does affect everyone but affects less aggressive people less noticeably.

4 *Imitation.* **Bandura** *et al.* (see unit 1.4.2) demonstrated that both the amount and kind of aggression can be learned through vicarious reinforcement and modelling. Further evidence for imitation comes from 'case studies' of copycat crimes, such as the role of the video 'Child's Play' in the murder of **James Bulger** (**Newson**, 1994).

Much of the violence in children's programmes is presented in rather unreal and stereotyped ways, as in cartoons, and therefore may not be imitated. Alternatively, Newson argues, when a victim is portrayed in subhuman ways we do not develop any empathy for them and therefore feel that no one really gets hurt. In traditional gruesome fairy tales the reader is more able to identify with the victim.

5 *Disinhibition.* The media present social *norms* which suggest that certain levels of violence are common and acceptable. Such norms disinhibit normal responses and increase the likelihood of aggressive responses. In America, the lawyer for a 15-year-old who shot his neighbour in the course of a burglary, claimed that the boy's sense of reality had been distorted through excessive exposure to television.

6 *Desensitisation.* Exposure to violence may desensitise us so that we tolerate it more easily in real life. **Drabman and Thomas** (1975) showed young children a film which was either violent or a non-violent but exciting. The participants were then asked to monitor the behaviour of two younger children via a TV link. When the confederates

started hitting each other, the children who were exposed to the violent film were slower to call for help.

7. *Arousal.* Watching violence may be arousing which could increase the likelihood of aggressive behaviour *if* a person has learned to deal with arousal in this way and/or if there were environmental triggers (**Geen and Berkowitz,** unit 1.4.2).

8. *Ethics.* The fact that *experimental* exposure of children to violent videos would be regarded as ethically objectionable indicates our intuitive understanding of its influence. Like all ethical decisions, violence on TV is a matter of balance.

1.4.4 INDIVIDUAL, SOCIAL AND CULTURAL DIVERSITY IN PRO- AND ANTISOCIAL BEHAVIOUR

1. *Individual differences* can be related to innate or environmental factors (see unit 1.4.2) so that aggressiveness and helpfulness vary with, for example, gender and parenting styles.

2. *Social norms* are critical in influencing individual behaviour, such as the differences between urban and rural behaviour (unit 1.4.1), and the effects of different childrearing styles.

3. *Cultural differences in prosocial behaviour.* Whiting and Whiting (1975) measured altruism in six cultures and found 100% of Kenyan children behaved altruistically compared with 8% of American children. Children on kibbutzim in Israel are more co-operative which can be related to the way their society is managed (**Eisenberg and Mussen,** 1989).

4. *Cultural differences in antisocial behaviour*
   - *Non-aggressive.* The *Amish* of Eastern America and people of the Quaker faith refuse to take part in aggressive encounters. **Mead** (1935) observed the *Arapesh* tribe of New Guinea and thought that their childrearing practices encouraged gentle and non-aggressive behaviour in both boys and girls.
   - *Aggressive.* The dominant culture in America is one of assertiveness and aggression; the murder rate is seven times higher than in Britain (**Smith and Bond,** 1993). **Mead** also observed the *Mundugumour* of New Guinea who were aggressive.

5. *Differences in amount and expression.* Interpersonal distance conveys different messages in different cultures. In Britain, close interpersonal distance communicates an intimate relationship or is interpreted as a threat, whereas Arabs tend to stand closer together in ordinary social intercourse. **Bond** *et al.* (1985) found that Hong Kong students judged insults between managers and subordinates differently than US students, demonstrating different rules of acceptable behaviour.

Chapter roundup

1.1   **Social cognition**: the way we *think* about other people.

1.1.1   Perception of people and groups (*social perception*) is biased by social factors and explained in terms of stereotypes, schema, social identity and social representation theory.

1.1.2   *Attribution theory* is a social psychological explanation of how individuals interpret the causes of behaviour. Inferences may be dispositional or situational, and are inevitably biased in the direction of the observer.

1.1.3   *Stereotypes, prejudice and discrimination* fulfil understandable and sometimes desirable individual and group needs.

1.1.4   Psychological research suggests that prejudice and discrimination may be *reduced* through equal status co-operation and slow political changes.

1.2 Social relationships

1.2.1 *Theories* describe relationships in terms of rewards and costs, reinforcement, needs, or biological adaptiveness.

1.2.2 Various factors, such as attractiveness, familiarity, and similarity, act as *filters* for selecting prospective friends or partners. Relationships are *maintained* through habit, disclosure and deliberate strategies. However certain factors, such as relocation, inequity, change or deception, may tip the balance and one or both partners will begin the process of *dissolving* the relationship.

1.2.3 Past research has focused on the commonalties in relationships. Another approach is to focus on individual experiences of relationships, such as *components*, and *variations* at an individual, social and cultural level.

1.2.4 Interpersonal relationships *affect* individual development, emotional stability, happiness and mental health.

1.3 Social influence

1.3.1 People *conform* to group norms which provide informational or normative social influence especially in ambiguous situations. People are more *obedient* than we expect, though studies of obedience may lack ecological validity. A more positive approach is to consider *independent behaviour* which is related to individual differences and culture norms.

1.3.2 *Leadership* is best understood in terms of an interaction between personality and situation. Social power and followership are elements of effective leadership.

1.3.3 The behaviour of a *collection of people* is different from that of individuals working separately. Issues include social facilitation, inhibition, contagion, mood enhancement and rule-governed mob behaviour.

1.4 Pro- and antisocial behaviour

1.4.1 Human *altruism* can be explained in terms of learned and innate factors. The presence of bystanders decreases *helping behaviour* is certain circumstances, especially when the situation is ambiguous and the costs are high.

1.4.2 *Antisocial behaviour* (aggression) is caused by a combination of social and biological factors, such as conditioning, imitation, arousal, diet, and genes. If aggression is caused by biological factors, it can be *reduced* using drugs. If the cause is environmental, then relearning and non-aggressive models are needed.

1.4.3 *Violence on TV* is probably a contributory rather than a primary cause of aggressive behaviour in all people.

1.4.4 There are *individual, social and cultural* differences in pro- and antisocial behaviour.

Illustrative question

(a) Describe some of the findings from research into obedience to authority. (14 marks)
(b) Evaluate procedures used in the study of this area. (10 marks)

(AEB A 1996)

Tutorial note

In part (a) the question requires a *description* (skill A) of *findings*. No extra credit would be awarded to an answer which provides details of the actual study or makes any evaluative comments. In part (b) you are given the opportunity to comment on the *procedures* but this time you must evaluate rather than describe. Such evaluation can include both practical and ethical considerations, and should present a balanced view rather than being all negative.

Don't feel that you would have to give exact percentages for full marks, though it obviously demonstrates detailed knowledge.

Suggested answer

(a) **Milgram** (1963) studied obedience to authority in a laboratory. He asked volunteers to take part in a learning experiment where the 'teacher' would give electric shocks to a 'learner' (confederate) every time a mistake was made. The experimenter was the authority figure. Before Milgram began his study he asked various people to say how experimental participants would behave. They thought at most only 3% of the participants might go as far as the highest level. When Milgram did the experiment, 65% of the participants, all males, went to the maximum limit.

Milgram subsequently altered various aspects of the experiment to see if obedience levels were affected. If the 'teacher' was placed in the same room as the 'learner' and had to press the learner's hand on the shock plate, obedience fell to 30%. If the experimenter gave instructions over the phone the 'teacher' often said they were giving the shocks when they weren't, nevertheless 21% continued to obey. When the experiment was conducted in a run-down building rather than a prestigious university setting, obedience fell to 47.5%. If the 'teacher' was paired with other two other 'teachers' (confederates) who dissented, then only 10% of the real participants continued to 450 volts. If the teacher thought that the learner had a heart condition obedience didn't change. Milgram found that educated participants were less obedient, and military participants were more obedient, and that females behaved the same as men. He also looked at other cultures and found some differences.

When he completed the study he debriefed his participants and asked them what they felt. Only 1% said they were sorry to have participated. Some felt the experience had been worthwhile, even if only to warn them about blind obedience in the future. One participant said she knew the learner wasn't really getting the shocks.

Zimbardo (1969) tried a different variation. He arranged for the 'teacher' to be introduced to the 'learner' and to wear a name tag , or to wear a lab coat and hood. The latter condition was called 'deindividuation', it increased the 'teacher's' sense of anonymity and led to increased electric shocks. Zimbardo's other well-known study, the Stanford Prison experiment, also looked at obedience to authority. Both prisoners and guards were college students who were taking part in a role-playing exercise. The prisoners displayed extreme obedience to their guards even though it wasn't real, for example they washed the toilets out with their bare hands.

Hofling *et al.* (1966) conducted a more realistic experiment where nurses were told to administer a drug to a patient despite the fact that this contravened institutional policy, 21 out of 22 nurses obeyed an unknown doctor over the telephone. The nurses defended themselves by saying it often happens, a doctor would be annoyed if they refused.

A study by **Langer *et al.*** (1978) found that people will obey mindless instructions as long as the request is not too large. Obedience may often occur because people are on auto-pilot.

(b) The procedures used in obedience research pose ethical and practical problems. The main criticism is deception. If participants knew the purpose of the experiment beforehand they would not behave normally. Therefore in both lab and field experiments the participants were deceived. **Aronson** (1988) says that deception is defensible when it is the only way to get certain results. He pointed out that people don't think they would be obedient but Milgram's evidence demonstrates how people do behave rather than how they think they would behave, therefore the deception is defensible.

Zimbardo did not deceive his participants but he nevertheless caused them severe distress. Milgram's participants also experienced distress both during the experiment when they thought the learner was in pain, and afterwards when they realised what they had done. The same could be said of Hofling's nurses. The fact that Zimbardo's participants volunteered for the study could be used in his defence, though some felt they had no idea of what they were letting themselves in for. The fact that the experimenter kept prodding them to continue might be seen as undue pressure and denying them the right to withdraw.

Milgram defended the distress he created by saying that he did not expect people to behave so obediently. However, he did go on to replicate the original experiment in many different situations when he knew how participants might well behave.

Milgram also defended his deception by pointing out that he did debrief all participants. The fact that most of them said they were glad to have taken part shows that they weren't that distressed by the experience.

There are several practical rather than ethical issues. Most important is the question of ecological validity. Since Milgram's experiment was conducted in a lab we cannot be sure that it is true to real llife. Participants respond to demand characteristics and especially because they were paid volunteers they feel they should obey norms about behaviour in experiments, i.e. obey the experimenter. In real life people have other options of how to respond. The fact that the participants were volunteers also means there may have been a bias since such people tend to have different characteristics such as being more willing to please.

Hofling's experiment was more realistic but it only tells us about a particular kind of obedience, where people have been trained to obey specific superiors. They may have been conforming to norms rather than being obedient.

Question bank

Allow 35-40 minutes for each question.

Social cognition

1 (a) Discuss errors and biases which may occur in the attribution process. (14 marks)
(b) Discuss **one** practical application based on research into attributions. (10 marks)

(AEB AS 1992)

Points: Candidates often know a lot about one part and very little of the other. It is useful to be familiar with applications throughout the syllabus as they are a good way to evaluate theories.

2 Critically consider the role played by stereotypes in how we perceive other people.

(AEB AS 1991)

Points: Unfortunately, the question lends itself to anecdotal answers. Empirical evidence from interpersonal perception will be relevant. Positive as well as negative stereotypes should be discussed.

3 (a) Consider psychological insights into the reduction of prejudice **and/or** discrimination. (14 marks)
(b) Critically evaluate the effectiveness of strategies for reducing prejudice **and/or** discrimination. (10 marks)

(AEB A 1995)

Points: Part (a) requires descriptions of 'insights' rather than any experimental procedures.

Social relationships

4 Describe and evaluate **two** psychological theories of and **two** investigations into either the formation or breakdown of relationships.

(AEB specimen)

Points: Make sure you do what is required, i.e. select formation or breakdown *not* both, and write about only two theories and two studies. Candidates often describe the material adequately but omit evaluation, especially of a positive nature (such as applications).

5 Critically consider some of the psychological explanations of why we are attracted to some people and not to others.

(AEB AS 1990)

Points: You obviously must do more than list factors which affect liking; you must evaluate them using empirical evidence, theories and alternative explanations.

6 (a) Define briefly the following three terms and give an example of each:
(i)   stereotyping; (3 marks)
(ii) racism; (3 marks)
(iii) sexism. (3 marks)
(b) Discuss, making reference to empirical studies, the main social factors influencing the choice of friends that a young person makes. (11 marks)

(NEAB A 1991)

Points: You might include conformity as well as factors of attraction in your answer. How does the phrase 'a young person' limit the question?

Social influence

7 Discuss some of the ways in which the presence of others may affect the behaviour of an individual.

(AEB A 1981)

Points: A straightforward question, which may lead to an oversimple answer. A good answer needs to go further than listing the ways. Relevant evidence is necessary, plus a critical appreciation of any theory or research.

8 Discuss psychological investigations of obedience in humans and consider the implications of this type of research.

(AEB A 1989)

Points: The question can be divided into two parts: description and evaluation of empirical studies, and a discussion of the ethical and social implications.

9 'Leaders are born not made'. Discuss.

(AEB AS 1990)

Points: Essentially a nature/nurture question, which should be discussed specifically in terms of leaders, rather than behaviour generally.

Pro- and antisocial behaviour

10 Describe and evaluate research into the bystander effect.

(AEB A 1995)

Points: The term 'research' covers both theory and empirical investigation.

11 (a) Discuss **two** of the social-psychological theories of aggression. (12 marks)
(b) Critically consider implications that social-psychological theories of aggression might have for the reduction of aggressive behaviour. (12 marks)

(AEB specimen)

Points: Theories which are biological may be used by way of evaluation in part (a) but are not relevant for part (b).

12 (a) Describe **one** study in which an attempt was made to assess the influence of television on social behaviour. (6 marks)

(b) Name and discuss **one** weakness and one strength in the methodology of the study you have described. (6 marks)

(c) Discuss **two** major problems which limit the extent to which clear-cut evidence can be found to show that television may influence social behaviour. (8 marks)

(NEAB A 1988)

Points: Television can have a pro- or antisocial influence on behaviour. The problem with much research in this area is its poor validity, a point addressed by part (c).

COMPARATIVE PSYCHOLOGY

Units in this chapter

Chapter overview

Animal psychology is called 'comparative psychology' because animal data is used to draw comparisons (similarities and differences) between species of animals, including humans. This chapter emphasises the adaptive significance of all behaviour.

2.1 EVOLUTIONARY DETERMINANTS OF BEHAVIOUR

2.1.1 EVOLUTION OF BEHAVIOUR IN NON-HUMAN ANIMALS

Evolution is a fact, living things evolve through a progressive sequence of changes. A theory is an attempt to explain the facts.

Darwin's theory of evolution

❶ *The theory*. Humans breed animals using *artificial* selection. Evolution occurs through *natural* selection.

- Individuals within a species *vary*. Some of this variation is caused by mutation and can be inherited.
- There is *competition* between individuals for scarce resources.
- The individuals who are best *adapted* to their *ecological niche* are *fittest*. Individuals who are fittest have a competitive advantage and are most likely to survive *and reproduce*. Fitness is measured in terms of the number of offspring produced by an individual.
- *Selective pressure* is the force by which one individual is favoured over another.
- Environmental change means that this process is ongoing.
- Only characteristics which are inherited can be naturally selected.

② *Understanding evolution in terms of genetics.* In the nineteenth century **Mendel** conducted experiments with plants and demonstrated that particles (genes) explained heredity. Each characteristic (such as flower colour) is determined by a pair of *alleles* (2 alleles = a gene), one inherited from each parent.

- The total set of genes is an individual's *genotype*. Some genes are dominant and some are recessive, so that only one is expressed.
- An individual's *phenotype* is the external character of an organism, recessive genes are not expressed unless they occur as a pair.
- It is genotype which is naturally selected, however selective pressure works on phenotype.
- Most behaviours are determined by more than one gene (*polygenetic inheritance*).

③ *Empirical evidence.* It follows from evolutionary theory that characteristics which a species possess are likely to be those which are most *adaptive*.

- *Comparative studies.* For example, most living and fossil vertebrates which share similar characteristics have the same bone structure in their arms.
- *Studying the effects of geographical isolation.* **Darwin** observed the physical differences between members of the same species living on different islands of the Galapagos. For example, on one island there were finches with thick beaks, whereas on another their beaks were elongated. He related this to dietary differences: hard-shelled seeds and insects under rocks respectively, and concluded that physical differences evolved as a result of selective pressure.
- *Studying the effects of environmental change.* Industrialisation in Britain led to a blackened environment, darker moths had an adaptive advantage in terms of camouflage. The peppered moth was light-coloured until a mutant darker variety appeared in 1850, by 1900 it had virtually replaced the lighter form (*industrial melanism*). **Kettlewell** (1955) demonstrated this by recording the frequency that birds took different types of moths on darker and lighter trees. Similar selective pressures have occurred with insecticides and antibiotic-resistant strains of bacteria.
- *Artificial selection experiments.* **Manning** (1961) bred fruit flies who were fast and slow maters, the progeny showed combined characteristics. Selective breeding programmes used by farmers with both plants and animals demonstrate artificial selection.
- *Shared behavioural patterns.* **Lorenz** (1958) argued that when individual members of the same species all exhibit the same behaviour, that behaviour must be largely inherited. Lorenz bred hybrid ducks, producing new combinations of motor patterns, evidence of the genetic basis of these behaviour patterns.

④ *Criticisms*

- Much of the empirical support is from *natural experiments*. The validity of the theory is demonstrated by its ability to explain observations, but cause and effect cannot be proven because no independent variable has been manipulated.
- How are *intermediate stages* of evolution selected? For example, when a species evolves a form of brightly coloured protective mimicry (see unit 2.1.3), there is a period during which the mimicry is not yet fully developed and the bright coloration must act as a positive disadvantage.

Other theories of evolution

① *Lamark's theory.* **Lamark** (1809) proposed that characteristics which are acquired during an organism's lifetime are inherited by subsequent generations. For example, a blacksmith's son would inherit large muscles developed during the father's lifetime. This cannot explain evolution because natural selection can only work on genetically determined characteristics. *Ontogeny* describes those changes which occur through experience whereas *phylogeny* are the changes which are genetically based.

② *Group selection.* Darwin's theory of evolution cannot explain altruism because any behaviour which decreases an individual's reproductive potential should not be naturally selected (see unit 2.3.1). **Wynne-Edwards** (1962) suggested that natural selection might operate at the level of the group (*group selection*). A group with more favourable characteristics would be more likely to survive to reproduce. However, selection takes place at the level of individual genes.

3 *Sociobiological explanations*

- **Hamilton** (1964) explained apparent altruism in terms of *inclusive fitness* rather than individual fitness; individuals behave altruistically towards their kin because they are promoting the reproduction of their gene pool. Evolution acts at the level of the genes and therefore selective pressure includes close genetic relations (*kin selection*). Inclusive fitness is measured in terms of the number of surviving descendants and relatives. [*Beware of explanations which sound as if the genes are actively developing strategies, evolutionary strategies are the* passive *result of natural selection.*]

- *Evolutionarily stable strategies (ESS)* are species-specific strategies which have evolved to a point where they cannot be bettered by any feasible alternative and therefore cannot be invaded by a mutant gene. For example, the *hawk–dove strategy* (**Maynard-Smith**, 1976), a balance between hawks (individuals who fight to kill) and doves (individuals who will threaten but avoid serious fighting). Another ESS is the '*owner wins*' *strategy*. **Davies and Houston** (1984) watched territorial speckled wood butterflies. When an intruder lost a contest, they removed the owner and the intruder was able to occupy the territory. If the original owner was reintroduced, the new owner won the contest. Ownership, not size, determined the winner in a territorial contest.

4 *Ethological explanations*. **Lorenz and Tinbergen** (1938) suggested that a behaviour (instinct) could be regarded as genetically determined (innate) if it was stereotyped, species-specific, and not present in individuals reared in isolation or those prevented from practising it. *Sign stimuli* produce an inevitable and distinct response, *fixed action pattern* (FAP). These are mainly innate, though they can be affected by experience (e.g. birdsong). The sign stimulus is also called a *releaser* because it releases the FAP under certain conditions.

The concept of instinct has become unfashionable because it attempts to distinguish between innate and learned behaviour, whereas there is no clear distinction (see unit 2.3.3).

5 *Cultural inheritance* is a form of evolutionary change but not as a result of natural selection. Behaviours which are successful or adaptive are imitated and passed on to future generations (ontogeny). Cultural transmission is more powerful and flexible because it is faster. Some examples of the influence of animal culture:

- Researchers left sweet potatoes on the beach for a troop of macaque monkeys, one of whom 'invented' the idea of washing the sand off the potatoes in the sea. Soon other monkeys imitated her, thus evolving a new kind of behaviour which was passed to subsequent generations (**Ridley**, 1986).

- Great tits and blue tits were first observed removing the foil tops of milk bottles and drinking the milk in 1921, within 10 years the habit had spread throughout Britain. The new behaviour was not due to natural selection because the change was too rapid. **Sherry and Galef** (1984) experimentally demonstrated that birds learn by a combination of imitation, spontaneous discovery and learning from drinking from already opened bottles.

The value of evolutionary concepts as explanations for non-human animal behaviour

1 *Explanations of sexual selection, parental investment, mating strategies, parent–offspring conflict* and *bonding* all use evolutionary concepts (see the whole of unit 2.2 and 2.3.3).

2 *Explanations of emotion* and *signalling systems*. **Darwin** suggested that some emotional responses are universal and innate (unit 3.4.2). Signalling systems (unit 2.3.4) have evolved from autonomic signals.

3 *Theories of aggression*. **Lorenz** (unit 1.4.2) explained aggression in terms of evolutionary pressures. Ritualised behaviour has evolved in animals as a means of communicating intent but limiting potential harm.

2.1.2 COMPETITION FOR RESOURCES

Limited availability of resources (food, water, mates and nesting sites) means that there must be competition between individuals. Those who are successful in attaining resources will have greater reproductive success.

① *Competition by exploitation* (competition resolved by sharing). In situations where there are sufficient resources all individuals are free to *exploit* (use) the resource. Efficient sharing of resources will be achieved using an *ideal free distribution* (**Fretwell**, 1972). Individual species members initially select the richest habitat. As more individuals arrive this area will be depleted and newcomers do better to select a poorer quality habitat, shared by fewer individuals. The model predicts three features:

- *Numerical*: more individuals should be in the richest habitats.
- *Equal intake*: individuals in all areas should have the same intake rate.
- *Prey risk*: mortality rates should be the same for all areas (**Kacelnik** *et al.*, 1992).

    Empirical support. **Milinski** (1979) placed six sticklebacks in a tank where one end received prey at twice the rate of the other end. The sticklebacks distributed themselves relative to resources – four at the fast end and two at the slow end. When delivery rate was switched, the fish redistributed themselves. **Power** (1984) found that algae-grazing catfish in the wild were distributed in an ideal free manner in relation to distribution of algae on the sides and bottoms of their pools.

② *Competition by resource defence* (despotic distribution). In situations of insufficient resources (scarcity), competition arises and can be resolved by using *territories* to defend the resource. This is an *interference strategy* because each individual suffers some loss – their efficient exploitation of resources is interfered with.

    The first individuals establish and defend territories in the richer habitats, subsequent individuals have to make do with poorer habitats or may be excluded altogether. Animals are not free to choose a habitat but are forced to accept the best available territory. The strongest individuals are called *despots*. Reasons for, and strategies of, resource defence:

- *Economy*. **Brown** (1964) suggested that territoriality should be naturally selected when the benefits outweigh the costs (energy expenditure, risk of predation). **Gill and Wolf** (1975) conducted time budget studies of the sunbird which defends patches of flowers. The metabolic gain (in terms of nectar) slightly outweighed the cost (in terms of flying and watching). But this does not apply when the resource is too scarce because a greater expenditure is necessary to defend the territory. When the resource is too abundant, defence is a waste of energy and may even incur a cost in terms of conspicuousness to predators.
- *Optimal territory size*. **Carpenter** *et al.* (1983) suggested that animals defend territories which maximise energy gain. A study of hummingbirds showed that they adjusted their territory size in relation to their weight; as their weight increased they reduced the space they defended.
- *Shared resource defence*. Individuals may share resources during mating, in some species sharing happens at other times. **Davies and Houston** (1981) studied pied wagtails who graze along river banks eating insects washed ashore. An individual returns to each spot every 40 minutes when the water has washed up a new supply. Watching for intruders reduces grazing efficiency, therefore when the bird can afford it (when food renewal rate is high), it makes economic sense for a territory owner to tolerate a 'satellite' who shares the resource and the defence.

③ *Combined model.* Both models usually operate in tandem. One reason is that competitors are not equal and therefore the ideal free distribution only operates up to a point. **Whitham** (1980) studied aphids who reproduce by entombing themselves on a leaf and feeding from it. The largest leaves are first occupied; subsequent females either have to share a large leaf or find a smaller leaf. The *average* success is the same for all leaves, as predicted by the ideal free model. However, in terms of each leaf not all females have the same success because of competition within that habitat. It is better to be near the base of the leaf to obtain most food from the leaf, confirmed by the fact that individuals removed from this spot are quickly replaced (despotic distribution).

④ *Resources and aggression.* The fact that competitors are unequal is related to their ability to threaten aggression. The theory of natural selection predicts that animals which are successful in competition will be selected, however natural selection actually favours those that threaten successfully but avoid unrestrained battles, and thus are more likely to survive. Control can be achieved through the use of territories, dominance hierarchies and/or ritualised fighting.

- A *territory* is a space which is exclusively used and defended by a solitary animal or family group. Territories can reduce aggression through the *owner wins strategy* (unit 2.1.1).
- *Ritualised fighting.* **Clutton-Brock and Albon** (1979) observed three stages of ritualised fighting in deer: roaring matches, parallel walking and locking antlers. The early stages allow rival males to assess each other's body size and condition, and back down rather than risk serious injury. Such encounters lead to dominance relations. There are many other ritualised signals which prevent aggressive escalation, such as appeasement, submission and displacement activities (see unit 2.3.4).
- *Dominance hierarchy* (see unit 2.2.3). Dominance reduces aggression because individuals know their place and don't engage in aggressive encounters.

2.1.3 PREDATOR–PREY AND SYMBIOTIC RELATIONSHIPS

Predator–prey relationships

Both getting food and avoiding predation lead to increased reproductive success. Efficient strategies will be favoured by natural selection.

① *Successful predation.* Searching, recognising, catching and handling prey are discussed in unit 2.4.2.

- *Economics.* A predator must maximise the success of any attack because stalking and chasing use up considerable energy. **Caro** (1986) experimentally demonstrated that cheetahs give up stalking gazelles as soon as the gazelle 'stotts'. The gazelle is faster than the cheetah so must be caught unawares. The 'stott' tells the cheetah that it has been spotted and therefore attack will be a waste of time.
- *Fixed action patterns* (unit 2.1.1). For example, the way a cat responds to a dangling piece of string by crouching down. It is obviously valuable for offspring to be born with successful predation techniques, or learn them early in life. Predatory-like play seen in kittens may function to tune up these behaviours.

② *Avoiding predation: successful prey.* Prey species have innate behavioural mechanisms for recognising and avoiding prey. For example, **Lorenz and Tinbergen** (1938) demonstrated that turkeys exhibit a fear response when they see the silhouette of a hawk (short neck, long tail) moving overhead but not when they see the same silhouette passed in the other direction, when it looks like a goose (long neck, short tail). They suggested that this is an innate response but **Schneirla** (1965) proposed that a triangle could have the same effect, the fear response may arise because an object which appears blunt end first is more surprising.

   Blanchard *et al.* (1990) suggested four key anti-predation behaviours:

- *Flight*, the most common response, works if the prey can get away fast enough but it may be counterproductive in eliciting a chase response. It may confuse the predator and therefore be successful, for example **Sherman** (1985) showed that squirrels respond to a predator with a high pitched warning call. The whole group dashes for cover and the scuffle confuses the predator and protects the animal who gave the warning. The schooling of fish has a similar effect.
- *Freeze* response allows the animal to make a sudden escape which may surprise the predator. It also allows the prey to assess the situation and determine whether they have been seen by the predator. The gazelle's stott may serve this function.
- *Defensive attack*. In some animals there is an intermediate state between freeze and attack where the animal indicates intention to act. For example, a cat hisses and arches its back.

- *Setting predators against each other*. The squirrels' warning call may attract other predators. The predators fight, giving the prey a chance to escape.

  There are other anti-predator techniques:
- Feeding at night, living in burrows, and living alone (less easy to detect).
- *Warning systems* can be an example of reciprocal altruism (unit 2.3.1). For example, when a flock of geese are grazing, individual members take turns as look-out.
- Poisonous species evolve warning signals to advertise their danger. Otherwise their poison would not protect the individual because they are not easily recognised.

③ *Mimicry* is used by both predator and prey, though it is hard to explain in terms of natural selection (see unit 2.1.1).
- *Aggressive mimicry*. The sabre-toothed blenny mimics the markings of the cleaner wrasse, which cleans parasites off bigger fish. The blenny therefore can approach a trusting bigger fish and take a bite before escaping. The angler fish dangles a worm-like bait on the end of a rod-like appendage attracting worm-eating animals, which it then eats.
- *Batesian mimicry*. A prey species may evolve the same markings as some other poisonous or distasteful animal. For example, one kind of harmless coral snake has the same colouring as its poisonous relative. Mimicry extends to behaviour as well as coloration, for example the hawk moth caterpillar inflates and wags its head around like a snake.
- *Mullerian mimicry* is based on universal indicators of poisonous prey. A number of species, all of which are noxious, share the same warning signals which trigger an innate response in the predator. This has advantages for both predator and prey because it enables a consistent and rapid response.

④ *Camouflage* is used by:
- Prey species. For example squid can change colour and shape to avoid detection. Even very slight disguise (*crypsis*) gives the prey species some advantage because the predator must delay longer in recognising the individual.
- Predators also use camouflage so that they can stalk prey unobtrusively.

⑤ *Predator–prey relationships*. As a predatory species improves its skill at detection and capture, the prey improve their abilities to avoid detection and capture. Therefore the two systems must *co-evolve*. **Krebs and Davies** (1993) offer three hypotheses about why this so-called *arms race* remains stable:
- *Prudent predation* may occur when an individual has exclusive use of a resource, as when defending a territory. This explanation cannot apply to group predation because this would involve group selection, a unit beyond the scope of natural selection (see unit 2.1.1).
- *Group extinctions*. If a predator kills off all its prey then it too will die because it cannot adapt to a new prey species quickly enough. If a predator disappears, the prey species overreproduce and strain their resources. The prey species may also suffer from a loss of selective pressure exerted by the predator. Only *unstable* predator–prey relations become extinct which is why only stable ones remain.
- *Prey are ahead in the arms race* because selective pressure is greater on them. A predator who often fails to catch prey will eventually die but may reproduce in the meantime; a prey who is killed has no further chance of reproduction. It may also be the case that prey have shorter life cycles and therefore evolve more quickly.

Symbiotic relationships

Symbiosis exists when members of different species derive mutual benefit from a relationship. For example, the cleaner wrasse and its host fish (above), or the fig tree and fig wasp (the tree relies on the wasp for fertilisation, the wasp relies on the tree for food).

- Symbiosis may appear to be altruistic but neither participant engages in it for the purpose of benefiting the other. Each animal has evolved a behaviour which is advantageous to itself, and which has not succumbed to selective pressure because it happens also to be beneficial to the other animal/plant.

- This relationship is open to exploitation by a third party who may mimic one of the symbiotic partners and potentially threaten the stable symbiotic relationship, as in the case sabre-toothed blenny and the cleaner wrasse (see above).

2.2 REPRODUCTIVE STRATEGIES

Sexual reproduction offers greater genetic variation than asexual reproduction, which increasing the likelihood of individual fitness and therefore favoured by natural selection.

2.2.1 SEXUAL SELECTION IN EVOLUTION

Sexual selection is the selection for traits which are *solely* concerned with increasing mating success. **Darwin** claimed sexual selection was the basis of sexual dimorphism (two forms, male and female) because only competition makes this necessary. Each sex behaves differently because of different selective pressures:

- *Males* can potentially fertilise hundreds of females at a minimal cost to future reproductive potential. Natural selection will favour strategies which maximise the number of fertilisations, this tends to lead to *intra*sexual competition.
- *Females* incur much greater cost per offspring. Natural selection will favour discrimination in females which leads to *inter*sexual selection strategies.
- *Mate choice vs. mate competition*: males usually compete to be selected whereas females usually select (choose the most suitable). At the most basic level females (eggs) choose and males (sperm) compete.

Male (*intrasexual*) strategies

❶ *Polygyny or monogamy.* A male can increase reproductive success by selecting many females (polygyny), or choosing one mate (monogamy) and being choosy.

❷ *Aggression.* When females are a scarce resource, males compete for their attention and/or for nesting sites. Therefore males evolve elaborate weaponry and rituals for fighting. Fighting may occur immediately before mating, during establishment of a dominance hierarchy or a harem, or after mating (sperm competition, below).

❸ *Sperm competition.* Once a male has inseminated the female, his sperm must continue to compete for the egg. The most recently arrived sperm appear to have an advantage. Male strategies include:
  - *Preventing subsequent copulation.* For example, male parasitic worms cement the female's genital opening after copulation and also copulate with other males, and cement their genital regions shut.
  - *Sneak copulation*: discreetly copulating when the first male is not looking. Some male elephant seals pretend to be females and are then able to join a harem and sneak copulation when the bull is occupied elsewhere. In order to counteract this males must be very possessive of their females and/or have sex in private.

❹ *Female intrasexual strategies.* In polyandrous species, one female has multiple male mates and the male usually does most of the parental care, meaning the males have the greater investment. In this situation males are the choosy ones whereas females are the competitive sex. For example, female spotted sandpipers compete to defend large territories in which they may have several males.

❺ *Factors which influence competitiveness*
  - The larger the difference in parental investment, the greater the competitiveness.
  - The larger the ratio of males to females, the greater the competition between males.
  - Where conditions favour polygyny, males must compete between each other (intersexual) and compete for female selection (intrasexual). Competition is less intense in monogamous species.

Female (*intersexual*) strategies

❶ *Choosing the right species.* Natural selection favours individuals which have distinctive markings so they can be readily identified by the opposite sex of the right species. It does not favour interbreeding which often results in sterile offspring.

❷ *Coy females.* Females do not always benefit from a sexual encounter and impregnation will reduce fitness. Therefore it is a good strategy for females to be coy, which allows time to assess the male's fitness. **Williams** (1966) suggested that courtship is a contest between male salesmanship and female sales resistance.

❸ *Genetic benefits.* A female wants 'good genes' so that her offspring are fitter. She can assess the fitness of any male using *sexual characteristics* and/or *courtship routines*. For this reason many males have elaborate and sometimes bizarre physical characteristics which incur a benefit (increased reproduction because they are chosen) but at a cost (in terms of energy and predation): examples include peacock's tails and stag's antlers. Explanations of how bizarre characteristics have evolved:

- *Runaway process: Fisher's hypothesis* ('sexy sons', 'good taste'). **Fisher** (1930) proposed that females mate with the most attractive males for the purpose of producing sons who will inherit those characteristics and be able to attract more females. Initially the characteristics would have had some survival value (e.g. antlers for fighting) but, because females actively selected mates with this feature, it became exaggerated. As long as the advantages outweigh the disadvantages the bizarre characteristic will be perpetuated. **Andersson** (1982) extended or shortened the tail length of long-tailed widow birds and found that breeding success was positively related to longer tail length. Other evidence comes from considering fossils of the extinct giant deer which show that their antlers spanned 3 metres; their extinction may have occurred because the disadvantages became too great.

- *Handicapping theory* ('good genes', 'good sense'). **Zahavi** (1975) proposed that females prefer mates with handicaps because this is evidence of their superior genetic quality. For example, if a male peacock can survive despite his tail he must be good in other respects. 'Good genes' are in terms of survival and reproduction as opposed to Fisher's hypothesis that the good genes would be for producing attractive male offspring. Critics of this view say that the same might then apply to males who have been injured but survived, but this 'handicap' would not be heritable and in fact might act detrimentally because individuals who get injured tend to be weaker to begin with.

- *Revisions of handicapping theory.* **Hamilton and Zuk** (1982) suggested that sexual displays are indicators of genetic resistance to disease. Only males who are disease free can fully develop secondary sexual characteristics. The fact that diseases continue to evolve means that this mechanism would be particularly advantageous because it must co-evolve. **Møller** (1990) studied barn swallows, a species troubled by the blood-sucking mite. He found that parents with longer tails had offspring with smaller mite loads even when they were reared in a foster nest (where the mites could not be passed through contact). **Møller** (1992) suggested that symmetry is a handicap because it requires a great deal of precision. Only good genes can produce a symmetrical body and this explains why symmetricality is attractive.

❹ *Non-genetic benefits*

- *Material resources.* In bullfrogs the strongest males (intrasexual strategy) get the best pond sites and the females choose (intersexual) the male with the best site.

- *Parental ability.* Male birds usually help feed the young; the male's ability to supply food during courtship is indicative of how well he will fare later.

2.2.2 PARENTAL INVESTMENT IN THE REARING OF THE YOUNG

Trivers (1972) used the term 'parental investment' to describe the balance between effort (time and resources) and reproductive success. Mating reduces the parent's future reproductive potential, therefore it is important to offset this by increased success.

❶ *Eggs and sperm.* Parental investment begins with the gametes, female investment is greater because the egg is larger and contains nutrients for the offspring. More often than not, females stay and males desert. Female fish make little investment, and both sexes are likely to desert though the male stickleback remains with the eggs gathered from a number of females until they hatch, and the male sea horse carries fertilised eggs around in a brood pouch.

❷ *Number of offspring.* Any species may employ one of these strategies, but within the species the sexes may each be employing a different strategy.

- A female may have a:
  - *r strategy*: many eggs and devote little resource, survival is ensured through numbers alone (with no parental care) or by having several mates and leaving the male to care (polyandry).
  - *K strategy*: relatively few eggs and devote more energy to ensuring their survival (parental care, monogamy or polygyny).
- The male may use a:
  - *r strategy*: mate with many females (polygyny) but spend little time with them.
  - *K strategy*: mate with one female (monogamy or polyandry) and devote some resources to promoting the survival of the offspring.

❸ *Mating systems* (unit 2.2.3)

- *Monogamy* is associated with shared care (found in 90% of birds).
- *Polygyny* results in female care (true for many mammals).
- *Polygynandry* or *promiscuity* may result in no care or care by one partner.
- *Polyandry* tends to lead to male care.

❹ *Mode of fertilisation* may be a way of explaining which sex becomes the carer:

- *Paternity certainty hypothesis.* **Ridley** (1978) proposed that males are more likely to care for young when fertilisation is external because the care increases the certainty that the offspring are his own. In the case of internal fertilisation the male can desert, knowing (or thinking, see sperm competition in unit 2.2.1) that the offspring are his.
- *Order of gamete release hypothesis.* **Dawkins and Carlisle** (1976) suggested that both sexes prefer not to be left 'holding the baby' because this decreases their own reproductive potential. Internal fertilisation allows the male to get away first, with external fertilisation the female can leave first.
- *Association hypothesis.* **Williams** (1975) suggested that the adult who is left in close proximity to the embryo tends to take care of the young. Where external fertilisation takes place this is the male, with internal fertilisation this is the female.

  Evaluation. External fertilisation does not always result in male care, nor does internal fertilisation always lead to maternal care. For example, the female jacana lays a clutch of eggs for each male in her harem and then leaves them for the male to incubate and rear entirely on his own. Mode of fertilisation explanations also cannot explain shared care or no parental care, but they are right much of the time (see below).

❺ *Mode of embryonic development* may further explain which partner makes the greater long-term investment.

- Mammals: offspring often have a prolonged period of gestation inside the female and, after birth, the young depend on the female's milk. The male may stay and feed and protect the female.
- Birds: one partner incubates the eggs (usually the female) and will benefit from help; feeding the young after hatching also places a demand on resources. **Lack** (1968) proposed (*Lack's hypothesis*) that the involvement of both parents will increase reproductive success. This doesn't explain why some male birds *do* desert. The incubator benefits from monogamy, the other partner (usually male) only benefits from monogamy when food is scarce and reproductive success depends on extra assistance. Birds are polygynous when resources are plentiful.

⑥ *Ecological factors*
- Scarcity leads to monogamy, as in birds, above.
- When resources are plentiful productivity is best served by having several mates.
- Breeding seasons are related to the availability of food, coinciding with seasonal increases in a target food such as insects.

⑦ *Sex-ratio.* When the male:female ratio is high, males are unlikely to succeed at polygyny because of intersexual rivalry. In general, the sex ratio remains close to 1:1 because any change leads to selective pressure on the scarcer sex – parents who produce more of that sex are selectively favoured.

⑧ *Behaviour of the other partner.* **Maynard Smith** (1977) suggested that male and female strategies form an evolutionarily stable strategy (ESS). The best strategy for one sex depends on the strategy adopted by the other sex. For example, a female should stay with her young unless she can depend on the male to care for them, in which case the best strategy for the female is to start on some more offspring. For the male, the best strategy is to depend on the female so that he can go off to reproduce elsewhere. For this reason the mode of fertilisation approach is likely to be right much of the time.

⑨ *Shared care by relatives.* In many social insect groups (e.g. ants) and in some other animals (e.g. the mongoose), only a few individuals mate and the rest of the society, who are genetically related, invest their resources in caring for the reproductive members and their offspring. This can be understood in terms of kin selection (unit 2.1.1) since those individuals who do not reproduce are still promoting their genetic line (inclusive fitness).

2.2.3 MATING STRATEGIES AND SOCIAL ORGANISATION

Both sexual selection and parental investment are related to particular mating strategies. The choices are: one (mono) mate or many (poly) mates; 'gamy' refers to joining, 'gyny' refers to females and 'andry' is male.

Mating systems

A mating system describes a set of behaviours which maximise reproductive success.

① *Monogamy*: a single male pairs with a single female. This is common in birds (90%) but rare in other animals. The male and female remain together for one or more mating seasons, both take part in care of offspring and tend to be similar in size. This is related to the fact that competition is decreased in monogamous species.

② *Polygyny* (a form of polygamy). A single male mates with several females.
- *Simultaneous polygyny*: as in a harem (see below).
- *Serial polygyny*. Males bond with one female at a time but, over a breeding season, have several females. Found in many songbirds, such as the pied flycatcher. The situation for the first female is like monogamy as she may continue to receive support from her partner. Why do subsequent females accept polygyny?
  - *'Sexy son' hypothesis.* **Waterhead and Robertson** (1979) suggested that secondary females' accept the situation because their sons will inherit their father's polygyny and therefore have increased reproductive success. This is unlikely because the gain would have to be considerable to offset the females' loss in reproductivity.
  - *Deception.* **Alatalo** *et al.* (1981) proposed that secondary females don't know that the male is polygynous until it's too late.
  - *Unmated males are hard to find.* **Dale** *et al.* (1990) suggested that second females settle for polygyny as their best option.

③ *Polyandry* (a form of polygamy). One female mates with several males. The female often develops the bizarre characteristics normally associated with males and the male usually cares for the young. Examples include the Tasmanian native hen and the spotted sandpiper, who mate with more than one male and provide each with a clutch of eggs.

④ *Polygynandry or promiscuity* (forms of polygamy). Both males and females mate with different members of the opposite sex. Multiple matings are advantageous for both sexes, there is increased reproduction (for males) and sperm competition (for females). Either sex may care for the eggs or young, or there may be no care.

- Polygynandry refers to social groups consisting of several males and several females where there are long-term breeding bonds, as in lions and chimpanzees.
- Promiscuity refers to random pairings, as in dunnocks.

Alternative strategies within a species

Mating behaviour may be better described in terms of a set of flexible strategies rather than a distinct system because:

- Many species have several alternative strategies rather than one system. It used to be thought that only abnormal individuals adopted less common strategies but it is now clear that it is adaptive for a species to have alternative strategies which are selected as a response to prevailing conditions. **Davies and Lunberg** (1984) found that dunnocks exhibited all four mating systems, each having different costs and benefits.
- A mating system only describes the experience for one partner, for example polygyny is experienced as monogamy for the first female.
- The concept of a mating system suggests that behaviour which is advantageous to the group will be selected whereas selection is made at the level of the individual's genes (see unit 2.1.1). Therefore it is more appropriate to discuss individual strategies rather than group behaviour.

Monogamy, polygyny, polyandry and polygynandry are examples of possible strategies. Other examples include:

① *Different coloration as a response to environment.* Members of a species live in different habitats, each with different selective pressures. For example, some male sticklebacks have brighter red underbellies than others: the advantage is attraction to females, the disadvantage is attractiveness to predators. Those males living in deeper and darker waters can afford to be brightly coloured because predators can't see them whereas those living in shallow waters do better being duller.

② *Different behaviour as a response to competition and size.* If an individual male is small they are unlikely to win intrasexual competitions. To achieve any reproductive success they must develop some 'sneak' strategies, such as sneak copulation (see unit 2.2.1). Another strategy is to adopt different behaviour. The male digger bee usually digs females out of their burrows and has to fight off competitors. Small males will never win, so instead they hover about waiting to catch a female who has escaped the diggers. They have little success but it is better than nothing. The strategy is, 'if you are big – fight, otherwise – sneak'.

③ *Dimorphic form as a response to competition.* In some species the males appear in two forms (dimorphic), each exploiting a particular strategy. For example, the Coho male salmon may either mature early, be small and lack secondary sexual characteristics. They lurk behind rocks (being small helps this) and fertilise female eggs surreptitiously. The longer maturing and larger, hook nose male fights for the opportunity to fertilise eggs with other males. The fact that both forms persist shows that both strategies pay off, they form an evolutionarily stable strategy (ESS).

④ *Sex change as a strategy.* For each individual actual gender does not matter, as long as their genes are maximally reproduced.

- *Protogynous hermaphroditism* is favoured when males compete for females and size is an advantage. In the blue-headed wrasse when an individual reaches a certain size it changes from a female to a male, and is able to reproduce throughout its life cycle.
- *Protandrous hermaphroditism* is favoured when male–male competition is low and therefore male size has little effect on breeding success. Large females are better because they produce more eggs. The clownfish is monogamous, the larger partner becomes female. If the female is removed, the male is joined by a smaller individual and the larger male changes to a female.

Social organisation

Mating strategies have implications for social organisation. The advantages of group living are listed in unit 2.3.2, and include reproductive success. **Crook** (1964) studied many species of weaver bird and related mating strategies and social organisation to ecology:

- In the forest insect food is dispersed and relatively scarce. Therefore parents form monogamous bonds and feed solitarily. They reduce predation risks through light colouration and camouflaged nests.
- In the savannah, seed food is abundant in patches. Efficient foraging is achieved by groups rather than individuals but there are few nesting sites, so what is there must be shared. This favours competition, intraspecies rivalry and brighter plumage. Polygyny is likely because the males who gain the best nest sites can attract several females.

Jarman (1974) reached similar conclusions when studying 74 species of ungulates. In the forest, the reproductive unit was a pair; in brushland there were usually harems, in river woodlands groups were territorial during the breeding season; and on the savannah large herds formed with male dominance hierarchies.

Each form of social organisation has selective advantages:

1 *Optimal group size and density.* **Krebs and Boonstra** (1979) noted that only larger voles mate successfully when the population density is high; when the density falls the smaller ones are allowed to mate as well. This regulates population in relation to available resources.

2 *Harems.* One male has exclusive rights to a group of females. Many males die without mating at all while others do most of the mating. The harem master has to fight for the privilege and tends to be larger. Females do most of the child care. Harem size is related to male strength and the length of time he can defend his harem. Being a harem master is exhausting and therefore most individuals don't last long.

- *Seasonal harems.* If females all come into oestrus at a particular time of year, males compete for the harem for that time and then go their own way, as in deer.
- *Permanent harems.* Where females only come into oestrus for limited periods, males defend the harem for their whole reproductive life, as in baboons.

3 *The lek.* Males defend a small territory which contains no resources and advertise themselves to females with great displays. Females visit several males before selecting, the most popular males mate with more than one female. Females gain clear advantages, but what do males get?

- *'Hotspots'.* Males increase their reproductivity by settling in areas frequented by females. This only explains some leks because many do not take place where encounter rates are likely to be high.
- *Safety in numbers.* Males congregate to reduce predation risks. However, predation rates are low in many leks.
- *Larger choruses may attract greater female attention.* It is difficult to establish cause and effect, it may be that larger leks form where there are likely to be more females.
- *Opportunity.* Leks give males the chance to display their wares to a large audience.

4 *Dominance hierarchies*

- *Dominant males* have greater reproductive success because of greater access to mates and other resources.
- *Dominant females* gain similar advantages. **Clutton-Brock** *et al.* (1982) found that dominant female deer had more sons, which is advantageous for their genes.
- *Subordinates* must gain some advantage or they wouldn't stay. Trying to join another hierarchy is not likely to be any better as newcomers start at the bottom, and life as a solitary individual is worse. There are gains in terms of food and safety, and there may be some mating opportunities. They may be relatives of the dominant individuals and therefore assisting reproduction promotes inclusive fitness.
- *Pecking-orders* as first studied in chickens by **Schjelderup-Ebbe** (1922), a simple kind of social structure found throughout the animal kingdom.
- *Matriline groups*: a group of sexually mature daughters and the dependent young of all of them, found in almost all primates.

⑤ *Dispersal.* Inbreeding reduces genetic variation, increases the expression of recessive genes and, overall, reduces reproductive success. One way of avoiding it is for one sex of offspring to disperse. In birds females are more likely to disperse because males defend a territory which may be in part inherited from their father. In polygynous societies, males disperse to locate a new group of females.

2.2.4 PARENT-OFFSPRING CONFLICT

Trivers (1974) predicted that parent–offspring conflict should occur because each offspring has a greater interest in their parents' care than parents have for each individual offspring. Parents have an equal interest in all offspring and want to distribute their investment evenly. This is true whether or not there is an overlap between successive generations because parents still wish to reserve resources for future reproductions.

① *Weaning conflict* occurs in mammals where offspring wish to prolong their easy and rich food source, whereas the mother needs to wean in order to prepare for the next pregnancy and conserve resources (lactation is a greater drain than pregnancy, and suppresses ovulation).

Who is likely to win? **Alexander** (1974) suggested that parents do because, in the long run, parents who are not manipulated will be the most successful reproducers. Parents are also larger and more powerful, but they may be manipulated because they have an interest in the offspring.

② *Sex-ratio conflict.* Social insects, such as wasps, have unusual genetic relationships. Queens are half-related to their male and female offspring, and daughters are three-quarters related to their sisters and one-quarter related to brothers. This occurs because males come from unfertilised cells and have only one half of each gene, females come from fertilised eggs and have full genes.

Queens produce fertilised eggs and should favour equal numbers of male and female offspring. Daughter workers tend the eggs and should favour more females. The sex ratio does tend to favour females, so the offspring appear to win the conflict. However, there are occasions when the overall ratio is 1:1 because queens produce more males at the beginning of the season, when few or no workers are around.

③ *Infanticide*

- *In birds*, especially raptors, the largest chicks (from the eggs laid first) are the ones given the majority of food by the parents. Ultimately the younger and smaller sibling may starve to death (selective neglect) and be fed to older siblings. This may be advantageous because:
  - *Insurance.* Parents lay more eggs than necessary in case some chicks die.
  - *Opportunistic.* In times of plenty all chicks may survive.

- *In harems*, such as lion prides, the first act of a male who takes over is to kill all offspring of the previous owner, freeing females to become pregnant (any lactating females will not ovulate), and ensuring his own offspring have no competition for care and resources.

- *Infanticide is not in a female's interests.* However, it will not benefit them to refuse sex with an infanticidal male because this reduces the female's reproductivity. There are some counter-tactics by females, for example an already pregnant female may show pseudo-oestrus so that paternity is uncertain. The new male cannot risk infanticide because the new offspring could be his.

- *Why isn't infanticide more common?* It only occurs in species where the male is bigger than the female (otherwise she wouldn't let him do it) and where the take-over rate is high, which pressures the male to reproduce quickly.

- *The Bruce effect* (**Bruce**, 1960). Pregnant female mice reabsorb their embryos when they smell strange male urine, perhaps because it signals the likelihood of eventual infanticide so the female will do better to abandon the investment now. Wild mares spontaneously abort after mating with a strange stallion (**Berger**, 1983).

❹ *Sibling conflict.* Siblings compete for limited parental resources. **Mock and Parker** (1986) studied siblicide in egrets and found that this worked to the siblings' advantage as long as one sibling remained. Once they were the only remaining offspring, the parents abandoned the nest to start again elsewhere thus committing infanticide by neglect.

2.3 KINSHIP AND SOCIAL BEHAVIOUR

2.3.1 APPARENT ALTRUISM

Biological altruism is behaviour which increases the survival potential of another while decreasing the altruist's survival and future reproductive potential. Human or psychological altruism is somewhat different (see unit 1.4.1). Altruism is distinct from co-operation (see unit 2.3.2) .

The paradox of altruism. The theory of natural selection predicts selfish rather than altruistic behaviour, to promote self-survival. The fact that animals do behave altruistically is a paradox. Why does it occur?

❶ *Group selection.* **Wynne-Edwards** (see unit 2.1.1) proposed that altruism benefits the group or species as a whole but natural selection acts on the individual not the group.

❷ *Kin selection: the selfish gene and 'apparent' altruism.* Sociobiologists such as **Hamilton** (see unit 2.1.1), **Wilson** (1975) and **Dawkins** (1976) proposed that group behaviour could be understood if the group consisted of close genetic relatives (i.e. kin). Behaviour may be unselfish at the level of the individual, but at the level of the genes it is selfish because it promotes their perpetuation. Altruism increases the fitness of the gene pool (*inclusive fitness*). Altruistic behaviour only *appears* to be unselfish. This can explain the evolution of:

- Any parental behaviour.
- Bees who die after they have stung a predator.
- Sterile workers in an ant colony and helpers at the nest in meerkats.
- Alarm calls in squirrels.

    Evaluation. This concept presupposes that individuals can recognise their relatives (see below) and assumes that genes directly cause behaviour. Sociobiological accounts are speculative, though they are supported by extensive observation.

❸ *Kin recognition*

- *Recognition by place.* Some species operate a simple rule: 'any individual in the nest is kin'. The hypothesis is likely to be correct but it allows for brood parasitism as in cuckoos.
- *Association mechanism.* Individuals learn to recognise each other, usually during early experience (imprinting). **Holmes and Sherman** (1982) reared squirrels in four groups: siblings reared together or apart, and non-siblings reared together or apart. When the squirrels were later placed together they found that animals reared together rarely fought, regardless of genetic relatedness. They also found that, of the animals reared apart the true siblings were *less* aggressive towards each other.
- *Phenotype matching.* External appearance, such as odour (phenotype rather than genotype) is evidence of apparent relatedness. **Kalmus and Ribbands** (in **Ridley**, 1986) noted that different diets led groups of honeybee to have different characteristic smells. When they moved two hives to the same location interhive fighting decreased because they fed on the same flowers and smelled the same. When they divided a hive and fed each half different diets, intrahive fighting increased. **Buckle and Greenberg** (1981) bred sweat bees. In a pure colony, any non-relative was challenged and not allowed in. In colonies composed of relatives and non-relatives (accepted because of recognition by place and association), relatives of either brood were admitted because of phenotype matching.

- *Green Beard effect.* **Dawkins** (1976) used this to describe the possibility that kin possess certain features which promote recognition. It is an unlikely possibility.
- *Distinguishing close and distant kin.* **Greenberg** (1979) found that hive admittance was relative to the closeness of genetic relation. **Holmes and Sherman** found that squirrels are more tolerant of full sisters than half sisters even when they are all part of the same litter.

④ *Reciprocal altruism* (**Trivers**, 1971) is an arrangement where one individual helps another organism, at some risk to themselves, in anticipation that the favour will be returned at some later date. For example, **Seyfarth and Cheyney** (1984) established that both relatives and non-relatives groomed each other, and observed that grooming increased the probability that individuals would come to each other's aid.

- It is adaptive because of mutual benefit.
- It is vulnerable to cheating and therefore will only evolve in species where individuals can recognise each other (see above).
- **Axelrod and Hamilton** (1981) proposed that reciprocal altruism was an ESS, as illustrated by the *Prisoner's dilemma*. Individual A and B can choose either to co-operate or defect. If they both co-operate, they both gain some reward. If one defects but the other co-operates the defector gets a large reward. If everyone defects there is no pay off. Under such conditions it pays occasional individuals to defect, but over a long period the ESS will be co-operation.

⑤ *Mutualism.* Two or more individuals may co-operate because there is a net gain in terms of survival and reproductive benefit. Non-relatives may collect food together because they offer increased protection from predation (as in geese grazing) or more effective capture techniques (as in lions hunting). This is not true altruism because *both* individuals benefit.

⑥ *Manipulated or induced altruism* is altruism in Darwinian terms (selfish individual interest). What looks like altruism on the part of the host, is manipulation by the recipient. Manipulated altruism can be:

- *Interspecies*, as in the cuckoo or any parasite.
- *Intraspecies*, as in cliff swallows who place their eggs in the nests of other females and avoid any further parental investment.

2.3.2 SOCIALITY IN NON-HUMAN ANIMALS

Collaboration or sociality increases individual survival and reproductive potential.

① *Facilitates mating* (see unit 2.2.3).

② *Co-operation in predators and foragers* (foraging is discussed in unit 2.4.2). Food location and capture is more effectively managed by an efficient group. For example:

- Insects share information about food sources with the whole community (see bee dance, in unit 2.3.3).
- Weaver birds living in the savannah can locate patches of food more efficiently if they search as a group.
- An organised group of lions can hunt more efficiently and tackle larger prey.
- There is a balance between loss (sharing resources) and gain (more food).

③ *Co-operation against predators* (see unit 2.1.3, avoiding predation).

- *Defence*: a group can more easily confuse a predator, as in schools of fish.
- *Safety in numbers*, the predator will only take part of the group.
- *Mutual protection.* **Hall and DeVore** (1965) found that baboons protect their young when on the move by forming a circle around them.
- *Lookout.* **Barnard** (1979) demonstrated that individual sparrows spent less time watching for predators and more time feeding in relation to increasing group size.
- *Attack.* A group of prey may be able to attack the predator and see them off, such as birds attacking a hawk.

④ *Optimality models* (see unit 2.4.2) predict a balance between costs and benefits, group size is related to increased protection but decreased resources. Groups maintain an optimal size, for example **Chapman** (1928) varied the quantities of flour placed in a jar with flour beetles. The ratio of beetles to food remained constant. Group size is often controlled either by variations in litter sizes or by how many group members are breeding. Group members may keep track of group size through flocking or a 'dawn chorus'.

⑤ *Solitary living* is the alternative. It is safer because a group can be spotted more easily, and may be necessary due to scarcity of food. Locating a mate is more difficult.

2.3.3 IMPRINTING AND BONDING SYSTEMS IN NON-HUMAN ANIMALS

Imprinting

Imprinting is the process of forming an association (learning) with another animal, object or class of items. It is an innate process which is influenced by experience.

① *Survival value.* Behaviours which promote survival will be favoured by natural selection and therefore we might expect their acqustion to be innately programmed.

- *Filial imprinting.* Learning to identify parents/carers who will provide food and protection. Parent–offspring interactions are FAPs, such as a gull pecking the orange spot on the parents' beak or the *following response*, as in ducklings. This is particularly important in *precocial species* (those who move around shortly after birth).
- *Sexual imprinting.* Future reproductive success depends on being able to identify the correct species otherwise mating is unlikely to be successful. **Immelmann** (1972) cross-fostered Zebra (Z) finches and Bengalese (B) finches. The finches preferred to mate with their foster species, even years later when given a free choice.
- *Kin selection* relies on early learning (see unit 2.3.1).
- *Homing* by salmon and birds is related to imprinting (see unit 2.4.2).
- Preferences for certain kinds of food, nesting materials, or habitat are learned through imprinting.

② *Visual imprinting.* **Lorenz** (1935) divided a clutch of greylag goose eggs into two groups: one raised naturally, the others in an incubator. When the latter group hatched the first living (moving) thing they saw was Lorenz and they followed him around. Lorenz marked the two groups to distinguish them and placed them together with their mother and Lorenz. The goslings went to their respective 'mother-figures'.

Lorenz found that goslings will also imprint on a cardboard box, a flashing light or a rubber ball. He also found that many other birds would imprint on these objects, such as pigeons and jackdaws, but not mallard ducks. Mallards imprinted on a quacking sound, an inborn reaction to a call note rather than a visual image.

③ *Aural imprinting.* **Grier** *et al.* (1967) exposed chicken eggs to continuous one-second beeps for a period of six days before hatching. After hatching the chicks showed a preference for this sound rather than a higher pitched version.

④ *Olfactory imprinting.* Salmon imprint on odours of home stream (see unit 2.4.2). **Klopfer and Gamble** (1966) found that mother goats are sensitive to the smell of their offspring for about an hour after birth; in fact contact with any kid for a five-minute period will mean that it is accepted as her own and she will allow it to suckle. This is shown in the practice of wrapping an orphaned lamb in the skin of a dead one so that the mother will suckle the adopted lamb.

⑤ *Applications.* Imprinting techniques are used by nature film makers. They rear a bird, such as an owl or swan, from the time it hatches. The bird will then always fly to their 'mother-figure' enabling unusual close-ups of the bird in flight. Imprinting is also used in cross-fostering to reintroduce animals back into the wild.

Imprinting versus learning

Ethologists suggest that imprinting can be distinguished from learning in five ways:

1 *A critical or sensitive period.* Unless learning takes place at a particular time, it will never happen. Lorenz took the concept of a critical period from *embryology*. During the development of the embryo there are exclusive short periods of vulnerability. For example, German measles only causes damage to hearing in the human foetus if it occurs during the third month of pregnancy, at other times there is no damage.

    Evidence for the capacity to acquire certain behaviours before a certain age:
- **Hess** (1958) placed newly hatched Mallard ducklings in a circular runway with a plastic duck suspended from a motor-driven arm. The strongest following response (imprinting) occurred between 13 and 16 hours after hatching. Ducklings who were first exposed 32 hours after hatching showed almost no imprinting response, and those who had to follow at model at a great distance, therefore exerting more effort, seemed to form stronger attachments.
- **Marler and Mundinger** (1971) found that sparrows kept in isolation between the age of 8 to 90 days failed to develop adult birdsong, though they were able to produce a basic version. This suggests the role of experience in modifying innate behaviours during a critical period. However, **Schjelderup-Ebbe** (1935) found that domestic chickens reared away from others still crowed as normal when they reached maturity.
- **Held and Hein** (1963) and **Blakemore and Cooper** (1970) demonstrated a critical period in the development of visual perception (see unit 5.1.2).
- *Physiological basis.* Hormones may have an organisational effect on brain development. **Landsberg** (1981) found that peaks of testosterone production in young zebra finches coincided with key periods of imprinting.

Evaluation
- **Sluckin** (1961) and **Bateson** (1964) found that some birds will imprint beyond the normal critical period. Therefore **Sluckin** (1965) coined the phrase 'sensitive period' to describe a time when an individual is optimally receptive to acquiring certain behaviours. Learning will be possible at other times but more difficult and less effective.

2 *Rapid change.* Unlike some other forms of learning, imprinting should take place with little effort and relatively quickly. **Hess** (1958, above) found ducklings imprinted after only 10 minutes of exposure.

3 *Supra-individual.* Imprinting is not to a specific individual but to a class of objects, as found by **Lorenz** (see above).

4 *Irreversible.* Once learned, subsequent experience should not modify an imprint. **Blakemore and Cooper**'s study (see unit 5.1.2) showed that neural changes accompany sensory deprivation, which would explain irreversibility.

    What happens if an individual is exposed to more than one imprinting experience?
- **Sluckin and Salzen** (1961) imprinted young chicks on a green ball and then, after a short delay, they were imprinted on a blue ball (a second group had the blue ball first). Three days later they were retested and showed a preference for their original colour. After another interval in isolation their preference changed to the second imprinting experience and this preference continued. This experiment was performed under laboratory conditions which may affect performance.
- **Guiton** (1966) found that leghorn chicks imprinted on a pair of yellow rubber gloves used in feeding them during their first six weeks, even trying to mate with them. However, the cocks later reverted to normal behaviour after spending time with other hens and would only mate with the hens and not the gloves. This suggests that imprinting has important effects, but that these can be reversed under suitable circumstances.

Evaluation
- It may be that the reason some behaviours *appear* reversible is because the researchers have tested them too early in the individual's life, when the sensitive period has not ended.

- The degree of irreversibility depends on, for example, the quality of the original imprinting experience.
- It is possible that *some* behaviours in *some* species are not reversible whereas others are.
- **Hinde** (1966) proposed that once imprinting has occurred, the organism is also programmed to avoid situations where imprinting might occur, e.g. being afraid of other potential mother-figures.

⑤ *Lasting effects.* The immediate effects of imprinting are for safety and food, the lasting effects are in terms of reproduction though these may be reversible. **Lorenz** (1935) noted that Barbary doves which imprinted on humans would often direct their subsequent sexual behaviour towards humans. **Immelmann** (see above) found evidence for lasting effects.

⑥ *Is imprinting really a special case?*

- Things which are imprinted can be learned at other times, though less easily.
- Learning can also be a rapid process.
- Imprinting is not always irreversible.
- Both learning and imprinting result in long-lasting neurological changes.

Imprinting is an innate *readiness* to learn certain things during sensitive periods. The actual change in behaviour is learning. **McFarland** (1993) concluded that imprinting is essentially the same as ordinary conditioning. **Bateson** (1990) suggested that the things which once made imprinting seem different are now seen as commonplace, as a result of changed views of learning.

Bonding and attachment

An attachment bond is an emotional tie, imprinting plus emotion. Bonding is often used to refer specifically to the relationship between a mother and her infant though adult–adult relationships also involve bonds. **Harlow** (1959) conducted extensive research on bonding in rhesus monkeys:

❶ *Learning experiments.* **Harlow** conducted experiments on learning using monkeys. He reared them apart from their mothers to reduce mortality and noticed that the young became very attached to the cotton nappy pads at the bottom of their cages and were distressed when their cages were cleaned. This led Harlow to question whether bodily contact and attachment bonds might be more important than the primary biological need of feeding.

❷ *The importance of physical contact.* Eight rhesus monkeys, separated from their mothers a few hours after birth, were each given two 'mothers', a wire one and a cloth one. Milk was provided through a nipple in one of the mothers. All of the monkeys spent more time with the cloth mother even if the other mother had the milk and, when frightened, went to the cloth mother. Later these monkeys had difficulties in mating, and those females who did become pregnant were poor mothers.

❸ *Experimental variations*

- **Rosenblum and Harlow** (1963) used two types of cloth mother: the one who blasted the infants with a strong current of compressed air at random intervals engendered the strongest attachments.
- **Novak and Harlow** (1975) raised infant monkeys in total isolation for one year and then introduced younger 'therapist' monkeys, who played and interacted with them. This led to a reversal of earlier privation.

❹ *Evaluation*

- This work was critical in demonstrating the importance of physical contact in emotional development, with important applications to childrearing.
- With hindsight, these experiments may appear unethical.
- Comparisons with human attachment may be inappropriate, see unit 6.1.1.

2.3.4 SIGNALLING SYSTEMS

A signal is any behaviour or feature which has the effect of changing the behaviour of another animal, through sensory perception rather than force. The message may not be intended. Language is a signalling system (see unit 2.4.3).

Sensory modalities

1 *Visual*

- *Location of food*. The dance of honey bees communicates where to find food (see unit 2.4.3).
- *Threat and dominance displays*: facial expression (bared teeth, staring eyes), posture (head lowered, swaying), movement (slow approach). Responses may be submissive or aggressive, signalled through posture (head down, or lying down).
- *Mood*. The octopus changes colour to indicate pleasure or anger. Cats signal embarrassment through displacement activities, humans blush.
- *Deceit and mimicry*. The cuckoo imitates another bird's eggs in order to deceive the host. Spots on caterpillars communicate danger to potential predators.
- *Identification*. Markings help to identify your own species, and individual members.
- *Parent–young*. The brightly coloured mouth of a young thrush elicits a feeding response in its parent.
- *Danger*. Rabbits raise their tail exposing a white patch as an alarm signal, wrens bob up and down.
- *Sexual displays* communicate readiness, for example a peacock's fan or a female primate's genitalia, which are blue and swollen in oestrus.

2 *Auditory* signals are effective over distances and where vision is limited.

- *Mating*. Birdsong is mainly to do with mating, and mainly by males. It either acts to defend and delineate a territory or to attract and stimulate females. **Krebs and Dawkins** (1984) removed pairs of great tits and replaced them either by loudspeakers or nothing. Where loudspeakers played a full repertoire of their birdsong it took longer for new pairs to occupy the territory (see also unit 2.4.3). Some whale species are solitary through most of the year and use 'songs' to locate each other for breeding.
- *Alarm call*. When Tyack (1983) played tape recordings of excited whales to a group of other whales, they all dispersed.
- *Aggression*, for example barking and growling.
- *'Vocabularies'*. **Marler** (1976) found about 13 categories of sound in chimpanzees, which communicated particular messages, such as greeting or food. **Seyfarth and Cheyney** (1980) observed three different types of alarm call in vervet monkeys, each related to a different predator (eagles, leopards and pythons). If an individual sees an eagle the call communicates 'look in the sky', if it sees a snake or leopard the call is 'look on the ground'.
- *Sociality*. A group of humpback whales all sing the same song, gradually adding new phrases so that the song evolves. This emphasises group membership.
- *Parent–young call*. Young birds cheep to elicit care, parents call to locate their young.
- *Group movement call*. A moving herd uses calls to aid organisation.

3 *Olfactory*. Odours can communicate effectively over both time and space. *Pheromones* are biochemical substances.

- *Mating*. The female silk moth produces bombykol, which can be detected by a male over a distance of a mile. Their taxic response is simply to fly upwind, if they lose the scent they zigzag. (A taxic response is an innate response to a specific stimulus.)
- *Location of food*. If an ant finds food it hurries back to the nest, leaving a trail of pheromones which is followed by the others using their antennae.
- *Identification*. Sweat bees and ants have colony odours to recognise each other and detect enemies.
- *Marking territory*, for example urination in dogs and defecation in hippopotami.

④ *Kinaesthetic* (touch)
  - *Sociality*. Grooming is partly functional but is also an important social signal, for bonding and the establishment and maintenance of dominance hierarchies. Gorillas don't groom as much as baboons, who have a much greater number of dominance conflicts. Submissive dogs lick the pack leader. Greeting often involves touch.
  - *Anxiety reducing*. Huddling is a response to fear.
  - *Parent–young*. Bonding is related to touch. Mouth-to-mouth contact elicits feeding.

⑤ *Electrical* signals are largely related to locating prey, as in the duckbilled platypus which has sensors around its bill to detect tiny electrical signals produced by the nervous system of all animals.

The origins of communication and rituals

Necessary acts inevitably take on a communicative function:
  - *Intention movements*, for example the first moves in an act of aggression become a signal for hostility.
  - *Antithesis*. A signal acquires its meaning by being the opposite of another one, for example, direct gaze communicates aggression and so gaze aversion comes to communicate submission.
  - *Displacement activities*. When an animal experiences conflicting motivations (approach/avoidance) they may yawn or groom themselves, thus communicating conflict.
  - *Autonomic displays* (emotion) such as bristling hair or panting, communicate arousal or exertion.
  - *Sexual displays* evolve as a by-product of competition between prospective mates as a means of communicating fitness.

Theoretical approaches

A signal may be naturally selected because it is:

① *Honest*. Signals evolve from their original form into a ritualised and less ambiguous form. Such 'honest' communication is important in courtship, parent–offspring interaction and forms of social interaction – all cases where mutual benefit occurs.

② *Dishonest: the manipulation hypothesis*. **Dawkins and Krebs** (1978) proposed that animals give signals to manipulate the behaviour of other animals into doing things for the benefit of the signaller. The signaller's fitness is increased at the expense of the receiver. When instances of dishonest signals outnumber honest versions, the signal becomes devalued and will no longer be effective. Therefore it progressively evolves into more and more extravagant forms. Examples include mimicry of poisonous prey (see unit 2.1.3), the behaviour of the cuckoo (the mouth gape of the young cuckoo is huge and acts as a super-releaser) and displays of aggression.

2.4 BEHAVIOUR ANALYSIS

2.4.1 CLASSICAL AND OPERANT CONDITIONING

Classical (Pavlovian) conditioning. Learning to *associate* a stimulus with a response.

Before	NS (neutral stimulus, bell)	→ no response
	UCS (unconditioned stimulus, food)	→ UCR (unconditioned response, salivation)
During conditioning	NS and UCS are paired by occurring together.	
After	CS (conditioned stimulus, bell)	→ CR (conditioned response, salivation)

Operant (instrumental) conditioning. Learning due to the *consequences* of a behaviour (response). The probability of a behaviour being repeated depends on strengthening or weakening S-R (stimulus-response) links. **Thorndike** (1913) first described this as the 'law of effect': behaviours are stamped in or out depending on their consequences. **Skinner** (1938) introduced the term operant because the learner *operates* on their environment, which brings certain consequences (in classical conditioning the learner *responds*, *respondent behaviour*).

> → Reinforcement (reward) strengthens response learning
>
> Situation (Antecedents) → Behaviour → Consequence [ABC]
>
> → Punishment weakens response, no learning takes place

❶ *Features of classical conditioning*

- *Extinction.* If the stimuli stop being paired, the CR is extinguished.
- *Spontaneous recovery.* If there is a rest interval after extinction, the CR will reappear. Therefore extinction is not unlearning but temporary suppression of the CR.
- *Generalisation.* The CR may occur in response to stimuli which are similar to the CS. For example, if the UCS was a circle, then other shapes (ellipse or square) may also elicit the CR.
- *Generalisation gradient*: the relationship between the new object (e.g. ellipse) to the original one. The more similar they are the stronger the response.
- *Discrimination.* If the circle continues to be paired with the food and the ellipse is shown without food, the organism learns to discriminate.
- *One trial learning.* Usually the NS and UCR have to be paired more than once for learning to take place, but under some conditions one trial is sufficient, for example one fearful incident in childhood may lead to a lifelong fear of dogs. **Guthrie** (1935) thought that all learning takes place on a single trial, the reason it appears to take longer is because a large number of simple components are being acquired.
- *First-order conditioning.* All initial conditioning acts on reflex responses.
- *Higher-order conditioning.* The CS from the original (first-order) conditioning series is used as the UCS in a new series. For example, a bell might be the first CS which can then be associated with a time of day.
- *Timing.* The strongest CR is produced when the NS appears half a second before the UCS and remains during the UCS (*delayed or forward* conditioning). If the NS comes after the UCS (*backward* conditioning) very little learning takes place. *Simultaneous* conditioning is most like real life and *trace* conditioning occurs when the CS is removed before the UCS and is remembered, resulting in weak conditioning.

❷ *Empirical evidence of classical conditioning*

- **Pavlov** (1927) was a physiologist investigating digestion and salivation. To observe salivation he redirected dogs' salivary duct through their cheeks and into a tube. He noticed that the dogs would salivate before they were given food. He proposed that learning took place through association and demonstrated conditioning using a bell, a metronome, the odour of vanilla, apomorphine (a drug which causes vomiting) and a rotating object.
- **Menzies** (1937) asked participants to put their hands in ice-cold water whenever a buzzer sounded, the cold temperature caused vasoconstriction (constriction of the blood vessels). Eventually the vasoconstriction occurred just in response to the sound of the buzzer.
- **Marquis** (1931) showed classical conditioning in ten newborns. By associating a buzzer with the presence of a bottle, they began sucking at the sound of the buzzer. He concluded that 'systematic training of the human infant can be started at birth'.
- **Watson and Rayner** (1920) conditioned Little Albert to fear white furry objects by pairing this with a loud noise, a CER (conditioned emotional response).

❸ *Features of operant conditioning*

- *Reinforcement and punishment.* Reinforcement (positive and negative) and rewards strengthen bonds, punishment weakens them. Negative reinforcement is the absence of, or escape from, a negative stimulus. Punishment is the *presence* of a negative stimulus. See unit 6.3.1 for discussion of the effectiveness of punishment and rewards.

- *Shaping*. It takes a long time for an organism to perform the right behaviour to receive a reward. This would suggest that learning is a time-consuming process, which it isn't. Therefore Skinner proposed the notion of shaping. Operant behaviours are gradually built up through progressive reinforcement as each behaviour becomes closer to the final goal.
- *Avoidance learning*. A type of operant conditioning where a response is learned as a means of avoiding an unpleasant (aversive) stimulus. However, the organism never has the chance to discover if the painful stimulus is still there, so it can't be extinguished.
- *Reinforcement schedules*. *Partial* reinforcement schedules are more effective and more resistant to extinction. This may be because, under *continuous* reinforcement, the organism 'expects' it on every trial and therefore 'notices' its absence more quickly. Partial reinforcement includes fixed, or variable ratios, and fixed or variable intervals.
- *Primary and secondary (conditioned) reinforcement*. Things which act as *primary* reinforcers are innate, such as food, approval or fear. *Secondary* reinforcers work because at some time they have been paired with a primary one. The classic example is money. An example of a negative secondary reinforcer is a hot cooker.
- *Generalisation, discrimination* and *extinction* also occur.

④ *Empirical evidence of operant conditioning*

- **Skinner** (1938) placed a pigeon in a Skinner box. If it pressed a lever (UCS), a door would open and food (reinforcer or reward) was delivered. The pigeon first pecks randomly around the box as part of its natural exploratory behaviour. Accidentally it presses the lever a few times and receives food. Each experience strengthens the S-R link. Reinforcement is both positive (when the lever is pressed) and negative (when pecking elsewhere no food appears). The lever becomes the CS and pressing the lever is a CR. Behaviour has been bought under *stimulus control*. If the pigeon learns to press a button whenever it is lit to get food, it is learning to discriminate the state of the button (a *discriminative stimulus*).
- **Wolfe** (1936) developed the token economy system, used in behaviour modification (see unit 4.4.1). Chimpanzees were given vending machines and learned that putting in tokens led to getting a grape. Even when the machine was not present the monkeys worked to get tokens (secondary reinforcers) to use later.

⑤ *Comparing classical and operant conditioning*

CLASSICAL	OPERANT
Learning through *association*.	Learning through *reinforcement*.
Concerned with a *reflex* or automatic response.	Concerned with *voluntary* behaviour, or any behaviour which is *naturally produced*.
Reinforcement is presented *before* the CR.	Reinforcement occurs *after* the CR.
The reinforcement is not related to anything the organism might do.	The organism is *instrumental* in obtaining reinforcement.
Both involve generalisation, extinction and discrimination.	

Despite apparently clear theoretical distinctions, in practice both classical and operant conditioning may occur at the same time and are hard to separate:

- In the classical conditioning experiment is food a UCS or a reward? The bell is a signal that the food is coming, salivating is an anticipatory response to food. If the bell comes immediately after the food it should still result in conditioning (backward conditioning) but such conditioning is rare, which suggests that the food is a reward and this paradigm is operant conditioning.
- It is not possible to set up an operant learning trial without also involving the conditions for classical conditioning, in which case it is possible that reinforcement is really not instrumental in forming learned responses.

⑥ *Evaluation of conditioning (learning) theory*. The Behaviourist approach generally is evaluated in unit 7.1.1, this includes a consideration of applications, and negative and positive points.

Learning theory cannot explain:

- *Innate learning*. **Seligman** (1970) suggested that a species is biologically predisposed to acquire certain conditioned responses more easily than others (*preparedness*). **Garcia and Koelling** (1966) demonstrated that rats had a predisposition to learn quickly to avoid substances which made them feel sick. There would be an adaptive advantage to individuals who avoided unfamiliar foods or sampled them cautiously. This 'bait shyness' can explain why rat poison isn't very effective.

- *Latent learning*: learning without reinforcement and in behavioural 'silence'. **Blodgett** (1929) demonstrated that rats which received no reward when placed in a maze did not appear to learn anything but when, after six days, food was placed in the goal box, they learned to go to that arm of the maze more rapidly than rats who had been rewarded from the beginning of the experiment. During the period before reward they had wandered around the maze and must have stored a *cognitive map* of the maze. **Tolman and Honzik** (1930) found that the experimental group did even better than the control, suggesting that latent learning may be more effective than learning with rewards. Furthermore, if a reward is removed from a previously rewarded group, performance declines (see **Lepper** *et al.* in unit 6.3.1).

- *Insight learning*. Some learning may take place because of a flash of insight, rather than by trial-and-error (see **Köhler**, unit 5.4.3). In defence of conditioning this behaviour could occur through generalisation.

- *The transfer of learning. Positive transfer* occurs when learning task A has a positive effect on learning task B, *negative transfer* occurs when learning task A interferes with learning task B. Both imply that some cognitive activity is mediating performance.

- *Imitation or observational learning*. See social learning theory, unit 1.4.2.

2.4.2 FORAGING AND HOMING BEHAVIOUR

Learning in the natural environment

Thorpe (1963) defined learning as 'that process which manifests itself by adaptive changes in individual behaviour as the result of experience', this excludes changes due to disease or maturation. There are many forms of learning:

- Imprinting and instinct (unit 2.3.3).
- Perceptual learning (unit 5.1.2).
- Habituation and sensitisation (non-associative forms of learning).
- Classical and operant conditioning (see unit 2.4.1).
- Cognitive activities (see unit 2.4.1).

Foraging

Foraging describes all those activities involved in satisfying nutritional requirements. Herbivores have to spend a greater part of the day grazing to obtain sufficient food whereas carnivores can eat less often but when they do, it often involves a great expenditure of energy. Larger animals need more food than smaller animals though smaller animals have a higher metabolic rate. There are omnivores, detrivores (consume dead organic matter) and parasites (eat but do not kill prey). The section on predator and prey relationships is relevant (see unit 2.1.3).

① *Optimal foraging* is the most efficient of all the possible foraging alternatives for an individual. There are physical constraints, such as the need to avoid predation, the individual's size and strength, encounter rates with prey, prey handling times, available search times, energy gain per item and environmental conditions.

- *Models of optimal foraging* predict behaviours which can then be tested against reality. The problem with these models is that, if they fail to match reality, it may be due to an error in the model or it may be because animals do not need to be as efficient as they could be. *Suboptimal strategies* are often selected because they are *sufficiently* good, especially in conditions when there is little competition.

- *Mixed strategies* are adopted in relation to environmental conditions and the behaviour of other animals. For example, **Barnard** (1980) studied the foraging behaviour of house sparrows on an English farm. In the cattlesheds, their behaviour was mainly influenced by the density of seeds. In the fields, they had to watch out for predators and therefore their rate of feeding was influenced by flock size. Mixed strategies are an example of optimal strategies and are an ESS (see unit 2.1.1).

② *Searching for food.* Some search behaviour may be innate, others may be learned through trial-and-error or problem-solving.

- *Static or nearly static food.* The animal must move around to find it, such as cattle grazing. Active search strategies for static foods are related to the distribution of food items in space. **Smith** (1974) experimented with thrushes by arranging pastry 'caterpillars' in different spacings. If the 'prey' were clumped the thrush ate one and then turned to one side, whereas with more spaced out food the thrush continued straight ahead. When food is clumped, the thrush will do well to stop and eat what's nearby, when food is evenly spaced out a straight path is a more efficient search strategy.
- *Mobile food: active searching* (hunting). Some carnivores hunt in packs, others are solitary; each has advantages (see unit 2.3.2). Some predators watch other predators and steal the felled prey, for instance gulls watch lapwings who adopt strategies to avoid such opportunism such as not crouching over their prey. A hunt may be 'called off' if the prey behaves in certain ways (see unit 2.1.3).
- *Mobile food: passive sit-and-wait strategies* work if prey are plentiful. The angler fish lures its prey by dangling a worm-like bait on the end of a rod-like antenna. Other strategies involve no specialist equipment but simply rely on passing trade, as in the case of a jelly fish which stings any passing fish with its immobile tentacles.

③ *Recognising food.* A hungry animal needs to distinguish edible from inedible food, and those species with specialist appetites need to recognise their target diet.

- *Innate recognition.* Toads have a diet mainly restricted to small insects. If you move a small dark piece of paper in front of a toad, it will snap at it. The toad's predisposition to snap at anything small, dark and moving works well in the natural environment because anything answering this description is invariably an insect. Toads' feeding responses are not much affected by learning.
- *Learned recognition.* Animals which have more catholic diets need a search image. They have to learn to distinguish figure from ground. **Dawkins** (1971) dyed grains of rice: some were a different colour from the background and therefore easy to see, some were the same colour as the background and therefore hard to see. Chickens pecked at the conspicuous grains first and then after a few minutes pecked at the camouflaged ones too. They learned to detect the camouflaged grains (see unit 5.1.2 on the development of perception).

④ *Handling time* is the time taken for the animal to search for, catch and eat its food. The profitability of the prey is the net energy value divided by the handling time. Given a choice an animal will select the most profitable prey. **Werner and Hall** (1974) found that if sunfish are placed in an aquarium with low densities of prey (water fleas) they eat fleas of any size, however if the prey are plentiful the sunfish chooses the largest fleas and ignores the smaller ones.

⑤ *Storage of food.* Some animals such as squirrels store their food, they then need some means of recognising the storage place (see below).

Homing behaviour

An animal uses homing behaviour to locate its home (nest, burrow, hive, etc.), origin or food store. This may require travel over land, air or sea.

① *Use of local landmarks* when travelling over short distances. **Tinbergen and Kruyt** (1938) placed a circle of pine cones around the entrance of a digger wasp's burrow. After a few days, they moved the circle a few metres away. When the wasp returned it looked for its burrow where the pine cones were.

② *Navigation* is required for long distances, and involves a compass (or directional sense) and some kind of map. In the case of migration, an animal may travel over great distances and will use both navigation and local landmarks to orient themselves. **Perdeck** (1967) followed starlings flying from the Baltic Sea to Spain. They were caught over Holland, ringed and released in Switzerland (a southerly displacement). The juveniles continued to fly south-west to France and Spain, using only compass navigation. The adults flew north-west to their usual winter grounds in northern France, they used true navigation and then landmarks as the destination approached.

Animals orient themselves using:

- *The sun*. **Santschi** (1911) shielded ants from direct sunlight and used a mirror to reflect sunlight from the opposite direction. This caused the ants to turn around and walk in the opposite direction until the shade was removed.
- *Smell*. Salmon return to the same river they were born in using smell. **Hasler** (1960) plugged the noses of salmon and found that they homed less accurately than untreated controls. Salmon probably use a sun compass to navigate across the ocean but, once they are at their home coast, they distinguish between rivers using smell. If they are transferred to another stream after the period of imprinting, they still return to their native tributary.
- *Magnetic information*. It is possible that magnetite, which is found in some species, acts as a magnetic sense. **Gould** *et al*. (1978) turned a bees' honeycomb round, thus disorienting them so they could not use their sun compass. However, it did not take long for them to reorient using their magnetic compass and then reset their sun compass.

③ *Homing pigeons*. In familiar terrain pigeons use physical cues. There is some debate about whether they ever truly experience unfamiliar terrains because they have a maximum range and within this range there may always be familiar landmarks. If they do use true navigation it might be based on:

- The position of the sun in the sky, making allowance for daily changes using an internal clock. Experiments have shown that pigeons make predictable errors when trained on a artificial light/dark schedule and are then exposed to the sun.
- A 'map' strategy – they work out latitude and longitude to home in on their target using magnetic information.
- A magnetic compass – pigeons with bar magnets on their head navigate incorrectly on cloudy days. This suggests that they do use magnetic fields and that they use this in conjunction with the sun.
- Smell – the pigeon may remember and orient to home odours. It has been found that pigeons do not home accurately if their noses are blocked.

2.4.3 ANIMAL LANGUAGE

All animals use signalling systems (see unit 2.3.4) but there is a distinction between these and true language. Language is often defined as 'the method of human communication' which excludes animals *ipso facto*. If we want to know whether animals can use language, then we must define language differently. **Hockett** (1958) suggested some 'design features' which jointly act as criteria for language. For example:

- It is a precise and specialised system.
- The units may be arbitrary (dance of the honey bees).
- The vocabulary is learned not inherited (birdsong).
- Meaning is communicated by order, a grammar (vervet monkeys).
- Displacement in time and space (urination in dogs).
- The system allows users to produce their own novel utterances (whales).
- Language can be used to lie or make jokes (monkeys).

Studies of natural animal language

① *The dance of honey bees* was first recorded by **von Frisch** (1914). For example, the 'waggle dance' is performed by a returning forager to tell other bees how far away the food is from the hive. The 'round' dance indicates the direction. If the dance is performed on a vertical instead of horizontal surface, the line represents the angle between the hive, the position of the sun, and the food. When a forager dances, the majority of (bee) observers are able to locate the food source accurately.

2 *Birdsong.* The functions of birdsong are to locate and identify members of the same species (courtship), to identify individuals, to solicit food (begging from chicks), to demarcate territory (aggression), to warn of predators (alarm calls) and simply to sing.

Bird species vary enormously in the extent to which their song development is innate. Some birds have almost no facility for learning and the full adult song is present even in birds raised in isolation, for example the alder flycatcher. Most birds need to hear the adult song to develop their innate version (cultural transmission). **Slater** (1981) showed that chaffinches produce a very basic song repertoire if hand reared and are strongly inclined to copy the song of any bird they hear. Some birds have a special ability for such interspecies imitation, such as parrots.

3 *Marine mammals* (cetaceans: whales and dolphins) use sound for communication because it travels a long way underwater (see unit 2.3.4). Dolphins whistle and click rather than sing. These sounds are used for social co-ordination, to warn of danger, and may even be used to communicate quite complex information. **Bastion** (1967) kept two dolphins in separate tanks, able to hear but not see each other. One dolphin was taught to press a paddle to receive a reward. When the other dolphin was given the same equipment, it knew the solution.

4 *Chimpanzee* communication is largely concerned with social relations, such as greeting, grooming, aggression, reconciliation and dominance. They use a combination of vocal and visual signals for complex communications. **Menzel** (1974) conducted an experiment with a group of six chimpanzees to see if they could convey information about a hidden object. Menzel took one of them with him when he hid some food or a snake. When the others were released they usually found the food very quickly. If a snake was hidden, they approached more cautiously. If two kinds of food were hidden, they usually went to the better one. This suggests that the 'leader' chimpanzee was communicating some very specific information about what was hidden and where it was. However, if the 'leader' did not go with the others on their search, they would just mill around. Also, if the 'leader' was a stranger the other chimpanzees paid him no attention.

5 *Vervet monkeys* have been shown to use a vocabulary (verbal as well as vocal) of alarm calls (see **Seyfarth and Cheyney**, unit 2.3.4).

Attempts to teach human language to non-humans

Psychologists have sought to teach animals to use human language in order to determine the extent to which it is a species-specific ability. If it is, this supports the nativist view of language acquisition (see unit 5.4.1). A second purpose of this research is as a means of differentiating humans from animals, this is especially important in terms of the rights we accord to animals (see unit 7.3.2). A further reason is that such communication could provide a more precise means of interspecies communication and a glimpse into unknown worlds.

1 *Empirical studies*

- **Kellogg and Kellogg** (1933) raised a chimpanzee called *Gua* who learned to recognise about 95 words and phrases, but was unable to speak. Circus animals learn to understand simple commands.
- **Gardner and Gardner** (1969) raised a female chimp, *Washoe*, and used operant conditioning (rewards such as tickling) to teach her American Sign Language (ASL or Ameslan), much of which is iconic, but some is arbitrary and includes tense and grammar in its gestures. Washoe was treated like a child and all conversation was held in ASL. By the age of 5 she had 133 signs and her development mirrored that of children, she spontaneously combined signs into strings of two to five words and talked about things which were not there. The Gardners claimed that her language was grammatical, for example she overgeneralised.
- **Fouts** (1973) continued work with Washoe to see if she would teach ASL to an adopted son, *Loulis* (cultural transmission). The researchers never signed directly to Loulis but, by the time he was 5 years old, he had learned 51 signs.
- **Patterson and Linden** (1981) taught *Koko*, a gorilla, ASL. After 7 years he knew almost all 700 signs and could understand many spoken equivalents. They claimed

that he used grammar and produced some novel sentences (his own form of swearing, 'you big dirty toilet') and invented his own combinations of signs, such as 'runny nose'.

- **Terrace** (1979) worked with a chimp called *Nim Chimpsky* (after Noam Chomsky, see unit 5.4.1). Nim never reached Washoe's level.
- **Premack** (1971) taught *Sarah* (a chimp) a language based on small, plastic, arbitrary symbols (lexigrams) to exclude any restrictions due to memory. She was able to interpret messages left for her on a magnetic board and to respond by placing the appropriate shapes on the board.
- **Rumbaugh** *et al.* (1973) used lexigrams to teach *Lana* to operate a computer with 50 keys, each key was a pattern representing a word in 'Yerkish'. The computer was able to recognise correct grammatical usage and reward her, it could also converse with her. She learned to correct mistaken displays (reading), conversed with the screen, initiated conversation and, when shown a new object, created a word for it.
- **Savage-Rumbaugh** (1991) has perhaps made the greatest progress with two chimpanzees, *Kanzi* and *Panbanisha*. She aimed to teach them language in the same way that children are taught: they were exposed to it in the course of everyday life, used it to talk about future plans and were enculturated by it. She conversed using lexigrams while roaming around a natural environment, the large forest surrounding her home. The results were a rich use of language: 90% accuracy in being able to identify pictures, novel combinations of words and introduction of new rules. Kanzi's skills were compared, on film, to the progress of a 2½-year-old child: they both showed correct comprehension about 75% of the time.
- **Pepperberg** (1983) taught her parrot *Alex* to name 40 objects. He could answer questions such as 'What colour or shape?' suggesting an understanding of abstract categories.
- **Herman** *et al.* (1990) worked with dolphins and **Schusterman and Gisiner** (1988) taught sea lions a series of commands, testing their comprehension with novel presentations.

② *Extent to which human language has been acquired*

- *Grammatical.* The key question is whether any of the efforts resulted in grammatical language (see unit 5.4.1). Washoe was never consistent, she would interchangeably say 'sweet go' and 'go sweet'. **Aitchison** (1983) suggested that this may have happened because she was not rewarded for grammatical expressions.
- *Social function of language.* Many of the attempts may have failed because the animals were not taught language within a social setting. Humans don't acquire language under such conditions either (see unit 5.4.1).
- *Limited system.* It is clear that certain features of language were acquired such as the ability to name objects, some novel utterances, and spontaneous production. **Terrace** (1979) suggested that primates reach a plateau which could be due to intellectual rather than linguistic competence. They may be using **Vygotsky**'s pre-intellectual language (see unit 6.2.1).

③ *Criticisms of empirical studies*

- *Subjective interpretation.* The question of whether an expression is grammatical or novel depends on the interpretation of the researcher.
- *Experimenter bias.* The animals may be responding to inadvertent cues from their trainers. The **Gardners** (1978) tested Washoe with questions to which they didn't know the answer, she was correct 72% of the time. Kanzi was tested with **Savage-Rumbaugh** behind him and performed well.
- *Ethics.* Do the ends justify the means? Teaching language involves enculturation.

④ *Conclusion.* Animals never acquire language without extensive training, unlike the speed and ease with which humans acquire language. This suggests that they do not have the same innate capacity.

2.4.4 EVOLUTIONARY EXPLANATIONS OF HUMAN BEHAVIOUR

Evolutionary psychology is an approach which explains behaviour in terms of its adaptiveness and innateness. Cross-cultural studies have been used to find universal behaviours, but this approach is fraught with difficulties (see unit 7.2.3). When considering human behaviour, learning and culture may have an overriding influence.

1. *Prejudice* is a possible example of kin selection in humans. **Ardrey** (1967) suggested that the hatred existing between races is an example of an inborn biological tendency similar to the animal's desire to protect its territory against predators.

2. *Aggression* (unit 1.4.2) may be an adaptive strategy in humans. This view has important consequences for the reduction of aggression since any treatment must also be biological (drugs, genetic engineering), or we should employ appeasement strategies and use social engineering (social skills training) to reduce aggression.

3. *Prosocial behaviour, altruism and co-operation* (units 2.3.1, 2.3.2 and 1.4.1). The reason that humans behave co-operatively and altruistically may be because we learn such behaviour or it may be that we have an innate tendency to protect our gene pool. Human altruism tends to be due to the former though parent–child caring can be understood in terms of kin selection.

4. *Sexual selection* (see unit 2.2.1). Men should prefer younger women because they are more fertile. Physical attractiveness is a means of assessing age and fitness. Females should be less concerned with age because males are fertile at any age, but more concerned with resource control to ensure good conditions for childrearing (see **Dunbar**, unit 1.2.1).

5. *Mating strategy* (see unit 2.2.3). Cases of polygyny (harems) occur in societies with powerful men, secondary females still gain because their sons may inherit some wealth. Males gain by maximising their reproduction.

   Cases of polyandry are rare, although in Tibet a woman may marry two or more brothers. This is necessitated by the harsh living conditions where it takes at least two men to manage a farm. With two brothers, all parents share a genetic interest in all the children (**Dickemann**, 1985).

   When humans were hunter-gatherers, their best strategy was monogamy (see **Crook**'s study of weaver birds in unit 2.2.3) because they had limited resources, therefore males were unlikely to attract more than one wife. The fact that humans exhibit dimorphism (see unit 2.2.1) is evidence of competition and polygyny but the differences are not as great as in some animals (such as peacocks) which suggests only a low degree of polygyny.

   Short (1991) investigated the testicular effect, males who have to compete (sperm competition) need to produce more sperm and hence have larger testicles. Chimpanzees have huge testicles, relative to body weight, in comparison with gorillas (60g:50kg compared with 10g:250kg). Therefore we would expect great competition among male chimpanzees but little in gorillas. This fits with the fact that chimpanzees have a mainly polygynandrous system whereas gorillas live in harems. Human male testicles are intermediate between chimpanzees and gorillas (10g:70kg).

   Altogether this suggests that humans are serial monogamists, an effect we can observe in Western society today. Like all species, humans have a set of alternative strategies which are selected in relation to prevailing conditions.

6. *Family conflicts* (see unit 2.2.4).

   - *Sibling rivalry* can be understood in terms of competition for limited parental resources. At the same time siblings have a genetic interest in each other. Overall, we would expect the relationship to be intense and ambivalent.
   - *Weaning conflict*. In poor countries women often prolong lactation as a means of birth control. In general human females maximise reproductive success by having a child once every four years.

- *Father–offspring conflict.* Males have an interest in restricting lactation so their females can continue to reproduce. **Palmer** (1993) suggested that wet nursing offered wealthy men greater reproductivity because their wives stopped breastfeeding, but it provided a method of birth control for poor women.
- *Step-parent–stepchild conflict.* The origin of the wicked step-parent may lie in the genetic threat posed by stepchildren (see 'Infanticide' in unit 2.2.4).

7 *Attachment* (imprinting and bonding, see units 2.2.3 and 6.1.1) is related to survival and reproductive success, and therefore an adaptive strategy. In non-human animals the imprinting template gives the offspring a means of recognising their own species. **Westermarck** (1891) suggested that humans negatively imprint on intimate associates during a critical period of early childhood (between 2 and 6 years of age). This is called the *Westermarck effect* and would be useful in avoiding incest. **Shepher** (1971) studied approximately 3,000 marriage records in Israel, not one was between individuals raised on the same kibbutz.

8 *The concept of preparedness.* Like bait shyness, there is evidence that humans have innate predispositions to avoid dangerous things. **Ohman** *et al.* (1975) demonstrated an innate fear of spiders and snakes in humans and **Bennett-Levy and Marteau** (1984) linked this to the animals' appearance.

Our dislike of characteristics associated with disease (such as mottled skin or withered limbs) may be an adaptive mechanism for avoiding contagion. Similarly, our dislike of faeces is a protective mechanism against the bacteria they harbour.

9 *Sleep* (unit 3.3.1). The *evolutionary theory* proposes that sleep is an adaptive response to environmental (predation) and internal (metabolic conservation) demands. However, this theory does not explain why animals who are sleep-deprived suffer serious, even fatal, consequences. This can be accounted for by the *restoration theory*.

10 *Motivation, emotion and stress* (section 3.4) are adaptive strategies.

11 *Language* (unit 5.4.1). **Chomsky**'s theory of language acquisition (the *nativist* view) proposes that humans have an innate capacity to acquire language (generate grammatical rules) which has evolved through selective pressure. In most people the language centres are located in the left hemisphere (see unit 3.2.2). The evolutionary advantage of such *brain lateralisation* is possibly that having language centres in both hemispheres would lead to stuttering. There is brain lateralisation in other animals who have systems of vocal communication.

12 *Territoriality.* The home field advantage may be related to the *owner wins strategy* (see unit 2.1.1). Examples include increased likelihood of winning a football match on your home ground, and people being less influenced by salespersons in their own home.

Research into overcrowding and defensible space (see unit 9.5.1) also suggests that we have inbuilt mechanisms for resource defence and for population control.

Chapter roundup

2.1 Evolutionary determinants of behaviour

2.1.1 The *evolution of non-human behaviour* occurs through natural selection of adaptive characteristics. Fitness in measured in terms of reproductive success. Selection operates at the level of the genes.

2.1.2 *Resources* are shared using an ideal free distribution, when supplies are plentiful, or using a resource defence strategy (despotic), when there is a scarcity. Aggression may be resolved using territories, ritualised behaviour and/or dominance hierarchies.

2.1.3 Both *predators* and *prey* develop efficient methods of recognition, attack and avoidance because of selective pressure. Examples include FAPs, mimicry and predator–prey co-evolution (the arms race).

2.1.4 *Symbiosis* describes an *apparently* altruistic interspecies relationship which evolves because of dual benefits which don't depend on reciprocation.

2.2 Reproductive strategies

2.2.1 *Sexual selection* promotes reproductive success through inter- or intrasexual strategies. Bizarre sexual characteristics can be explained by the runaway process or handicapping theory.

2.2.2 *Parental investment* can be explained in terms of sex gametes, numbers, mating systems, mode of fertilisation and embryonic development, ecological conditions, the behaviour of the partner and care by relatives.

2.2.3 The strategy of having alternative *mating strategies* best describes mating behaviour, as opposed to using *mating systems*. Various forms of social organisation (harems, leks and dominance hierarchies) can be related to mating strategies.

2.2.4 *Parent–offspring conflict* arises because offspring have a greater interest in parental investment than their parents. Examples include weaning conflict and infanticide.

2.3 Kinship and social behaviour

2.3.1 Most cases of *altruism* appear to be unselfish but in fact are selfish at the level of the genes (inclusive fitness). There is also reciprocal and manipulated altruism.

2.3.2 Group living or *sociality* has many benefits for individual members in terms of mating, food and anti-predation. Cost-benefit principles guide optimal group size.

2.3.3 Non-human animal *signals* evolve from functional displays which communicate information about the sender. These may remain honest or become dishonest, and can use visual, auditory, olfactory or kinaesthetic modalities.

2.4 Behaviour analysis

2.4.1 *Classical conditioning* is by association, *operant conditioning* is by consequences. Key concepts include generalisation, extinction, discrimination, reinforcement and punishment.

2.4.2 Efficient *foraging and homing behaviour* depends on a combination of innate and learned strategies. Foraging includes searching for, recognising, capturing, handling and storing food. Homing cues may be visual, olfactory, auditory or magnetic.

2.4.3 Many *animals* have sophisticated systems of communication which could be described as *languages*. Non-human animals may be able to acquire a limited system of human language but do not appear to have an innate capacity for this.

2.4.4 Evolutionary explanations can be used to understand *human behaviour* in terms of its adaptive significance. Learning and free will can override innate tendencies.

Illustrative question

Discuss the role of **both** reinforcement **and** punishment in the learning process.

(AEB A 1993)

Tutorial note

You are directed both to describe *and* evaluate how reinforcement *and* punishment contribute to learning. A good answer should be balanced (covering all four). Where possible, any arguments should be backed up by psychological knowledge rather than common-sense material. Evaluation can be achieved through the use of empirical evidence, reference to theories, and a critical appreciation of the concepts. It is important that you can distinguish between punishment and negative reinforcement.

Suggested answer

Skinner proposed that learning occurs as a result of the consequences of behaviour. If a behaviour is reinforced it is more likely to occur in the future, if a behaviour is punished it is less likely to reoccur. Thorndike called this 'stamping in' and 'stamping out'. This is operant conditioning because the learner operates on their environment, rather than responding as in respondent or classical conditioning.

ABC = antecedents → behaviour → consequences (which strengthen or weaken S-R links)

Reinforcement can be positive or negative, both are pleasant and encourage the organism to repeat the behaviour. An example of positive reinforcement is the use of praise or a gold star. An example of negative reinforcement is escaping from an aversive stimulus such as when you manage to avoid punishment because you apologised profusely. The success of the apology should encourage you to repeat it in the future.

Skinner demonstrated operant conditioning with pigeons in a Skinner box. There is a lever which, when pressed causes a door to open and a pellet of food to appear. The lever is an unconditioned stimulus and the food is a reinforcer or reward. The pigeon first pecks randomly around the box as part of its natural exploratory behaviour. Accidentally it presses the lever on a number of occasions and is rewarded with food. The reward strengthens the link between the stimulus and response, and increases the likelihood of the behaviour being repeated. Reinforcement is both positive and negative. When the lever is pressed, it is positive. Receiving no food when pecking elsewhere is negative reinforcement. The lever becomes the conditioned stimulus and pressing the lever is a conditioned response. Skinner described the process as bringing behaviour under stimulus control.

It often takes a long time for an organism to perform the right behaviour to receive a reward, however learning often takes place quickly. Skinner proposed the concept of shaping: operant behaviours are gradually built up through progressive reinforcement as each behaviour becomes closer to the final goal. This has been applied to the acquisition of language in young children. Skinner suggested that children start by producing random sounds (mands) which progressively come to sound like real words because adults first reinforce words which vaguely sound like something recognisable. Gradually the mands come to sound more and more like the real thing. Reinforcement takes place through a child getting what it wants (like a biscuit) or getting attention. **Brown et al.** (1969) found that mothers reinforce meaning rather than grammatical correctness, therefore language acquisition could not be explained entirely using operant conditioning.

Behaviours may also be *unlearned* when reinforcement ceases. However, in avoidance learning this is not possible. In this case an individual learns to avoid a particular response but then it can't find out if the unpleasant stimulus is still there and doesn't unlearn the response.

Reinforcement may be given at regular intervals but this is rare in real life. The concept of 'reinforcement schedules' describes the frequency of a reinforcer. Partial reinforcement schedules are more effective and more resistant to extinction. This may be because continuous reinforcement leads to an expectation of a reward every time the behaviour is produced, when this doesn't happen the behaviour starts to be unlearned. Partial reinforcement may be fixed or variable ratios or intervals.

The kind of reinforcement that Skinner used with pigeons is called primary. Primary reinforcers are innate things, such as food, approval or fear. Secondary reinforcers work because at some time they have been paired with a primary one, for example money. This concept has been applied in token economies, a treatment of mental patients. Patients are given tokens (secondary reinforcers) which can later be exchanged for primary reinforcers such as food or privileges. **Wolfe** (1936) demonstrated this technique with chimpanzees and it has proved to be a successful therapy. Some people object on ethical grounds because it manipulates patients' behaviour and takes away their free will.

Another successful application of operant conditioning is the 'time out' method where difficult children are placed in temporary isolation when they misbehave instead of being told off. Telling off is a kind of attention, even though it is negative, and is reinforcing. Isolation leads to unlearning. The system works best if the children are given extra attention (positive reinforcement) when they behave well.

Punishment also weakens S-R links, it discourages an individual from repeating a behaviour. Punishment doesn't always work well. As suggested above this may be because the attention associated with punishment may be positively reinforcing. Some children are naughty because it is an easy way of gaining attention. It may be as effective to ignore bad behaviour, which will then disappear through lack of reinforcement.

Punishment may produce hostility and a desire to rebel. A person may get used to punishment, which means it continually has to be increased to be effective. The threat of punishment may be sufficient, though this cannot be included in learning theory because it refers to the existence of cognitive factors.

Punishment is useful in situations where an immediate effect is needed, such as a child putting its hand near the fire. It is most effective if it is consistent and immediate, if it is not too severe and if you also show the person the right way to behave.

It has been shown that prosocial behaviour is learned better through direct imitation rather than the use of reward and punishment. **Rosenhan** (1970) interviewed people who participated in the US civil rights movement. Those who were most active had parents who had similar views and had also been active. They also had warmer relations with their children which promotes prosocial development.

Hoffman (1970) found that childrearing methods which used rewards and punishment were the least effective way to promote moral development. The best way is 'induction', explaining why a behaviour is wrong and encouraging independent thought. **Hartshorne and May** (1928) conducted a large study of children's moral behaviour and concluded that direct instruction made children more rather than less honest. **Lepper et al.** (1973) showed that rewards destroyed children's intrinsic motivation to do things because they offer an extrinsic motive. So rewards, like punishment, can be counter-productive.

Reinforcement and punishment alone cannot explain learning because there are many situations where other cognitive factors are involved, for example social learning where children model behaviour on what they have observed. **Bandura et al.** (1961) demonstrated how children learned to be aggressive by observing an adult behaving that way. Latent learning also involves cognitive factors. This is learning in behavioural 'silence'. **Blodgett** (1929) demonstrated this with rats in a maze, those who were not rewarded at the start later learned the maze more quickly, suggesting that they had stored a 'cognitive map' of the maze when exploring. Insight learning is another cognitive explanation of learning, using a flash of insight rather than trial-and-error.

There are also situations where learning takes place through association alone (classical conditioning) or due to innate predisposition. **Garcia and Koelling** (1966) demonstrated 'bait shyness' in rats, a predisposition to learn quickly to avoid substances which made them feel sick.

Reinforcement and punishment are powerful concepts which explain some aspects of learning. They have led to many useful applications such as in the treatment of abnormal behaviour, education by parents and teachers, and programmed learning. However they cannot explain all learning.

Question bank

Allow 35-40 minutes for each question.

Evolutionary determinants of behaviour

1   To what extent do evolutionary concepts contribute to our understanding of the behaviour of non-human animals?

(AEB A 1990)

Points: Many candidates answer questions in this section on the basis of a wealth of knowledge gleaned from wildlife programmes. This is by no means irrelevant, but a good answer requires evaluation skills, evidenced by making some theoretical sense out of the descriptive data. It is also tempting to be anthropomorphic (e.g. talk about animals 'falling in love') but this suggests a superficial level of understanding.

2 (a) Describe **two** methods that non-human animals use to exploit and compete for resources. (10 marks)
  (b) Assess the consequences of these methods in terms of their evolutionary value. (14 marks)

Points: Take care to separate the strands of describe and assess in your answer. You should use actual examples to support your description and can evaluate the evolutionary consequences with reference to the examples. Try to describe evolution as a *passive* process not one where the genes are actually 'deciding' anything.

3 Discuss the nature of predator–prey and symbiotic relationships.

Points: Describe such relationships. You can evaluate them using actual examples and by assessing their evolutionary significance. Make sure that your examples are based on detailed knowledge.

Reproductive strategies

4 Discuss how sexual selection contributes to physical and psychological differences between males and females in non-human animal species.

Points: You must restrict your answer to non-human animals only. Focus on sexual differences, such as size, colouration and coyness, and explain these in terms of selective pressure arising from the process of sexual selection.

5 (a) Explain the concept of parental investment. (5 marks)
  (b) Compare and contrast **two** explanations for the differential investments of males and females in the rearing of their young. (19 marks)

Points: In part (a) the question requests skill A only, a description which can be amplified by using examples. Part (b) is 'compare and contrast' which means you should suggest both similarities and differences for your chosen explanations. These comparisons are the skill B element of the question, for skill A you should describe each explanation. You must give two explanations, even if one is only very briefly described, otherwise the 'compare and contrast' is not addressed.

6 (a) Consider **two** mating systems used by non-human animals. (14 marks).
  (b) Assess the advantages of each of these to the animals concerned. (10 marks)

(AEB A 1996)

Points: 'Consider' is a skill A term, therefore part (a) requires a description of two *non-human* animal *systems*. In part (b) you can assess the advantages probably in evolutionary terms to all the animals concerned. Make sure you refer to the same mating systems in (a) and (b).

7 Discuss the nature and implications of parent–offspring conflict.

Points: A broad question which permits use of both non-human and human material in a discussion (description and evaluation) of anything related to parent–offspring conflict.

Kinship and social behaviour

8 Using examples, show what is meant by apparent altruistic and selfish behaviour in non-human species. Discuss how these behaviours may have potential survival value.

(AEB A 1991)

Points: A classic question on this area of the syllabus. Descriptive skills are clearly distinguished from evaluation skills (discuss...) yet many candidates do little more than describe, without comment on survival value.

9 (a) Describe any **two** types of social organisation found in non-human animals. (10 marks).
   (b) Consider the selective advantage of these arrangements to the animals concerned. (14 marks)

(AEB A 1993)

Points: Part (a) is a straightforward description which should include reference to actual examples. However, a description of arrangements in different species is not enough without reference to the type of structure they exemplify. Only two types should be described but you can use many examples. Part (b) involves an assessment in terms of selective advantages, a discussion which can include the disadvantages.

10 Describe studies of imprinting in non-human animals and discuss how the imprinting process may be beneficial to animals.

(AEB A 1991)

Points: Candidates in examinations dwell too much on the original work by Lorenz rather than branching out to the many other classic studies. A good essay should consider more than visual imprinting, and comment on more than the immediate effects.

11 Discuss the evolutionary development and significance of communication in non-human animals.

(AEB A 1992)

Points: The descriptive element of this question includes listing different kinds of communication in non-human animals but the question as a whole involves significantly more than this. Communication systems should be presented in terms of their evolutionary development.

Behaviour analysis

12 (a) Outline the main processes involved in operant conditioning. (10 marks)
   (b) Critically consider the usefulness of operant conditioning as a concept for explaining learning in humans. (14 marks)

(AEB AS 1995)

Points: Part (a) is much simpler than part (b) which involves a consideration of the usefulness of the concept and its ability to explain learning in *humans*. For practice, you could change the wording and write about classical conditioning.

13 (a) Consider ways in which non-human animals might learn in the natural environment. (14 marks)
   (b) Assess the effectiveness of such learning to the adaptation of behaviour in non-human animals. (10 marks)

(AEB A 1994)

Points: Since the question is about the natural environment you must restrict your discussion to this. Evidence relating to classical and operant conditioning is mainly laboratory based and therefore should be introduced cautiously. Parts (a) and (b) involve skill A and skill B respectively. Evaluation should be in terms of adaptiveness.

14 (a) Explain what psychologists mean by the term 'language'. (4 marks)
   (b) Critically consider **one** study of natural animal language. (10 marks)
   (c) Critically consider **one** study of an attempt to teach human language to non-humans. (10 marks)

Points: Use the marks to guide the structure of your answer: define, and describe and evaluate two studies in about equal measure. Evaluation can be in terms of adaptiveness, ethics, application or methodology.

15 Describe and evaluate evolutionary explanations of two aspects of human behaviour.

(AEB specimen)

Points: Select two areas which contain a wealth of material. It could be argued that sexual behaviour is one 'area' and includes sexual selection, parental investment, and mating strategy. Your evaluation must be in evolutionary terms not simply looking at the innateness of a behaviour. Ensure that your answer is well-informed rather than anecdotal.

BIO-PSYCHOLOGY

Units in this chapter

Chapter overview

Biology refers to all the physiological systems we find in the body: muscles, blood, hormones (the autonomic nervous system), nerves and the brain (the central nervous system). It also includes genetic explanations, such as heredity and maturation. The biological approach to explaining human behaviour is regarded as reductionist and determinist but it is an important *level* of explanation. A recent development has been a combined approach, called 'bio-psychosocial'.

3.1 BASIC NEURAL AND HORMONAL PROCESSES AND THEIR INFLUENCE ON BEHAVIOUR

3.1.1 THE NERVOUS SYSTEM

- The *central nervous system* (CNS) comprises the brain and spinal cord, containing about 12 billion nerve cells (*neurons*), and about 10 times as many *glia cells*, packing cells which provide nutrition and waste removal. The neurons are bathed in *cerebrospinal fluid*, which supplies nutrients and cushions the CNS from damage.
- The *peripheral nervous system* comprises:
  - The *somatic nervous system* (soma = body) messages are sent out to control voluntary movement and sent back regarding sensations.
  - The *autonomic nervous system* (ANS) controls involuntary muscles, such as the stomach and the heart, and the *endocrine system* which produces and distributes hormones. The ANS is largely self-regulating (autonomous).
- Communication throughout the nervous system is affected by *electrical potentials* (nerve impulses), *neurotransmitters* (chemical substances) and *hormones*.

The central nervous system

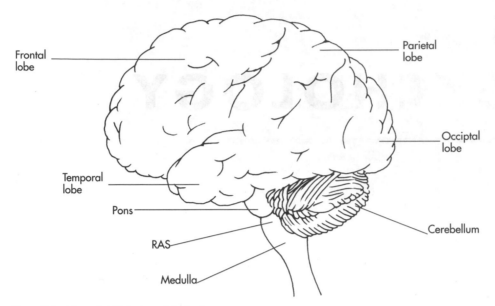

Figure 3.1 A lateral (side) view of the brain

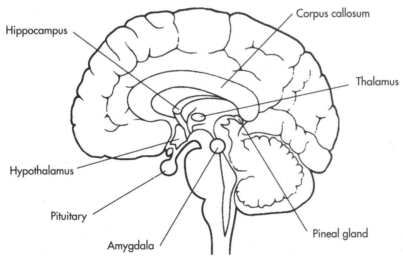

Figure 3.2 A simplified cross-section of the brain, showing important subcortical areas

❶ *Forebrain*

- *Cerebral cortex*. Responsible for higher cognitive functions, it is not very important in lower animals but accounts for 50% of the human nervous system. It is divided into two halves (*hemispheres*) joined by fibres (including the *corpus callosum*). Each half has four lobes:

  - *Frontal* cortex: controls fine voluntary movements, inhibits inappropriate behaviours and is associated with thinking and planning.
  - *Parietal* cortex, somatosensory: touch, pain, pressure and temperature.
  - *Temporal* cortex: contains auditory cortex for hearing and balance, contributes to memory, language, emotion and perception.
  - *Occipital* cortex: primarily responsible for vision (visual cortex).

- *Thalamus*. Great relay station of the brain, receives sensory data, performs some processing before passing information on to the cerebral cortex.
- *Limbic system*. Chiefly emotion and motivation, includes parts of the cortex and:

  - *Hypothalamus*: integrates the ANS, important in homeostasis and stress.
  - *Pituitary gland*: controls ANS activity (below).

- *Pineal gland*: controls bodily rhythms (see unit 3.3.2).
- *Hippocampus*: involved in learning and storing new information.
- *Amygdala*: important in aggression, and also involved with memory.

② *Midbrain.* A small area connecting the forebrain to the hindbrain.

- *Reticular activating system* (RAS): sleep, arousal, consciousness and attention. The ascending system (ARAS) sends signals to the cortex; the descending system (DRAS) sends signals down the spinal column.
- *Raphe system*: located in the hindbrain and extending into the midbrain, promotes sleep.

③ *Hindbrain*

- *Medulla*: the 'vital centre' controlling heartbeat, breathing, digestion, blood pressure, etc. It connects the spinal column to the higher brain.
- *Cerebellum*: controls voluntary movement, muscle tone and balance.
- *Pons*: possibly related to sleep.
- *Brainstem*: the region connecting the spinal cord to the brain, including most of the hindbrain except the cerebellum.

④ *Spinal cord.* Conducts messages to and from the brain, and integrates many complex reflexes without the mediation of the brain.

⑤ *Division of the CNS following the evolution of the brain.* **Maclean** (1982) proposed the *triune model* which identifies three main parts of the CNS:

- *Reptilian brain.* The central core, whose structures are found in modern reptiles.
- *Old mammalian brain.* The limbic system, first appeared in mammals 100 million years ago.
- *New mammalian brain.* The cerebral cortex, only present in some mammals and first appeared about 2 million years ago.

The autonomic nervous system

The two divisions of the ANS work in a correlated but antagonistic fashion to maintain internal equilibrium (*homeostasis*):

- The *sympathetic branch*: activates internal organs for vigorous activities and emergencies; 'fight or flight'.
- The *parasympathetic branch*: conserves and stores resources, monitors the relaxed state, promotes digestion and metabolism.

Effect on:	Sympathetic	Parasympathetic
pupils	dilates	constricts
saliva	inhibits (mouth feels dry)	stimulates
heart beat	accelerates	slows
digestive processes	inhibits	promotes
liver	sugar is released	sugar is stored
bladder	contracts	inhibits contraction

The endocrine system and hormones

The *endocrine* system is a collection of ductless glands, controlled by the ANS, which secrete hormones directly into the blood. [The *exocrine* system comprises glands *with* ducts, for example, the bile duct or sweat glands.]

Hormones are biochemicals which profoundly affect behaviour and development. They are present in very small doses and the individual molecules have a very short life, so their effects quickly disappear if not secreted continuously. Their action is rapid but slower than the nervous system because they are transported by the blood.

The main endocrine glands and their functions are:

- *Pituitary gland* in the forebrain, controls much of the endocrine system by producing hormones itself, such as *growth hormone*, *prolactin* (responsible for milk production), *oxytocin* (causes the uterus to contract in childbirth), *anti-diuretic* hormone (ADH, regulates the amount of water secreted by the kidneys), *vasopressin* (which acts on the kidneys and controls blood pressure) and *adrenocorticotrophic* hormones (ACTH, which target the adrenal gland, thyroid and gonads).

- *Pineal gland* in the forebrain, secretes *melatonin*, which regulates sleep and other bodily rhythms.
- *Adrenal gland*, located just above the kidneys, consists of:
  - *Adrenal cortex* secretes at least 20 different hormones, including *corticosteroids* which mobilise glucose and reduce immune responses, *mineralosteroids* which control salt retention, and *sex steroids* (androgens and estrogens).
  - *Adrenal medulla* produces *adrenalin* (also called epinephrine) and *noradrenalin* (norepinephrine), which are associated with arousal via the sympathetic branch of the ANS and also act as neurotransmitters.
- *Thyroid gland* controls metabolism and growth through the release of *thyroxin*. Over- and underproduction results in hyper- or hypothyroidism and over- or undereating respectively.
- *Parathyroid gland* produces *parathormone* which controls calcium deposits in the bones and levels of phosphates in the body.
- *Pancreas* produces *insulin* and *glucagon*, which work in opposition to keep blood-sugar levels balanced.
- *Gonads* (ovaries or testes) produce sex hormones such as *testosterone* and *oestrogen* which promote and maintain secondary sexual characteristics, and control the menstrual cycle and pregnancy.

3.1.2 INFLUENCES ON PHYSIOLOGICAL AND BEHAVIOURAL FUNCTIONS

The behavioural effects of the CNS and ANS are described in units on:
- Perception, memory and language (3.2.3, 5.3.1 and 5.4.1).
- Levels of awareness, arousal, bodily rhythms, sleep and hypnosis (3.3).
- Motivation, emotion and stress (3.4).
- Atypical and abnormal behaviour (4.1.1 and 4.3.1).
- Sexual development (6.3.2).

Homeostasis (homeo = same, stasis = state) is a state of dynamic equilibrium which is important for survival. Continuous small changes, governed by negative feedback, ensure that uniform conditions prevail in the body, in the same way that a thermostat controls room temperature.

The hypothalamus and ANS largely control biological homeostatic mechanisms.

➊ *Temperature control.* Constant temperature enables an animal to be independent of the environment and to evolve chemical reactions that are precisely co-ordinated. It is regulated *behaviourally* by, for example, putting on more or less clothing. *Physiologically* temperature is monitored by the preoptic area (in front of the hypothalamus), which leads to various ANS functions such as sweating, shivering and vasodilation. *Fever* is caused by the release of prostaglandin E from white cells in the blood, which stimulate the preoptic cells to raise the temperature. A moderate fever helps combat infection.

➋ *Thirst.* When tissue fluid levels are low we feel thirsty (*behavioural* effect).
Physiological mechanisms
- *Intracellular fluid loss* (inside body cells) raises levels of salt in the blood. These are detected by osmoreceptors in the hypothalamus which shrivel. The changed cell shape is detected by a comparator in the anterior hypothalamus, which in turn alerts the pituitary to secrete ADH, which results in the kidneys secreting more concentrated urine.
- *Extracellular fluid loss.* Loss of blood or water from the blood (sweating) leads to decreased pressure, which is detected by receptors in the heart and kidneys. The kidneys secrete renin causing vasoconstriction, preventing further blood loss.

➌ *Hunger.* Hunger pangs cause an individual to seek food and eat (*behavioural* mechanism). Such sensations do not arise in the stomach because people with no stomach still feel hungry.

Physiological explanations for why people feel hungry:

- *Glucostatic theory* suggests that the brain monitors blood-glucose levels; glucoreceptors may be located in the ventromedial hypothalamas (VMH).
- *Lipostatic theory*. Body fat is normally maintained at a steady level and therefore fat levels are monitored and affect sensations of hunger. This might explain why short-term diets do not effect long-term weight loss.

Physiological explanations for why people feel full:

- *Cognitive*. 'I have eaten therefore I am full'.
- *Stretch sensors* in the stomach report fullness, which is why liquids make you feel full.
- *Physiological mechanisms*. The intestine produces *cholectystokinin* (CCK) in response to the presence of food, CCK causes the liver to produce glucose and to signal the brain via the vagus nerve.
- *Satiety and hunger centres in the brain*. Animals who overeat (aphagia) or undereat have been found to have a damaged *ventromedial hypothalamas* (VMH) and *lateral hypothalamus* (LH) respectively in post-mortem examinations. **Reeves and Plum** (1969) performed a post-mortem examination of a patient who had doubled her body weight in two years, finding a tumour in the VMH. **Quaade** (1971) found that electrical stimulation of the LH in obese patients led to reports of feeling hungry. However, **Teitelbaum and Stellar** (1954) showed that rats with LH lesions could recover normal appetites.

④ *Pleasure*. **Olds and Milner** (1954) found that rats would increase their lever-pressing if certain 'pleasure centres' located in the hypothalamus were subject to ESB (electrical stimulation of the brain). **Campbell** (1973) found that human patients with electrodes implanted in their hypothalamus (as a means of relief from severe pain) stimulated themselves as often as they could. The 'pleasure centre' may be linked to homeostasis: imbalance creates tension, restoring balance leads to tension-relief (pleasure). This can explain reinforcement and drive reduction.

3.1.3 NEURAL AND SYNAPTIC ACTIVITY

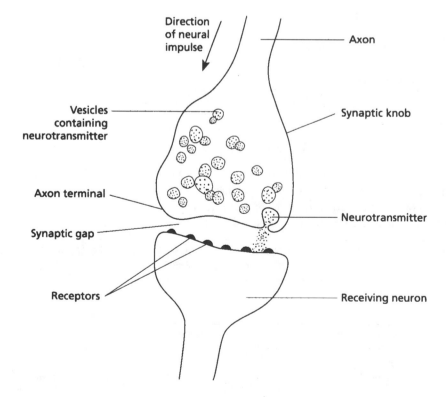

Figure 3.3 A synapse

❶ *Neurons*

- *Sensory or receptor cells* (temperature, touch, taste, hearing, light) convert environmental stimuli into the electrochemical activity of the neurons (*sensory transduction*).
- *Motor or effector cells*: muscles or glands, which secrete chemicals (neurotransmitters or hormones) to stimulate or relax the muscles.
- *Neurons*: generally connect receptors to effectors, they may be several metres long.
- Each neuron ends in numerous *dendrites*, so that each neuron has a multiplicity of connections.
- *Electrical activity* is created by changes in the concentration of sodium and potassium ions across the membrane of the *axon* (nerve fibre).
- A *nerve* is a bundle of neurons.

❷ *Synapses*. The junctions between nerve cells – a 200 angstrom gap (see Fig. 3.3).

- *Neurotransmitters* are released from *presynaptic vesicles* when these are stimulated by an electrical signal. The receptor site of the adjoining dendrite is excited or inhibited by the action of the chemical.
- *Subthreshold*. A single release of neurotransmitter is usually *insufficient* to trigger a nervous impulse.
- The *threshold* is achieved through
  - *Spatial summation*: release of neurotransmitter from more than one dendrite.
  - *Temporal summation*: repeated release within a certain time frame.

❸ *Neurotransmitters*. Each cell produces and responds to more than one type of neurotransmitter. Each neurotransmitter has a variety of effects, depending where it is injected. The main transmitter substances (there are more than 40) are:

- *Acetycholine*: among its actions is the stimulation of parasympathetic muscles. Reduced production is associated with senile dementia.
- *Dopamine*: functions as an inhibitor, also a hormone. Parkinson's disease and schizophrenia are linked with a deficit or overproduction (respectively) (see unit 4.3.1).
- *Serotonin*: low amounts lead to high arousal, linked with aggression and sleep (units 1.4.2 and 3.3.3).
- *Adrenalin* and *noradrenalin* (epinephrine and norepinephrine): hormones which also act as neurotransmitters and have an excitory/inhibitory effect on the nervous system.
- *GABA* (gamma aminobutyric acid): inhibitory action, decreases anxiety.
- *Endorphins* and enkephalins: neuromodulators that relieve pain by inhibiting neurons which produce substance P.
- *Catecholamines*: a term referring collectively to adrenalin, noradrenalin and dopamine, which are chemically related.

3.1.4 DRUGS AND BEHAVIOUR

All drugs have only partly predictable influences. Their effects are related to dosage (high or low); ongoing processes in each individual such as movement, arousal, and diet; and the fact that all drugs (and neurotransmitters) have multiple effects.

Julien (1992) lists the following classes of drugs:

CLASS	DRUG e.g.	NEURAL LOCATION	IMMEDIATE EFFECT	EFFECT ON BEHAVIOUR
Non selective CNS depressants	barbiturates and injected general anaesthetics	RAS and neuron thresholds	depressed	reduces nervous activity and lowers cortical arousal
	centrally-acting, inhaled general anaesthetics	RAS and nerve membranes (lipids)	nervous transmission depressed	loss of consciousness, overdose results in respiratory failure
	alcohol	inhibitory synapses	depressed	elation, long-term shrinkage of dendrites leading to memory loss

CLASS	DRUG e.g.	NEURAL LOCATION	IMMEDIATE EFFECT	EFFECT ON BEHAVIOUR
Anti-anxiety (minor tranquillisers)	benzodiazepines, Valium	GABA	release promoted	relieves anxiety
Psychostimulants	caffeine	dopamine and serotonin	release affected	arousing at cellular level
Antidepressants	tricyclics	acetylcholine	receptors blocked	increases arousal, followed by rebound effect (below)
Mood stabilisers	lithium	noradrenalin and serotonin	decreases release	does not effect normal individuals
Narcotic agents	heroin, morphine, codeine	endorphins	mimic natural processes	relieves pain
Antipsychotic agents (major tranquillisers)	Chlorpromazine	dopamine	blocks receptor sites	strong side effects, e.g. Parkinsonianism
Hallucinogens	cannabis	noradrenalin	releases	moods or emotions
	LSD, angel dust, PCP	serotonin	blocks receptor sites	inhibits thought processes and emotions
Neurological drugs	non-narcotic, peripherally-acting analgesics, e.g. aspirin	endorphins	block pain receptors	relieves pain (placebos are thought to act in same way)
	local anaesthetics, e.g. procaine	sodium ions	paralyses local electric	Affects sensory and motor neurons, no pain potential

Kalat (1988) classifies drugs according to the ways they affect synapses:

EFFECT OF DRUG	EXAMPLE	SOME EFFECTS
Mimics the effect of a neurotransmitter by stimulating the receptor of a post-synaptic cell.	Nicotine stimulates one kind acetylcholine receptor.	Increases heart rate, arouses cerebral cortex.
Stimulates the release of a transmitter from its storage in the presynaptic neuron.	Amphetamine increases the release of noradrenalin.	Rebound effect: the brain is unable to resynthesize new transmitter fast enough; after a few hours the opposite effect is felt. For amphetamine, depression often occurs after the initial euphoria.
Slows the presynaptic neuron's reuptake of the transmitters it released.	Cocaine blocks the reuptake of noradrenalin and dopamine.	Prolongs the effect of the transmitter on the post-synaptic cell.
Interferes with an enzyme which usually inactivates transmitters after they have stimulated the post-synaptic receptor.	Nerve gas destroys the enzyme which breaks acetylcholine down.	Prolongs the effect of the transmitter.
Inhibits the reactions necessary for the production of a particular transmitter.	Curare blocks acetylcholine receptor sites.	Therefore decreases production of noradrenalin and dopamine.
Blocks the receptors for a particular transmitter.	Curare blocks acetylcholine receptor sites.	Paralysis as long as drug is present; if breathing artificially maintained the person can recover.
	Ergot (a fungus) blocks serotonin receptor sites.	May have been cause of Salem witchcraft episode.
Attaches to a receptor and modifies the sensitivity of a neighbouring receptor.	Benzodiazepine attaches to receptors adjacent to GABA receptors.	Increases sensitivity of GABA receptors.

3.2 CORTICAL FUNCTIONS

3.2.1 TECHNIQUES USED TO INVESTIGATE CORTICAL FUNCTIONS

① *Techniques with no side-effects*

- *Temporary lesions.* Sodium amytal, an anaesthetic, can be used to deactivate a hemisphere for short periods in a fully conscious patient (the *Wada test*).
- *Electrical stimulation.* A weak current is applied to a small region of the brain in a conscious patient to see what experience they report. **Penfield** (1955) produced recollections of specific memories and sounds by stimulating specific areas.
- *EEG* (electro–encephalogram). Microelectrodes are attached to the patient's scalp to detect electrical activity in specific parts of the brain; useful in understanding states of awareness.
- *X-ray tomography* (CAT and PET scans). Brain tissue is dyed using radioactive substances which are injected into the bloodstream. Active areas of the brain take up more of these substances, so enabling detection of tumour growth or determining what part of the brain is working and relate this to concurrent behaviour, such as learning activity.
- *NMR.* Uses magnetic fields and radio waves to construct a picture of the brain.
- *Neurospinal fluid, blood and urine.* Can be checked for traces of chemicals. For example, large amounts of cortisol in the urine indicates stress.

   Evaluation. You cannot be certain that a primary cause has been located. For example, if you sever a person's vocal chords they cannot speak but that doesn't mean the chords are central to speech.

② *Techniques involving deliberate damage*

- *Ablation.* Removal of parts of the brain, for example the removal of **H.M.**'s (see unit 5.3.1) hippocampus resulted in memory loss. **Lashley** (1950) removed large sections of rats' cortex to discover what areas were important in learning.
- *Lesions.* Cutting connections in the brain and therefore *functionally* destroying a section of the brain. Prefrontal *lobotomies* sever the connections within the frontal lobes resulting in personality changes (see unit 4.4.1).
- *Implanting electrodes.* **Hubel and Wiesel** (unit 3.2.3) placed electrodes in cats' visual cortex to trace the activity of individual neurons. This is different from EEG.

Evaluation

- You cannot be certain that a primary cause has been located.
- The damage caused in surgery may not be limited to specific parts.
- Conclusions drawn from animals may not always generalise to humans.
- Ethical considerations are important.

③ *Effects of chemicals*

- *Drugs* mimic the action of neurotransmitters, indicating what may be happening normally. **Grossman** (1964) found that noradrenalin injected into a rat's brain elicited feeding, while acetylcholine elicited drinking. The action of dopamine has been observed in its link with L-dopa and psychosis (see unit 4.3.1).
- *Diet.* Certain foodstuffs are precursors of neurotransmitters and therefore affect production; diets with or without such substances may be associated with certain behaviours. For example, acetylcholine is synthesised from choline which is present in, for example, cauliflower and egg yolks. Eating such substances leads to a brief increase in acetylcholine levels in the brain. Corn promotes the production of serotonin and may be linked with aggressiveness (**Mawson and Jacobs**, unit 1.4.2).

   Evaluation. It is difficult to prove the precise effect of any chemical substance, particularly as the effects vary from one person to the next and most chemicals have more than one effect.

4 *Observations of brain injuries or illness*

- *Accidental damage.* In 1848 **Phineas Gage** had a crowbar fired through his skull when working with explosives. He survived, but became mild-mannered leading experts to suppose that prefrontal cortical damage (i.e. lobotomies, see unit 4.4.1) might reduce aggressiveness. **Grafman** *et al.* (1986) observed that soldiers with brain damage had reduced IQ scores.
- *Brain operations.* Split-brain operations have been used to demonstrate the functional asymmetry of the brain (unit 3.2.2).
- *Brain illnesses and tumours.* The brains of stroke or tumour patients can be examined with PET scans, and damage can be related to behavioural changes. Tumours in the limbic system have been associated with increased aggressiveness.
- *Post-mortem examinations* of the brains of people with known problems. For example, schizophrenics' brains have been found to be about 6% lighter than other mental patients.

Evaluation

- Observations of human behaviour can confirm the results of animal studies.
- It is difficult to know whether a primary or peripheral cause *or* effect has been identified.
- It is usually not possible to make before and after comparisons of patients, therefore comparisons are made between normal and abnormal individuals and lack control for individual differences.
- The process of brain injury is traumatic, which in itself changes behaviour.

3.2.2 LOCALISATION OF FUNCTION

Localisation refers to the fact that particular areas of the cerebral cortex are associated with specific physical or behavioural functions. Localisation of function allows more specialised development, for example if an area of the brain is pre-set to interpret visual information it reduces the amount of learning which is necessary. *Phrenology* is a pseudoscience that links specific areas of the brain to specific behaviours; the principle is correct but the details are not based on empirical research.

1 *Laterality* (sidedness). Lateral means 'side'.

- *Bilateral.* Functions which are equally represented in the same areas on both sides (hemispheres) of the brain. The study of **H.M.** showed that bilateral loss of the hippocampus led to anterograde amnesia (see unit 5.3.1).
- *Contralateral.* One hemisphere controls the *opposite* side of the body as in *sensory* and *motor processes*. The main connections between muscles and sense receptors on the right side of the body are connected to the left hemisphere and vice versa.
- *Ipsilateral.* Connections are between the same side of the brain and body. *Hearing* is both contralateral and ipsilateral because most of the information from one ear travels to the auditory cortex on the opposite side of the brain but some also goes to the same side. This allows comparisons to be made so that the direction of the sound can be calculated. *Vision* (unit 3.2.3) is organised so that each hemisphere receives the input of one side of the visual field, again contra- and ipsilateral. This means that, if one eye is damaged, both hemispheres continue to get visual input.
- *Laterality.* One hemisphere is *preferred* over the other even though both sides are capable, as illustrated by *handedness*. Analysis of drawings shows that about 90% of people all over the world and even in prehistoric times are right-handed (their *left* hemisphere is dominant).

2 *Language* is usually unilateral (one-sided) and also localised.

- *Broca's area* is in the anterior frontal lobe of the left cerebral cortex. It has sensory-motor connections and is associated with speaking and understanding grammatical connections. When normal people speak, there is increased blood flow to Broca's area, the motor cortex, the left thalamus and basal ganglia. These areas show damage when a patient is permanently unable to speak. Broca's aphasia results in difficulty with language production (slow and poorly articulated, difficulties writing), telegraphic speech, some difficulties with comprehension (fairly similar to children's speech).

- *Wernicke's area* is in the posterior temporal lobe of the left cerebral cortex. It is connected to the visual and auditory cortex and is related to language production. Wernicke's aphasia is shown by poor language comprehension and difficulty finding the right word but no difficulty with articulation; speech is grammatical but makes little sense.
- Damage to the connection between Broca's and Wernicke's areas is called *conduction aphasia*, patients can't repeat what others say, and can't name objects.

Left hemisphere language dominance may cause some problems for left-handers. For example, for left-handers writing is controlled by the right hemisphere (contralateral), this may explain the strange inverted writing posture used by some left-handed people.

Not everyone has language centres on the left, when brain damage to either side of the brain results in impaired language this indicates bilateral dominance which is the case for about 25% of left-handers (**Satz**, 1979). About 5% of right-handers have right-side language dominance. **Kimura** (1993) reports that speech is more bilaterally organised in women.

③ *Hemispheric (cerebral) asymmetry* or *dominance.* The side of the brain which has greater control over a particular function is dominant.

- The left hemisphere is dominant for right-handed people, it is also dominant for language.
- The right hemisphere controls *emotional* expression and the understanding of other people's expressions. It contributes emotional content to speech. The left side of the face (controlled by the right hemisphere) generally smiles more broadly and expresses more emotion than the right side. *Visual and spatial tasks*, such as imagery, artistic expression, and pattern recognition are often performed better by the right hemisphere.

Why? *Mixed dominance* is associated with a variety of problems such as stuttering and dyslexia. Such language difficulties may be due to the presence of two competing language centres. The linguistic confusions (as between b and d) which are typical of some dyslexics may be due to having bilateral language centres. More stutterers than non-stutterers have been found to have mixed or right-hand dominance for speech. **Jones** (1966) used sodium amytal to establish where patients' speech centres were located so that he could operate on tumours (if they could still talk when the left side was paralysed, the centre must be on the right). He found that all patients with mixed dominance stuttered but after the left hemisphere centres were removed (with the tumour) their stuttering stopped.

④ *Hemispheric asymmetry and the split brain.* If the fibres connecting the two cerebral hemispheres are cut, two functionally independent brains are created. This procedure is used in patients suffering from severe epileptic seizures. **Sperry and Gazzaniga** (1967) tested patients' cognitive functions by placing them behind a screen with their hands free to handle objects unseen. If a word was flashed to the left side of the screen it was 'seen' by the right hemisphere only. If the participant was asked to pick up the object they could only do this with their left hand, and could not say what the object was. Patients did learn ways of communicating between hemispheres, for example, if a letter was shown to the left visual field and the patient asked if it was 'A', the left hemisphere guessed the answer, the right hemisphere (which knew the answer) heard this and made a frown if the answer was wrong, the left hemisphere felt the frown and corrected the mistake (both sides control and feel the facial muscles).

The problem with these experiments is that they use a relatively small sample of abnormal individuals (their brains may have been damaged by severe epilepsy). **Jeeves** (1984) reports that individuals who are born without a corpus callosum can say words they see in either visual field (they probably have two language centres), they are slow on tasks requiring co-ordination of two hands and when asked to move the fingers of one hand they involuntarily move the fingers of the other hand.

The split-brain procedure raises an interesting philosophical point (*Fechner's question*), do split-brain patients have two minds or one?

⑤ *Plasticity.* After a critical or sensitive period, the brain may be unable to recover or regenerate specialised functions (see development of perception and language in chapter 5). **Lashley** (1950) proposed the *law of equipotentiality* to describe the brain's ability to take over the function of damaged parts. Certain areas of the brain are capable of generating new neurons even after maturity and dendritic branches can grow or retract, thus forming new connections.

Levy *et al.* (1992) described a 3-year-old with a massive left hemisphere lesion who nevertheless developed normal linguistic function. Presumably he was young enough for the right hemisphere to take over language functions. Recovery is always related to the location, type and extent of damage, as much as to age.

The *Kennard principle* (**Kennard**, 1938) states that it is easier to recover from brain damage earlier rather than later in life. However, sometimes damage in younger children is more serious, as when a neonate suffers brain damage through oxygen-deprivation.

3.2.3 NEUROPHYSIOLOGICAL BASIS OF VISUAL PERCEPTION

The structure of the eye

The eye is formed from neural tissue during embryonic development. Vision is critical for survival and therefore it is not surprising that the eye is a very intricate organ.

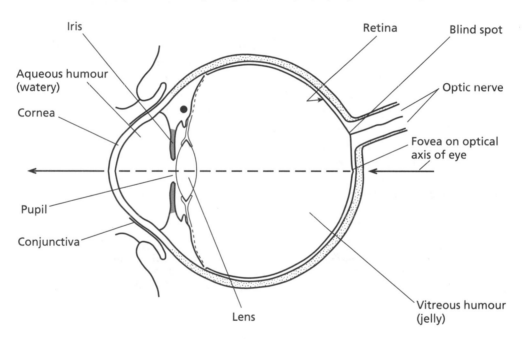

Figure 3.4 The human eye

① *The parts of the eye.* The *iris* is the coloured part around the *pupil*, muscles control the amount of light admitted. The *cornea* and *lens* bend incoming light so that it is focused on the fovea. The lens is round for near focus (attached muscles contract) and flat for distant vision (muscles relax). This is called *accommodation*. The *retina* is a thin sheet of interconnected nerve cells.

② *Cellular structure of the retina* (see Fig. 3.5). *Photoreceptors* (photosensitive) are specialised cells which convert light (*sensory transduction*) into a nervous impulse. *Rod*-like photosensitive cells (124 million of them) respond to shades of grey, to movement and edges. They function in conditions of low lighting and are concentrated in the outer parts of the retina. *Cone*-shaped photosensitive cells report colour and function in daylight conditions. They (12 million of them) are not present in the outer parts of the retina. Every photoreceptor is connected to more than one *bipolar cell*, and each bipolar

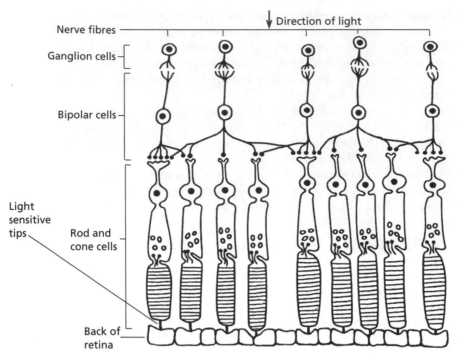

Figure 3.5 Cellular structure of the retina

cell receives impulses from more than one photoreceptor. One or more bipolar cells are connected to *ganglion cells*, the third layer closest to the light source, which in turn are bundled into the *optic nerve*. The area of the retina where the optic nerve passes through is called the *blind spot* or *optic disc*, it generally doesn't disrupt vision because the brain 'fills in gaps' in data. The *fovea* is specialised for detailed vision, it contains densely packed photoreceptors, mainly cones.

③ *Pathways of the optic nerve.* The *optic chiasma* is the point of crossover, each side of the brain receives information from *both* eyes (see Fig. 3.6). The *lateral geniculate nucleus* (LGN) is a relay station, nerves from the retina synapse with nerves to the *visual cortex* in the occipital cortical lobe (at the back). The *striate* cortex is the primary visual cortex surrounded by the *parastriate* cortex.

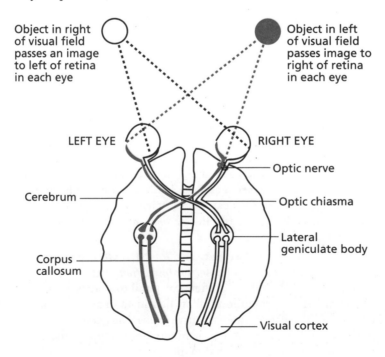

Figure 3.6 Pathways of the optic nerve

Neurophysiological explanations of perception

Sensations are the raw data of the perceptual system, the unaltered record of the physical stimulus. *Perceptions* are based on sensations, but they are altered through summation and interpretation so that what is 'seen' has meaning. Visual perception is either based on the sensory data itself (*bottom-up processing*) or influenced by expectations (*top-down processing*, discussed in unit 5.1.1).

1 *The eye is not like a camera* because of:
- *Poor quality*. The retinal image is blurred due to imperfections in the lens and the cells lying in front of the photoreceptors. It is also curved and constantly in motion.
- *Too much data* to be processed rapidly or usefully. The retina collects 136 million points of light, much of which is repetitive. Therefore some information is summarised at the retina (perceiving rather than sensing). *Lateral inhibition* is an example of this – when one retinal cell is stimulated, it inhibits activity in surrounding cells, which emphasises the borders between light and dark.

2 *The visual cortex*. **Hubel and Wiesel** (1962) placed microelectrodes in different parts of a cat's visual cortex. They found that each cell only fired when the cat was shown a line of unique orientation in a particular part of the visual field. They called these *simple cells*.

They also found cells sensitive to other features (such as a stationary or moving dot or the direction of movement), *complex cells* which responded to several simple cells, and *hypercomplex cells* which responded to simple patterns or shapes (such as angles) from the information they received from many complex cells.

They found that simple, complex and hypercomplex cells are organised into *functional columns* which all respond to a particular feature from one eye. The functional columns may predispose the brain to be able to make certain comparisons, such as those used in depth perception.

3 *The perception of depth* involves turning the two-dimensional proximal image into three dimensions. One source of depth information comes from *disparity (stereoscopic vision)* – the slight difference between two retinal images produced when viewing an object. **Julesz** (1964) produced computer-generated random dot patterns with some of the dots in one picture shifted horizontally in relation to corresponding dots in the other picture so that, when viewed stereoscopically, an illusion of depth is created and an 'image' emerges. Binocular cells in the visual cortex compare corresponding points from both retinas and compute depth from the disparity. Aerial reconnaissance uses disparity to detect images.

4 *The perception of brightness*. Brightness or illumination is found in the simplest 'eyes' (for example, a limpet). The stronger the light, the faster the rate of firing from the photoreceptor. This straightforward coding is dependent on two other factors:
- *Dark–light adaptation*. When an eye is kept in a low light for some time, it grows more sensitive and a given light will look brighter.
- *Differences in illumination*. Contrasts between adjacent areas which are most information-rich – brightness is a function of: intensity of light at a particular point, the intensity of light the retina has been exposed to in the recent past, and the intensities of light falling on other regions of the retina.

  The Pulfrich effect (**Pulfrich**, 1922) shows how a dark filter covering one eye can make a pendulum swing look elliptical because, as the pendulum swings, the delay is greater for the covered eye causing disparity. This retinal delay has important implications for night driving.

5 *The perception of movement*. Movement is detected by changes in brightness and can be understood in terms of various retinal activities:
- *Apparent motion* (phi phenomenon). When a row of lights flash in sequence, they look like one moving light if the physical and temporal distance is right. The cells of the retina 'don't notice' a limited gap. Television relies on our inability to notice the gaps, the screen is 'refreshed' nearly once a second.
- *Nystagmus* is the random tremors which stop the photoreceptors adapting to stimuli and ceasing to respond. **Pritchard** (1961) mounted a tiny slide projector on the retina

so that any movement of the participant's eye while looking at a picture were exactly followed. After a few seconds the participant no longer saw the picture. Blinking may be a means of renewing the retinal image.

6 *The perception of colour*
- *Young-Helmholtz* (*trichromatic*) theory proposes the existent of three types of cone: red-, green- and blue-sensitive contain photopigments which respond maximally to particular wavelengths (short, medium and long respectively). This account explains how the perception of colour is created by mixing signals from each receptor and is supported by evidence of only three types of cone pigment. However, it cannot explain colour blindness or negative afterimages.
- *Opponent-process* theory (**Hering**, 1870) suggests that there are three pairs of receptor systems, red-green, blue-yellow and black-white, which work in opposition. Stimulation of one of the pair results in inhibition of the other. It is probable that when information leaves the cones (i.e. bipolar and ganglion cells) it is then coded in the opponent-process fashion (**DeValois and Jacobs**, 1968).
- *Retinex* theory (**Land** *et al.*, 1983) accounts for the fact that colour constancy depends on simultaneous contrasts; if you wear red tinted glasses you still perceive colour differences but if (still wearing the red-tinted glasses) you focus on a blue object it will start to look red because there is no contrast. The visual cortex compares the wavelengths of light coming from different parts of the retina at a given time and determines a colour perception for each object.

7 *Visual disturbances and visual illusions.* The ray figure is disturbing to look at probably because it 'upsets' the visual system by overstimulating the edge detectors. Stroboscopes, television flicker and driving past a row of trees can be annoying because they overload the visual system with rapidly changing intensities. The white diamond illusion is due to an overload on movement and edge detectors. Positive and negative afterimages are created by overstimulation of the photoreceptors.

Figure 3.7 The ray and white diamond figures

3.3 AWARENESS

3.3.1 STATES OF AWARENESS

1 *Consciousness has three levels.* States of awareness are equivalent to different levels of consciousness. The concept of 'consciousness' was regarded as 'epiphenomenal flotsam of bodily activity' and rejected by many psychologists.
- *Conscious.* The individual is capable of self-awareness: monitoring themselves and their environment, having sensations and thoughts. The individual is also capable of self-control, which implies free will and moral 'consciousness' (conscience). In cognitive psychology consciousness is equivalent to 'attention'.

- *Preconscious* (subconscious). Information at the edge of consciousness which can be made conscious if desired, such as daydreaming. The cocktail party effect (unit 5.2.1) shows that processing occurs outside consciousness.
- *Unconscious*. Lacking in awareness either as in 'he lost consciousness' (coma) or 'I was not conscious of the rules' (not knowing). *Freudians* use the term in a special sense to refer to repressed thoughts; 'unconscious awareness' is essentially a contradiction.

2 *Kinds of awareness.* **Oakley** (1985) has suggested a way to divide awareness:

- *Consciousness*: representational systems for external events, located in the limbic system.
- *Self-awareness*: awareness of being aware, associated with a highly developed cortex as in humans and other primates.
- *Simple awareness*: reflex systems and associative learning, located in subcortical structures.

3 *Investigating states of awareness*

- *EEG* measures electrical activity in the brain. Different states have different characteristic waves: *alpha* waves (relaxed state), *beta* (aroused), *delta* (sleep, also present in infants and adults with tumours) and *theta* (preschool children, possibly related to memory storage and frustration).
- *Self-recognition.* **Gallop** (1977) painted red dye on the eyebrow and opposite ear of chimpanzees. When they looked in a mirror they repeatedly touched these body parts, demonstrating self-recognition and self-awareness. **Lewis and Brooks-Gunn** (1979) put rouge on infants' noses and found, by the age of 20 months, that most of them showed self-awareness.

4 *Altered states of awareness*

- *Drugs* such as LSD lead to a loss of self-awareness, hallucinations lead to a sense of new awareness.
- *Schizophrenics* have been described as 'divided selves' (see unit 4.3.1). **Firth** (1992) suggested that schizophrenic delusions result from altered awareness – thinking that others are controlling one's own actions and thoughts.
- *Autism* and the *theory of mind*. Part of self-awareness is being aware of other people's point of view, which means we can interpret their actions. **Firth** (1989) proposed that autism results from a lack of this kind of awareness (see unit 4.1.3).

5 *Multiple consciousness*

- *Neo-dissociation* and the 'hidden observer' (see 'Hypnotism', unit 3.3.4).
- *Dissociation identity disorder* (multiple personality). **Thigpen and Cleckley** (1957) described a woman with three personalities in 'The Three Faces of Eve'. Her consciousness had become pathologically disassociated as a way of coping with emotional problems. The different personalities had different voices and postures, and were only dimly aware of each other.
- *Split-brain patients* (see unit 3.2.2). Do they have more than one consciousness?

6 *Philosophical questions related to states of awareness*

- Is suffering (rather than pain) a conscious activity? Do animals and neonates suffer?
- Does consciousness distinguish humans from animals?

3.3.2 BODILY RHYTHMS

A *rhythm* is a periodically repeated feature. *Biorhythms* are a pseudoscientific technique using biological rhythms to predict a person's behaviour on a given day.

Bodily rhythms are set off or triggered by:

- *External* stimuli which may themselves be rhythmic. Day length is the dominant *zeitgeber* ('time-giver' in German), also important are the seasons, weather, temperature, phases of the moon, tides (in aquatic animals), availability of food, pheromones and social stimuli.
- *Internal* stimuli. Rhythms persist even in the absence of external physical stimuli because of internal biological clocks. In the mammalian hypothalamus, the

suprachiasmatic nucleus (*SCN*) generates circadian rhythms from protein synthesis and is 'fine tuned' by light and other stimuli, receiving information about light directly from the retina. The SCN regulates production of *melatonin* in the *pineal* gland. Increases in melatonin are associated with decreases in arousal.

Empirical evidence

① *Circadian rhythms*: a cycle that lasts about 24 hours. How are human circadian rhythms controlled?

- *Cave experiments.* **Siffre** (1972) spent six months in an underground cave finding that his sleep/waking cycle settled down to 25–30 hours. **Kleitman** (1963) studied two volunteers living in a cave on a 28-hour cycle controlled by artificial lights; neither participant was fully able to adjust to this cycle. **Folkard** *et al*. (1985) used artificial light to reduce the clock cycle, participants coped at a 23-hour cycle, but when it was reduced to 22 hours their bodies reverted to a natural cycle. It appears that light can have a profound influence but that our 'free-running' cycle is not 24 hours, which means that we have to adjust our clocks each day.

- *Individual differences.* **Aschoff and Wever** (1976) observed that some people, when isolated from daylight, maintain 24–5 hour cycles whereas others develop idiosyncrasies such as 29 hours awake and 21 hours asleep. **Marks and Folkard** (1985) suggested that 'morning' types may peak in their daily rhythms a few hours earlier than 'evening' types.

- *Two clocks?* In cave experiments all other circadian rhythms follow the sleep-waking pattern except temperature, which stayed at a 24-hour cycle, suggesting that there are two clocks at work. The study by **Hawkins and Armstrong-Esther** (1978) of nurses on shift duty, described below, also found that temperature cycles did not change.

- *Body temperature* covaries with heart rate, urine secretion, or any measure which indicates metabolic rate. It reaches a trough around 4 a.m. and returns to normal level by about 8 p.m. **Colquhuon** (1970) concluded from a review of research that cognitive performance is positively correlated with temperature. **Folkard** *et al*. (1977) found that STM performance is better in the morning than the afternoon while the reverse is true for LTM, possibly higher temperature leads to increased arousal which impairs STM but benefits LTM.

② *Ultradian rhythms*: shorter than a day; such as sleep stages (see unit 3.3.3), heart beat and breathing.

- *Basic rest activity cycle* (BRAC). **Klein and Armitage** (1979) tested participants' performance on verbal and spatial tasks through the day and found a 96-minute cycle. This may be related to REM activity.

- *Tidal.* Marine animals such as crabs respond to tidal rhythms even when kept in constant conditions, suggesting an internal lunar clock (**Palmer**, 1989).

③ *Infradian rhythms*: longer than a day, such as seasonal mating and:

- *Menstrual cycle* (circa-lunar) is controlled by hormones (internal factors) and may be synchronised by external factors. **Russell** *et al*. (1980) collected daily samples of women's underarm sweat, mixed it with alcohol and applied this to the upper lip of their female participants. The participants' menstrual cycles began to synchronise, possibly due to *pheromones* (biochemical substances).

- *Migration* (circa-annual). **Gwinner** (1986) kept wild birds in cages for three years, exposing them to 12 hours of light and 12 hours of darkness daily. Despite a lack of external stimuli they still showed signs of migratory restlessness.

- *Hibernation.* **Pengelly and Fisher** (1957) artificially controlled squirrels' exposure to light (12 hours on/off) and temperature (0°C). Nevertheless the squirrel hibernated from October to April probably because of a fall in internally regulated body temperature.

- *Seasonal affective disorder* (SAD). Darkness rather than temperature causes some people to become depressed at the onset of winter, probably because of increased production of melatonin which affects mood. It can be relieved using bright lights.

Practical applications of bodily rhythms

1. *Shift work.* There are large individual differences, on average it takes about three days to adjust to a 12-hour shift in time (which applies to jet lag as well). **Folkard** *et al.* (1993) suggested that rhythmic changes in body temperature might lead to industrial accidents in shift work conditions (such as Bhopal and Chernobyl). **Novak** *et al.* (1990) found higher injury rates for shift workers in a chemical plant. **Hawkins and Armstrong-Esther** (1978) studied 11 nurses during the first seven nights of their duty. Performance was significantly impaired on the first night but improved through the week, though body temperature was still not adjusted by the last night.

   Considerable research focuses on ways of improving shift work performance. **Dawson and Campbell** (1991) exposed participants to a four-hour pulse of bright light on their first night and found that this helped their subsequent adjustment as measured by body temperature.

2. *Jet lag* leads to tiredness, headaches and cognitive confusion, at least in part due to desynchronisation of circadian rhythms. Body temperature changes within a week but the rhythm of adrenocortical hormone production takes much longer so that the return home is often much easier. **Redfern** (1989) suggested the use of benzodiazepines to increase melatonin levels and resynchronise the body clock. **Webb and Agnew** (1971) interviewed regular travellers and found they used various non-pharmacological approaches, such as a rigid schedule of meals, exposure to light and outdoor activity.

3. *Pre-menstrual syndrome* (PMS). **Floody** (1968) reviewed a large body of research indicating that PMS was positively associated with child abuse, irritability, hostility, crime and aggression generally (see unit 1.4.2). Such findings have led to its use as a criminal defence.

4. *Medical diagnosis.* Time of day is taken into account in medical checks of blood pressure, urine or temperature.

3.3.3 SLEEP AND DREAM STATES

Sleep is not unconsciousness, it is an altered state of consciousness such that there is a decreased responsiveness to the external environment. It occurs daily (circadian) and has distinct stages.

Sleep stages

Stage	EEG recording		Behaviour
Relaxed, awake	alpha waves, 8–12 hertz	synchronised	
REM sleep	theta		associated with dreams
1	desynchronised		transition to deeper state
2	sleep spindles, k-complexes	deep or slow wave	progressively harder to wake, familiar
3	delta waves, 1–2 hertz	sleep (SWS),	names cause more EEG activity, sound
4	mainly delta waves	synchronised	of baby crying may rouse sleeper

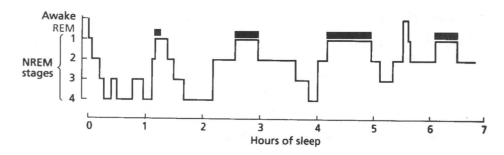

Figure 3.8 Sleep stages alternate through the night, starting with a rapid descent into deep sleep, followed by progressively increased episodes of lighter sleep and REM sleep (coloured area).

Empirical studies of sleep

1 *Rapid eye movement (REM) sleep.* **Jouvet** called this *paradoxical sleep* because of the contradictions: eye movement, heart rate, breathing, etc. are increased but the body is in a state of near paralysis and it is difficult to wake a person up.

- *Dreams.* **Dement and Kleitman** (1957) woke participants during REM episodes, 80–90% of the time they reported dreaming, i.e. most but not all of the time. Dreams do also occur in NREM sleep.
- *REM deprivation.* **Jouvet** (1967) used the *flowerpot technique*: an animal is placed on a small platform surrounded by water. During slow wave sleep the animal snoozes, but loss of muscle tone in REM sleep causes them to slip off. Cats deprived of REM sleep became hypersexual and eventually died.
- *REM rebound*: **Dement** (1960) woke eight volunteers during each REM episode. The rebound effect was that they needed progressively more REM sleep, they were woken 12 times on the first night and 26 times by the seventh night. Dement originally claimed that his volunteers exhibited psychiatric symptoms, but subsequently he recognised that these were due to experimenter bias.
- REM occurs in mammals, but it is not clear whether it extends to fish and reptiles, because even when awake the eyes of these animals do not move much.

2 *Studies of total sleep deprivation*

- *Case studies.* **Dement** (1972) reported the cases of a disc jockey, Peter Tripp, and a student, Randy Gardner who spent over 200 hours without sleep. Towards the end Tripp experienced hallucinations and profound delusions but Gardner wasn't affected except finding it difficult to perform some tasks. At the end Gardner only slept for 15 hours but this sleep consisted of mainly *core sleep* (stage 4 and REM). It's possible that Gardner benefited from episodes of *micro-sleep* (staring into space for a moment).
- *Controlled studies.* **Webb** (1985): found that sleep loss over 48 hours had little effect on precision and cognitive processing tasks, whereas subjective and attention measures suffered. Depressed performance may be more due to motivational factors than cognitive components. **Hüber-Weidman** (1976) identified several psychological effects of deprivation in a review of research: after one night there was an increased urge to sleep, after four nights increased episodes of *micro-sleep*, and after six nights a loss of identity and sense of reality (*sleep deprivation psychosis*).

3 *Increased activity and sleep.* **Shapiro et al.** (1981) found that marathon runners did require extra sleep, whereas **Horne and Minard** (1985) tried to exhaust their participants with numerous activities and found that they went to sleep faster but not for longer.

4 *Neural mechanisms. SCN* (see unit 3.3.2) responds to changes in light and controls production of *melatonin* in the *pineal gland* which, in turn leads to production of *serotonin* in the *raphe nuclei*, which has an arousing effect on the *RAS* (reticular activating system). Stimulation of the RAS awakens a sleeping individual or increases alertness. Damage or lesions to the RAS lead to prolonged sleep or inactivity.

Any strong stimulation activates the ascending RAS (ARAS), which then activates the entire cortex. Lack of stimulation decreases arousal of RAS and sleep occurs.

Theories of sleep

1 *The repair and restoration (R&R) theory.* Sleep allows various physiological and psychological states to be recovered. Infancy is a time of high sleep needs because there is enormous brain and body growth and learning.

During slow wave sleep the body makes repairs, for example removing waste products and replenishing synaptic transmitters. Certain metabolic processes also increase at night, for example there is increased production of growth hormone and increased protein synthesis, particularly in REM sleep. Also during REM sleep memory may be consolidated and emotional experience relived (see below).

However, if R&R was the only function of sleep we would expect to observe deprivation effects, and increased sleep in relation to increased activity. However, the evidence suggests that effects of sleep deprivation are not great. On the other hand **Empson** (1989) reported that it is impossible to go without sleep and remain OK and **Horne** (1988) pointed out that sleep-deprived participants do show a rebound effect. It may be that only *core sleep* is essential and that some recovery can take place during relaxed wakefulness and micro-sleep.

② *The evolutionary theory*. Sleep is an adaptive response to environmental and internal demands, akin to hibernation. Animals have evolved an innate programme to protect them at times of danger (such as darkness or daylight), protect them from excessive wear and tear, and conserve energy by limiting metabolic requirements. Infant sleep could be explained as an innate mechanism to help exhausted parents cope with finding food and other things.

If protection was the only function of sleep we would expect an inverse relationship between the time needed to search for food and the time needed for sleep. This is true for cows which graze all the time and sleep little, and cats who eat rapidly and sleep a lot. We would also expect that animals likely to be attacked will sleep little and lightly. Predators do sleep more than animals who are preyed upon, and animals who are preyed upon often sleep in burrows and feed at night, such as rabbits. But, taken to its logical conclusion, some animals shouldn't sleep at all to ensure their safety.

Support for the evolutionary theory comes from looking at how species adapt their mode of sleep to suit their lifestyle. For example, dolphins sleep one hemisphere at a time which probably is related to the fact that if they will drown unless they surface regularly to breathe and need to remain partly conscious to do this. (Beware of evolutionary arguments which sound as if the animal has made some deliberate choice about behaviour, the 'choice' is made through natural selection.)

③ *A combined approach*. Neither theory accounts for why animals lose consciousness when sleeping. It is not necessary for R&R, and from a safety (adaptive) point of view it makes little sense. The fact that all animals sleep means that it must perform some R&R function. The fact that each species evolves a particular style suggests an adaptive element as well.

Theories of REM sleep and dreams

① *Activation-synthesis model*. **Hobson and McCarley** (1977) suggested that dreams arise because external stimuli (a dripping tap) or internal stimuli (memories) produce nonsensical neural activity and dreams are an attempt to impose some meaning.

② *Cognitive restoration*. **Crick and Mitchison** (1983) used a computer analogy to liken dreams to updating memory files and discarding redundant data. The actual content of dreams is an accidental by-product. **Evans** (1984) suggested that, while sorting memory files, we reorganise material and some problem-solving may occur. This could explain why infants need more REM sleep.

③ *Emotional catharsis*. **Freud** (1900) suggested that dreams are 'the royal road' to the unconscious enabling repressed desires or memories to become known. **Webb and Cartwright** (1978) suggested that dreams are a way of working out problems. This approach cannot explain why animals dream, if they do.

④ *Periodic arousal* of the brain may be necessary to maintain minimum levels of CNS activity.

3.3.4 HYPNOSIS

Hypnosis is 'a social interaction in which one person responds to suggestions offered by another' (**Kihlstrom**, 1985). A hypnotised person ceases to initiate activity, their attention narrows, reality testing is reduced and there can be age regression, posthypnotic amnesia, and sensory changes like blindness and reduced pain perception.

Empirical studies of hypnosis

1. *Personality and hypnosis.* Susceptibility can be tested using the *Stanford Hypnotic Susceptibility Scale*: a hypnotised person is given a series of suggestions ranging from arm lowering ('your arm is getting heavy') to posthypnotic amnesia ('you will forget what has happened'). Between 5–10% are highly resistant while about 15% are highly sensitive. The latter tend to be more imaginative and fantasy-prone, and have positive attitudes towards hypnosis. **Orne and Evans** (1965) claim that the difference between hypnotised 'reals' and 'simulators' is that the latter know they are pretending while the former believe their responses are involuntary.

2. *Transcending normal capacity.* Hypnotised people are said to be able to do things beyond their normal capacity, such as remember past events or lift heavy objects. Many uses of hypnosis involve *recovered memories* (see below) but it is not possible to confirm the accuracy of such recall. Claims of increased capacity are often made with no rigorous before and after comparisons.

3. *Trance logic* is the behavioural differences observed between hypnotised and non-hypnotised persons. **Orne** *et al.* (1968) told hypnotised and non-hypnotised participants that they should touch their forehead everytime they heard the word 'experiment' in the next 48 hours. When a confederate said the word, 30% of the hypnotised participants obeyed compared with 8% of the non-hypnotised. **Bowers** (1976) showed that hypnotised participants, when told they could not see a chair, will walk round it but non-hypnotised participants bump into it. **Wagstaff** (1995) reported that even when tasks involve dangerous or antisocial activities 'simulators' are just as likely and sometimes more likely to perform than 'reals'.

4. *Availability of information.* **Miller** *et al.* (1973) showed the Ponzo illusion to hypnotised participants, and told them that the sloping lines had disappeared. They continued to perceive the top line as longer therefore demonstrating that the visual system was still processing all the information. **Coe and Yashinski** (1985) demonstrated that posthypnotic amnesia is significantly reduced if a person is told they will be given a lie detector test.

   Hilgard (1977) investigated the *hidden observer phenomenon*: he told a hypnotised participant that he would not hear anything, but then said if there was some part of him which could hear, he should raise a finger. The finger was raised. Later, the participant was asked if he heard anything, he said he was aware of the finger moving but not why.

5. *Pain.* There is considerable evidence of the analgesic properties of hypnosis in susceptible individuals, though when patients claim to feel no pain they may show other pain behaviours such as grimacing (**Bakal**, 1979). Hilgard used the *cold pressor test* (putting your arm in very cold water), hypnotised people can tolerate about 40 seconds of the resultant pain whereas normally levels are around 25 seconds. If a hidden observer is asked they report feeling more pain than the 'hypnotised' part.

Theories of hypnosis

1. *Neo-dissociation theory* (a state theory). Hilgard suggested that hypnosis is the dissociation of consciousness into several streams somewhat independent of each other. This explains the hidden observer phenomenon, altered sensitivity and access to memories not usually available.

2. *The non-state approach.* **Barber** (1969) suggested that hypnosis is a superfluous concept, it is not a distinctive state but a consequence of role-playing and/or the influence of a number of social or experimental variables such as demand characteristics and experimenter bias. For example, **Spanos** (1989) showed that the hidden observer in the cold pressor test will report more, less or the same perceptions of pain as the 'hypnotised' part *if* those expectations are conveyed to it. Spanos also claimed that hypnotic suggestions are less effective than other pain-reducing strategies, such as distraction.

3. *Physiological explanation.* The brain wave patterns accompanying hypnosis show a state of deep relaxation. This may promote the release of endorphins (see unit 3.1.3), a form of natural painkillers which are similar to opiates.

Applications of hypnosis

❶ *Analgesia.* There is considerable evidence that patients can be helped to tolerate pain in dentistry, childbirth and surgery through the use of hypnosis.

❷ *Solving crime.* Police witnesses may remember specific details under hypnosis and, in America, this information can now be used in court. Such apparent 'facts' should be treated with caution because suggestions from the hypnotist may be reproduced as facts and spoken with great confidence. Both the American Medical Association and the British Psychological Society have concluded that information recalled under hypnosis is unreliable, it *may* be accurate but cannot be validated.

❸ *Psychotherapy.* Psychoanalysts use hypnosis to uncover repressed memories and relive childhood experiences. Recovered memories are susceptible to the *false memory syndrome* for the same reasons as listed above.

❹ *Behaviour change.* People undergo hypnosis in an effort to, for example, give up smoking, control overeating or overcome phobias. Success may be related to social support, attitudes and compliance (**Wagstaff**, 1995).

❺ *Entertainment.* The use of hypnosis to 'make' people behave antisocially or foolishly is ethically objectionable and regulated by the Federation of Ethical Stage Hypnotists. There is some doubt whether anyone can actually be forced to do such things.

3.4 MOTIVATION, EMOTION AND STRESS

3.4.1 MOTIVATION

Motivation is an internal state that drives an organism to action.

The brain and motivation

Drives for hunger, thirst, and temperature control are regulated by tissue needs. Levels of glucose, water and temperature are signalled to the hypothalamus, which then influences higher cortical centres and behaviour. Some specific mechanisms are discussed in unit 3.1.2.

Physiological theories of motivation

❶ *Homeostatic drive theory.* **Cannon** (1929) coined the term 'homeostasis' (see unit 3.1.2) to describe the organism's motivation to return to a state of balance when basic needs are not fulfilled. He thought that hunger arises from the contractions of an empty stomach and thirst from dryness in the mouth. **Cannon and Washburn** (1912) demonstrated this in an experiment where Washburn swallowed a balloon so his stomach contractions could be measured. They found a high correlation between hunger and contraction. However this doesn't prove that one causes the other, and people with no stomachs still get hungry.

    Evaluation. The principle of homeostasis is valid but it does not account for all biological needs, such as for vitamins, nor does it explain higher-order needs.

❷ *Drive-reduction theory.* **Hull** (1943) suggested that drive-reduction (physiological) is reinforcing (psychological) which leads to learning. For example, physiological depletion of glucose leads to a homeostatic need and results in a drive; this increases activity which eventually brings the animal in contact which something which will satisfy the need (i.e. food); eating reduces the drive (hunger) thus reinforcing the behaviour which brought about food. Hull believed that all human behaviour is a result of satisfying primary needs.

Evaluation

- This theory offers a useful distinction between needs (physiological) and drives (psychological).

- It is limited to biological, homeostatic mechanisms, but the principle of reinforcement can be adapted to cope with secondary motives.
- It produces testable equations and does explain *some* behaviour. However, **Tolman and Honzik** (1930) demonstrated that learning can take place without reinforcement (see unit 2.4.1).
- It does not explain behaviour which is not drive-reducing. **Sheffield and Roby** (1950) found that rats will continue eating saccharin for hours even though it has no nutritional value and even if it did, saturation must have been reached.

❸ *Optimum levels of arousal theory* is a generalised concept which can be used to explain the motivations behind many behaviours (see social facilitation in unit 1.3.3, bystander behaviour and aggression in units 1.4.1 and 1.4.2 and emotion and stress, units 3.4.2 and 3.4.3).

- *Physiological level.* Arousal is important to the function of the nervous system and therefore it is important to maintain optimum levels.
- *Psychological level.* Optimum cognitive functioning is related to arousal (the *Yerkes-Dodson Law*, see unit 3.4.3). Curiosity is related to arousal, and boredom (lack of curiosity drive) may have profound psychological consequences. Animals in zoos suffer from boredom because, in the wild most of their time is occupied searching for food but when this is provided they have little to do. The motive to play games may provide necessary arousal for children and adults.

Evaluation. We can only establish optimum levels of arousal by observing behaviour, a circular argument and one which cannot really support a theory. In any case, arousal theory has not been specifically formulated as a theory of motivation.

Non-physiological theories of motivation

❶ *Needs theories.* Physiological theories present a mechanistic view of motivation and one that emphasises *extrinsic* rather than *intrinsic* motives (see unit 6.3.1). They also cannot account for non-homeostatic drives. *Humanistic* psychologists suggest that humans have higher-order needs as well as physiological ones.

Murray (1938) described 20 different human motives (needs), such as for achievement (nAch), play, affiliation, aggression, nurturance and understanding.

McClelland (1961) measured the need for achievement (nAch) and demonstrated its importance in many behaviours; nPower has also been suggested and measured (**Winter,** 1973). **Rogers** (unit 4.2.2) explained development in terms of the desire for social approval and self-actualisation.

White (1959) described competence as the 'master reinforcer' because our capacity to deal effectively with and to control our environment is intrinsically rewarding. The *theory of cognitive dissonance* (**Festinger,** 1957) suggests that people have a need for cognitive balance and this drives attitude change.

Evaluation. The humanistic approach can account for the social environment, individual differences and long-term goals. It reflects the complexity of human behaviour, but is less relevant to animal behaviour.

❷ *Hierarchy of needs.* **Maslow** (1954) suggested that physiological needs are *prepotent* (more powerful when unfulfilled) to intermediate and meta needs, proposing a hierarchy:

- Levels 1 & 2 basic needs: *physiological* (food, water), and *safety* (physical danger).
- Levels 3 & 4 psychological needs: *love and belonging* (affiliation), *esteem* (respect from achievement, competence).
- Levels 5, 6 & 7 self-actualisation needs: *cognitive* (knowledge, understanding, curiosity), *aesthetic* (order, beauty, art) and *self-actualisation* (self-fulfilment, realisation of potential).

Alderfer's (1972) ERG (Existence Relatedness Growth needs) theory suggests that people also move downwards, using lower level needs as a substitute when frustrated at a higher level.

Evaluation

- A more powerful explanation than just a list of needs.

- There is some question about whether the hierarchy is strictly followed, for example many sports (meta-need) involve considerable danger (physiological need).
- It is difficult to collect empirical support.

❸ *Psychoanalytic theory.* Freud suggested that the infant and id are driven by innate, biological (sexual) forces, governed by the pleasure principle and homeostatic forces (tension is reduced by satisfying basic needs). As the child gets older, the ego and superego regulate the expression of id, and provide higher order motives learned from society.

Evaluation. A holistic approach that does not account for free will and learning because of emphasis on unconscious, innate forces.

❹ *Hydraulic model.* Ethologists proposed that fixed action patterns (FAPs) are initiated by an innate releasing mechanism (IRM) which produces action-specific energy (ASE) to 'power' the appropriate behaviour. ASE is stored in a reservoir in between demand. If demand is non-existent it builds up until it overflows triggering the IRM and FAP in the absence of a sign stimulus, like a cistern which has to be flushed. Catharsis is another means of 'flushing' the system.

Evaluation. A mechanistic description which is appropriate to animal behaviour. The concept of instinct has been challenged (see unit 2.1.1).

3.4.2 EMOTION

Emotion comes from the Latin meaning 'to move, excite, stir up or agitate'. It is a state of physiological arousal with important motivational properties.

❶ *Physiological arousal.* The *limbic system* and *hypothalamus* stimulate production of *adrenalin*, which arouses the *sympathetic branch* of the ANS (see unit 3.1.1). This creates a physiological response (e.g. increased heart rate) and a behavioural response (e.g. increased attention) in readiness to deal with the stimulus.

❷ *Subjective experience* of emotion is a 'read-out' of the physiological state, though physiological arousal is not necessary for all emotional experiences (see below) and the interpretation is affected by cognitive factors. *Primary* emotions (such as joy and sadness) are universal and innate, *secondary* emotions (such as contempt) are a blend of the former and are culturally determined.

❸ *Emotional expression* is a 'read-out' for the benefit of others, which is either innate or learned. **Ekman** *et al.* (1987) showed pictures of Western emotional expressions to 10 cultural groups and found better than 80% recognition for happiness, sadness, anger and disgust. Innate emotional expression may be important for survival and social interaction. *Display rules* are culturally based. We often show our emotions without conscious awareness (*non-verbal leakage*).

❹ *Measurement of emotion* can be achieved through self-report or direct observation. **Ekman** *et al.* (1971) developed a list of 70 facial expressions (facial affect scoring technique, FAST), including eight positions of the brows and forehead, to record expression. ANS arousal, such as increased heart rate, can be measured. The *galvanic skin response* (GSR) registers arousal because sweat increases the electrical conductivity of the skin. Experimental anxiety may also increase ANS arousal.

The brain and emotion

❶ *The limbic system.* **Papez** (1937) and **Maclean** (1949) proposed the *Papez-Maclean limbic theory* of emotion which distinguished three circuits:

- The *amygdala* and *hippocampus*: self-preservation, such as aggression.
- The *cingulate gyrus*, *septum* and other structures: pleasure, sex.
- The *hypothalamus* and *thalamus*: co-operative social behaviour, certain aspects of sexuality and motivation.

Aronson and Cooper (1979) studied male cats with lesions of the amygdala and found that they mounted anything, they were not just hypersexual but became indiscriminate about partners. Therefore the lesions did not simply cause or prevent a behaviour, but seemed to change how the animals interpreted information.

Evaluation. The theory accounts well for animal behaviour but is less relevant to humans where experience is a key element of emotions. It is difficult to collect empirical evidence of the limbic system's role in human emotion. The model deals mainly with high intensity emotions, such as rage and fear.

❷ *The cortex*. **Bard** (1929) ablated the cerebral cortex in cats, which led to *sham rage*, a kind of 'cool' aggression. If the hypothalamus was also removed the rage stopped, suggesting that the cortex ordinarily inhibits and organises attacks, whereas the hypothalamus is necessary for expression of rage. In humans the situation may be more complicated. **Jacobsen** (1968) found no emotional experience in association with stimulation of the human hypothalamus nor evidence that damage to this area is associated with emotional abnormality.

❸ *The temporal cortex*. **Klüver and Bucy** (1939) found that bilateral removal of the temporal cortical lobe resulted in profound changes in affective and social behaviour in monkeys (the *Klüver-Bucy syndrome*). This research led **Moniz** (see unit 4.4.1) to develop prefrontal lobotomies (which include the temporal lobes). It has also been observed that rabies leads to violent behaviour and is associated with infection of temporal lobes and amygdala, and that some cases of temporal lobe epilepsy have affective overtones. For example, Dostoyevskian epilepsy (named after the novelist) is associated with feelings of extreme happiness.

❹ *Lateralisation*. Generally, the right hemisphere is involved with recognition of emotion and negative affect, while the left hemisphere is involved with positive affects. **Gainotti** (1972) found that patients with damage to the left cortical hemisphere could perceive the emotional tone of a statement even though they couldn't understand the words. The opposite was true of people with right hemisphere damage.

❺ *Neurotransmitters*. Low levels of *serotonin* are associated with increases in aggressive behaviour (see unit 1.4.2). *Adrenalin*, which is both a hormone and a neurotransmitter, has an excitatory effect on the nervous system.

Theories of emotion

❶ *James-Lange theory*. **James** (1884) and **Lange** (1887) independently proposed the view that bodily changes come first and form the basis of an emotional experience. This is the reverse of the common-sense view that the mental state triggers the emotional response. Evidence *for* the James-Lange view:

- *Physical action causes subjective experience*. James said you are frightened when you see a bear *because* you run, not the reverse, that you run because you are frightened. **Laird** (1974) told participants that he was measuring activity of facial muscles using electrodes and instructed them to relax and contract muscles; cartoons viewed when 'smiling' were rated as funnier. Participants were amused because they were smiling, not smiling because they were amused.

- *For each emotion there should be a different physiological state*. **Schwartz** *et al*. (1981) and **Ekman** *et al*. (1983) asked participants to imagine scenes involving primary emotions or to watch themselves in a mirror as they tried to look happy, sad, etc.; each produced a different physiological 'signature' (e.g. heart rate). Primary emotions appear to have individual physiological states, which supports one aspect of James' theory but also indicates that physiological changes can be *caused* by the subjective experience, rather than vice versa.

- *The more intense the arousal the greater the emotion*. **White** *et al*. (1981) asked male college students to run on the spot. Those that ran for 120 seconds found videos of attractive women more attractive than those who ran for only 15 seconds, whereas the opposite was true if the woman was unattractive, suggesting that arousal enhances existing emotional states.

Evaluation. It offers a reasonable account of some of the evidence, but it cannot explain emotion before or without any arousal, nor can it explain the role of learning and cognitive control.

❷ *Cannon-Bard theory*. **Cannon** (1927) criticised the James-Lange view and put forward his own ideas, which were later modified by **Bard**. This model suggested that changes of emotional state and changes in the ANS occur *simultaneously* but *independently*, both caused by the arrival of the same sensory input. Evidence *against* the James-Lange theory:

- *Each emotion needs a corresponding physiological state*. Even if there are different physiological states, there are not as many as there are emotions. Some aspects of emotion *are* determined by mental state (**Schachter and Singer**, below).
- *It is difficult to perceive different physiological states accurately*. People are not very aware of increases or decreases in their blood pressure (**Valins**, below).
- *Emotional experiences occur rapidly* yet the ANS is slow to react.
- *Physiological changes can occur without any emotional experience*. **Marañon** (1924) injected patients with adrenalin, 71% were aware of physical sensations but had no emotional experience, the rest used phrases like 'it's *as if* I was afraid'.
- *Emotional states may occur without any physiological changes*. **Hohmann** (1966) interviewed patients with spinal-cord injuries (brain and ANS were disconnected). They had 'as if' experiences especially in the presence of appropriate cognitive stimuli. **Valins** (1966) showed male participants slides of semi-nude women and gave them false feedback about their heart rate. Ratings of attractiveness were positively related to supposed increases in heart rate (the *Valins effect*).

Evaluation. The criticisms are all only partly true.

❸ *Cognitive Labelling Theory*. **Schachter and Singer** (1962) proposed that all emotional experiences are preceded by a generalised state of arousal, but the nature of the subjective experience is determined ('labelled') by the individual's cognitive assessment based on external, situational cues or internal ones such as imagination.

Evidence for the cognitive labelling theory:

- **Schachter and Singer** (1962) injected 185 male undergraduates with a new vitamin, Suproxin, which was in fact adrenalin. The participants were either correctly informed (told they would feel aroused), misinformed (told their feet would feel numb), uninformed or given a placebo and uninformed. After the injection, they were placed in a room with a confederate who behaved euphorically or angrily. The correctly informed were least affected by stooge's behaviour because they could 'explain' the arousal. The other groups mimicked the emotional behaviour of the stooge because there was no explanation for their state of arousal and therefore they used situational cues. (The placebo participants may have experienced some arousal through anxiety.)

  Evaluation. The researchers excluded participants who did not report any physiological sensations, if their data had been included the results may not have been so significant. The research equates drug-induced arousal states with real-life emotions. Several studies have failed to replicate this finding (e.g. **Marshall and Zimbardo**, 1979).

- **Dutton and Aron** (1974) arranged for attractive women to conduct a questionnaire with men either on a high suspension bridge (high arousal) or a low bridge, and to give out their phone numbers (measure of attraction). The high arousal condition led to greater attraction presumably because, in the presence of an attractive female interviewer, the men had labelled or *misattributed* the arousal they felt as sexual attraction rather than fear (**Bersheid and Walster**'s *two-factor theory of emotion*).

Evidence against the cognitive labelling theory:

- *There are occasions when cognition comes before or without arousal* (the **Valins** Effect, above). **Darley and Katz** (1973) told participants that a task was either a test or a game; their heart rate increased or decreased accordingly, suggesting that cognitive appraisal may lead to different states of arousal.
- *There are different physiological states* (**Schwartz et al.** above).
- *You can have an emotional response with no cognitive awareness*. **McGinnies'** (1949) research on 'perceptual defence' (see unit 5.1.3) demonstrated an emotional response (GSR) to subliminal words. **Lazarus and McCleary** (1951) classically conditioned participants, pairing random words with electric shocks. Later, when the words were presented subliminally the participants had a strong GSR.

Evaluation. This view can explain how emotions are learned because an emotional 'label' is derived from previous experiences of emotion in a similar situation. It has stimulated a lot of research and it offers the best account of the available evidence.

④ *Cognitive appraisal theory* is an extension of Cognitive Labelling Theory. This theory offers a kind of calculus for predicting the emotion that will be felt when arousal is experienced. There have been a number of formulations, such as one by **Smith and Ellsworth** (1987), who described emotions in terms of the different cognitive expectations, for example: the desirability of the situation, effort one anticipates spending, certainty of the situation and control one feels. For example, an unpleasant situation may lead variously to anger (if caused by another), or guilt (if brought about by self), or sadness (when controlled by external circumstances).

Lazarus (1982) suggested that cognitive processing and conscious control of emotions and arousal are key elements in emotional experiences.

⑤ *A combined approach.* The evidence suggests that both factors, arousal and cognitive appraisal, are sufficient but not necessary conditions:

- Physiological arousal *alone* is sufficient but not always necessary.
- *Arousal* may come *first*, and then receives an appropriate label.
- The *cognition* (label) may come *first* and lead to arousal.
- You can have an emotional response with *no cognitive awareness*.

There are different kinds of emotional experience: a physiological experience such as a jet screaming overhead (the emotional experience will be relative to the label: fear, surprise, elation), or a cognitive experience (you hear that you passed your driving test which makes you feel excited/aroused).

3.4.3 STRESS

- *Stressor* = a physical or psychological stimulus which threatens an individual's psychological and/or physiological well-being.
- *Stress response* = an innate, defensive reaction to promote survival; however not all stress situations result in a response.
- *Stress* = an emotion, a state of psychological tension and physiological arousal produced by a stressor which makes the individual *ready* to respond.

Cox (1975) suggested that there are three models of stress:

- The *engineering model*: causes of stress.
- The *physiological model*: internal processes accompanying stress (e.g. GAS).
- **Cox's** *transactional model*. Stress is experienced when the perceived demands of the environment are greater than the individual's perceived ability to cope.

Psychological effects of stress

There are four main responses to stress: anxiety, anger, aggression and depression.

① *Adaptive. Innate* stress responses may help to remove a stressor (e.g. aggression) or to cope (e.g. depression). **Yerkes-Dodson law** (1908) suggests a curvilinear relationship between arousal and performance, *optimum* levels are adaptive.

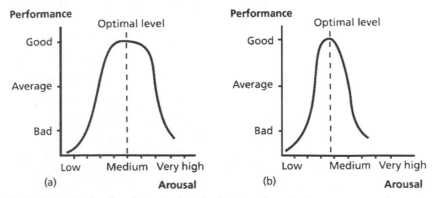

Figure 3.9 The Yerkes-Dodson law (a) a simple task, (b) a complicated task

② *Pleasurable.* Emotional highs or loud music produce agreeable pressure. **Selye** (1956) used the term *eustress* to signify pleasant stress associated with fulfilment.

③ *Maladaptive.* Extreme levels of stress lead to impaired performance especially on cognitive tasks. Some maladaptive stress responses are *learned*, **Watson and Rayner** (1920) demonstrated conditioned emotional responses (CERs) in Little Albert by pairing a loud noise with white rat; subsequently he had an abnormal fear response to anything white and furry. Anxiety may be learned in the same way, for example, an examination room may create anxiety because of past associations.

Depression (withdrawal) may be an innate and healthy response but chronic depression (helplessness) is not healthy. **Seligman** (1975) suggested that *learned helplessness* occurs when a person experiences no control when trying to remove a stressor. This may lead to depression *when* the individual blames their failure on themselves (internal) and such failure is seen as unchanging (stable) and relevant to all aspects of their personality (global) (see attribution, unit 1.1.2).

④ *Compensatory behaviour.* Smoking, excess drinking or eating, and deviant sexual behaviour may result from stress. These may contribute to poor health (see below).

⑤ *Individual and cultural differences.* A person's ability to cope and the social support available will affect the degree to which any stressor disturbs their psychic resources. This may be socially learned, for example, Japanese coping style is to accept problems whereas Westerners are taught to take control and change a stressful problem.

Coping style may be due to innate temperamental differences. **Kobasa** (1979) suggested that 'hardy' types are better able to cope with stress because they regard stressors as challenges which are a necessary part of meaningful activities and they have a high internal locus of control (**Rotter**, in unit 1.1.2). **Friedman and Rosenman** and **Morris** *et al.* (below) provided evidence of how different personality types are more prone to stress and illness.

The effect of stress on the body

① *Short-term effects.* Stress is an emotion and therefore physiological reactions are similar (see unit 3.3.2). Stress activates the *hypothalamus* and the *pituitary* in the brain, which stimulate the autonomic nervous system (ANS) and the production of *ACTH* (adrenocorticotrophic hormone). ACTH leads to production of *adrenalin* from the *adrenal glands* located just on top of both kidneys. The result is ANS arousal which causes increases in heart rate, respiration, sweating and so on.

② *Long-term effects: general adaptation syndrome (GAS).* Selye (1956) described a model for prolonged stress from observations of his patients:

- *Alarm reaction.* The sympathetic branch of the ANS is aroused, ACTH and adrenalin are released in readiness for fight or flight.
- *Resistance.* If the stressor persists, hormone production is maintained but at a lower level.
- *Exhaustion.* Eventually the body's resources are depleted. Adrenal glands are not functioning properly leading to drop in blood sugar levels and leading to various psychosomatic disorders such as high blood pressure and ulcers.

Evaluation. Selye thought that GAS was a non-specific response to *any* stressor, but in fact different stimuli lead to different responses (stimulus differences). No two people respond in the same way (individual differences) nor does the same person always respond in the same way (situational differences). Selye's contribution was to alert medicine to the importance of stress.

③ *Long term effects: reduced immune response.* The immune system protects us from disease. The main components of the system are antibodies, T-cells and B-cells. The presence of adrenalin seems to inhibit the production of these components. **Kiecolt-Glaser** *et al.* (1984) tested students' blood a month before and during their final examinations. They found that T-cell activity was significantly lower on the second occasion, and that it was particularly low for students who reported feeling most lonely, and those experiencing other stressful life events. **Kamarck** *et al.* (1990) found that friends had a good effect on stress responses (see unit 1.2.4).

The relationship between stress and illness

① *Life events.* Two doctors, **Holmes and Rahe** (1967), observed that poor health was associated with life events which involved *change* from a steady state, even when the change was for the better. Changes absorb 'psychic energy', leaving less available for other matters such as physical defence against illness. Analysis of 5,000 patient records led them to identify 43 life events which seemed to precede illness (the *Social Readjustment Rating Scale*, SRRS). The top two are: death of spouse (100), divorce (73); the bottom two are: Christmas (12), minor violations of the law (11). The figure in brackets is the 'stress value' of event (out of 100) in 'life change units' (LCUs).

Rahe *et al.* (1970) monitored 2,500 naval personnel during a six-month tour of duty, administering the SRRS beforehand. They found a small but significant positive correlation between LCUs and illness. **Rahe and Arthur** (1977) found an increase of various psychological illnesses, athletic injuries, physical illness and even traffic accidents, when LCUs were raised.

Evaluation

- The results are correlational, the data about LCUs was retrospective.
- The scale muddles different kinds of life events, such as those over which you do or do not have some control.
- The scale does not allow for individual differences, effects will be moderated by personality, past experience and coping skills.
- It is a flawed but useful tool which has stimulated much research.

② *Daily events.* DeLongis *et al.* (1982) noted that most people do not often experience major life events, therefore strains of everyday life might be a better measure of stress and predictor of physical illness. They followed 100 individuals for a year, monitoring their health, life events, and daily hassles and uplifts (using their *Hassles and Uplifts Scale*) and found a significant positive correlation between health and hassles but not uplifts or life events. **DeLongis** *et al.* (1988) studied married couples over a period of six months and found a significant relationship between hassles and health problems, and evidence of individual differences in stress responses: people high in self-esteem and social support were not as affected by stress.

DeLongis *et al.* pointed out that chronic, ongoing sources of stress (e.g. poor housing, strains of family life, unsatisfying work) are also important. Health is affected by all three: hassles, chronic situations and life changes. It is a circular model because hassles affect health and health affects the subjective experience of hassles.

③ *Coronary heart disease.* **Friedman and Rosenman** (1974) tested 3,000 men and found that, over a period of eight years, type A individuals were twice as likely as type B to develop coronary heart disease (CHD). Type A individuals are described as 'competitive, ambitious, impatient, pressurised', i.e. they respond to stress badly. Type B lacks the characteristics of type A. Twenty-two years later, marginally more type As had died from CHD than type Bs; it is possible that death is not as good an indicator as illness, because some people take preventive measures once they know they are ill.

④ *Cancer.* **Morris** *et al.* (1981) found evidence that cancer is associated with type C individuals (nice, industrious, repressed emotional reactions, tendency to feel helpless). In their study women who developed malignant rather than non-malignant breast cancer reported that they both experienced and expressed far less anger. Emotional suppression is linked with increased stress, lowered effectiveness of the immune system and illness (above).

⑤ *Ulcers.* After an episode of stress, parasympathetic rebound causes a release of noradrenalin and increases in digestive juices which may led to ulcers. **Brady** (1958) strapped a monkey in a chair and gave it electric shocks unless it pressed a lever every 20 seconds. The monkeys invariably died and post-mortem examination revealed ulcers. To test whether the cause was the restraint or the stress, he used a yoked control – another monkey also received the shocks but had no control over the lever, only the 'executive' monkey experienced psychological stress. After 23 days the executive monkey died due to a perforated ulcer. Some variations in the relative amounts of stress and rest significantly reduced the damaging effects, and they found that acidity was greatest during the rest period, leading Brady to conclude that rest time was also important.

Evaluation

- The executive monkeys were not randomly selected, but were chosen because they were faster at learning an avoidance response (i.e. type A).
- The study shows stress in animals and may not apply to humans.
- It is an ethically dubious study.
- More recently evidence has emerged that ulcers may be due to the presence of a bacterium, *helicobacter pylorii*, which creates increased acidity and causes duodenal ulcers (**Northfield** *et al.*, 1993). Stress may still lower immune response and make infection more likely.

⑥ *Psychological stress-related disorders* such as burnout (due to work stress), post-traumatic stress disorder (shell shock, see unit 4.3.3) and repetitive strain injury. Psychological shock may produce stress responses disabling the individual emotionally.

3.4.4 METHODS USED TO REDUCE STRESS

Some methods are physiological while others are psychological (cognitive or behavioural). **Lazarus and Folkman** (1984) distinguished between problem- and emotion-focused strategies.

❶ *Direct action (problem-focused).* In some cases the stressor can be removed.

❷ *Other problem-focused strategies*

- *Avoidance.* Do something else to 'take your mind off' the problem.
- *Take control.* A person who feels in control suffers less harmful consequences of stress. **Glass** *et al.* (1969) found that participants who were given a button purported to control random noise were more persistent on an insoluble task. **Cohen** *et al.* (1991) found that participants who felt that their lives were unpredictable and uncontrollable (high stress) were twice as likely to develop colds as those suffering low stress. *Attribution retraining* helps people reassign control to themselves (see unit 1.1.2).
- *Cognitive redefinition.* Intellectualisation and rationalisation are ways of consciously reshaping the problem.

❸ *Biofeedback and relaxation (emotion-focused).* A technique to learn voluntary control of involuntary muscles or voluntary muscles which are not normally controlled, such as blood pressure and heart rate. Learning occurs through feedback, a patient is connected to various monitoring devices and a light or tone signals when a correct alteration occurs. Biofeedback certainly works with *voluntary* responses. Apparent changes in involuntary control may be due to relaxation and control of unused voluntary muscles. Such strategies are costly and time-consuming.

❹ *Other emotion-focused strategies*

- *Anxiolytic drugs* such as Librium and Valium act directly on the ANS and synapses (see table of drug effects in unit 3.1.4). In the long term, drugs may lead to problems of dependence.
- *Stress management programmes* such as time management or assertiveness training teach people to pace themselves better and avoid stress.
- *Physical activity and exercise* promote better circulation which strengthens the heart. **Goldwater and Collis** (1985) found that exercise was positively related to decreased anxiety.
- *Rest periods* may be a potentially dangerous time physiologically. The advice is not to stop suddenly and to have a meal to absorb the digestive juices.
- *Emotional discharge (catharsis).* Expressing tension through crying, anger or humour, or using alcohol or non-prescription drugs.
- *Social support* (**Kamarck** *et al.*, unit 3.4.3).

Chapter roundup

3.1   Basic neural and hormonal processes and their influence on behaviour

3.1.1   The *CNS*, *ANS* and *endocrine systems* interact via electrical signals and biochemical substances (neurotransmitters and hormones).

3.1.2   *Homeostasis* illustrates the importance of feedback, and can be seen in the control of temperature, thirst and hunger.

3.1.3   *Neural and synaptic activity* is the most basic level of behavioural analysis.

3.1.4   *Drugs* have variable effects on behaviour and often mimic the activity of neurotransmitters.

3.2   Cortical functions

3.2.1   *Techniques used to investigate cortical activity* may or may not cause damage, and have inherent problems in determining cause and effect.

3.2.2   Physical and behavioural functions may be bilateral (memory), unilateral (language), contralateral (motor responses) or ipsilateral (vision). Both *lateralisation* and *localisation* confer advantages.

3.2.3   Neurophysiological explanations of *vision* provide considerable understanding of many perceptual processes such as depth, brightness, movement, colour and visual illusions.

3.3   Awareness

3.3.1   *States of awareness* (consciousness) account for differences between humans and animals, and for abnormal states of mind.

3.3.2   Understanding *bodily rhythms* has many useful applications, such as for shift work and jet lag.

3.3.3   All animals *sleep* but differently suggesting that (a) sleep is necessary physiologically and (b) the way it is achieved is adaptive. *Dreams* may have real meaning or are the subjective interpretation of spontaneous neural activity created by cognitive repair and restoration.

3.3.4   People who can be *hypnotised* may be able to separate streams of consciousness (disassociation) or they may be responding to social cues from the hypnotist.

3.4   Motivation, emotion and stress

3.4.1   Human *motivation* can be understood as a combination of prepotent biological needs and higher-order drives such as for self-actualisation.

3.4.2   *Emotional experiences* are due to a combination of arousal and cognition, either of which may be sufficient.

3.4.3   Poor health may result from psychological and physiological *stress*, though there are individual differences in how stressors are experienced.

3.4.4   Methods used to *reduce stress* may be problem- or emotion-focused.

Illustrative question

Critically consider the extent to which behaviours can be explained in terms of activity of the nervous system.

(AEB A 1992)

Tutorial note

This question is at the root of this chapter. Students find it difficult to construct a suitable response despite the fact that they probably know a lot of relevant material. Such a broad question can be answered in depth or breadth. The answer below takes the breadth approach, a 'depth' answer might have selected only one or two behaviours and offered detailed descriptions and evaluation. The question lends itself to description; the evaluative element can be tackled by comparing physiological explanations with other possibilities or criticising the empirical evidence.

Suggested answer

What is 'the nervous system'? The central nervous system consists of the brain, spinal cord and neurons. The peripheral nervous system includes the nerves of the body (somatic nervous system) and the autonomic nervous system, which is associated with hormone production. Activity in the nervous system is electrical and chemical: nervous impulses, neurotransmitters and hormones.

Just about any behaviour you could think of has been given some explanation in terms of nervous system activity, but to what extent are such explanations sufficient?

One might expect there to be a relatively simple correlation between a drug, the nervous system and behaviour. However, just about every drug has multiple effects. Some effects, the primary ones, are fairly predictable and can be shown in terms of the effect on synaptic transmission. The secondary effects vary from person to person, which explains why it is impossible to predict the exact behavioural corollaries of a drug. For example, of the women who took thalidomide during the critical period of pregnancy, only about 20% gave birth to deformed babies.

Sight is another example of interaction. It can be explained in terms of the properties of rods and cones, and the specialised nature of the cells in the visual cortex which respond to very specific stimuli and begin the process of perception. For example, **Hubel and Wiesel** (1977) showed how hypercomplex cells of the visual cortex organise sensory data. However, perception is also influenced by top-down processes. **Bruner and Minturn** (1955) showed that perceptual set alters the way we interpret a 13 (as a letter B or number 13).

The process of motivation has been explained at various levels. The most basic needs such as body temperature and thirst are controlled by autonomic homeostatic mechanisms. Maslow suggested that 'meta' needs, such as curiosity and self-actualisation, are needed to explain human rather than animal behaviour. Even basic needs are sometimes mediated by cognitive factors, for example we often feel hungry not because of real hunger but because the food looks good.

Attempts to explain the processes involved in an emotional experience involve strands from both physiology and psychology. It is clear that in some cases arousal alone can account for a person's emotional state; for example **Schachter and Singer**'s (1962) classic experiment demonstrated that injected epinephrine can lead to an emotional experience. However, the tone of the experience depended on cognitive factors.

Much work on sleep has focused on nervous activity. It is an example of arousal, or the lack of it, mediated by areas of the brain, such as the reticular activating system. One explanation for the need for sleep is as a time for the nervous system to be 'restored'. **Crick and Mitchison** (1986) suggest that dreams may also serve a restorative function; they are the subjective experience of random neural firing needed for the daily debugging and fine tuning of the neural network. However, the evidence for sleep as a necessary physiological need is equivocal. Deprivation studies have failed to find consistent ill effects. Alternative explanations suggest that sleep is a form of protection. For example, **Meddis** (1979) has suggested that the long sleep periods of babies have evolved in order to help their mothers to cope.

In recent years, mental illnesses have been more clearly linked with neural activity. One example comes from studies of the Amish, which have provided evidence that a chromosome defect predisposes a person to manic-depression (**Rosenhan and Seligman**, 1984). This genetic defect has been associated with a lack of certain neurotransmitters (catecholamines) which in turn affects brain activity. One important practical consequence is the link with suitable drug therapies. However, not everyone with the defect becomes mentally ill, which suggests that the defect only 'predisposes' a person to become ill.

Bodily rhythms can be explained in terms of a biological clock, the suprachiasmatic nucleus located in the hypothalamus. Experiments in caves have shown that this is set to a cycle of just under 25 hours. **Weitzman *et al.*** (1981) investigated delayed sleep phase disorder. In some individuals, staying up late a few nights in a row or travelling eastwards resets their biological clock and they then maintain a pattern of staying up late and waking late. The researchers recommend that the only way to reset the clock is to take some time off work and stay up a few hours later each night until a suitable bedtime is reached.

Some of the effects of hypnosis and relaxation, in particular for pain relief, may be due to the production of endorphins – neuromodulators which block pain. There is emerging evidence that endorphins may have other effects as well, such as the control of blood pressure and thermoregulation. Such processes are under the control of the autonomic nervous system, and relaxation is generally associated with the parasympathetic activity of the ANS.

The original question as to the 'extent' that behaviour can be 'explained in terms of nervous system activity' is a reductionist one: can we reduce all behaviour to such units? The current failure to do so completely may simply be because we do not know sufficient detail, but theoretically it will one day be possible. Alternatively, Gestalt, or humanist, psychologists take the view that such data is illuminating, but will never explain the complexity of human behaviour and that such an approach is not even relevant to some aspects of behaviour. For example, language, which has long been identified with specific areas of the brain and, being closely associated with memory, clearly has a biochemical basis. However, other aspects of language, such as dialect, are explained in terms of in-group processes. Nervous activity may underlie such behaviour but as an explanation it makes no sense. **Rose** (1976) suggests that we need to see all explanations as part of a hierarchy of different universes of discourse, there are higher and lower levels of explanation each of which separately contribute to our understanding.

Question bank

Allow 35–40 minutes for each question.

Basic neural and hormonal processes and their influence on behaviour

1 Discuss the influence of the nervous system **and** the endocrine system upon homeostasis.

(AEB A 1996)

Points: Try to avoid too much description of neurons, glands, etc., and try to include material on how the systems interact and how they relate to specific behaviours such as eating and drinking.

2 (a) Outline the main processes involved in neural and synaptic transmission. (10 marks)
(b) Critically consider the contribution which knowledge of these processes has made to an understanding of **one or more** aspects of human behaviour. (14 marks)

(AEB AS 1996)

Points:: Part (a) is straightforward if you have the requisite biological knowledge. Part (b) could draw on the effects of drugs or knowledge from other sections of the syllabus, such as abnormal behaviour. You only need to address one of these but if you take this 'depth' approach your critical consideration should be very detailed.

3 How may drugs affect the nervous system in terms of neural activity and what are the consequent effects upon behaviour?

(AEB A 1990)

Points: A question like this is either answered very badly, with common knowledge about alcohol and LSD, or answered extremely well, covering neural and behavioural effects.

Cortical functions

4 Critically consider the methods/techniques that have been used to study how brain activity is related to behaviour.

(AEB A 1995)

Points: The descriptive element is a matter of writing a list but remember to evaluate each method/technique. This can be done by using empirical examples and by assessing the advantages and disadvantages of the method.

5 Discuss some of the findings of research into localisation of function in the human cerebral cortex.

(AEB AS 1993)

Points: Describing the necessary material is fairly straightforward. Evaluation is more difficult but can be done using empirical evidence and assessing the importance of such localisation. It is best to discriminate between cortical and subcortical structures, and avoid dwelling on split-brain studies and lateralisation.

6 Discuss the contribution which *physiological* research has made to our understanding of visual perception.

(AEB AS 1995)

Points: This is an easy question to misunderstand, whether deliberately or not. The key words are 'discuss' (do more than describe), 'physiological' (i.e. not psychological), 'research' (which can be theories or empirical studies), and 'perception' (not just sensation). Material which is psychological could be used as a means of evaluation but this must be explicit.

Awareness

7 Describe and evaluate the evidence that has been produced by studies of bodily rhythms.

(AEB A 1993)

Points: A discussion of stages of sleep would be perfectly acceptable but note that the question asks for 'studies' not theories, the latter can be used to evaluate the empirical evidence. A broader approach would be to consider a variety of bodily rhythms which would mean less time for detailed evaluations of each.

8 Describe and evaluate physiological and neurochemical theories of sleep.

(AEB AS 1994)

Points: Any non-physiological or non-neurochemical theories of sleep may be used to evaluate the designated theories for this question. Empirical evidence can be used to evaluate the theories, and dream theories can be presented to account for REM sleep.

9 Using psychological evidence, critically consider whether hypnosis should be regarded as an altered state of awareness.

(AEB AS 1991)

Points: This is a popular topic which attracts common-sense answers. Be sure to use psychological theory and evidence to argue your case.

Motivation, emotion and stress

10 Compare and contrast any **two** theories of **either** motivation **or** emotion.

(AEB A 1995)

Points: Students find it difficult to 'compare and contrast'. Don't just describe the two theories and offer evaluative material for each, you must set them against each other. And remember to highlight similarities as well as differences.

11 (a) Distinguish between the terms **eustress** and **distress** and give **one** example of **each**. (4 marks).

(b) Outline the role of the endocrine system in stress responses. (6 marks)

(c) Individuals respond differently to a variety of potential sources of stress, such as sitting an examination or moving house. Using **either** of these examples, discuss how any **one** theory of stress might explain why only some people experience stress with a particular life event. (10 marks)

(NEAB module 8 Summer 1995)

Points: In part (b) good answers should include both the action of the pituitary and the adrenal glands; the GAS theory could also be relevant. In part (c) you must discuss one theory only (but could use others for evaluation) and make sure that your answer is relevant to the example you have selected.

ATYPICAL DEVELOPMENT AND ABNORMAL BEHAVIOUR

Units in this chapter

4.1 *Atypical development*
4.2 *Conceptions and models of abnormality*
4.3 *Psychopathology*
4.4 *Therapeutic approaches*

Chapter overview

Abnormal psychology is the study of behaviour outside the 'normal' range. There is considerable debate about definitions, explanations and treatments; driven by practical necessity.

4.1 ATYPICAL DEVELOPMENT

A disability is a condition which impairs individuals or those around them, and hinders some aspect of human performance. The term 'atypical' seems to express this better than 'abnormal', meaning 'not having the characteristics of the group'. Many atypical behaviours are ones which are typical at an earlier age, for example bedwetting. Atypical behaviour is quantitatively not qualitatively different from 'normal'.

4.1.1 LEARNING DIFFICULTIES

❶ *What are 'learning difficulties'?*

- *Mental retardation* is an old fashioned term, as are the terms 'idiot', 'moron' and 'imbecile'. All were official labels in their time. It is defined by the American Association on Mental Deficiency as an IQ of less than 70, a deficit in general intellectual functioning which appears before the age of 18. It can be further subdivided into mild (55–69 IQ), moderate (40–54), severe (25–39) and profound (below 25).

- *Specific learning difficulties* are delays which are not global but specific perceptual and/or intellectual deficits found in children of 'normal' or superior intelligence. This is diagnosed when the delay is of a magnitude of at least 2 years and the child's IQ and background indicate that the child should be functioning at the expected level. Such disabilities are believed to be neurologically rather than psychologically caused. Examples include developmental dyslexia (see unit 4.1.3), developmental arithmetic disorder and developmental articulation disorder.

② *Intrinsic causes*

- *Inherited conditions* such as cretinism.
- *Malformation* such as *hydrocephalus* (fluid around the brain) which is associated with *spina bifida*, can cause brain damage if the fluid is not drained.
- *Genetic abnormalities*. *Fragile X* syndrome occurs when an individual has a weak 'spot' on their X sex chromosome. This has a greater effect on a boy than a girl because there is no other X chromosome to compensate. Boys with fragile X syndrome almost always experience developmental delays. They may also suffer severe mental impairment and behave autistically. Girls may experience some intellectual, social, or emotional problems. *Down's syndrome* occurs when an individual has three copies of chromosome 21 rather than the usual two. The incidence of such mutations increases with maternal and possibly paternal age. Down's syndrome babies have distinctive facial features, and have some physical defects, such as heart or gastrointestinal problems. Behaviourally, such children are usually very friendly and affectionate. Cognitive impairment varies enormously from moderate to severe depending on constitutional and experiential factors.
- *Metabolic disorders* such as *phenylketonuria* (PKU) and *Tay-Sachs disease*. PKU occurs when a baby is born with an inherited inability to metabolise phenylalanine, a substance found in all proteins. Phenylalanine builds up and poisons the central nervous system causing irreversible brain damage. If a baby has such a defect it can be given a diet which controls the levels of phenylalanine which avoids mental retardation.

③ *Extrinsic causes*

- *Prenatal or perinatal influences*. Prenatal anoxia is associated with low birth weight and reduced cell growth throughout the body including the brain. This is called *intra-uterine growth retardation* (IUGR). **Resnick** *et al.* (1990) followed about 500 children born with very low birth weight (VLBW) and found depressed cognitive development, though sociodemographic factors were critical in exacerbating this.
- *Disease and head injury*, such as brain tumours, measles and encephalitis.
- *Absence of essential vitamins/proteins*. **Benton and Cook** (1991) demonstrated that vitamin supplements can lead to IQ gains, which suggests that reduced vitamins minimises development. Too little folic acid is associated with spina bifida.
- *Presence of harmful substances* such as cadmium, mercury lead or other pollutants.
- *Cultural-familial retardation*. About two-thirds of the cases of retardation have no clear injury or disease, in which case it is assumed to be the result of innately low intelligence combined with an environmental deficit.
- *Reaction range*. The severity of all disabilities is determined by an interaction between innate predispositions and life events. A mentally retarded child from an economically disadvantaged home will never achieve as much as a retarded child from a middle-class home because of differences in cognitive stimulation and a range of other factors associated with low social class, such as foetal alcohol syndrome, smoking in pregnancy, low birth weight, malnourishment and poor health. **Sameroff** *et al.* (1993) showed that 'risk factors' such as family size and stressful life events, were associated with an average decrease of 4 IQ points each in 'normal' children.

④ *Treatments*

- *Remedial help*. Language training and special education programmes are offered in school. Remedial schemes are not always successful because many problems remain outside the clinic or educational setting. In fact, such schemes may be ultimately counterproductive because they encourage retarded children to have unrealistic expectations. **Ringness** (1961) found that mentally retarded children had a larger gap between their expectations and reality than groups of average and high intelligence children. He suggested that such unrealistic attitudes later would cause difficulty when the children had to function in the real world.

- *Special schools.* Learning disabled children can benefit cognitively (greater variety) and socially (intermixing) from mainstream education. Increased contact should also lead to more realistic and favourable attitudes in 'normal' children. For this reason legislation in both America and Britain has abolished special schools. However, in the short term 'normal' children may continue to be biased which means that disabled children continue to learn negative self-attitudes and also have a greater sense of what they cannot do. Research on the reduction of prejudice (unit 1.1.4) shows that equal status may not be enough. **Abrams** *et al.* (1990) found that increased contact had little affect on attitudes and suggested that social identity theory (unit 1.1.1) can be used to explain why hostility is perpetuated at an intergroup level. **Hastings and Graham** (1995) found no attitude differences between 'normal' children in integrated and non-integrated schools, though frequency of contact was associated with more positive attitudes and girls were more positive than boys.
- *Prevention of secondary problems* may be helped by early diagnosis and treatment. However, diagnosis leads to a label (see below) which may be self-fulfilling.

5 *Issues*

- The identification of learning difficulties depends on the use of *IQ tests*, which may be unreliable or invalid (see unit 7.2.1).
- *Mainstream vs. special education* (see above).
- *Labelling.* Labels ('hearing impaired', 'dyslexic', 'retarded') arise from diagnoses and should lead to beneficial treatment. It may be preferable to be labelled 'autistic' rather than being thought of as a 'difficult and wayward child'. However, a label creates a negative stereotype and leads to lower self-expectations. This shapes self-image and has a self-fulfilling effect. The label may be a second handicap which is even more difficult to overcome.

4.1.2 PHYSICAL AND SENSORY HANDICAPS

The World Health Organisation defines:

- *Impairment* as an objective pathology or psychological difficulty.
- *Disability* as the effects of impairment on everyday activities.
- *Handicap* as the effect of impairment on social roles.

Cerebral palsy

1 *Incidence.* About 0.2% of the population.

2 *Cause.* Cerebral palsy is due to brain cell death in the immature motor cortex, usually because of a lack of oxygen (anoxia) before or during birth, or during infancy. It may also be caused by bleeding in the brain, early jaundice, injury or infections.

3 *Primary consequences*

- Cerebral palsy is a motor disability where individuals have difficulty controlling the muscles of their arms, legs and/or head. About 50% can walk by the age of 5.
- Other areas of the brain may also be directly affected, such as the visual or auditory cortex, so that palsied children often have multiple disabilities.
- *Language.* **Wilson** (1970) reported that 7% of palsied children in a survey could not speak and 9% produced speech which was hard to understand, with a further 16% requiring speech therapy.
- *Cognitive impairments* may be a direct result of brain damage or an indirect result of other impairments such as language difficulty which restrict cognitive development. Assessment is difficult in children with poor motor or language skills.
- *Mild anoxia* may cause minimal brain damage and lead to clumsiness and poor intellect. This often goes undiagnosed.

④ *Secondary consequences*

- *Sensorimotor development.* **Held and Hein**'s research (unit 5.1.2) showed that a lack of motor stimulus may damage sensory development. Children with poor co-ordination may experience sensory and cognitive deficits as a result.
- *Social development.* The physical strangeness of palsied children means that some people find social contact difficult with them, leading to a negative self-image. Poor language also makes social contact difficult.
- *Self-image.* As a palsied child gets older (s)he may become depressed by the difficulties of their condition (see unit 6.3.3). Persistent problems such as incontinence or immobility and lack of independence may be chronically depressing.
- *Early separation.* Children who are ill may be separated from parents and even institutionalised (see unit 6.1.2). This impairs cognitive and emotional development.
- *Mild problems* may be unrecognised. This has the advantage of avoiding labelling and the associated negative stereotype, the child will have greater self-expectations and may achieve more as a result. However, if the child finds school difficult, progress may be hindered by feelings of failure and labels of being 'stupid'. The child may be relieved to know the reason for their slow progress and prefer to have been labelled and to have received appropriate remedial education.

⑤ *Treatment*

- *Conductive education* originated by the Peto Institute in Hungary, concentrates on intensive physiotherapy to develop motor skills.

Hearing impairment and deafness

① *Incidence.* Approximately two children in every thousand have some hearing impairment, any such hearing loss deteriorates with age. Only 1% of these children will be profoundly deaf.

② *Causes.* There are three main forms of hearing impairment, which may occur together:

- *Nerve deafness* occurs when parts of the inner ear or auditory nerve are damaged, resulting in the loss of a particular range of auditory frequencies, usually the high ones. Hearing aids can compensate for this loss. The reason for such loss may be due to inherited factors or may have happened in pregnancy from rubella, or as a side effect from some diseases such as multiple sclerosis, it may even develop from prolonged exposure to loud noise.
- *Conductive deafness* occurs when the bones of the middle ear don't transmit noise properly. Such damage is usually caused by infection. Some hearing remains because the inner ear is still functional and sound is transmitted through the skull. It may be possible to correct this surgically.
- *'Glue' or sticky ear* (secretory otitis media) is a common problem in young children. It is caused by the build up of catarrh in the middle ear and, with age, will drain naturally as the Eustachian tubes get larger. However, the child may suffer some cognitive delay because of hearing loss during a critical period of their development and so it is usually treated with surgically implaced grommets.

③ *Primary consequence* is hearing loss. The fact that deaf children often have other visual, mental or learning disorders means that it is rarely possible to observe the effects of deafness in isolation.

④ *Secondary consequences*

- *Language development* is hampered by limited feedback (see unit 5.4.1). About 10% of hearing-impaired children have parents with similar problems.
- *Cognitive impairment.* **Phelps and Branyan** (1990) found that non-verbal IQ scores for pre-linguistically deaf children are consistently one standard deviation or more below normal. This is probably because linguistic deficits hamper learning.
- *Reading difficulties.* **Conrad** (1979) suggested that deaf children inevitably suffer reading deficits because reading is taught through saying words out loud.

- *Social and emotional development.* Social interactions are difficult with impaired language, which affects social, emotional and self-development. Children in residential schools may also be affected emotionally.

⑤ *Treatment.* Early diagnosis is important to minimise secondary consequences.

- *Oral.* Children are helped to communicate with the hearing world through the use of hearing aids and lip reading. Individuals who are deaf from birth are rarely able to communicate effectively orally.
- *Sign languages* are naturally occurring languages, not just adaptations of native languages (see unit 5.4.1 and the development of Nicaraguan sign language). They are fully grammatical and do not restrict cognitive development or thought.
- *Sign systems* are a set of signs which correspond to a native language and permit hearing-impaired people to communicate effortlessly with others. They are not fully grammatical and are slower.

Visual impairment and blindness

① *Incidence.* Total blindness is rare, most so-called 'blind' people in fact have some degree of vision, if only for light and dark. Statutory blindness is defined in terms of acuity and the width of a person's visual field. The incidence is about 0.01% of school children. It is more common in Third World countries due to the prevalence of diseases which cause blindness.

② *Causes*

- Brain damage may cause blindness and such children will have other severe handicaps.
- Congenital cataracts, glaucoma or deformity of the eye.
- Disease: maternal rubella causes visual impairment as does meningitis during childhood.

③ *Primary consequence* is restricted vision.

④ *Secondary consequences*

- *Age.* The effects of such impairment vary depending on the age of onset. If a child has had some experience of sight this makes learning very much easier. Case studies of individuals blind from birth who later become able to see (unit 5.1.2) suggest that, after a certain age, it is not possible to develop visual perception.
- *Cognitive development* starts with sensorimotor development (unit 6.2.1). Visual impairment has a drastic effect on this resulting in a developmental lag in motor, perceptual and cognitive capacities in blind children. **Tait** (1990) found that blind children performed less well than same-age sighted children on Piagetian conservation tasks.
- *Reading.* Braille is a poor substitute for reading because it has a smaller visual field, places greater demand on short-term memory and is harder to learn and slower to process.
- *Social and emotional development.* **Fraiberg** (1977) pointed out that visually impaired children suffer emotionally and cognitively because smiling is important for attachment and eye gaze is a part of pre-speech. Lack of visual contact continues to handicap such children in social intercourse.

Coping with disability

① *Multiple and secondary handicaps.* Most impaired persons experience multiple disabilities and disabilities/handicaps which are not simply additive. Secondary handicaps are not to be confused with multiple disabilities/handicaps. They develop as a direct or indirect result of the primary impairment, for example delays in motor, cognitive, linguistic, social and/or emotional development.

② *Individual differences* influence the degree of difficulty experienced:

- *Personality* and coping skills (see below).
- *Motivation*: some people view their disability/handicap as a challenge.

- *Age* and stage of life.
- *Financial* and *social support* available.
- *Impact on daily life*. In some families, certain disabilities are less of a problem. For example, a sport-oriented family would find it more difficult to adjust to a child with physical disabilities whereas an academic family might find a mentally retarded child more difficult. Similarly, disabilities are more of a disadvantage in fast-moving, urban settings than in a rural community.

3 *Personal development* (see unit 6.3.3)

- *'Looking-glass' self* (unit 6.3.3) will be seriously affected by the negative reactions of others. Disabled children learn to dislike themselves. **Thomas** (1995) reports that negative stereotyping begins at birth because the newborn baby picks up non-verbal signals of sadness and disaffection.
- *Role models* are less available to impaired children. For some impaired, it's not clear whether they belong to the 'handicapped' or the 'normal' population, and this further confuses their sense of identity. **Cowen and Bobrove** (1966) found that the totally disabled were better adjusted than those who had partial disabilities, presumably because their group identity was clearer. In this way, labelling can act as a positive influence.
- *Labelling* (see above).
- *'The sick role'*: expecting to be looked after, being absolved of responsibility, and relinquishing control for major decisions. This is a form of *learned helplessness* (see unit 3.4.3). Overprotection probably only encourages the sick role and prolongs recovery and/or adjustment. If disabled persons are given, and take, greater control, this may lead to improvements in their self-image.
- *Institutionalised care* or residential schools may cause privation and/or disrupted bonds (see unit 6.1.2).

4 *Prejudices*

- *Public attitudes* may be improved through increased contact (see unit 4.1.1).
- *Media images* of disabled persons which elicit pity tend to reinforce outdated stereotypes. The 'charity ethic' directly contradicts the 'independent living ethic'. This suggests that it is better to portray the disabled as people who are as 'in control' and on a par with others, rather than people who need our help.

5 *Strategies for coping* are needed both by disabled individuals and their families.

- *Minimise the seriousness*: prevents a person from being overwhelmed by the various implications.
- *Gather information* about the problem and ways of treating it.
- *Take control*, e.g. the diabetic learning to give self-injections.
- Set concrete, achievable *goals* which give the patient things to look forward to.
- *Recruit help* and emotional support, talk through the future and prepare for unexpected difficulties.
- Find *long-term meaning* for the experience. This may be provided by religion and/or joining a pressure group.

4.1.3 EMOTIONAL DISTURBANCES AND BEHAVIOURAL PROBLEMS

Attention-deficit hyperactivity disorder (ADHD)

1 *Description*. ADHD is characterised by inappropriate inattention, impulsiveness and motor hyperactivity for the child's age. It affects more boys than girls, and tends to appear early.

2 *Possible causes*. The cause is thought to lie with the brain's arousal mechanism, either due to:

- *Overarousal* which leads to continual switching of attention.

- *Underarousal*, the inability to maintain attention. This view is supported by the fact that stimulants appear to reduce hyperactivity. **Whalen** (1989) suggested that ADHD children need extra stimulation because of minimal and undetected brain damage.
- Both may be caused by innate neurological differences or environmental factors such as diet.

3 *Treatment*

- *The Feingold diet* is a diet free of additives. Other programmes have been suggested to avoid specific foods such as milk, chocolate and wheat. **Mattes and Gittelman** (1981) concluded that research has not found evidence that diet and ADHD are linked. **Varley** (1984) suggested that families latch on to the idea of dietary control because it gives them something concrete to do but that any behavioural change is probably due to a placebo effect.
- *Drugs* such as Ritalin. The use of drugs has become widespread in America but is far from desirable when dealing with children because of side effects such as insomnia and loss of appetite.
- *Behaviour modification*, for example the 'time out' method aims to teach parents how to give the child attention for positive rather than negative reasons (see unit 4.4.1).

Autism

1 *Description*. The term autism means 'self-orientation' and it is used to refer to any inwardly directed activities, such as autistic thought. The pathological condition occurs in about 3 children per 10,000 and boys outnumber girls by 3 to 1. It is more common in high socio-economic families, though this may be because it goes unrecognised elsewhere or is labelled differently. It is apparent very early in life and is almost always diagnosed before school age.

Typical features:

- *Social impairment*. The most characteristic behaviour is their aloneness and aversion to physical and social contact with other people. Autistics have few facial expressions, lack empathy and emotion, and fail to develop normal attachments.
- *Linguistic impairments*. The child may be mute or use words in idiosyncratic ways, such as echolalia (to repeat and echo words) or pronominal reversals (swapping 'you' and 'I').
- *Bizarre, stereotyped behaviours* including a fascination with and intense attachment for inanimate objects, mechanical and repetitive behaviour, greater interest in pattern than functional or imaginative play. Such behaviours may be due to difficulty coping with change.
- *Altered sensitivity*. Some autistics have heightened sensitivity, such as feeling overstimulated by crowds of people, whereas others are less sensitive than normal, for example, they may feel little pain.
- *Intelligence*. Children with infantile autism tend to perform poorly on verbal intelligence tests but have 'islands' of intelligence, such as talents in rote memory, music or drawing. This kind of autism was first described by **Kanner** (1943). A second kind of autistic condition exists, called *Asperger's syndrome*, which is associated with normal or even superior intelligence and few neurological problems.
- *Other problems* sometimes co-occur with autism including epileptic seizures or problems of co-ordination.
- *Primary or secondary symptoms?* Some symptoms may only be secondary, for example a lack of sociability may be directly due to innate differences or may result from linguistic deficits in turn caused by cognitive impairments.

2 *Possible causes*. The different symptoms suggest there may be more than one cause.

- *Genetic factors* are implied by the association found between fragile X and autism.
- *Biological factors*. A neurological basis is suggested by the fact that many autistics are also epileptic, have abnormal brain waves and altered sensitivities. Also many typical autistic behaviours, such as repetitive movements, tics and rocking are also seen in people who have some brain damage. The patchy intelligence and linguistic deficits

are also consistent with a brain damage hypothesis. Such damage might be the result of viral infections. For example, in the 1960s, an epidemic of rubella resulted in many babies being affected prenatally and some of them became autistic.

- *Experiential factors.* It is possible that vulnerable individuals only become autistic when they are exposed to what **Kanner** described as emotional refrigeration (parents who are introverted, distant, intellectual and meticulous). **Bettleheim** (1967) suggested the behaviour of autistics was similar to children in concentration camps who withdrew psychologically from their hostile surroundings. However it is unlikely that parents are the *primary* cause, there may well be a poor 'fit' between certain parents and an emotionally difficult child and this leads to autism.
- *Psychological explanations.* **Gardner** (1983) suggested that intelligence is subdivided into different abilities, one of which is *personal intelligence* (the ability to perceive one's own and other people's state of mind). **Hobson** (1986) thought that autistic children might lack a personal intelligence which would mean that they were unable to understand the emotional states of other people and can't develop an understanding that other people can hold different thoughts. He supported this with empirical evidence that autistic children were far less able to match pictures of facial expressions to an emotion. This would explain their lack of pretend play and other social deficits. **Baron-Cohen** (1989) and **Leslie and Frith** (1990) proposed that autistics lack a *Theory of Mind* (ToM). **Baron-Cohen** *et al.* (1985) showed that autistic children had difficulty with a task involving false belief, demonstrating that they could not separate their own thoughts from reality (see unit 3.3.1). (False belief task: if Sally places a marble in her basket, leaves the room and Anne puts it in a box; where will Sally look? Autistic children say she will look in the box.)

❸ *Treatment* includes behaviour therapy, structured education and play therapy.

Developmental dyslexia

❶ *Description.* Dyslexia is a specific learning disability, a difficulty with reading, spelling and writing which is out of proportion to the child's intellectual development and instruction. Boys are more likely to have dyslexia than girls.

- One group of dyslexics tend to have general language disorders in addition to their reading difficulties, such as problems with language acquisition and speech disorders.
- A second broad group have problems generally with visual perception and memory, for example reversals of the letters 'b' and 'd'.
- Associated problems. **Fawcett** (1994) suggested that forgetfulness and clumsiness may be associated with dyslexia.

❷ *Possible causes. Acquired* dyslexia results from either accidental injury or brain disease. *Developmental* dyslexia is suggested to be due to:

- *Genetic factors* because it is more common in boys (sex linked) and has a higher incidence in monozygotic twins (**Wadsworth** *et al.*, 1989).
- *Mixed cerebral dominance.* **Geschwind and Behan** (1982) reported that a disproportionate number of developmental dyslexics are left handed which would mean they had competing language centres (see unit 3.2.2). However not all children with defective lateralisation have reading problems.
- *Minimal brain damage.* If brain damage later in life leads to dyslexia perhaps developmental dyslexia is also caused by brain damage. **Galaburda and Geschwind** (1984) reported evidence of an association between left-sided EEG abnormalities and developmental dyslexics.
- *The effects of experience.* **Vellutino** *et al.* (1973) found that dyslexic children were less able to copy from memory words of about four letters, but they were just as good as normal readers when they were given words in Hebrew. This suggests that reading failure at least compounds the problem.

There are difficulties separating causes from effects, though it has been suggested that dyslexics have problems:

- *Processing visual information.* **Vellutino** (1979) showed that dyslexic children were slower at matching visual and verbal images than 'normal' readers. **Farnham-Diggory** (1978) showed that dyslexic children were slower at processing visual images: they needed nearly double the exposure time as normal children before they could say or draw a figure.
- *Processing speech sounds.* **Olsen** *et al.* (1989) found that dyslexic children had more difficulty moving a sound from one part of a word to another part.

❸ *Criticisms*

- **Whittaker** (1982) suggested that the concept had become too broad to be useful. Simply labelling a problem does not lead to a magical cure.
- **Snowling** (1987) has criticised the definition of dyslexia because it lacks preciseness. It might be better described as difficulty learning to read, erratic spelling and problems manipulating written as opposed to spoken words.
- The label may have a detrimental effect because it encourages the parent or child to give up any further efforts to change the situation, accepting that the cause is constitutional and something which has to be lived with.
- People prefer the label 'dyslexic' to 'slow reader' because the former suggests underachievement and should promote remedial efforts.
- There is a debate over whether dyslexia represents a specific problem or is one end of a continuum.

❹ *Treatment*

- *Structured multisensory method.* **Gillingham and Stillman** (1956) suggested that a child should be introduced to new spelling patterns as a total experience: see it, say it, read it and feel it (as wooden letters). **Hulme** (1981) demonstrated that poor readers were better able to remember strings of letters if they traced them.
- *Miscue analysis.* Teachers should analyse mistakes.

4.2 CONCEPTIONS AND MODELS OF ABNORMALITY

4.2.1 DEFINITIONS AND CLASSIFICATIONS OF NORMAL AND ABNORMAL BEHAVIOURS

Defining abnormal behaviour

Definitions are required for legal and social purposes.

❶ *Deviation from a statistical norm.* 'Abnormal' means 'deviating from what is usual'. A norm is a standard, something which is most frequent, typical, usual or average. The normal curve delineates areas of normal behaviour, 95% of the population lie within two standard deviations of the mean on any measure which is normally distributed such as shoe size or intelligence.

Criticisms

- Many unusual behaviours, such as genius, are statistically uncommon but not aberrant, in fact they may be highly desirable.
- Some undesirable behaviours or disorders, such as chicken pox, anxiety, divorce or depression, are *statistically* normal.
- What is common at a certain age or in a certain context, is not universally applicable – there are different developmental and cultural norms.
- How far does one need to deviate to be considered abnormal?

② *Social deviation.* Abnormality can be defined in terms of certain standards of social behaviour. Examples of deviation through history have been witchcraft, homosexuality, unmarried motherhood, delinquency and political dissent.

Criticisms. Social deviations vary according to prevailing moral perspectives and this approach allows serious abuse of individual rights.

③ *Deviation from mental health.* Doctors use the concept of physical health as a yardstick to measure ill-health (for example a body temperature outside the normal range indicates illness). **Jahoda** (1958) suggested that we could define psychological well-being in order to recognise mental illness. The key features would be: self-acceptance, potential for growth and development, autonomy, accurate perception of reality, environmental competence and positive interpersonal relations. **Rogers** (1959) also defined abnormality in terms of the characteristics of a mentally healthy person, namely a sense of self and self-acceptance.

Criticisms

- Such approaches are influenced by cultural attitudes, for example autonomy is not a universal ideal (see unit 7.2.3).
- The list is idealistic, few people actually manage to achieve most of them.
- The concepts are too vague for the purpose of diagnosis.

④ *Dysfunction and distress.* Certain behaviours are dysfunctional for the individual. For example, they disrupt the ability to work and/or to conduct satisfying relations with people. This approach is similar to the concept of mental health because it suggests a 'functional' state. In some situations apparently dysfunctional behaviour may be functional, for example depression can be an adaptive response to stress.

Many people seek psychiatric help because they feel distressed, however not all mental disorders are accompanied by a state of distress (e.g. antisocial personality disorder) while in other situations distress is a 'healthy' response (e.g. the death of a close friend). It might be preferable to include the distress of others as a feature of mental illness.

Rosenhan and Seligman (1989) suggested that certain elements *jointly* determine abnormality, singly they may cause no problem but when several co-occur they are symptomatic of abnormality: suffering, maladaptiveness (personally and socially), irrationality and incomprehensibility, unpredictability and loss of control, vividness and unconventionality, observer discomfort, and violation of moral and ideal standards.

Criticisms

- Using the concepts of dysfunction and distress acknowledges the subjective experience of the individual.
- Diagnoses of dysfunction and distress require judgements to be made by others, which are inevitably influenced by social and cultural mores.

The classification of abnormal behaviour

① *Classification schemes.* A group of symptoms which regularly co-occur are called a *syndrome*. If there is sufficient agreement among clinicians a syndrome may be regarded as a *category* of mental disorder. Such categories form a classification scheme. The DSM-IV is used in America. The ICD-10 (1993) is published by the World Health Organisation and used in Britain:

Category	Examples
Organic mental disorders	Alzheimer's, senile dementia, brain disease
Substance abuse disorders	alcohol, cannabis, cocaine, hallucinogens
Schizophrenia	e.g. catatonic, disorganised; also persistent delusional disorders
Mood (affective) disorders	depression, manic-depression
Neurotic, stress-related and somatoform disorders	phobias, anxiety disorders, obsessive-compulsive, post-traumatic stress, dissociative (multiple personality)
Behavioural syndromes	eating disorders, non-organic sleep disorders (e.g. night terrors) *(contd)*

Category	Examples
Disorders of adult personality	specific personality disorders (e.g. schizoid), habit disorders (e.g. pathological gambling), gender, identity and sexual disorders (e.g. transsexualism, pedophilia)
Mental retardation	
Disorders of psychological development	specific learning disorders (developmental dyslexia), autism
Childhood emotional and behavioural disorders	conduct disorder, stuttering, non-organic enuresis
Unspecified mental disorder	

② *Psychoses and neuroses.* The traditional distinction between psychoses and neuroses has been dropped from current classification schemes because it is an inaccurate dichotomy. However, the terms remain in use probably because they reflect some important characteristics of mental illness.

	Psychoses	Neuroses
Example	schizophrenia	phobia
The whole personality is affected	yes	no
Contact with reality is maintained	no	yes
The patient has insight into their condition	no	yes
Behaviour is different	qualitatively	quantitatively
Relationship with 'normal' behaviour	discontinuous	exaggerated
Related to patient's premorbid personality	no	yes
Most likely treatment	psychological	physical

Using classification schemes: diagnosis

Diagnosis is the identification of a disease by its symptoms, using a scheme of classification.

① *Tools of diagnosis*
- *Structured interviews* enable standardised judgements to be made and can be scored by a computer, e.g. SADS (Schedule of Affective Disorders and Schizophrenia).
- *Unstructured interviews* are influenced by the clinician's perspective.
- *Testing*: intelligence tests, or personality tests (see unit 7.2.1).
- *Classification scheme*: DSM and ICD.

② *Advantages of diagnosis and classification*
- Form of communication shorthand.
- May indicate a cause, and lead to an appropriate treatment.
- Useful in assessing any later improvement or deterioration.
- Helpful for empirical research.

③ *Limitations of diagnosis and classification.* Is diagnosis an effective tool?

Reliability. Are diagnoses consistent?
- **Beck** *et al.* (1962) found that the agreement among diagnosticians was at about the level of chance. **Zigler and Phillips** (1961) found between 54–84% agreement.

Validity. Are diagnoses based on reality?
- The *prestige effect*: psychiatrists influence each other's diagnoses, particularly where one is held in esteem.
- **Heather** (1976) claimed that the same diagnosis had a 50:50 chance of leading to the same or a different treatment, which suggests that diagnoses lack validity.
- **Zigler and Phillips** (1961) found that the symptom of depression was just as likely to be found in someone diagnosed as manic–depressive as in someone labelled 'neurotic', and in 25% of those termed schizophrenic. This suggests that a diagnosis conveys little information about a patient.

- **Rosenhan** (1973) arranged for eight 'normal' students to be examined by admitting doctors in psychiatric hospitals. They were instructed to behave normally except for reporting that they heard a voice. All except one was admitted as schizophrenic, and later released (between 2 and 52 days later) as schizophrenics in remission (a rare diagnosis which might suggest a recognition of unusual circumstances). It would seem that the context mattered more than the symptoms. Though it might be a case of a type II error, psychiatrists preferred to call a healthy person sick rather than a sick person healthy.
- What would happen if the hospital knew some new patients were stooges? **Rosenhan** arranged that a hospital expected one or more pseudopatients over a period of three months. In that time 193 patients were admitted and all staff were asked to rate the likelihood of whether they were 'real'. In fact all patients were genuine but more than 20% were judged as pseudopatients by one member of staff and 10% were judged so by two members of staff.

  Conclusion. The fact that diagnoses can be unreliable and inaccurate (invalid) suggests they should not be used. However, the same is at least partly true of medical diagnosis generally, yet we wouldn't suggest abandoning that. Diagnosis and assessment are fundamental to treatment and necessary for scientific advancement. The latest revisions (DSM-IV and ICD-10) claim to be more reliable.

④ *Ethical considerations*

- *Labelling* a collection of symptoms creates an illusion of causation and cure. Labels related to mental illness are global (a person becomes a schizophrenic rather than an individual with schizophrenia) and 'sticky' (hard to remove).
- *Culture bias.* Western classification systems are an imposed etic (see unit 7.2.3). They are biased against people from different cultures (see unit 4.2.3)

4.2.2 MODELS OF ABNORMAL PSYCHOLOGY

Reference should be made to unit 4.4.1, for the therapies related to each of the models.

① *The medical model* asserts that psychological symptoms are manifestations of an underlying biochemical or physiological dysfunction, which may or may not have a known cause. Symptoms need to be identified and syndromes diagnosed, followed by appropriate somatic treatment(s).

Support

- *General paresis* was a mental disorder known since the 16th century. **Krafft-Ebing** (1897) was able to demonstrate that the symptoms had an organic cause, the syphilis bacterium. The medical treatment of insanity was a move in the direction of humanity: the illness rather than the patient was blamed.
- Knowledge about genetic inheritance, biochemicals and other diseases provides further support for the medical model (see units 4.3.1 and 4.3.2).

Criticisms

- **Szasz** ('The Myth of Mental Illness', 1960) argued that the medical model is 'worthless and misleading' and 'scientifically crippling' because it prevents us investigating the true problems, it undermines personal responsibility, and it ignores socially expressed symptoms which are better viewed as problems in living. He claimed that it is a modern day version of demonology and serves the same political purposes, namely social control by those invested with undisputed authority – the medical profession.
- **Heather** (1976) argued that whereas psychoses may be found to have organic causes, the same is not true for neuroses.

Evaluation

- The approach purports to be value-free and scientific, but is just as subject to prevailing attitudes as other models. **Clare** (1980) pointed out that all illness has a physical and mental component and is defined in terms of current views and knowledge. Therefore Szasz's criticisms apply to physical as well as mental illnesses.

- It overlooks the fact that mental disturbance is defined in terms of social difficulties and therefore the application of medical principles is inappropriate.
- At least some disorders have a biological basis, however an exclusive emphasis on biological bases may mean that other factors are overlooked.
- Control is taken away from the patient, who relies on expert guidance.
- The use of medical (drug) therapies has changed the face of psychiatry for good and bad (see unit 4.4.1).

2 *The psychodynamic model.* Freud (a doctor) challenged the physical origin of mental illness. His view was that mental illness was caused by unresolved, unconscious conflicts originating in childhood. Recovery depends on insight and working through past problems (see unit 7.1.1 for more on the psychodynamic perspective).

- Instinctual drives are satisfied during the stages of childhood (oral, anal and phallic), any disturbance results in a fixation and anxiety.
- Defence mechanisms, such as the repression of unpleasant memories, serve to protect the ego.
- Neurotic symptoms are the result of conflicts between repressed or unfulfilled desires and attempts to control or resolve them.

Evaluation

- It is not a scientifically rigorous approach, the model is based on research with a limited sample (Freud's middle-class Viennese clients), but it is supported by extensive theory and practice.
- It is a reductionist model, suggesting that the patient is controlled by instinctual forces and help must come from an expert.
- It is a determinist model based on innate, biological mechanisms with some room for cultural influences.

3 *The behavioural model.* Behaviourists (see unit 7.1.1) suggest that abnormal behaviours are learned, like any other behaviour.

- Psychological problems are seen as maladaptive behaviour patterns which have arisen through traumatic or inappropriate learning.
- What was learned can be re- or unlearned using classical or operant conditioning techniques
- Only behaviours which are currently observable are important, the patient's history doesn't matter.

Evaluation

- The therapies are successful for certain disorders.
- It is an empirical approach, which facilitates research and assessment.
- As only symptoms are treated, the underlying problems remain, though behaviourists argue that the symptoms are all that matters.
- It is a reductionist, deterministic approach.

4 *The cognitive model* emphasises the role of thoughts, expectations and attitudes (i.e. cognitions) in mental illness, either as causes or mediating factors. It is the way you think about a situation which is maladaptive.

- **Ellis** (1962) suggested that *irrational assumptions* lead to mental disorders. **Beck** (1967) used the phrase *cognitive errors* and **Meichenbaum** (1976) described them as *counterproductive self-statements*.
- The approach grew out of the behavioural perspective, and a dissatisfaction with the emphasis on external factors only.
- Cognitive therapies aim to restructure a patient's thinking and enable them to change their self-beliefs and motivations. The psychotherapy is client-centred – only the client knows their own cognitions.

Evaluation

- Behaviourists regard cognitive concepts as unnecessary, humanists regard them as mechanistic.

- Like the behavioural model, this approach does not investigate causes but just treats behaviours.
- The therapies have been successful.

5 *The humanist model* (see unit 7.1.1). **Rogers** (1959) suggested that *unconditional positive regard* from significant others enables healthy personality development, particularly high self-esteem and self-acceptance. Only under such conditions is a person able to assimilate contradictory emotions and thereby accept themselves. This frees the individual from striving for social approval and enables him/her to seek self-actualisation. Conditional love leads to maladjustment because the self and ideal self are in conflict.

A therapist offers unconditional positive regard to allow the patient to enable healthy self-development and self-determination.

Evaluation

- This is an approach of our age. Rogers said that he had 'expressed an idea whose time had come'.
- The therapy has wide application and has been very influential.
- The model lacks rigour and is not readily susceptible to scientific analysis.
- It is class- and culture-specific, for example the goal of self-actualisation is a middle-class Western ideal.

Summary table

Model:	Medical	Psychodynamic	Behavioural	Cognitive	Humanist
Cause of mental illness	organic	unresolved problems	inappropriate learning	irrational thoughts	poor sense of self-worth
Location of cause	internal	internal	external	internal	internal
Treatment	somatic	psychotherapy	conditioning	cognitive restructuring	counselling
Who is in control?	the doctor	the therapist	the therapist	the patient	the client

4.2.3 CULTURAL AND SUBCULTURAL DIFFERENCES

1 *Gender and mental illness.* Women are more likely to experience depression than men. This may be explained:

- *Biologically.* Women experience hormonal changes during their menstrual cycle, the menopause and pregnancy.
- *Non-biologically.* **Cochrane** (1995) pointed out that men are encouraged to take control of their lives whereas the traditional female gender role is one of unquestioning acceptance, similar to learned helplessness which can lead to depression (see unit 3.4.3). Girls are also more likely to be abused than boys, and this could explain why overall they suffer depression more frequently.
- **Bem** (1993) proposed that attempts to explain female behaviour as 'sick', as in the battered woman's syndrome, are mistaken. Female behaviour is a sane response to a male-centred world but society makes female behaviour appear pathological (see unit 7.2.3). This is similar to Laing's view that abnormal behaviour was a normal response to an insane world.

2 *Social class and mental illness.* **Srole et al.** (1961) found a negative correlation between social class and psychiatric impairment in New York City, **Cochrane and Stopes-Roe** (1980) found a similar correlation in Britain. Possible reasons for an positive association between low social class and mental illness:

- *Stress.* Low socio-economic status is associated with many disadvantages, such as economic uncertainty, poor housing and difficult relationships. These create stress which, in turn, is related to poor health (see unit 3.4.3). Lower-class individuals may have less access to coping resources (see unit 3.4.4).
- *'Drift'.* Individuals suffering from mental illness may sink to low socio-economic status so that it *appears* that class is a causal factor whereas it is an effect. **Turner and**

Wagenfeld (1967) surveyed schizophrenics in the whole of New York State. They found an equal number of sufferers whose fathers had low occupational status as high status, which does not support a drift hypothesis. However, overall the schizophrenics had lower occupational levels than the general population which suggests some drift.

- *Bias in diagnosis.* It is possible that lower-class people receive less favourable judgements because of professional biases. **Johnstone** (1989) found that lower-class patients were more likely to spend longer in hospital, be prescribed physical treatments and had a poorer prognosis. They may be less able to benefit from treatments which require good verbal skills, which removes their autonomy.

③ *Culture and mental illness.* **Berry *et al.*** (1992) suggested that particular mental illnesses are either:

- *Absolute*: found in all cultures in the same form.
- *Universal*: found in all cultures but expression is different and affected by prevailing beliefs. It is unlikely that any mental illnesses are absolute, even those which are specific to organic states vary in expression and can be linked to cultural expectations. For example, in the 1920s schizophrenics complained of mind invasions by radio waves, in the 1950s this was TV signals, and, in cultures where witchcraft persists, the invasion is by spirits.
- *Culturally relative.* There are some illnesses which are only found in particular cultures, such as *koro*, a culture-bound disorder found in Southeast Asian males who fear that their penis will retract into their abdomen and cause their death.

④ *Culture and the diagnosis of mental illness.* **Cochrane** (1977) found that more people of African-Caribbean origins were diagnosed as schizophrenic than whites (possibly seven times as many). This may be because:

- The disease has a *genetic origin* and its incidence is higher in this group of people, like sickle cell anaemia. But diagnosis rates for African-Caribbeans are not as high elsewhere in the world.
- Members of minority ethnic groups in Britain have *more stressful lives* (see above).
- Some of the *characteristics symptoms* of schizophrenia are 'abnormal' for white British people but 'normal' for other cultural groups, such as hearing voices. The reverse is also true, what we regard as normal or desirable is a cultural ideal, such as the desire for self-actualisation.
- Delusions of persecution may be a response to the experience of discrimination – a sane response to an insane world. **Littlewood and Lipsedge** (1989) suggest that the majority of West Indian patients in British hospitals diagnosed as schizophrenic are actually suffering from an acute stress reaction ('West Indian Psychosis') to their disadvantaged social conditions. Feeling that 'someone is out to get me' may be a real fear but may be diagnosed as a mental illness.

4.3 PSYCHOPATHOLOGY

4.3.1 SCHIZOPHRENIA

① *Description.* Schizophrenia means literally 'split-mind' but is wrongly confused with split or multiple personality. It is a group of psychoses which are characterised by:

- Loss of contact with reality.
- *Thought disturbance* (positive symptoms) such as thought insertion (e.g. thoughts controlled by aliens), hallucinations (e.g. hearing voices) and delusions (e.g. of grandeur).
- *Disturbances of affect/volition* (negative symptoms) such as withdrawal, flattened and inappropriate affect, reduced motivation, and difficulty planning and carrying out actions.

- *Psychomotor disturbances* such as catatonia (immobility, bizarre statues), stereotypy (e.g. rocking) and frenetic activity (e.g. strange grimaces).
- The symptoms should last for more than six months, and appear before the age of 45. It was once called 'dementia praecox' (early senility).

② *Types of schizophrenia.* In the past a distinction was made between type I (positive/acute/functional cause) and type II (negative/chronic/organic cause) schizophrenia. DSM-IV includes:

- *Paranoid* type: positive symptoms such as delusions and auditory hallucinations. Sufferers are able to carry on daily functions because awareness and language are relatively unimpaired.
- *Disorganised* type: disorganised speech and behaviour, vivid hallucinations, flat emotion, and inappropriate affect. The most severe form appears in adolescence/early adulthood and is progressive and irreversible.
- *Catatonic type*: apathy and psychomotor disturbances.

③ *Recovery.* The prognosis is divided equally between three groups:

- One or a few acute episodes followed by full recovery.
- Periodic acute episodes throughout life, near normal life during remission.
- Persistent deterioration which may be partly alleviated by drug therapy.

④ *Possible causes: genetic*

- *Twin* studies. **Gottesman and Shields** (1972) found that concordance rates for schizophrenia in non-identical twins is about 9% whereas it rises to 42% in identical twins, indicating some environmental influence but a larger genetic component.
- *Adoption* studies. **Heston** (1966) found that adopted children whose natural mothers were schizophrenic were five times more likely to be diagnosed schizophrenic than those of normal natural mothers.
- *Family* studies. **Kendler** *et al.* (1985) found that first-degree relatives of schizophrenics are 18 times more likely to be similarly diagnosed. Family similarities can also be explained by shared environmental influences.
- *Viral.* **Crow** (1984) proposed that a retrovirus, which becomes incorporated into DNA, causes schizophrenia and is passed on to offspring. This is consistent with a number of facts, including gradual brain damage and the appearance of schizophrenia in families where it never occurred before.
- *Chromosomes.* **Sherrington** *et al.* (1988) found evidence for a cluster of genes on chromosome 5, which might make an individual susceptible. Subsequent studies have not confirmed this.

Evaluation. Genetic factors are involved but are not solely responsible.

⑤ *Possible causes: neurological.* If schizophrenia is transmitted genetically then there should be neurological differences.

- *Neuroanatomical* evidence. Post-mortem examinations of some schizophrenics show that their brains are 6% lighter and have fewer neurons in the cerebral cortex. PET and CAT scans show that schizophrenics have larger ventricles in their brains and they have a smaller than normal frontal cortex.
- *Neurochemical* evidence. Dopamine activity has been linked to psychotic-type behaviour:
  - Drugs used to alleviate schizophrenic symptoms (antipsychotic drugs) block dopamine synapses and the release of dopamine.
  - The side-effects of antipsychotic drugs are similar to the symptoms of Parkinson's disease, a condition associated with low levels of dopamine which is improved through the use of L-dopa.
  - Psychotic states can be induced by large doses of amphetamines, cocaine, LSD and L-dopa. All of these drugs stimulate the dopamine synapses.
  - If L-dopa is given to schizophrenics it aggravates their symptoms.
  - Post-mortem examinations of schizophrenics show abnormally high levels of dopamine.

- *Known organic disorders*, such as brain tumours, lead to psychotic states suggesting an organic basis for schizophrenia.

   Evaluation. Neurological differences may be causes or effects. They may be due to genetic factors or could arise from:

- *Birth complications.* **Harrison** (1995) found that at least some schizophrenics may have experienced brain damage from anoxia at birth.
- *Viral infections.* **Torrey** (1988) confirmed that schizophrenics are more likely to be born in late winter and early spring, which may be due to seasonal viral variation (e.g. chickenpox) leading to poor prenatal brain development. **Barr** *et al.* (1990) found an increased incidence of schizophrenia in children whose mothers had flu when five months pregnant during the 1957 pandemic. Studies in some other countries have not confirmed this (**O'Callaghan** *et al.*, 1994).

6 *Possible causes: psychological*

- *Schizophrenogenic families* (**Fromm-Reichman**, 1948) have high emotional tension and many secrets, their mothers are cold and promote feelings of guilt, their fathers are ineffectual. **Wynne** *et al.* (1977) suggested that some families have deviant communication systems which confuse their children.
- *A learned response.* **Bateson** *et al.* (1956) proposed that schizophrenia is a learned response to mutually exclusive demands being made on a child, neither of which can be made or avoided (a *double-bind* theory). **Laing** (1959) also regarded schizophrenia as a sane response to a disordered environment.
- *Social factors* (see unit 4.2.3).

Evaluation

- The genetic evidence shows that any account must include biological factors.
- It is wrong to conclude that observed family relations are a cause, they may be an effect because studies of schizophrenogenic families usually occur considerably after the onset of the disease and therefore the dynamics have probably been altered by the stresses of having an ill son/daughter.
- Family abnormalities may be a reasonable response to an unusual child (i.e. one with brain damage).
- Why do only some family members suffer? If the family is at fault, all children should develop the disorder. This suggests that only vulnerable individuals are affected or those who are a scapegoat.
- Environmental factors may be more important in understanding the course rather than the cause of schizophrenia. The *EE model* proposes that schizophrenics with families expressing high levels of emotion (high EE) such as criticism and over-concern, are less likely to recover. **Vaughn and Leff** (1976) found 51% relapse in schizophrenics returning to high EE homes compared with 13% relapse for those returning to low EE homes. **Doune** *et al.* (1985) found that recurrence rates were lower if families learned to reduce their criticism and intrusiveness.

7 *Possible causes: the diathesis-stress model* describes an interaction between biological and environmental factors. 'Diathesis' means susceptibility to illness, 'stress' is the psychological reaction to meaningful events. The more susceptible you are the less stress is required to *trigger* schizophrenic symptoms. Possible triggers include:

- Adverse family circumstances.
- Major life events.
- Traumatic experiences.

   Evaluation. This seems to present the best summary of available evidence though **Rabkin** (1980) found that schizophrenics do not report significantly more stressful episodes during the months preceding the initial onset of the disorder.

4.3.2 DEPRESSION

Depression is a disorder of mood or affect. It may exist on its own or is often just one symptom of a more involved disorder.

Major depression

1 *Description.* The symptoms of clinical depression are similar to 'normal' depression, but more intense and long-lasting:

- *Emotional*: sadness, melancholy, self-involvement, guilt, thoughts of suicide.
- *Motivational*: passivity, loss of interest and energy.
- *Cognitive*: hopelessness, pessimism, lack of self-esteem.
- *Somatic*: loss or increase of appetite and weight; sleep disturbance (insomnia or oversleeping).

2 *Prognosis.* On average chronically depressed patients recover spontaneously after about three months. About 10% of patients remain depressed.

3 *Possible causes: biological*

- *Genetic.* **Allen** (1976) found that identical twins showed concordance for major depression only 40% of the time compared with 72% for bipolar depression.
- *Neurochemical.* **Schildkraut** (1965) suggested that too little noradrenalin results in depression. **Teuting** *et al.* (1981) analysed the urine of depressed and normal people and found lower levels of products associated with noradrenalin in the former. Antidepressant drugs do increase the availability of noradrenalin, though the effects are not the same for everyone.
- *Hormonal.* Some forms of depression, such as post-partum depression, pre-menstrual syndrome and seasonal affective disorder (see unit 3.3.1) are linked to hormonal changes.

4 *Possible causes: psychological*

- *Stress.* Depression can be an adaptive response to stress (see unit 3.4.3).
- *Behavioural.* **Seligman** (1975) proposed that 'learned helplessness' can explain the occurrence of depression (see units 1.1.2 and 3.4.3). **Lewinsohn** (1974) suggested that depressed persons become trapped in a cycle of social withdrawal which leads to a lack of positive reinforcement which perpetuates the depression. Socially unskilled individuals may be more prone to depression.
- *Psychodynamic.* Loss in early life leads to depression later. **Bifulco** *et al.* (1992) followed 249 women who had lost mothers, through separation or death before they were 17. This group were twice as likely to suffer from depressive or anxiety disorders as adults.
- *Social and gender* factors (see unit 4.2.3).
- *The diathesis-stress model*: life events may be triggering factors for vulnerable individuals.

Bipolar depression: manic depression

1 *Description*

- *Depression* (see characteristics, above).
- *Elation*: euphoria, hyperactivity, sleeplessness; the person behaves in socially unacceptable ways and makes grandiose and unrealistic plans.

The two phases (mania/elation and depression) may occur independently or oscillate over weeks and months with normal spells in between. The syndrome is associated with creativity and its attendant grandiosity may lead to great achievements. Many successful and famous people (e.g. Winston Churchill and Abraham Lincoln) were sufferers. However, for many it is a crippling disorder which ruins their lives.

2 *Possible causes: biological*

- *Twin* studies. **Allen** (1976) found that identical twins had a concordance rate of 72%.
- *Adoption* studies. **Gershon** (1983) looked at adopted persons with manic depression, 2% of their adoptive parents had the disorder whereas 30% of their biological parents had it.
- *Chromosome* evidence. **Egeland** *et al.* (1987) studied the Amish, an American religious sect with a comparatively undiluted gene pool and high incidence of manic depression. They found a cluster of genes on chromosome 11 which were present in

63% of those with the disorder. This may explain a predisposition but does not account for all incidence. It may be that more than one chromosome is involved. **Baron** *et al.* (1987) found a marker on the X chromosome. Other studies of families (e.g. **Hodgkinson** *et al.*, 1987) with high incidence rates have failed to find any common marker on chromosome 11.

- *Neurological* evidence. **Kety** (1975) suggested that serotonin regulates noradrenalin levels, when serotonin is low noradrenalin fluctuates wildly causing highs and lows (serotonin and noradrenalin are biogenic amines, therefore it is called the *permissive amine theory of mood disorder*).

❸ *Possible causes: psychological*

- *Psychodynamic* theory suggests that bipolar depression results from alternating dominance of the personality by the superego (depression) and the ego (elation).
- *Diathesis-stress model.* Vulnerable individuals will develop mania and/or depression under stressful conditions.

4.3.3 ANXIETY DISORDERS

Anxiety, like depression, can be an adaptive response to stress (see unit 3.4.3).

Phobias

❶ *Description*: extreme, persistent, irrational fear with lack of control, which is strongly out of proportion with the danger. A fear becomes a phobia when it interferes with normal functioning. Three categories are distinguished by DSM–IV:

- *Agoraphobia*: fear of open spaces, often associated with panic attacks.
- *Social phobias* such as talking or eating in public, an exaggeration of fears we all have of being anxious in social situations.
- *Specific phobias*: such as zoophobias (animals).

❷ *Possible causes: biological*

- *Twin* studies. **Torgersen** (1983) found 31% concordance in 13 identical twins versus zero concordance in non-identical twins.
- *Family* studies. **Solyom** *et al.* (1974) found that 45% of phobic patients studied had a family history of the disorder compared with 17% of 'normal' controls.
- *Biological preparedness.* **Seligman** (1971) suggested that we have an innate predisposition to develop certain fears (see units 2.4.1 and 2.4.4).

❸ *Possible causes: psychological*

- *Psychodynamic*. **Freud** (1909) suggested that phobias arise when anxieties are displaced onto the phobic object which symbolises the initial conflict, if the conflict is resolved the phobia will disappear. This theory was based on his case study of 'Little Hans' whose fear of horses stopped him leaving the house. Freud suggested that the fear represented the boy's unconscious fear of his father. It is equally possible that Hans developed his fear through classical conditioning and it would have disappeared without Freud's intervention.
- *Classical conditioning*: **Watson and Rayner** (1920) conditioned 'Little Albert' to fear white furry objects by pairing a loud noise with a furry object. It is likely that most phobias are learned through the association of trauma with some neutral stimulus, a case of aversion learning (see unit 2.4.1). However, some fears may be innate (see above) and not everyone who is exposed to such conditioning develops phobias.
- *Social learning*. People learn fears from cultural beliefs, which explains cultural differences.
- *Cognitive*. Phobias are the result of irrational thoughts (see unit 4.2.2 on cognitive explanations). For example, the sensation of crowding in a lift may evolve into an cognition that lifts are associated with suffocation.
- *Diathesis-stress model.* An individual who has vulnerability (through biological factors or early life experiences) will be more likely to develop a phobic reaction when stressed through life events and/or hassles (see unit 3.4.3).

Post-traumatic stress disorder (PTSD)

① *Description.* PTSD is a disabling reaction to stress following a traumatic event. These are exceptional events which threaten survival. The response does not always appear immediately after the event but may be delayed. The reactions are long-lasting:

- *Reliving*: the person relives the event recurrently in flashbacks and dreams.
- *Emotional numbness* and avoidance of things which serve as a reminder.
- *General anxiety* and arousal not previously present, including overalertness, trouble concentrating, impairments of memory, irritability and outbursts of anger.
- *Guilt* about surviving.

The label PTSD is relatively new but the symptoms have been long recognised and called, for example, shell shock or combat fatigue.

② *Possible causes: biological*

- *Physiological stress response* (see unit 3.4.3). **Kosten** *et al.* (1987) found that PTSD patients had higher than normal levels of noradrenalin. Trauma may damage the noradrenalin system and the raised levels lead to heightened sensitivity.
- *Prolonged stress* leads to a depletion of noradrenalin and lowered resilience to stress.

③ *Possible causes: psychological*

- *Traumatic experience* is the prime cause but not everyone involved in the trauma develops PTSD. Therefore the diathesis-stress model should be used to explain the cause.
- *One-trial conditioning.* The individual may be learning a severe avoidance reaction.
- *Cognitive.* Lack of control may be one of the key factors, since such traumas disorder our orderly world.

4.3.4 EATING DISORDERS

Anorexia nervosa

① *Description.* Anorexia is literally a 'nervous lack of appetite'.

- The deliberate and prolonged restriction of calorie intake and considerable weight loss (less than 85% of normal weight).
- Accompanied by amenorrhea (no menstrual cycle).
- Anorexics have a disturbed body image, they usually continue to see themselves as overweight despite large weight loss and have an intense fear of gaining weight.
- Anorexics are often very hungry and preoccupied with food.
- It is largely a problem of middle-class, adolescent girls. It affects about 0.5–1% of all 12–18 year olds, 90% of those affected are women.
- Mortality: **Crisp** *et al.* (1992) estimated around 10% mortality arising from starvation, electrolyte imbalance or suicide.
- It is sometimes seen as a modern problem, however **Tolstrup** (1990) documented cases prior to 1600, when the condition was described in connection with religious life.

② *Possible causes: biological*

- *Twin* studies. **Holland** *et al.* (1984) found a 55% concordance rate for identical twins compared with only 7% for non-identical.
- *Neuroanatomy.* Damage to the hypothalamus may result in a loss of appetite (see unit 3.1.2). There is no specific evidence to link this with anorexia.
- *Hormones.* Amenorrhea may occur before weight loss which suggests a disorder of the endocrine system. However, it is difficult to separate cause and effect.

③ *Possible causes: psychological*

- *Feminine stereotypes* in the media and the current emphasis on dieting promote a desire to be thin which is exaggerated by vulnerable individuals. Anorexia is more common in, for example, models (**Garfinkel and Garner**, 1982).
- *Behavioural view.* People praise weight loss, this is positively reinforcing and self-perpetuating. Anorexia may also be a kind of phobia.

- *Traumatic experience.* Anorexics often report experiences of sexual abuse. This may lead to a desire to destroy their own body.
- *Rejection of womanhood.* Weight loss is a means of warding off maturity by preventing the full female form developing. It also stops menstruation. This cannot explain male anorexia.
- *Autonomy.* Anorexics may be conformists with domineering parents. During adolescence they feel lacking in self-determination and wish to separate themselves from their parents. Anorexia is a means of exerting control over their body. The fact that most anorexics came from middle-class families where there are high expectations supports this.
- *Personality.* Anorexics tend to be somewhat obsessive personalities, with low self-esteem and a fear of their own autonomy. **Bruch** (1987) suggested that certain mothers wish their daughters to remain dependent and therefore encourage anorexia, equally the daughters wish to remain as children.

Bulimia nervosa

1 *Description.* A more common problem than anorexia and probably more related to dieting.

- It is characterised by periods of compulsive bingeing followed by forced vomiting or the use of laxatives or other means.
- Their weight is usually nearer normal.
- It is estimated to affect 1–5% of the female population over 20, and very few males.
- 'Binge eating' is fairly normal, as a means of dieting. However, when it occurs more than three times a week it is abnormal. The abnormal behaviour also involves eating enormous amounts of high calorie food and then purging.
- Secondary problems arise from the persistent vomiting, for example tooth decay from the acid of the vomit.
- Some anorexics become bulimics.

2 *Possible causes: biological*

- *Twin* studies. **Kendler** *et al.* (1991) found a 23% concordance rate for identical twins compared with about 9% in non-identical twins.
- *Neuroanatomical.* As for anorexia.

3 *Possible causes: psychological*

- Associated with depression and sexual abuse.
- Binge-purge is a means of relieving anxiety and anger. It also provides a sense of control, as for anorexics.
- *Personality: disinhibition hypothesis.* **Ruderman** (1986) suggested that when a dieter is very rigid they respond to situations of overeating by going over the top (becoming disinhibited). Once they have overeaten they purge to rectify their mistake.

4.4 THERAPEUTIC APPROACHES

4.4.1 THERAPIES AND TREATMENTS

This part should be read in conjunction with unit 4.2.2 'Models of abnormal psychology'.

The somatic approach

Somatic treatment (soma = body) is justified if one believes that mental illnesses have a physical basis like physical illnesses (the biomedical approach).

1 *ECT (electroconvulsive therapy)* was a popular treatment prior to the advent of drug therapies and gained a bad reputation for its indiscriminate use and lack of refinement in application. Today it involves little discomfort, as the patient is given an anaesthetic and muscle relaxant. An electric shock is applied to the non-dominant cerebral hemisphere (unilateral) to produce a seizure. The individual awakens soon after and remembers nothing of the treatment, which is desirable, but they may also suffer some long-term memory loss. A course of treatment usually involves six sessions.

The origins of ECT lie in the observation that epilepsy and schizophrenia appear to be negatively correlated. In the 1930s insulin shock was used to induce a seizure but later **Cerletti and Bini** (1938) introduced the use of electric shock.

ECT is now rarely used for schizophrenia, however it appears to be successful for cases of severe depression. **Janicak** *et al.* (1985) found that 80% of all severely depressed patients respond well to ECT, compared with 64% given drug therapy. **Fink** (1985) concluded, from a review of studies on ECT using measures such as suicide rates, that it is effective in over 60% of psychotic-depressive patients.

Current understanding suggests three possible explanations for its effectiveness:

- *Punishment.* ECT extinguishes undesirable behaviours because it is seen as a punishment which weakens the S-R link. However, sub-convulsive shocks do not appear to change behaviour but are equally unpleasant.
- *Memory loss* allows restructuring of disordered thinking. However, unilateral ECT leads to minimal memory disruption yet is still effective.
- *Biochemical changes.* The shock activates noradrenalin transmission, reduces serotonin re-uptake and increases sensitivity of dopamine receptors, all of which may help alleviate depression.

Evaluation

- There is some discomfort about using a method which cannot be explained, it may not be the seizure which is important at all.
- The method is potentially dangerous. In the past patients had to be forcibly restrained and broke limbs, now the current is smaller and breathing is monitored carefully but there is still some attendant risk. Drug therapies are considerably safer.

② *Psychosurgery.* **Moniz** (1937) introduced the practice of lobotomy as a means of reducing antisocial behaviour. The operation involved removing large portions of the frontal cerebral cortex to induce personality changes and make a patient more controllable.

Today, it is used only rarely, in cases of severe depression, obsessive-compulsive disorder or pain where all other treatment has failed (**Griest**, 1992). The technique is much refined, electric probes destroy specific nerve fibres and cause minimal intellectual damage.

Evaluation

- It is irreversible.
- It lacks a scientific basis.
- The effects are not consistent.

③ *Drug therapy (chemotherapy).* The main classes of drugs (see also unit 3.1.4):

- *Anxiolytic drugs* (*antianxiety, minor tranquillisers*) e.g. Valium and Librium, reduce anxiety and tension by reducing activity in the nervous system. Side effects include drowsiness and addiction.
- *Neuroleptic drugs* (*antipsychotic, major tranquillisers*) e.g. chlorpromazine, which is used to treat schizophrenia. They block dopamine receptor sites (see unit 4.3.1). Possible side effects include blurred vision and a decrease in white blood cells (can be fatal).
- *Antidepressant* drugs (stimulants) e.g. Prozac. They promote activity of noradrenalin and serotonin which leads to increased arousal but can be affected by rebound (depression after initial euphoria, see unit 3.1.4). Side effects include heart problems and brain haemorrhage unless certain foods are avoided.
- *Antimanic drugs* e.g. Lithium, used to control mania in bipolar depression, is 80% effective.

Evaluation

- The use of drug therapies has offered significant relief to many sufferers.

- It has led to reduced institutionalisation. In 1955 there were 560,000 patients in American psychiatric institutions, by 1977 this had declined to 160,000, with a comparable increase in outpatient care.
- There are problems of addiction and dangerous side-effects.
- Drugs are not cures, they are short-term remedies which inevitably become long-term. A patient may overcome their initial psychological disorder but become addicted to the drug.
- It leads to the *revolving-door phenomenon*, where patients are discharged and readmitted.
- The fact that effectiveness varies considerably between individuals detracts from its power as a therapy. For example, **Spiegel** (1989) found that 65% of depressed patients improved using tricyclics.
- Drugs can be particularly effective when used in conjunction with psychotherapy, they can relieve some of the disabling symptoms and allow the contributing psychological factors to be dealt with.

The psychodynamic approach

❶ *Method. Psychoanalysis* relies on the therapist's ability to make the unconscious conscious and guide the patient in resolving underlying conflicts.

- *Free association.* The therapist introduces a topic and the patient talks freely about anything that comes into their mind.
- *Rich interpretation.* The therapist explains the patient's thoughts and feelings using Freud's dynamics of personality development.
- *Analysis of dreams.* Dreams express the innermost workings of the mind. In Freudian therapy dreams are repressed 'wishes', in Jungian analysis dreams reflect attempts to solve particular problems.
- *Transference.* The patient transfers their feelings about others onto the therapist. During the course of therapy these may have to be dealt with as an additional 'problem'.

❷ *Related approaches*

- *Psychodrama.* Participants act out each other's emotional conflicts. **Moreno** (1946) developed this as a means of enabling individuals to express deep and irrational feelings.
- *Transactional analysis (TA).* **Berne** (1964) suggested that there are three ego states: the child which is impulsive, the adult state which is rational and the parent state which stands for social prohibitions. In normal social intercourse transactions are at an adult–adult level but sometimes the interactions are *crossed*. Berne suggests crossed transactions are 'games', one person is manipulating the other. TA looks at the games people play and uses role play to uncross the transactions. This has been a very productive approach, concentrating on the present and giving control back to the individual.

❸ *Research*

- **Eysenck** (1952) analysed two outcome studies and found that 66% of control patients improved spontaneously, whereas only 44% of the patients receiving psychoanalysis improved. However, when **Bergin** (1971) reanalysed his results using different outcome criteria the psychoanalysis success rose to 83% and the control group fell to 30%.

❹ *Evaluation*

- The emphasis on early conflicts means that present conflicts may be overlooked.
- It has somewhat limited applicability, being suitable for intelligent and verbally able patients and for wealthy clients with time on their hands since appointments are usually several times a week over a period of years.
- It is only suitable for mental illnesses where some insight is retained.
- It has been adapted for children in the form of play therapy.
- It is not scientifically rigorous.

Humanistic therapies

❶ *Description.* Counselling takes a non-directive, client-centred, empathetic and accepting approach.

- *An enabling process.* The therapist's warmth and accepting manner enables the client to express their problems, revealing them to the therapist and to themselves.
- *The therapist's role is non-judgemental*: to listen, reflect and accept the client's feelings by showing unconditional positive regard.
- *Person-centred.* What matters is the problem as experienced by the client.
- The emphasis is on *the present*, though the past may be important.
- The aim is for the client to become self-accepting and self-directing. It is the client not the therapist who must formulate a solution.

❷ *Research*

- **Rogers and Dymond** (1954) studied 75 adults divided into three groups: one group received counselling immediately, one had to wait 60 days and the last group was a control. When the groups were compared after six months the first group showed significant changes in personality (greater confidence, self-understanding and self-direction) which must be due to counselling rather than spontaneous changes.
- **Campbell** (1965) followed a group of undergraduates who received counselling, they did better at college and were more successful 25 years later.
- **Lawrence** (1971) developed a programme of remedial reading which included counselling sessions. He found that those readers who received counselling on its own did better than those receiving either remedial reading lessons or lessons plus counselling. He suggested that this was because the lessons serve to reinforce the poor readers' sense of low self-esteem, counselling can raise this which will then lead to greater self-expectations and performance.

❸ *Evaluation*

- It is a widely applicable approach for non-serious disturbances: addiction, depression, play therapy with children and family conciliation services. It can be used with a minimum of training, for example the Samaritans or marriage guidance. Groups may function with or without an expert leader.
- It is class- and culture-specific. Like psychoanalysis, it relies on good communication skills.
- It lacks rigour and is not readily susceptible to scientific analysis. It may be little more than a good relationship rather than a specialist psychotherapy.

Behavioural therapies

❶ *Classical conditioning techniques: behaviour therapy*

- *Aversion therapy.* For example, alcoholics are injected with a drug which makes them vomit when drinking, eventually the nausea becomes a conditioned response to the presentation of alcohol (conditioned stimulus). **Meter and Chesser** (1970) found that at least half their patients abstained for a year after therapy. The use of an unpleasant stimulus is ethically questionable. The drop-out rate tends to be high and patients may become anxious and hostile.
- *Systematic desensitisation* (SD) is used to treat phobias. The patient learns to pair the feared thing with relaxation rather than anxiety. **Wolpe** (1958) described the following steps:
  - Patient learns deep muscle relaxation.
  - Patient constructs a hierarchy of increasingly threatening situations.
  - Patient asked to imagine each scene while deeply relaxed.
    At any time, if the patient feels anxious, the image is stopped and relaxation regained. The concept of reciprocal inhibition describes the fact that it is impossible to maintain two incompatible emotional responses simultaneously (anxiety and relaxation). **Marks** (1973) suggests that SD works because of exposure to the feared stimulus, not the relaxation. The technique can be explained in terms of cognitive restructuring rather than classic learning theory.

- *Implosion therapy or flooding* presents the patient with maximum exposure to the feared stimulus, which continues until their fear subsides, thus extinguishing the conditioned response. This can be done in one's imagination but real-life exposure is more effective; virtual reality may be a useful alternative with fewer anxieties. The classic example is throwing someone in at the deep end of a swimming pool to overcome their fear of water.

❷ *Operant conditioning techniques: behaviour modification*

- *Modelling.* The patient first watches the therapist experiencing the phobic situation calmly, then the patient does the same. This is based on social learning theory.
- *Token economy* (TE). Patients are given tokens as secondary reinforcers when they engage in correct/socially desirable behaviours (see unit 2.4.1). The tokens can then be exchanged for primary reinforcers – food or privileges. This mirrors the system of rewards used by parents. **Allyon and Azrin** (1968) used TE to control the behaviour of 45 chronic schizophrenics. The drawback to this therapy is that it often fails to transfer to life outside the institution though **Woods *et al.*** (1984) found that short-term changes did lead on to more fundamental long-term ones possibly because newly acquired behaviours are 'trapped' by social reinforcers. The effectiveness of tokens may be due to other factors, such as being positively reinforcing for the nursing staff, who feel they are making positive gains and therefore are stimulated to persist. They also help to structure the situation and ensure consistent rewards. **Paul and Lentz** (1977) compared the outcome of chronic mental patients under different treatment regimes. Those in TE did as well as those in a therapeutic community in terms of full release or reduction of medication, and they did considerably better than those in a hospital setting.
- *Social skills training.* For example, **Lovaas *et al.*** (1967) trained autistic children in language skills using shaping and positive reinforcement '*Time out*' is a technique used to train hyperactive children. When they behave uncontrollably they receive attention which, despite being negative, is positively reinforcing. In order to break this cycle, unacceptable behaviour is treated with time in temporary isolation until they calm down. To be effective this should be accompanied by child-centred attention for good behaviour. **Goddard and Cross** (1987) described a course developed for disruptive pupils which included skills such as: listening, apologising, dealing with teasing and bullying, and gaining feedback from video recordings. In all cases long-term benefits were gained by training the parents so that they could continue the training programmes at home.

❸ *Evaluation*

- There are ethical questions about manipulating behaviour.
- The therapies are successful for the target range of disorders, e.g. phobias, obsessive-compulsive and developmental disorders. In fact for some disorders it is the only viable option, e.g. the brain injured.
- The firm scientific basis and operationalised procedures makes the therapies easy to research.
- Treatment is of symptoms not underlying causes, which may remain, but behaviourists argue that the symptoms are all that matters.
- The success of behavioural therapies may be quite unrelated to learning theory, for example it may be a matter of giving increased attention.

Cognitive-behavioural therapies

❶ *Descriptions*

- **Ellis** (1962) developed *rational-emotional therapy* (RET). He suggested that patients develop a set of irrational beliefs which lead them react to situations with undesirable emotions (ABC – *A*ctivating event – *B*eliefs about the activating event – *C*onsequences). For example, a person might believe that he must be competent in everything he does in order to be worthwhile. When he fails at something, he is plunged into despair. The therapist is directive and aggressive and challenges beliefs, 'who says you must be perfect?' leading the patient to ask the same questions.

- **Beck** (1976) developed *cognitive restructuring therapy* to deal with depressed patients. The therapist identifies the patient's self-defeating assumptions and substitutes more adaptive ones. This should disprove the patient's negative self-image. The therapy may be effective with eating disorders and even schizophrenia.
- **Meichenbaum** (1975) developed *stress inoculation therapy*. First, the therapist identifies the patient's maladaptive coping mechanisms for a stress situation (cognitive preparation), second, the patient learns more adaptive responses and self-statements (skill acquisition) and third, the patient applies these. The cycle starts again with a more difficult stress situation.

❷ *Research*

- **Bradsma** *et al.* (1978) reported that RET is effective with certain types of patient (those who are perfectionist) but not with patients with thought disorders.
- **Hollon** *et al.* (1988) gave 64 adults suffering from major depression either drug or cognitive therapy, or both for 12 weeks. Each treatment lead to improvements. In the drug only group there were no changes in 'explanatory style' but there were considerable changes in the other groups. There was some evidence of relapse in the drug only group over the next two years but not in the other patients.

❸ *Evaluation*

- In general these therapies are quick, and are becoming increasingly popular.
- They are successful for a target range of disorders (depression, anxiety and eating disorders, and sexual problems).
- They do not treat underlying causes, which appeals to some patients who prefer not to search for deep meanings.
- They lend themselves to assessment because there are measurable outcomes.

Evaluating and comparing effectiveness

Is any one therapy better than another one? Therapy outcome studies are used to try to establish this but they are fraught with difficulties.

❶ *What constitutes a cure or improvement?*

- Improvements in therapy may not carry over into real life or be long-lasting.
- The concept of 'cure' varies from one approach to another. For example, a psychoanalyst would not regard simply removing the symptoms as evidence that underlying problems had been cured, whereas a behaviourist would.

❷ *What measures are valid for assessing effectiveness?*

- The client's self-report may suffer from the *hello–goodbye effect*. People tend to exaggerate their unhappiness at the beginning of therapy to convince the therapist that they are in genuine need. At the end of therapy the reverse is true, in order to express thanks to therapist, the patient exaggerates their well-being.   The therapist is not likely to be an objective judge.
- Psychometric tests may be unreliable, self-report methods rely on patient honesty.
- Changes in a target behaviour can be used, such as counting the time an agoraphobic spends away from home or hours of sleep in a depressed patient. However, in the long term, it is difficult to reliably obtain such information.

❸ *How do we know what caused the change?*

- *Spontaneous remission*. In the case of depression particularly, time alone may affect an improvement. **Eysenck** (see above) found evidence for spontaneous remission. However, **Smith** *et al.* (1980) reviewed 475 studies which compared patients who underwent therapy with an untreated control group and concluded that the average 'treated' patient showed greater improvement on such measures as self-esteem, anxiety and achievement than 80% of the untreated patients.
- *A self-fulfilling prophecy*. If a patient believes a therapy will cure them, the expectations themselves may be the cause of success.
- *Increased attention* (the *Hawthorne effect*) may account for any change, all methods involve this.

④ *Ethical and practical considerations*

- *Obtaining a control group* is difficult. If a waiting list exists, it may be possible to withhold therapy from some patients for a while but this still does not permit random selection.
- *Random allocation* to therapy would be unethical, the alternative is that any participants are volunteers which introduces a research bias.
- The information required may be considered *confidential*.

⑤ *Are they comparable?*

- Each therapy works best with a particular set of problems therefore it is inappropriate to try to compare them. **Kazdin** (1986) found that behavioural methods are the most effective means of treating phobias, that drug therapies are most successful with schizophrenia, and that cognitive-behavioural methods are best for sexual problems.
- Each therapy has different goals which makes comparison difficult.
- Individual differences in patients and therapists affect effectiveness. Psychoanalysis and counselling work best with intelligent patients able to verbalise. Clearly some therapists will be better than others.
- Treatments in reality usually use a mixture of approaches such as drugs and psychotherapy or cognitive restructuring with social skills training. CCRT (core conflicting relationship theme) combines cognitive, behavioural and psychodynamic approaches. **Hock** (1992) reports that 40% of all therapists claim to be eclectic, which vastly outnumbers any other single approach. An eclectic approach means selecting the technique which seems most appropriate for a particular patient.

4.4.2 ETHICAL ISSUES INVOLVED IN THERAPY AND INTERVENTION

① *The need to identify mental illness*

- *For the patient's protection*. Where people are not capable of looking after themselves a caring society should provide care for them, in institutions, sheltered housing or other communities.
- *The protection of others*. Some of the mentally ill are a danger to others, which gives society the right to enforce some kind of treatment, possibly incarceration.

② *Labelling a person 'mentally ill'*

- *Reliability and validity of diagnosis* (see unit 4.2.1 and 4.2.3). If diagnoses are unreliable or invalid, a label is not justified. This is especially true in the case of minority groups.
- *Rights of the mentally ill*. Once a person is labelled, they may be stigmatised for life.
- *Rights of the public*. If someone has been diagnosed mentally disturbed do 'we', as a prospective employer or a neighbour, have a right to know this?

③ *The rights of the mentally ill*

- *Confidentiality*. Information is usually restricted to those working within the therapist's agency. In law a therapist is not required to report a criminal offence committed by a client.
- *Informed consent*. Clients should be informed about the range of therapies and treatments available, their likely success, effects and costs. In practice this is difficult because assessment of therapies is not objective (see above) and many patients are not in a suitable state of mind to make a rational choice. **Irwin** *et al.* (1985) found that even though patients said they understood what they were told, only 25% actually did (as demonstrated when questioned specifically). Frequently consent is given by relatives.

④ *Legal considerations*

- *Criminal insanity*. If a person is found to have behaved irrationally at the time of a crime they are judged insane and they may serve an indefinite sentence in a mental institution. **Szasz** (1974) described the case of Joe Skulski, who was imprisoned indefinitely, for a relatively minor crime, because the district attorney declared him unfit to stand trial. A plea of insanity may act against the defendant's interests and discourages people from taking this course of action. The GBMI verdict (guilty but mentally ill) is becoming common in the US, the person is sent to a mental institution rather than a prison but the question of whether the person has or has not any responsibility is side-stepped.

- *Involuntary commitment and treatment*. It is possible for a person to be committed to a mental institution against their will, if they are judged to be a danger to themselves or others. In Britain, initial committal (called 'sectioning' because of the use of sections of the Mental Health Act) involves two professional people, usually the person's own GP and a social worker, and only lasts for a maximum of six months. The Mental Health Review Tribunal can be appealed to. Any sectioned patient can be given medication for three months and/or ECT if they give informed consent or a second independent medical opinion is obtained. Psychosurgery or hormone treatment (e.g. for birth control) requires the patient's consent.

⑤ *Mad or bad?*

- If you label the illness as 'mad' and suggest that the person is suffering an illness, you remove responsibility and place the patient in the care of others, creating a potential victim. This approach works, at least to some extent, if there is a known cause and cure, though even then (as with genetic and neurochemical causes) the patient is an unequal partner.
- If you use the idea of 'bad' (or maladapted) you hold the person responsible for their ills and make them responsible for resolving them.
- The judgement 'bad' can also be applied to those who do the locking up. In the right hands locking up can be humane, not bad. But there is a potential for abuse and this gives it a bad name.

⑥ *The problems of deinstitutionalisation*

- A person who has been cared for in an institution for a prolonged period becomes incapable of life in the real world.
- The theory of releasing mental patients into the care of the community (deinstitutionalisation) has been described as enlightened social policy. It may work if there is adequate community care and it depends upon the continuing use of drugs. However, the practice of such a social policy has led to an increase in homeless persons.

⑦ *The responsibilities of therapists* (see unit 7.3.3).

Chapter roundup

4.1   Atypical development

4.1.1   *Learning difficulties* may be global or specific, and may be caused by intrinsic or extrinsic factors. In most cases the cause is unknown and/or exacerbated by poor home environment (cultural-familial retardation).

4.1.2   *Physical and sensory handicaps* have secondary consequences such as cognitive, motor and social deficits. These compound the original problem but may be alleviated by coping mechanisms.

4.1.3   ADHD, autism and dyslexia are familiar *emotional and behavioural problems* of childhood though they are relatively rare. Their underlying causes are not yet fully understood. The picture is complicated by considerable variations within the conditions.

4.2   Conceptions and models of abnormality

4.2.1   Abnormality has been *defined* in terms of statistical frequency, social deviation, mental healthiness and dysfunctionality, and *classified* using the ICD-10 and DSM-IV, based on clusters of symptoms.

4.2.2   The main *models of abnormal behaviour* (medical, psychodynamic, behavioural, cognitive and humanist) can be compared in terms of how they explain the causes of mental illness, and their associated therapies.

4.2.3 The expression of mental illness varies across gender, social and cultural groups. Cultural and sub–cultural differences may lead to mistaken diagnoses in certain social groups.

4.3 Psychopathology

4.3.1 *Schizophrenia* is characterised by a loss of contact with reality. The cause is probably an interaction between genetic predisposition and environmental triggers (the diathesis–stress model).

4.3.2 Major *depression* appears to have some neurochemical basis but is influenced by psychological factors such as learned patterns of behaviour (learned helplessness), early experience, and social and gender factors. Bipolar depression is more likely to have a genetic basis.

4.3.3 *Anxiety disorders*: Phobias can be explained using psychodynamic, behavioural or cognitive theories. Post-traumatic stress disorder (PTSD) can be understood as a physiological response to stress and a sense of lack of control.

4.3.4 *Eating disorders*: Anorexia nervosa and bulimia nervosa involve weight loss beyond what is normal. They affect mainly girls and may have some genetic basis. Psychological explanations include thin stereotypes, sexual abuse, lack of autonomy, overdependence, avoidance of womanhood and personality differences.

4.4 Therapeutic approaches

4.4.1 The main types of *therapies and treatments* are somatic (medical approach), psychodynamic, humanistic, behavioural and cognitive-behavioural. Evaluating comparable effectiveness is difficult.

4.4.2 *Ethical issues* involved in therapy and intervention include consideration of the need to identify mental illness, the rights of the public and the patient, the law, the view of mad versus bad, the problems of deinstitutionalisation, and the responsibilities of therapists.

Illustrative question

Jane is a 15-year old female with Down's syndrome. She is a pupil at a local school at which she enjoys using computers, playing hockey, singing and the company of boys. Jane's condition was obvious at birth, but her parents never considered treating her differently from their other children. She was the first pupil with Down's syndrome to attend the school and now there are three other such pupils younger than her at school. Jane has learned to read and write, she takes regular classes as well as some special education classes. Her parents report that she has a positive self-image, and is aware that she is different from most other children. Her classmates accept her most of the time though she does get teased and called names. Jane would like to find work when she leaves school, be independent and perhaps have children of her own.

(a) Describe problems Jane's peers and teachers might have had integrating Jane into school. (6 marks)
(b) Describe problems Jane might encounter in trying to realise her ambitions as an adult. (6 marks)
(c) Discuss, citing empirical evidence, how the cognitive development of a person who is mentally retarded may be affected by their self-image. (8 marks)

(NEAB A 1992)

Tutorial note

These questions, like many from this area of the syllabus, tend to attract common-sense answers, particular where candidates have personal knowledge of Down's syndrome children. In order to score high marks answers must draw specifically on psychological theory and empirical research. This question is an example of one that can use knowledge that you have but don't realise you have, from many other areas of psychology, and therefore makes extra demands in an examination situation.

Suggested answer

(a) There has been a move in this country to integrate those with special educational requirements into mainstream education. **The Warnock Report** (1978) suggested that decisions should be based on each individual's needs. Some very seriously disabled children require special schools but others would benefit from integration into ordinary education. The Education Reform Act (1988) states that the national curriculum should be broad enough to cover most of the ability range. However, current pressures on the accountability of schools may mean that in practice teachers are not able to devote sufficient time to this end of the spectrum. It will be necessary to enlist the help of specialist teachers for support and surveillance.

The presence of a child like Jane gives both teachers and the other pupils the chance to develop positive attitudes towards her disability based on understanding rather than prejudice. For Jane, and children like her, who have some retardation, there are many benefits. An ordinary school offers better facilities to develop their potential, such as sports or library amenities, and a full range of school subjects. Perhaps even more importantly there is the opportunity to mix with ordinary children and learn the social skills necessary for survival in adult life. Since Down's syndrome children are particularly responsive to social stimuli they will be able to make good use of the human interactions.

However, there are many problems. Even given time, teachers may lack the specialist skills necessary to adapt the lessons to special needs. It is possible that resentment from other children may arise from the extra time spent on the Down's syndrome child and this could exacerbate their feelings of being stigmatised, undoing any positive effects of integration. Any initial problems would only serve to confirm the stereotypes held by the teachers and other children. **Hastings and Graham** (1995) compared children in integrated and non-integrated schools in terms of their attitudes towards the disabled and found no differences, though frequency of contact was associated with more positive expectations. They used Social Identity Theory to explain why stereotypes of the disabled persist – members of an outgroup are perceived in stereotypical ways as a means of maintaining personal social/group identity. This means that, if contact between members of different groups (disabled and non-disabled) is only made at an intergroup level, then negative attitudes are unlikely to change. If contact is made at an interpersonal level, then negative stereotypes may break down.

(b) Most Down's syndrome sufferers spend their adult years in an institution because they are not able to be economically self-sufficient, particularly as such people are most often born to older parents who will eventually not be able to care for them. Jane's competence in reading and writing suggests that she might be able to find some work but might have to live in some form of institution. It is unlikely that she would have children. This is partly because her children might inherit her disorder, but also because her inability to care for herself would lead carers to ensure that she didn't become pregnant. This is an important ethical question relevant to all mentally retarded adults in institutions. From the point of view of health, 25% of Down's syndrome children don't survive beyond their first few years, largely because of associated congenital heart defects. Those who do survive may still have a number of other linked problems, such as disorders of the digestive system or cancers, particularly leukaemia. Most Down's syndrome sufferers who survive until middle age almost invariably suffer from Alzheimer's disease, which, like Down's syndrome, is controlled by chromosome 21.

(c) A child with Down's syndrome starts life with a lowered potential intelligence. Their cognitive development may be further slowed because of a poor self-image. All development is affected by self-image, in particular self-esteem. The self-fulfilling prophecy is one way of explaining how a positive self-image can lead to successful performance.

Coopersmith (1968) found that boys with high self-esteem were more confident and academically successful.

Self-efficacy is a person's expectation of their own future performance. Being labelled 'mentally retarded' would lead a person to expect to do poorly. **Weinberg *et al.*** (1979) demonstrated how performance on a physical task was depressed when participants were given a sense of low self-efficacy. In Russia they show athletes films of their own performance which are edited to make it look better, thus raising the athletes' sense of their own self-efficacy and in turn improving performance. However, **Ringness** (1961) found evidence to suggest that some mentally retarded children have artificially high expectations because their educational environment is overaccepting and overencouraging. Unrealistic expectations would eventually cause difficulties when they could not be fulfilled.

Some Down's children have nearly normal intelligence so that the potentially detrimental effects of a poor self-image could be disastrous for their cognitive development. **Lewis** (1987) reported that most Down's children start with an IQ around 70 but this tends to decline with age. A key factor in this deterioration is the amount of stimulation they experience. **Brinkworth** (1975) developed an early stimulation programme and reported that Down's children who had followed this had an average score on the Griffiths Developmental Scale by the time they were over 1.

Down's syndrome children are particularly responsive to social support, so their self-esteem should benefit from outside interest. An important way of raising self-esteem is to place the mentally retarded in mainstream education, to increase their social contact and raise their self-image by seeing themselves as more 'normal'. At the same time they can benefit cognitively from increased variety. But many studies (e.g. **Abrams *et al.*** 1990) have found that negative attitudes persist and this confirms the retarded child's negative self-image.

Question bank

Allow 35–40 minutes for each question.

Atypical development

1 (a) Explain the meaning of the term 'specific learning disabilities'. (4 marks)
　　(b) Describe and evaluate research into **one** specific learning disability. (10 marks)
　　(c) Critically consider practical applications of research in helping individuals cope with this specific learning disability. (10 marks)

(AEB AS 1995)

Points: In part (a) your explanation might refer to actual examples. Part (b) requires reference to research (theory or studies) in relation to one disability. In part (c) you should stay with the same disability, this time considering how research might be practically applied (a skill B activity).

2 (a) A person born with the loss of a major sense is bound to be affected to a considerable extent. What, in your view, are the most serious adverse consequences for a person with the loss of a major sense? Choose either blindness or deafness to answer this question and justify your answer using empirical evidence. (12 marks)
　　(b) With reference to either blindness or deafness, examine evidence for 'compensation' of one sense by another. (8 marks)

(NEAB A 1991)

Points: A question which attracts anecdotal answers based on personal experience. A good answer must use empirical evidence to support the named consequences and must be limited to either blindness or deafness. In part (b) you are not restricted to answer on the same sensory impairment as part (a). You should discuss how the individual uses their other senses.

3 (a) Outline **one or more** psychological problem(s) in childhood or adolescence.
(b) Discuss the contribution of psychological research to our understanding of the problem(s).

(AEB AS 1994)

Points: You can chose the 'depth' route and discuss only one problem but provide considerable detail in part (a) and ample research (theory and studies) in part (b). Or you can chose the 'breadth' route and discuss many different problems, providing a limited amount of information for each.

Conceptions and models of abnormality

4 Critically consider difficulties involved in diagnosing and explaining mental disorders.

(AEB A 1994)

Points: Avoid writing everything you know about the diagnosis and explanation of mental disorders. Instead concentrate on the difficulties which are encountered such as validity and reliability of diagnoses, and the problems researching the causes of mental disorders. It may help to focus on a particular disorder such as schizophrenia.

5 (a) Describe the assumptions made about the origins of abnormality by **either** the medical model **or** the behavioural model of abnormality. (10 marks).
(b) Compare and contrast current models of abnormality in terms of **either** their ethical **or** practical implications. (14 marks).

(AEB A 1994)

Points: There is a temptation, in part (a) to present evaluative material. However this part is skill A only – 'describe'. In part (b) you may select a range of models and compare them in terms of either ethical or practical implications. It is important to be clear which of these implications you are discussing and to discuss only one of them. Comparing and contrasting can be done serially (discuss each one separately, covering the same points each time) or point-by-point, i.e. making a comparison on an issue such as informed consent.

Psychopathology

6 (a) Describe any **one** psychological disorder. (12 marks)
(b) Evaluate psychological explanations given for this disorder. (12 marks)

(AEB specimen)

Points: You must describe only one disorder and keep your evaluations for part (b). It is arguable whether certain disorders are one or several, for example anorexia and bulimia are eating disorders and schizophrenia can be broken down into different types. If you do present a cluster, be explicit about why they constitute one disorder.

7 (a) Outline what is meant by 'schizophrenia'. (6 marks)
(b) Discuss **two** possible causes of schizophrenia suggested by psychologists and evaluate evidence supporting each. (14 marks)

(NEAB A 1991)

Points: A straightforward essay, which should include evaluation rather than just description. Part (b) calls for the use of empirical evidence.

8 'It is now clear beyond reasonable doubt that biological factors play a major part in the onset and development of depression.'
Critically consider the extent to which research supports the view expressed in this quotation.

(AEB AS 1996)

Points: You must use research (theory and studies) to evaluate the importance of biological factors. This means that you should consider the alternative – non-biological factors – as well.

9 (a) Outline the main features of:
  (i) anorexia nervosa; (5 marks)
  (ii) bulimia nervosa. (5 marks)
  (b) Discuss the effectiveness of **two** different treatments for one of the above disorders. Make reference to empirical studies in your answer. (10 marks)

(NEAB A 1992)

Points: The question does not ask for theories of anorexia or bulimia, but only descriptions (in part a) and treatments (in part b). Anecdotal descriptions of counselling should be avoided and, where possible, you should use empirical evidence.

Therapeutic approaches

10 Discuss **two** types of treatment/therapy for abnormal behaviour, including reference to research studies of their effectiveness.

(AEB A 1996)

Points: Your discussion should include a description of the two therapies and an evaluation in terms of effectiveness and other issues such as ethics. The question specifically asks for research evidence about effectiveness, when discussing this you can raise the problem of assessing effectiveness.

11 In 'A Code of Conduct for Psychologists' (1985), the British Psychological Society says that 'In all their work, psychologists shall seek to establish the highest ethical standards.'

Identify the major ethical constraints on the work of practising psychologists. Discuss the difficulties faced by psychologists involved in the treatment of abnormal behaviours in staying within these guidelines.

(AEB AS 1990)

Points: The quotation in the question must be addressed. You should list ethical constraints (see chapter 7) and discuss how these are difficult to apply in the context of the treatment of abnormal behaviours.

COGNITIVE PSYCHOLOGY

Units in this chapter:

Chapter overview

Cognition is the activity of internal mental processing. Early psychologists investigated mental (cognitive) activity using introspection; behaviourists rejected this approach and regarded mental concepts as 'explanatory fictions'; cognitive psychology enjoyed a revival in the 1950s using computer metaphors to explain internal processing. Most recently, this latter approach has also been criticised as overly mechanistic and lacking in social, motivational and emotional factors.

5.1   PERCEPTUAL PROCESSES

Perception is the act of giving coherence and unity to sensory input. The five senses are: vision (sight), audition (hearing), olfaction (smell), tactition (touch) and gustation (taste); plus proprioception (internal senses) which include kinaesthetic (muscular movement) and vestibular (balance) senses.

The AEB syllabus concentrates on the visual system.

5.1.1   THEORIES OF PERCEPTION

❶ *Bottom-up or data-driven processing.* Perception is primarily determined by the physical stimulus. **James Gibson** (1979) argued in his *direct perception theory* that the amount of data contained in the retinal image (the *optic array*) is underestimated. It is sufficiently rich in information to explain perception.

- *Optic flow patterns* are produced as we move around the environment. Gibson was asked to prepare training films for Second World War pilots and observed that the 'flow' of data past a viewer (the pilot) provided unambiguous perceptual information about direction, speed and altitude.

- *Texture gradients* provide information of depth from sensory data alone, as do *motion parallax* and *linear perspective*.

- *Affordances* = the potential uses of objects. Gibson proposed that a chair 'affords' sitting and a post-box 'affords' letter-mailing to a person who has knowledge of the postal system. Sensory data can provide information about meaning and there is a close relationship between perception and action.
- *Resonance*. We collect visual data in the same way that a radio collects radio waves; once a stimulus is tuned in to, processing is automatic and effortless.
- *Differentiation theory* (see end of unit 5.1.2).
- **Lee and Lishman** (1975) built a swaying room so that they could manipulate optic flow patterns. Children typically fell over but adults were able to adjust, showing that sensory and motor processes are linked and that we learn to adjust them.

Evaluation

- This theory explains the functioning of animal perception and some aspects of human perception, particularly situations where data is unambiguous (such as conditions of good lighting).
- **Fodor and Pylyshyn** (1981) distinguished between 'seeing' and 'seeing as', the latter is what you 'know about what you are seeing' and cannot be explained by Gibson's theory.
- It can't explain the effects of perceptual set, the lack of recovery of cataract patients, and some constancies and illusions. Gibson defends himself by saying that illusions, and many experiments testing perception, are artificial and therefore do not represent perceptual behaviour in the real world.
- It can't cope with concept-driven processing or internal representations. **Menzel** (1978) demonstrated that monkeys, shown the location of 20 pieces of food, could later locate these. They must have relied on cognitive maps and not solely on sensory data.

Application: Gibson produced pilot training films based on his principles of data–driven perception.

2. *Top-down, constructivist or concept-driven processing.* **Gregory** (1966) suggested that a perceived object is a hypothesis, which is suggested and then tested by sensory data . The stimulus provided to our senses is often incomplete or ambiguous; perception is therefore 'driven' by cognitive expectations.

- *Visual illusions* demonstrate that perception is sometimes inaccurate. Gregory offered an explanation in terms of mistaken hypotheses (see unit 5.1.3), but this can only account for some illusions.
- *Perceptual constancy and set.* Empirical evidence (unit 5.1.3) shows that perception is influenced by expectations.
- *Enrichment theory* (see unit 5.1.2).

Evaluation

- The theory explains how incomplete and ambiguous visual stimuli are perceived.
- It can't explain why vision is generally so accurate even in novel situations.
- It can't explain why the system is sometimes slow to adjust (as in inverted images) and sometimes faster (as in seeing ambiguous images).
- It can't explain how the system reacts so fast when having to search through a store of cognitive schemas.

Application: It is possible to explain, for example airplane accidents, how preconceived ideas affect what is 'seen' and lead people to make errors.

3. *Interactive theories.* Bottom–up and top–down processing can be seen as complementary. The former may represent innate sensory mechanisms whereas the latter depend on learned experience. Their relative importance varies with particular circumstances. **Neisser**'s (1976) *analysis-by-synthesis* or *cyclic model* shows how the two systems might interact.

- Perception starts with a *sampling* of available information (bottom-up), for example, four legs might generate the hypothesis 'dog'.
- Attention is *directed* towards specific features which are generated from existing cognitive schema (top-down), e.g. a wet nose and a hairy body.

- If these are not found, the original hypothesis must be *modified*, and the process restarted.

Evaluation

- Gibson would argue that it is not necessary to complicate matters.
- Such a perceptual cycle would be slower than observed speeds of functioning.

④ *Computer models.* **Marr** (1982) put forward the *computational theory* of vision. The function of the visual system is to build 3D images and to extract meaning, this involves three steps:

- Forming the *primal sketch*: the pattern of light falling on the retina, using data about edges, blobs, textures.
- *2½D sketch*. The primal sketch converted to an image from the observer's point of view, using further data such as depth and orientation of visible surfaces.
- *3D model*. The image independent of the observer; this must be compared with stored representations to arrive at recognition.

Evaluation

- This specifies details of the exact processes, a criticism of other approaches.
- Combines bottom-up and top-down processing.
- Marr used it to construct a computer program which could recognise simple outlines but it required additional information to cope with ambiguous stimuli.
- The fact that a computer program can accomplish the same task as the eye and the brain does not mean that the methods are the same.
  Application. Constructing pattern recognition machines.

⑤ *Gestalt theory.* Gestalt psychologists explained perception using innate Laws of Pràgnanz (meaning) which emphasise the whole (*gestalten*) rather than constituent parts. The same principles explain how a melody remains recognisable despite changes in instrument or key.

- *Figure/ground*. When looking at a picture we see figures set against a background.
- *Similarity*. Tendency to visually group similar objects together, e.g. oooxxxoooxxx.
- *Proximity* in space and time organises sensory data, e.g. •• ••• • ••.
- *Closure*. We tend to complete images with sections missing.
- *Continuity*. A series of dots which make a recognisable shape, such as a square, are seen as a square rather than their constituent parts.

  Navon (1977) tested participants with a 'global' stimulus letter (an H or an S) which was made up of smaller 'local' letters (either Hs and Ss). Global letters were more quickly identified, and when local and global letters were in conflict, participants were slowed in their identification of the local letters but not the global ones. This supports the view that initial perceptions are based on the overall representation rather than the overall picture being built up from its individual elements (top-down rather than bottom-up). It is a desirable feature of the perceptual process so that important objects in the visual scene can be identified with minimal delay and before the image changes.
  Evaluation. A top-down theory which placed undue emphasis on inherited factors.
  Application. Instrument panels may use analogue displays (provide better immediate impressions) or digital displays (provide more exact information).

5.1.2 PERCEPTUAL DEVELOPMENT

Human neonate studies

❶ *Sensory abilities at birth* are not fully mature. The human visual system is sensitive to colour, brightness, movement and visual patterns which have sufficient light/dark contrast. The lens cannot change shape and therefore visual acuity is limited to a fixed focal length of about 20 centimetres (the distance between mother and infant when feeding).
  Perceptual development is the beginning of cognitive development, learning to make sense of the mass of data (**James'** 'blooming, buzzing confusion'). **Piaget** (see unit 6.2.1) described the first stage as one of sensorimotor development.

② *Perceptual abilities at birth.* **Fantz** (1961) showed that neonates (up to 6 months old) could easily discriminate certain visual forms. They preferred more complex patterns and a real face rather than a scrambled set of the same features (point of fixation, i.e. preference, was determined by noting the reflections in the infant's eyes). An interest in complexity may be important in stimulating the visual development of the brain, however the preference for a face cannot be explained solely in terms of pattern complexity because the scrambled version was less preferred. It may be due to a liking for things which are symmetrical or it may have adaptive importance: a neonate who can recognise and respond to its own species will better elicit attachment and caring.

Bower (1966) investigated size and shape constancy in 6- to 8-week-old infants, too young to be capable of reaching or crawling. He conditioned the infants to turn their heads towards a certain sized or shaped cube by rewarding them with a game of 'peek-a-boo' every time the correct response was made. When he changed the distance or angle, they continued to produce the conditioned response even though the retinal image had changed, thus demonstrating size and shape constancy. If the infant had a patch over one eye, their performance remained the same. This was not true if they were shown slides of the stimulus, which means that the infants were using motion parallax to determine depth.

Bower *et al.* (1970) tested depth perception in infants aged 6 to 20 days old, by observing their response to an approaching object. The infants signalled awareness by opening their eyes, moving their head back and putting their hands in front of their face. If the infant had no depth perception their response to a large disc stopping further should be the same as their response to a smaller, closer one because they both create the same *retinal* image. In fact the infants were so upset by the smaller, closer one that the experiment was abandoned.

Gibson and Walk (1960) used the *visual cliff* to test depth perception in infants aged 6 to 14 months. Most of the infants (92%) refused to crawl over the 'cliff' even if they had a patch across one eye, which showed that they were using monocular cues only. This may be due to learned rather than innate factors, though maturation (innate) rather than learning could explain any developmental delay.

③ *Human deprivation studies.* **Banks** *et al.* (1975) found that if children with squints are operated on before the age of 3, they subsequently develop normal vision but if the operation is left any later the deprivation appears to result in some degree of abnormal binocular vision. Experience can also be enriching, see **White and Held** (in unit 6.1.2).

④ *Techniques:* spontaneous visual preference (SVP), conditioning, avoidance response, visual cliff and abnormal visual development. *Sucking rate* is measured using a dummy with sensor, interest increases sucking. **Butterfield and Siperstein** (1972) found that babies increased their sucking rate when played folk music, but decreased it when the sound was non-rythmical.

⑤ *Problems*

- Testing a somewhat immobile and unresponsive participant is difficult and prone to subjective interpretation and experimenter bias.
- Conclusions about behaviour are always based on inference.
- Research tends to be laboratory-based and possibly atypical.
- It is impossible to test an infant who has had no experience, since activity in the womb has a major impact, e.g. in sensorimotor development.
- Separating maturation from learning is difficult. An ability may still be innate even if an infant has not developed it yet.

⑥ *Ethical considerations*

- Infants are especially affected by experience and perhaps should not be exposed to *any* research treatment.
- Parents should never be deceived, though informed consent might bias the research.

Other studies of perceptual development

① *Animal neonate studies.* Many of the human neonate studies were also conducted with animals. **Gibson and Walk** (above) found that goats and kittens refused to cross the visual cliff. They compared 3–month–old rats who had been reared in the dark with normal rats and found no differences, suggesting that depth perception was innate. **Hess** (below) found that chickens could not adapt to new environmental situations.

Evaluation. Most animals are more mature at birth than humans, so such evidence may have little bearing on the *human* nature-nurture debate.

② *Deprived environments.* **Riesen** (1950) raised chimpanzees in total darkness until the age of 16 months. They couldn't distinguish simple patterns and were developmentally deprived in other respects, such as not responding to conditioning. **Wiesel** (1982) sewed one eye of a kitten shut. If this is done early enough and long enough the eye becomes blind, suggesting that experience is necessary to maintain the innate system.

Evaluation. Sensory deprivation has major emotional effects, which could explain retardation.

③ *Restricted environments.* **Held and Hein** (1963) showed that the effects of visual deprivation are tied to sensorimotor experiences. When one kitten is allowed to walk in a *kitten carousel* its sensorimotor co-ordination develops normally whereas a yoked control, kept in a basket and not allowed to walk, has no such co-ordination. The yoked control had an intact visual system but seemed unable to use the information.

Blakemore and Cooper (1970) placed kittens in a drum which had only vertical or only horizontal lines. The kittens later showed difficulties with depth perception and were virtually blind for the contours perpendicular to those they had experienced. Examination of their visual cortex showed that no cells responded electrically to the orientation *not* experienced by the cat (**Hubel and Wiesel**, in unit 3.2.3), supporting the view that physical degeneration results from a lack of experience during a critical period.

④ *Readjustment studies: adults who have regained their sight.* **Gregory and Wallace** (1963) studied a man who was blind from birth due to having cataracts. In later life they were removed but he was never fully able to use his newly acquired sight. Other studies confirm this incomplete recovery (e.g. **von Senden**, 1932).

Evaluation

- Cataract patients may have undergone physical and psychological trauma when their eyesight was restored.
- Such patients may have learned to rely on other senses.
- Using adults as participants means they can provide verbal reports of their experiences.

⑤ *Distortion studies.* **Stratton** (1986) and **Snyder and Pronko** (1952) experimented with goggles which turned the world upside down. Within a few days the world appeared right way up. **Hess** (1956) placed prism lenses on chickens so things appeared ten degrees to one side, the chickens continued to peck in the wrong place. **Kohler** (1966) gave coloured goggles to participants, and found that apparent colour soon returns to normal.

Evaluation. This suggests that experience leads to new interpretations of visual data by the brain, a feature not present in a fully innate system.

⑥ *Cross-cultural studies.* **Turnbull** (1961) described how a pygmy guide thought a herd of buffalo grazing in the distance were insects. Having lived in a forest all his life the guide had acquired no knowledge of depth cues nor of size constancy. **Hudson** (1960) tested over 500 children and adults, Black and White, from southern Africa. He showed them pictures of a hunting scene or a flying bird and found that the 'school-going' participants interpreted the depth cues correctly whereas the 'non-school-going' participants did not, suggesting that the ability to decode depth cues is learned.

Evaluation. See criticisms of case studies and cross-cultural studies in units 7.2.3 and 8.1.2.

Theories of perceptual development

❶ *Enrichment theory.* **Piaget** (unit 6.2.1) suggested that perceptual (and cognitive development) depends on the individual *enriching* their sensory input using cognitive schemas.

❷ *Differentiation theory.* **Eleanor Gibson** (1987) proposed that sensory information alone and without the influence of expectations can account for perceptual development. The infant learns to *differentiate* between the distinctive features of different classes of objects and to ignore irrelevant features in order to build up an accurate perception. **Bower** (1982) suggested that infants can *register* most of the information that adults can, but are not able to *handle* it.

❸ *Nature versus nurture.* The process of differentiation or bottom-up processing may explain innate systems of perception whereas enrichment or top-down processing is related to those perceptual abilities which are learned. In any one situation the relative contributions of each will vary according to particular circumstances.

The empirical evidence suggests that innate systems may be incomplete at birth and require experiential input to be maintained and to adapt to changed circumstances.

5.1.3 PERCEPTUAL ORGANISATION

Perception involves *organising* sensory data into meaningful patterns. Some organisation can be explained neurophysiologically (see unit 3.2.3), other organisation relies on cognitive schema (experience and expectations).

❶ *Perception of space (depth).* Apparent distance influences the perception of size, and apparent size influences the perception of distance. There are many cues related to distance perception, though none absolutely determine it. The perceptual system selects the most likely solution according to experience:

- *Disparity* (see unit 3.2.3).
- *Convergence* of eyes acts as a range finder.
- *Relative size*: more distant objects are smaller.
- *Linear perspective*: parallel lines converge, as in the Ponzo illusion (see Fig. 5.2).
- *Texture gradients*: distant parts of a surface appear denser.
- *Shade*: shading on an object or shadow behind it.
- *Brightness*: a brighter object appears closer.
- *Relative clarity*: things in the distance are less in focus and also bluer, due to refracted light (aerial haze).
- *Interposition*: one object overlapping another makes it appear to be closer.
- *Motion parallax*: things which are closer move faster.

❷ *Perception of movement (location constancy).* Systematic movements in the visual field give cues of movement:

- The movements of the head and eyeball flicker give the appearance of movement, therefore the perceptual system needs feedback to eliminate this data.
- *Motion parallax* (see above), sense of speed is determined by how quickly objects move across the eye. This has an application in the use of optical brakes at road traffic junctions, parallel lines which progressively become closer together.

❸ *Pattern recognition*

- *Templates* in the visual system recognise certain shapes; if this was the only system there would have to be a large number of templates. **Neisser** (1964) found that participants took longer to search for 'not Q' than 'Q' in a list of letters; if they had been using a template both searches should take the same time.
- *Prototypes* (abstract forms) represent the typical features of a category, such as a letter A. These could be fewer in number than templates, but the details of how such systems might work remains imprecise, e.g. *fuzzy boundaries* (see unit 5.4.3).
- *Feature detection model* proposes a hierarchy of attributes. Neisser also found that visual search was slowed if participants were asked to search for a 'Z' imbedded in a list of letters with similar features (e.g. M and V rather than O and G). This explains

much but not all of pattern recognition, empirical work on perceptual set (below) demonstrates the importance of expectations. Also the interrelationships between features is given little emphasis, whereas the Gestalt approach would predict that the whole stimulus is perceived before its parts (**Navon**, unit 5.1.1, and 'Feature detection', unit 5.2.1).

❹ *Perceptual constancies.* We 'see' the same object despite changed retinal images.

- *Shape constancy.* A book 'looks' rectangular from any angle.
- *Brightness constancy.* A white shirt 'looks' white in any light.
- *Colour constancy.* A blue shirt 'looks' blue even in red light ('Retinex theory' in unit 3.2.3).
- *Size constancy. Apparent distance* is the key to understanding size constancy. In the Ponzo illusion, the line which appears to be more distant 'looks' longer. In the Ames Room (see Fig. 5.1), one person appears larger because constancy cues are confused. One corner of the room is actually further away but the ceiling is adjusted to maintain the appearance of a rectangular room. If the person in the far corner is very familiar, the size effect disappears and the room is seen as distorted.

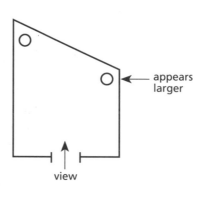

Figure 5.1: Ames room illustrations

❺ *Visual illusions* are not 'mistakes' of perception, they illustrate normal functioning in abnormal conditions.

- *Neurophysiological* explanations (see unit 3.2.3).
- *Size constancy.* The converging lines of the Ponzo illusion make the top line appear more distant and therefore longer. **Gregory** (1966) suggested that the Müller-Lyer illusion can also be explained this way: the line with the ingoing fins suggests the outside corner of a building, and therefore is in some sense farther away from us (and longer). The outgoing fins suggest the inside of a room we are in and therefore the line appears closer (and smaller). **Segall** *et al.* (1963) and **Annis and Frost** (1973) found that Africans and traditional Canadian Cree Indians (respectively) were less able to perceive visual illusions than Americans, and suggested that people in the Western world live in *carpentered* environments where they experience sharp corners (rectangularity), whereas Africans may have less experience of this and therefore have not learned the cues for distance which are exploited by illusions. However, it may be that some people do not 'see' the illusions because they are unused to interpreting paper-and-pencil drawings (see Figure 5.2).
- *Movement constancy.* The moon appears to move when clouds move across it.
- *Depth perception.* Shading makes a picture appear to be 3D.
- *Experience.* Far-off objects are projected higher on the retina than nearer ones; the same length lower line appears shorter in the vertical-horizontal line illusion.
- *Gestalt principles.* The Kanizsa triangle shows our tendency to organisation of data on the basis of sufficient cues.
- *Expectations.* **Warren and Warren** (1970) investigated *auditory illusions*, for example a sentence is tampered with so that a bleep occurs instead of a particular phoneme, the listener still 'hears' the phoneme even when they know it's missing (*phonemic restoration*).

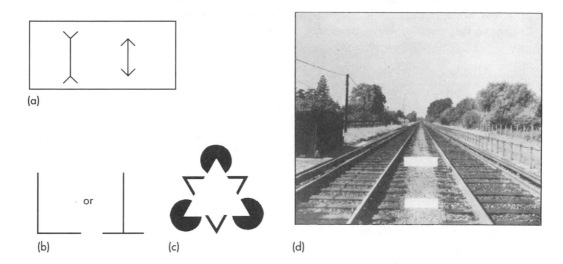

Figure 5.2: (a) The Muller-Lyer illusion , (b) the vertical-horizontal illusion, (c) the Kanizsa triangle illusion and (d) the Ponzo illusion

❻ *Perceptual set.* 'Set' is the tendency to respond in a certain manner, a parallel process to visual constancy. Set may be influenced by external (situational) or internal (e.g. emotion) information; set may enhance or suppress information.

- *Attention.* Intensity, repetition, movement or internal decisions determine what you look at, your attentional set (**Neisser and Becklen** in unit 5.2.1).
- *Context.* Often visual data is incomplete or ambiguous. **Bruner and Minturn** (1955) showed that the characters '13' were interpreted as thirteen or the letter B depending on the rest of the context (L,M,Y,A,13 or 16,17,10,12,13). **Carmichael** *et al.* (unit 5.4.4) showed how language affects perception.
- *Expectations* lead to quicker but not always more accurate identification. **Tulving and Gold** (1963) showed participants sentences with 4, 6, or 7 words missing. The fewer words missing, the quicker they would correctly guess the target word. **Bruner and Postman** (1949) showed incongruous cards (e.g. a red six of clubs) to participants. Past experience and expectation led to perceptual conflict, which is subconsciously resolved, e.g. the card looked purple. The more trick cards a person was shown, the less fooled they were – their 'set' changed in line with experience.
- *Motivation.* **Gilchrist and Nesburg** (1952) found that if a person is experiencing a 'need', this distorts their perception of objects related to that need. Participants who were hungry perceived photographs of food as brighter.
- *Emotion.* **McGinnies** (1949) found that more 'emotional' words (as measured by galvanic skin response) took longer to be recognised. **Solley and Haigh** (1958) showed that emotion can also be sensitising, children drew larger pictures of Santa before as compared with after Christmas.

5.1.4 INDIVIDUAL, SOCIAL AND CULTURAL VARIATIONS

❶ *Individual differences* can be related to experience. For example, the case of **S.B.** (unit 5.1.2) illustrates how extreme deprivation severely restricts perceptual ability. **Mitchell** *et al.* (1973) found that when adult astigmatics have their vision corrected many of them are still unable to see parallel lines in all orientations equally. Enrichment may also affect visual development (see **White and Held**, unit 6.1.2).

❷ *Cultural factors.* Culture has a major impact on the way perceptual organisation is learned, as in the perception of depth and of visual illusions (see unit 5.1.2). It may also affect perceptual set. **Pettigrew** *et al.* (1958) tested five racial groups in South Africa on a task involving binocular rivalry (each eye is presented with a different picture: in this case a member of a different racial group). Afrikaners tended to perceive the pictures as black or white, rather than less well-defined racial groups (e.g. Indians). This helps maintain their view of white supremacy.

5.2 ATTENTION AND PERFORMANCE LIMITATIONS

Attention is the concentration of mental effort on sensory or mental events, equivalent to consciousness.

- *Selective or focused attention.* At any one time an organism selects one input out of the mass of existing sensations.
- *Divided attention or concentration.* Often organisms perform several tasks at once (dual-task performance). Strategies are developed to allocate limited mental resources.

5.2.1 FOCUSED ATTENTION

Focused auditory attention

① *Single channel filter model.* **Broadbent** (1958) described attention in terms of a *filter* – a structural bottleneck which is needed for a limited capacity system to select a single channel from the mass of parallel inputs. All later filter models are essentially modified versions of this, the difference lies in where the filter is placed. Broadbent suggested that (1) the filter was located at or just prior to perceptual analysis and (2) that messages are filtered on the basis of physical characteristics.

Evidence for

- *Cocktail party phenomenon.* A person can follow one conversation when several people are talking at once. **Cherry** (1953) presented two auditory messages to participants and asked them to repeat (*shadow*) one of the messages and ignore the other (*dichotic listening task*). Participants were unaware of the content of the non-attended message (e.g. they didn't notice if it was in a foreign language) but they *did* notice physical aspects of the non-attended message, such as sex of speaker (i.e. physical characteristics).
- *Single channel, serial processing.* **Broadbent** (1958) presented two sets of digits dichotically and concurrently (e.g. 493 to one ear, 852 to the other). He found that participants usually recalled the digits ear by ear (493852) rather than in the sequence they were heard (489532).

Evidence against

- *Non-serial recall.* **Gray and Wedderburn** (1960) tested Broadbent's predictions by presenting 'DEAR, 5, JANE' to the one ear and '3, AUNT, 4' to the other. They found that participants recall by meaning rather than ear by ear (DEAR AUNT JANE rather than DEAR 5 JANE 3 AUNT 4) refuting Broadbent's finding.
- *Monitoring the unattended message.* **Moray** (1959) found that information played to the 'deaf' ear was not remembered even if it was repeated 35 times. However, if the unattended message contained the person's name it was remembered one-third of the time.

Evaluation

- Far more processing takes place on the non-attended message than Broadbent's relatively rigid system allows.
- The filter acts not just on physical attributes but on meaning as well.

② *Attenuation model.* **Treisman** (1964) proposed that the incoming signals become progressively attenuated (weakened) as they pass through successively more sophisticated filters. Therefore messages are not blocked completely but subjected to some analysis: if a weak signal triggers a person's 'dictionary' of important words, the signal is enhanced. If at any time, there is insufficient capacity in the system (due to other demands) the more sophisticated filters are omitted.

Evidence for

- **Gray and Wedderburn** (1960) and **Moray** (1959), above.
- *Processing two messages.* **Treisman** (1964) used bilingual participants and a time delay between a speech given dichotically in French and in English. As the offset was reduced between the two messages, the participants realised they were the same but in French and English.
- *GSR.* **von Wright** *et al.* (1975) paired certain words with an electric shock. If these words, or their synonyms, were later presented to the non-attended ear, the participant produced a galvanic skin response (see unit 3.4.2) indicating some semantic processing of the unattended message.

Evaluation

- This model is more flexible but is still essentially a single channel theory, ignoring parallel processing.
- The attenuation process has not been precisely specified.

③ *Late selection models.* **Deutsch and Deutsch** (1963) and **Norman** (1968) proposed that all information receives limited processing for meaning before selection takes place on the basis of salience.

Evidence for

- *Unconscious semantic processing.* **McKay** (1973) played an ambiguous sentence to participants' shadowed side, e.g. containing the word 'bank'. Another word was played to the non-attended ear, e.g. either 'river' or 'money'. Participants had no recall of the non-attended words but their interpretation of the ambiguous sentence was affected.

Evidence against

- *Unequal processing.* **Treisman and Riley** (1969) asked participants to shadow one message and tap whenever a target word was presented to either ear. Detection rates were much higher in the shadowed message. The late selection model would predict there should be no difference because both channels have complete perceptual analysis, whereas in Treisman's model the weakened non-attended signal would account for poorer performance.

Evaluation

- This model allows for the effects of, for example, perceptual set, semantic and physical content, and parallel processing.
- It is possible that participants are switching attention between channels rather than truly parallel processing, i.e. they are multiprocessing.
- Treisman's model can account for the same evidence.
- It is a rather rigid and unnecessarily complicated system.

④ *A flexible model.* **Johnston and Heinz** (1978) suggested that selection occurs as early in processing as possible, depending on the prevailing circumstances and task demands. Semantic processing makes a greater demand on resources than physical messages and therefore makes early filtering necessary.

Evidence for

- *Semantic processing does not necessarily take place.* **Johnston and Wilson** (1980) presented pairs of words dichotically, the task was to identify various target items. When participants were told to attend to both ears all the words were processed for meaning. When participants knew that the target words would arrive in the left ear, words of a similar nature presented to the right side had no effect on target detection. See also **Sullivan**, unit 5.2.4.

⑤ *Conclusion.* It is difficult to establish which is correct. **Eysenck and Keane** (1995) conclude that the attenuation model is adequate with the addition of some concept of flexibility. Models of divided attention offer further alternatives (see unit 5.2.2).

Criticisms of focused attention research

- The failure to shadow may be an effect of *practice*. **Underwood** (1974) found that naive participants were only able to detect 8% of the digits presented to the unshadowed ear whereas well-practiced participants reported 67% of the words.
- All empirical studies are lab experiments and lack *ecological validity*.
- Experimental participants may have been influenced by *experimenter bias*.
- The research concerned *audition only*. **Allport et al.** (1972) found that if participants had to monitor two messages in different sensory modalities (a tape and a film), their performance improved enormously.

Applications: radar operations and vigilance.

Focused visual attention

① *Zoom-lens model.* **Eriksen** (1990) proposed that the visual attention acts like a spotlight, the 'beam' can be adjusted to cover a greater or smaller area.

Evidence for

- *Faster response in region of focused attention.* **LaBerge** (1983) presented five-letter words and asked participants either to report the middle letter or to categorise the whole word. On some trials a 'probe' was presented in place of the word in the same space. When attending to the central position participants were slower at responding to peripherally positioned probes.

Evidence against

- *Focus can be on specific objects rather than a particular field.* **Neisser and Becklen** (1975) showed participants a video of two superimposed sequences, a handgame and a ballgame. Participants only reported the details of the one they were told to shadow and did not appear to process any 'odd' occurrences which appeared in the non-shadowed version.

Evaluation. Focused visual attention is more flexible than this model suggests.

② *Unattended visual stimuli.* **Navon**'s research (unit 5.1.1) indicated that performance is slowed by the presence of inconsistent stimuli, therefore stimuli which are ignored are still processed at some level. **Francolini and Egeth** (1980) told participants to count a set of red letters or numerals and ignore any black items. When the numerals were in conflict with the actual answer, performance was slowed but there was no distraction effect from the black items suggesting that unattended stimuli only interfere when they are relevant.

③ *Visual search and feature detection.* When conducting a visual search, a person must process all stimuli to a limited extent in order to reject them. **Neisser** (unit 5.1.3) showed that people locate letters in a visual search task by looking for critical features rather than template matching. The *word superiority effect* shows that expectations also influence visual detection. **Reicher** (1969) found that participants were able to identify a letter in a target position more quickly if the string was a word (or a familiar spelling pattern) rather than a non-word. The person's initial hypothesis generates expectations about what letters might appear and facilitates letter recognition (unit 5.4.2).

5.2.2 DIVIDED ATTENTION

① *Bottleneck theories.* **Welford** (1952) suggested that performance is severely limited when a person has to make two decisions almost simultaneously (a bottleneck).

Evidence for

- *Psychological refractory period effect*: one stimulus is presented very shortly after another, for each stimulus the participant has to make a specific response; this is much slower for the second response. **Pashler** (1993) showed that even when participants practice, the effect remains and that, even when the stimuli and responses are very different, the effect remains, e.g. a tone requiring a vocal response and a visual letter requiring a button–push response.

Evidence against

- *Practice does facilitate dual-task performance.* **Spelke** *et al.* (1976) were able to train two participants to perform two quite complex tasks simultaneously (read for comprehension and take down dictation). **Allport** *et al.* (1972) found that expert pianists could play from seen music and shadow auditory messages. **Shaffer** (1975) found that typists could type and shadow.

Evaluation. A bottleneck cannot be the only explanation.

❷ *Central capacity theories.* **Kahneman** (1973) and **Johnston and Heinz** (1978) suggested that attention can be understood in terms of a central processor which allocates one central pool of attention. The amount of capacity varies with circumstances: if you are wide awake you have more attentional capacity, different tasks take up different capacity, and motivation increases capacity. When two tasks do not overload capacity, they do not interfere with each other.

Evidence for

- *Dual-task performance.* Practice means that some processes become more automatic therefore placing fewer demands on central capacity (see above).

Evidence against

- *Task similarity may be more important than central capacity.* **Segal and Fusella** (1970) combined image construction (task A) with signal detection (task B), both in visual (C) and auditory (D) modes. According to central capacity theory, if A interferes with C more than B does we would expect the same to hold true for A, B and D. However, they found that the auditory image task interfered more than the visual one with auditory signals whereas the opposite was true for the visual signal task, in both cases due to task similarity.

Evaluation. This theory can explain both focused and divided attention, and can incorporate top–down and bottom–up processing.

❸ *Modular theories.* **Allport** (1980) proposed a system consisting of independent processors responsible for different tasks and with individual capacities.

Evidence for

- This model can account for task interference on similar tasks and lack of interference on different or automated tasks.
- *Neurophysiological evidence.* For example, individuals with tumours in Broca's area lose specific linguistic abilities (unit 3.2.2).

Evaluation. This is a difficult theory to disprove. It also does not explain how modules are co-ordinated, unless there is a central processor.

❹ *Synthesis theories.* **Baddeley** (1986) combined the above approaches in the form of a hierarchy of processes: specific processors function independently of each other and are co-ordinated by a central processor.

Evidence for

- *Neurophysiological* evidence. Dual-task performance where both tasks are organised by the same brain hemisphere should result in interference. **Kinsbourne and McMurray** (1975) demonstrated that this is true in young children who couldn't recite a nursery rhyme (controlled by left hemisphere) and tap with their right finger as fast as with their left finger (controlled by right hemisphere). However, adults can tap with either hand as quickly because they have developed *synergisms*, co–ordinated systems with a unified aim.

Evaluation. Information processing theories are mechanistic, they don't take social, motivational and emotional factors into account.

5.2.3 AUTOMATIC PROCESSING

Automatic processing: (1) occurs without intention, (2) is concealed from consciousness and (3) consumes few or no conscious resources (**Posner and Snyder**, 1974). Like attention generally, it is a way to use resources efficiently.

❶ *Controlled versus automatic processes.* **Shiffrin and Schneider** (1977) proposed a distinction between:

- *Controlled (attentional) processes* have limited capacity, involve serial processing and focused attention, and can be modified easily.
- *Automatic processes* have no capacity limitations, do not require attention and are difficult to modify once learned. They are examples of parallel processing.

   Stroop (1935) found that the task of naming the colour of a conflicting colour word (e.g. RED is written in green) is slower than naming the colour when the word and ink are the same. This *Stroop effect* is due to the automatic tendency to read words. The effect is strongest in children who are just learning to read and is used to test brain damage (a NFER test). **Navon** (unit 5.1.1) used a variant of the Stroop task to show that, when local and global letters are in conflict, processing of local letters is slowed down because participants automatically process the global ones.

   Evaluation

- It is a descriptive rather than explanatory account.
- Automatic processes require some attentional control.

❷ *Fully versus partially automatic processes.* **Kahneman and Henik** (1979) found that the Stroop effect was less likely to occur when distracting information (the colour name) was in an adjacent location, which suggests that the effect is not entirely unavoidable and therefore not fully automatic. **Logan and Zbrodoff** (1979) showed that practice could reduce the effect: participants had to say the position of the word 'ABOVE' or 'BELOW' when it appeared above or below a line. They were able to develop strategies for dividing attention.

   Therefore, **Norman and Shallice** (1986) suggested that controlled and automatic processes should be located on a continuum rather than being seen as discrete:

- *Fully automatic processes* are controlled by schemas and receive minimal conscious awareness.
- *Partially automatic processes* occur when there is conflict, this is automatically resolved by contention scheduling. If this didn't happen automatic processes would disrupt behaviour.
- *Deliberate control* by a *supervisory attention system* (the second source of control).

❸ *Memory and automatic processing.* **Logan** (1988) proposed that automatic processes are fast because they involve 'single-step direct-access retrieval of past solutions'. Prolonged practice means we no longer have to think about what we are doing because the information can be supplied directly from memory; memory retrieval does not require attentional control (**Norman**'s model, unit 5.2.4).

5.2.4 PERFORMANCE DEFICITS (ATTENTIONAL ERRORS)

❶ *Action slips* (absent-mindedness) are the performance of an unintended action. **Reason** (1979) asked 35 people to keep diaries over a two-week period. Of the 400 errors reported 40% were storage failures (intentions or actions were forgotten or recalled incorrectly), 20% were test failures (diversions from a planned activity) and 18% were subroutine failures (small alterations of a well-used routine). In a laboratory study of action slips, participants were asked to respond as quickly as possible to a series of questions, for example 'What do we call a tree that grows from acorns?' , 'What do you call the white of an egg?'; 85% said 'yolk' because the misleading context activates an automatic and incorrect response (similar to mental set, unit 5.4.3) (**Reason**, 1992).

Reason suggested two modes of control over motor performance to account for the fact that action slips and errors tend to occur during highly practised and overlearned activities, rather than, as one might expect, during learning.

- *Closed-loop* (feedback) method of control used during skill acquisition to monitor motor performance and provide feedback; attention is required.
- *Open-loop* methods of control result from practice. Subroutines (predetermined sequences of action) are linked together and performed automatically (without attention) thus freeing central resources to engage in other processing activities. Sometimes a person who is operating in open-loop mode may fail to return to closed-loop mode (direct attention) when necessary, resulting in an action slip because the wrong motor programme is activated or runs on.

Norman (1981) proposed an alternative model, a hierarchy of schemas. The highest level is the overall intention, and the lower levels are like Reason's subroutines. At any time an intention or environmental cue will trigger a particular schema, which is performed with attentional control. According to this schema model there are three reasons why action slips occur: (1) errors in forming the intention to do something, e.g. discrimination errors, (2) faulty activation of a schema leading to the performance of the wrong schema, e.g. storage failures, (3) faulty triggering of active schema, e.g.. programme assembly failures.

Application. Action slips may explain the causes of many accidents, such as pilot and machine–operator errors. The study of vigilance (sustained attention) looks at how to avoid such difficulties. **Mackworth** (1950) gave participants a task similar to radar-watching, and found that they were 85% correct in the first 30 minutes but this decreased to around 70% thereafter. In order to compensate it may be necessary to take a break and thoroughly rearouse the system – advice given to sleepy drivers.

② *Dual-task limitations* can be understood in terms of:

- *Task similarity.* **McLeod** (1977) asked participants to manually respond to a tracking task with one hand and, at the same time, to make a verbal or manual response (with their other hand) to a tone. They could do the verbal response better than the manual one. It is difficult to test task similarity because it is not always possible to decide how similar two tasks are (e.g. playing the piano and singing a song).
- *Task difficulty.* **Sullivan** (1976) arranged for participants to shadow one message and report the presence of target words in the non-shadowed ear. If the shadowing task was made more difficult, the performance with the non-shadowed ear fell.
- *Practice* (**Spelke** *et al.*, unit 5.2.2).

③ *Attentional deficit hyperactivity disorder* (see unit 4.1.3) is characterised by an inability to concentrate for lengths of time, and being continually distracted. Sufferers may be chronically overaroused (easily aroused and therefore distracted), or it may be that they are underaroused (they can't maintain attention and therefore continually switch).

5.3 MEMORY

Memory is the mental function of retaining data (i.e. learning), the storage system holding the data, and the data which is retained.

5.3.1 THE NATURE OF MEMORY

Stages of memory

Each is a necessary but not sufficient condition for memory to have taken place.

- *Input* (*registering / encoding information*). Sensory data is translated into a *memory trace* (the neurological representation).

- *Storage*, temporary or permanent.
- *Output* (*retrieval*). Memories are useless unless they can retrieved through recognition, recall, reconstruction, reproduction (rote learning) and/or confabulation.

Structure of memory

Memory can be separated into:

- *Sensory memory* (SM or sensory input store, SIS). The sensory form of a stimulus remains unaltered in the mind for a brief time, there are different stores for each modality. Information is rapidly lost through decay.
- *Short-term memory* (STM). It has relatively limited capacity (about seven items) and rapidly decays unless maintained through rehearsal. Also called primary or working memory.
- *Long-term memory* (LTM). Relatively permanent storage which has unlimited capacity. Information is held in enactive, iconic or symbolic forms and structured in some way. Also called secondary or permanent memory; subdivided into procedural, declarative, semantic and episodic memory (see unit 5.3.2).

The evidence for separate stores comes from empirical studies of:

1 *Duration.* **Sperling** (1960) briefly showed participants a display of 12 letters organised in three rows, and asked them to immediately recall the letters. If a tone was presented after the display, signalling which row to report, recall was three times better demonstrating that available information disappears very rapidly. **Peterson and Peterson** (1959) found that delayed recall of trigrams reduces performance from 80% after 3 seconds to 10% after 18 seconds (participants did an interpolated task between presentation and recall to prevent rehearsal). **Atkinson and Shiffrin** (1971) reported a longer duration of 15–30 seconds, suggesting an upper limit for STM of 30 seconds. LTM is potentially unlimited ('Forgetting', unit 5.3.4).

2 *Capacity.* SM is limited by duration, LTM is potentially unlimited. **Miller** (1956) suggested that the span of STM is limited *not* by bits of information but by the *chunks*; people can remember the same number of 10-letter words as 5-letter ones. The number of chunks which can be remembered is 7±2 (which might explain why categories often consist of 7 items: days of the week, wonders of the world, etc.). However, **Simon** (1974) found that there is a limit beyond which chunk size does have an effect – participants had a shorter memory span for larger chunks, such as 8-word phrases, than smaller chunks, such as one-syllable words.

Chunking relies on LTM in order to determine meaningfulness. **Bower and Springston** (1970) showed that participants recalled meaningful chunks (e.g. 'FBI ... PHD ... TWA') better than meaningless groups ('FB ... IPH ... DWT').

Applications. Post codes and telephone numbers.

3 *Coding differences.* **Baddeley** (1966) showed that STM recall was poorer when word lists were acoustically similar (e.g. man, mad, cab, can) whereas LTM recall was worse when words were semantically similar (e.g. great, large, big). **Conrad** (1964) demonstrated that visually presented letters suffer from acoustic errors in immediate recall (B is confused with P rather than F), therefore they must be acoustically coded in STM.

4 *Serial position effect.* **Glanzer and Cunitz** (1966) asked participants to recall word lists. If this was done immediately there was a *primacy* and a *recency* effect (early and later words were better recalled), both STM and LTM were involved. If there was delay of ten seconds or more there was only a primacy effect – LTM alone was affected. Primacy is due to the fact that the first items are more likely to have entered LTM. Recency occurs because the last items in the list are still in STM.

5 *Brain damage. Retrograde amnesia* affects STM, it may be caused by an accident or ECT; events immediately prior to the trauma are permanently forgotten presumably because information is lost from STM at the time of trauma. *Anterograde amnesia* affects LTM, permanent memories remain intact but sufferers cannot remember any new information for more than the normal STM span. This is probably because transfer from STM to LTM is lost. Examples include *Korsakoff's syndrome*, due to severe alcohol poisoning, and the case study of **H.M.** whose hippocampus was removed because of severe epilepsy. He could still recall all the skills he previously knew but he perpetually thought he was 27 and that the year was 1953. After a while he realised this was absurd and tried guessing the answer. **Baddeley** (1990) described another case of such anterograde amnesia, Clive Wearing, whose hippocampus was damaged by infection.

6 *Forgetting.* Explanations are different for STM and LTM, see unit 5.3.4.

5.3.2 THEORIES OF MEMORY

1 *The multistore model*, e.g. **Atkinson and Shriffrin** (1968). The evidence described in unit 5.2.1 suggests three distinct stores. Information enters SM, and is initially stored in STM. If it is not rehearsed, it is lost; continued rehearsal leads to LTM storage.

Evaluation

- It is a useful model, based on empirical evidence. Many subsequent theories are derived from it.
- Rehearsal doesn't adequately explain LTM, it may be an artefact of memory experiments.
- Alternative explanations can account for the empirical findings, e.g. the levels of processing model can explain differences in the amount of material recalled.
- The model is oversimplified, in practice there are not clear distinctions between stages of memory.
- It presents a passive view of memory and cannot account for active processes such as reconstruction.

2 *Modifications of the multistore model: divisions of LTM*

Cohen and Squire (1980) divided LTM into:

- *Procedural system*: knowing how to do things.
- *Declarative system*: knowledge about facts.

Tulving (1972) further divided the procedural system into:

- *Episodic memory*: personal events and people.
- *Semantic memory*: language and other general knowledge .

Evaluation

- These subdivisions make more sense of the experimental data, such as the effects of brain damage.
- This explains why laboratory studies, which involve episodic memory only, may not be applicable to real life.

3 *Modifications of the multistore model: working memory* (WM). **Baddeley and Hitch** (1974) and **Baddeley** (1986) suggested an active WM in place of passive STM:

- A modality-free *central executive* resembles attention, allocates resources to other components and may function like **Norman and Shallice**'s supervisory attentional system (see unit 5.2.3). It has a limited capacity and brief duration. Empirical support comes from studies which show that task similarity impairs performance (see unit 5.2.4). This must be due to competition within the same system.
- A *phonological loop* deals with verbal material and consists of a *phonological store* and an *articulatory process*. **Baddeley *et al.*** (1975) gave participants a sequence of words to recall. Normally, they could perform the task better with short rather than long words (*word-length effect*) but when an articulatory suppression task (counting backwards) was included there was no difference, demonstrating that the word–length effect depends on an articulatory process. Subsequent research (**Baddeley and Lewis**, 1981) found that articulatory suppression did *not* affect decisions involving acoustic (phonological) differences and therefore there must be a separate store for this.
- A *visuo-spatial sketchpad* is specialised for spatial and visual coding. **Baddeley, Grant *et al.*** (1975) gave participants the task of visualising a matrix of digits which was

presented auditorially; if this was combined with tracking a moving light, the ability to visualise was impaired.

Evaluation

- This model is relevant to a wider set of activities, such as verbal reasoning and comprehension, because it is active.
- The model describes rehearsal (the articulatory process) as only one component, which seems more appropriate.
- The division of STM into further components more accurately reflects evidence from brain damaged patients, who experience specific kinds of attentional disorders. For example, frontal lobe damage results in behaviour which appears to be lacking a control system (**Eysenck and Keane**, 1995).
- The central executive is somewhat vague and may not be unitary.

④ *Levels of processing model.* **Craik and Lockhart** (1972) argued that when information is given more meaning (*depth*) it is processed more and this, rather than rehearsal alone, makes it more memorable. Memory is a by-product of processing.

Evidence for

- **Craik and Tulving** (1975) asked participants a series of yes/no questions about a list of words. Questions were either: shallow ('Is the word in capital letters?'), phonemic ('Does the word rhyme with able?') or semantic ('Would the word fit in the sentence "They met a ---- in the street"?'). Participant's recall (with or without warning) was best with semantic processing and worst with shallow processing.
- **Hyde and Jenkins** (1973) gave participants five different tasks: they were asked to rate a list of words for pleasantness, estimate their frequency of usage, count the letters 'e' and 'g', decide what part of speech it was or decide if the word fitted into certain sentences. When tested for incidental learning (recall without warning), recall was best in the first two conditions which involved semantic processing.
- **Mandler**'s (1967) experiment which involved sorting word cards into categories, also demonstrated incidental learning, though in this case processing occurred through organisation.

Evidence against

- It is possible that the better recall of meaningful material is due to the way the participants' memories were tested. **Morris *et al.*** (1977) found that if participants were given a rhyming recognition test they remembered the words which had received shallow processing better than the more deeply processed ones.

Evaluation

- This is also an oversimplified account. Depth is not the only factor which affects memorability, relevance can be important.
- This model describes rather than explains.
- The concept of 'depth' is hard to define and it is circular.
- This model emphasises processes of memory.

Application. Giving meaning to material is one means of improving your memory.

⑤ *Schema theory.* **Bartlett** (1932) suggested that recall is not simply matter of accessing a piece of information but often involves some reconstruction. Prior knowledge, or schema, lead to predictable distortions during both storage and recall. Schema are organised packets of information which facilitate understanding and generate expectations.

Bartlett tested this using successive reproduction. He gave people one of eight passages to read, most famously the 'War of the Ghosts' an Inuit legend with strange references to battles and black stuff coming out of someone's mouth. He repeatedly asked his participants to recall the story and noted that the kind of transformations they made were consistent with the Western assumptions and expectations, for example the 'something black' was translated to 'foaming at the mouth'. He concluded that the process of remembering is not passive recording but active processing. ('Organisation of memory', unit 5.3.3 and 'Models of thought', unit 5.4.3).

Evaluation

- Memory is influenced by social factors which may be obscured by laboratory methods.
- Schema theory is a more general approach to cognitive processes than just memory (stereotypes, unit 1.1.3, and Piaget, unit 6.2.1).
- It does not explain some important features of memory, such as why some material cannot be retrieved.

6 *Connectionist networks.* **McClelland**'s (1981) *parallel distributed processing* (PDP) model suggested that information about a person, object or event, is stored in several interconnected units rather than a single place (hence, distributed), and retrieval involves accessing one or more of these units.

Evaluation

- Networks are a powerful conceptual framework, and used in many cognitive explanations.
- Such a model accounts for many features of memory, such as: reconstructive recall, hierarchical organisation, spontaneous generalisations and physiological descriptions of interconnected pathways.
- Can be tested using computer modelling techniques.
- The differences between this and earlier models are so great that comparison is difficult.

5.3.3 ORGANISATION OF MEMORY

1 *Theories of memory (unit 5.3.2)* all provide information about how memory is structured and organised. LTM cannot function without some structure.

2 *Hierarchical semantic networks.* **Collins and Quillan**'s (1969) model proposes that concepts are arranged in hierarchies so that any concept has all the attributes of those which are superordinate). A hierarchy enables efficient storage and retrieval.

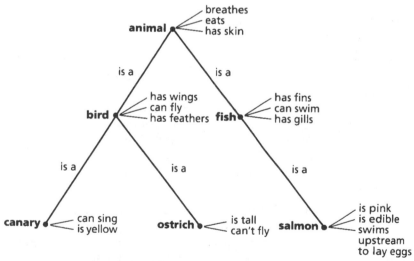

Figure 5.3 Hierarchical semantic network

Evidence for

- *Hierarchical recall.* **Bousfield** (1953) found that participants recalled words in clusters despite the fact that they were given items from various categories (e.g. vegetables, animals) in random order.
- *Increased retrieval.* **Bower** *et al.* (1969) gave participants 112 words belonging to several categories; if the words were presented in random order recall was worse than if the same words were arranged in conceptual hierarchies.
- *Search time.* **Collins and Quillan** asked participants to verify a series of statements. The time taken was related to the distance between the subject and predicate in the sentence, e.g. 'a canary can fly' took longer than 'a canary can sing'.

Evidence against

- *Search time.* **Rips et al.** (1973) found it took longer to verify 'a bear is a mammal' than 'a bear is an animal', the reverse of Collins and Quillan.
- *Salience.* **Conrad** (1972) found that speed on the sentence verification task could be due to the commonness of an attribute, e.g. we hear the phrase 'a salmon is pink' more often than 'a salmon has fins'.
- *Typicality effect.* It takes longer to verify statements involving less typical members (e.g. 'a penguin is a bird' compared with 'a robin is a bird').
- *Fuzzy boundaries.* Most of our concepts are probabilistic, rather than having definite attributes (unit 5.4.3).

❸ *Interconnected semantic networks.* **Collins and Loftus** (1975) revised the original model in response to the above criticisms.

- *Flexible* rather than logical structure allows for personal experience.
- *Semantic distance.* All concepts are linked, the more similar ones are closer.
- *Negative links,* e.g. 'a penguin is *not* a fish'.
- *Spreading activation.* When two concepts are simultaneously activated, a link is formed. This explains how personal and negative links are formed.

    Evaluation. This model continues to pose difficulties for fuzzy boundaries and fails to account for the way that real-world knowledge affects interpretation.

❹ *Schema theory* offers a means of understanding dynamic organisation and suggests that memory is more than a set of interconnected concepts (see unit 5.3.2).

5.3.4 FORGETTING

'Forgetting' assumes that something was once stored in STM or LTM, and now either it has disappeared (not available), or can't be 'brought to mind' (not accessible).

Failures of availability

❶ *Encoding failure.* You may think you've forgotten something, but in fact you never remembered it, i.e. it was not stored in STM or LTM.

❷ *Trace decay.* The physical form of memory disappears with time due to neural decay.

- It can explain SM and STM 'forgetting', and the effect of rehearsal.
- LTM: some *kinds* of memory clearly do not decay, e.g. you never forget to ride a bicycle even if you haven't done it for a long time (procedural system). Other kinds may not decay but they become *inaccessible*, support comes from the success of recall under hypnosis (not always accurate), electrical stimulation of the brain (recovery of some long-lost memories), relearning studies (see below) and the effectiveness of cues (see below). It may be that the reconstructive nature of memory gives the illusion of long-term memories.

❸ *Displacement.* As STM appears to be limited in capacity, any excess would be displaced or overwritten. This cannot apply to LTM, which is unlimited in capacity. **Shallice** (1967) presented digits rapidly to participants and found that speed of presentation affected recall less than the number of subsequent items, which means that displacement must have caused the effect.

❹ *Lack of consolidation.* When people are given ECT or experience concussion, they may have retrograde amnesia (see unit 5.3.1). The trauma prevents the consolidation of immediate memories and therefore they are lost. REM sleep may enable memories to be consolidated.

❺ *Interference.* One set of information competes with another, causing it to be 'overwritten' or physically lost.

- *Similarity* causes greater interference. **McGeoch and McDonald** (1931) found that if the interference task was a list of synonyms to the original list, recall was poor (12%), nonsense syllables interfered less (26% recall) and numbers (37% recall). Only interference can explain such findings.

- *RI is stronger than PI.* Interference can be tested by giving participants two *similar* lists: the same nonsense syllable paired with different words, A-B (e.g. BEM and lawn) and A-C (e.g. BEM and aisle). If participants learn A-B, then A-C; recall on A-B is affected by *retroactive interference* (RI). If they learn A-C, then A-B, recall on A-B is affected by *proactive inhibition* (PI).
- *Inaccessible not unavailable.* **Ceraso** (1967) found that, if memory was tested again after 24 hours, recognition (accessibility) showed considerable spontaneous recovery, whereas recall (availability) remained the same.

   Evaluation. Interference has limited application, it is relevant to occasions when two sets of data are very similar. This is rare in everyday life.

⑥ *Brain damage* (i.e. neural tissue loss). This may occur through ageing, illness or injury. Studies of the effects of such damage in terms of memory failure highlight the way memory works at a neurophysiological level (see unit 3.1.1).

⑦ *Gestalt theory of forgetting.* Gestalt psychologists suggested that the form of memory is important (i.e. the '*gestalten*'). Memories spontaneously change over time to maintain consistency. This is similar to reconstructive memory except that it is spontaneous.

Failures of accessibility

① *Cue-dependent forgetting.* **Tulving** (1962) presented participants with a list of words followed by three successive recall trials. The *specific* words recalled each time differed though the response rate remained a fairly steady 50%. This suggests that information is there but not always retrieved. The fact that recognition is better than recall also points to lack of accessibility which could be improved by using cues.

Evidence for

- **Tulving and Pearlstone** (1966) found that performance was three times better when participants were given appropriate retrieval cues.
- *Context-dependent recall.* **Abernethy** (1940) found recall was better for a group of participants who sat in the same room and seat when tested than those tested in different surroundings. **Godden and Baddeley** (1975) gave divers lists of words to learn on land or underwater, recall was better when the context was constant.
- *State dependent recall.* **Goodwin** *et al.* (1969) reported clinical evidence of drinkers who hid money when drunk and couldn't remember where when sober. However, they could recall when drunk again.

② *Repressed memories* (motivated forgetting). **Freud** suggested that painful or disturbing memories are put beyond conscious recall, this may range from sexual abuse to more commonplace situations like 'forgetting' to clean your room or go to the dentist. Hypnosis is one means of retrieving inaccessible memories, though it may rely on reconstructions and therefore inaccurate recall (unit 3.3.4). **Levinger and Clark** (1993) gave participants word lists, including some emotionally charged words (such as 'fear'). Subsequent recall was poorer for the emotional words. However, when **Parkin** *et al.* (1982) repeated this experiment with delayed recall, they found improvement, which suggests that arousal had led to initial repression (see also the effects of emotion on perception, unit 5.1.3).

③ *Underprocessing.* **Ebbinghaus** (1885) read hundreds of nonsense syllables out loud and tested his own recall. One of his conclusions was about *relearning savings*, relearning is faster than original learning which must be due to an inaccessible but faint trace remaining.

5.3.5 PRACTICAL APPLICATIONS OF MEMORY RESEARCH

① *Eyewitness testimony.* **Loftus** (1979) was called as an expert witness in a trial where a shop assistant, Melville, had identified a robber, José Garcia. She based her advice on the following:

- Identification was made two weeks after the crime, **Ebbinghaus** (1885) found that memory decays rapidly at first and then more gradually (the *forgetting curve*).
- The assistant was in a state of extreme distress after seeing his colleague shot, psychologists have found that arousal and stress have a negative effect on recall, especially STM ('Bodily rhythms' and 'Stress' in chapter 3).
- Garcia was a Mexican–American, Melville was White. People are less good at identifying members of a different race (see unit 5.1.4).

Melville was probably unconsciously filling in the gaps in his memory on the basis of expectations and prejudices. The jury was not able to agree on a verdict.

Wells *et al.* (1979) left a participant in a cubicle with a calculator, a confederate appeared and took it. When the experimenter asked the participant (witness) to identify the 'thief ' from six pictures, 58% were correct. Moreover, in a follow-up mock trial, 80% of the witnesses were believed. Such unreliability and subsequent believability needs careful monitoring. (See also **Loftus** *et al.*, 1978, in unit 5.4.4.)

② *Memory for medical information.* **Ley** (1978) prepared a booklet for doctors with suggestions about how to improve patients' recall of medical advice or information:

- Give instructions and advice *before* other information.
- *Stress* the importance of the instructions and advice you give.
- Use *short* words and *short* sentences.
- Use *explicit terms* where possible.
- Repeat information.
- Give *specific* detailed advice rather than general rules.

All of these suggestions are based on the findings of psychological studies. A group of doctors used the booklet and found that their patients' recall improved from 55% to 70%.

③ *Mnemonics* (technique for improving memory) can be explained using memory research:

- *Repetition*. Rehearsal and relearning enhance long-term memories.
- *Organisation*. The act of categorising is equivalent to memorising.
- *Elaboration*. Expanding and discussing material increases its meaning.
- *Chunking*, e.g. using keyword headings and numbered lists.
- *Cues*, e.g. subheadings and keywords.
- *Visual imagery*: Images help connect or organise pieces of information, form links, impose structure and reduce the chunks.
- *Loci system* (method of locations). Objects are 'placed' by forming strong visual images; relies on contextual cues, organisation of material and imagery.
- *Keyword system*. A word which sounds very similar to a foreign word is linked to the foreign word using an image, e.g. the Spanish word for chicken (*pollo*) sounds like 'pole', imagine a chicken holding a pole.
- *Peg word system*. A previously learned system of words are used as *pegs* on which to hang data. You could use the list: one-bun, two-shoe, etc. and associate each new word with a known word in the list.
- *Abbreviations and meaning*. Giving meaning (deeper processing) to otherwise meaningless material. For example, *acronyms* (using a letter from each word: ROY G. BIV for the colours of the spectrum), *acrostics* (using the same first letter: 'Some old hippies can always have tankards of ale' for the trigonometry formula sine = opp/hyp, etc.) and *rhymes* (such as 'thirty days hath September ...').

5.4 LANGUAGE AND THOUGHT

5.4.1 LANGUAGE ACQUISITION

Stages of language acquisition

PHASE	AGE (approx)	BEHAVIOUR
Pre-linguistic	0-1	Cooing, crying, turn-taking, babbling, echolalia, gestures.
One word utterances	1-1½	Holophrases, first words.
First sentences	2 – 4	**Bee and Mitchel** (1980) distinguished two stages: • *Stage 1 grammar*: two word utterances, telegraphic speech. **Braine** (1963) described a *pivot grammar*: pivot words (e.g. 'see') combined with 'open' or 'x' words. • *Stage 2 grammar*: overgeneralising, over- and underextension, pragmatics. Complex sentences with MLU of 4 ((MLU=mean length of utterance measured in morphemes, 'to' is one morpheme, 'toes' and 'today' are two).
Later speech	4 plus	Improving pronunciation and complexity, use of metalanguage in poems and jokes.

Empirical studies of language acquisition

① *Non-verbal behaviours.* **Trevarthen** (1974) observed that very young babies 'take turns' in conversations, practising elements of linguistic interaction. **Bates** *et al.* (1979) found that 10-month-olds used gestures to say 'What's that?' or 'Look at that'. These are part of the pragmatics of language. Babble reflects the sound of adult speech, **Bates** *et al.* (1987) say that they are 'learning the tune before the words'.

② *Early words.* **Nelson** (1973) conducted a longitudnal naturalistic study and found that first words tended to be for objects which were prone to change (movement) such as 'ball' or 'car'. She also found that, from the beginning, children used all types of words and ones which were quite specific such as 'pigeon' rather than 'bird'. Vocabulary was typically 10 words at 15 months, 50 words at 19 months and 200 words by 2 years.

③ *Grammatical speech.* **Brown** *et al.* (1973) recorded the speech development of Adam and Eve.

- *Imitation preserving word order.* The mother might say 'He's going out' whereas the child would repeat 'He go out'. Order (grammar) not content was preserved.
- *Reduction of sentence length* is not because of memory limitations, otherwise they would only repeat the first two or three words. The key words sustain the sentence's meaning.
- *Imitation with expansion.* The mothers responded to telegraphese by expanding the sentence with the order preserved. This is a 'meaning check' for the mother and a lesson in how to create detailed meaning for the child.
- *Overgeneralisations.* **Berko** (1958) showed children a picture of a '*wug*', and then a picture of two, children easily completed the sentence : 'There are two ...' demonstrating grammatical knowledge.

④ *Sensitive period.* **Lenneberg** (1967) suggested that, if language is biologically controlled, it should not be possible to acquire it after puberty.

- *Deprived children.* Genie (**Curtiss**, 1977) spent her early life in extreme isolation. At 13 she joined the real world, unable to speak and very underdeveloped. After many years it became clear that her word combinations could never be called grammatical. Her poor recovery may have been due to brain damage and/or the emotional deprivation she experienced. In other cases of extreme early deprivation (unit 6.1.2), children have recovered the ability to use language *but* they were either younger when 'discovered' (e.g. Isabelle) or they had been isolated with a brother or sister (e.g. the Koluchova twins).

- *Deaf children* offer a kind of 'natural experiment' when their exposure to language is restricted. **Singleton and Newport** (1993) studied a deaf family, the parents only learned sign language after the age of 15 and it remained ungrammatical. Their son, Simon, was able to generate a grammatical system from this defective linguistic input. **Pinker** (1994) described how a group of older deaf Nicaraguans invented their own sign system (LSN) when deaf schools opened for the first time. Younger deaf children were able to develop a grammatical version, called ISN.

⑤ *Social factors*

- **Sachs** *et al.* (1981) studied a young boy, Jim, whose parents were both deaf and dumb. Jim heard language on TV and briefly at nursery school, but by the age of 4 his speech was backwards. Speech therapy led to quick improvements emphasising the importance of a social context.
- The Nicaraguan deaf children (above) did not learn sign language from their teachers but invented it themselves in the playground.
- **Brown** (1973) studied an autistic boy, John, and suggested that his lack of social interaction might have caused his idiosyncratic forms of communication.

⑥ *Cross-cultural studies.* **Pinker** (1994) noted that all societies develop language and that, while 'there are Stone Age societies, ... there is no such thing as a Stone Age language'. There are *linguistic universals*, forms of speech which can be found in all languages (e.g. nouns, verbs, clauses) and there is a *universal sequence* of language acquisition (as described in the table above).

⑦ *Studies of animal language* (unit 2.4.3) suggest that animals cannot acquire grammar which is probably due to innate neurophysiological differences.

Theories of language acquisition

① *Learning theory.* **Skinner** (1957) claimed that language is acquired in the same way as any other behaviour, and therefore the same laws of learning apply.

- Random sounds (*mands*) are selectively *reinforced* by the child getting what it wants, such as a biscuit or parental attention. However, **deVilliers and deVilliers** (1979) found that mands are not used meaningfully, and **Slobin** (1977) noted that adults reinforce incorrect grammar.
- Through the process of *shaping* these sounds come closer to the real thing. **Brown** *et al.* (1969) found that mothers reinforced meaning rather than grammatical structure, therefore they were not shaping performance.
- *Echoic responses*: a child imitates the sounds made by others and is positively reinforced. However, babbling is not imitative.
- A child learns to produce actual words through *imitation*. **Gelman and Shatz** (1977) found that children are helped by adults' use of *motherese* (Baby Talk Register, BTR), a special form of language which is repetitive and uses a simplified grammar (e.g. 'pat the doggie').

Evaluation

- Skinner's theory explains some aspects of language acquisition such as learning speech sounds, simple meanings, vocabulary and accent.
- It cannot account for overgeneralisations nor the universal sequence of acquisition.
- Empirical evidence is poor; learning theory is largely supported by animal research.

② *Nativist theory.* **Chomsky** (1959) proposed that language is biologically driven; humans have an innate capacity to generate the rules of grammar from a native vocabulary (i.e. acquire language), similar to the innate capacity to walk.

- *Language acquisition device* (LAD or LAS). An innate, biological system which produces universal linguistic rules.
- *Generativity of language.* An infinite number of expressions can be generated from a finite set of sounds using grammatical rules.

- *Transformational grammar.* The ability to move between *surface structure* (the actual words and phrases expressed) and *deep structure* (the meaning) is achieved using grammatical rules. 'The peasants are revolting' has two deep structures; 'the cat chased the dog' and 'the dog is chased by the cat' have the same deep structure.
- *The evolution of language.* **McNeill** (1966) argued that the development of a language relies on the reformulation made by children as they acquire language; each new generation of children reinvent and simplify the linguistic corpus.

Evaluation

- Chomsky's views were revolutionary, opening up the study of language.
- This account explains overgeneralisations, linguistic universals, the universal sequence acquisition, the ease of acquisition even when working on an incomplete sample, the lack of true language in animals, sensitive periods and language localisation in the brain (unit 3.2.2).
- This model combines nature and nurture (innate grammar and learned vocabulary).
- Children reared in social isolation don't develop language on their own, therefore exposure and innate potential are necessary but not sufficient factors.

③ *Functional theories.* **Halliday** (1975) has criticised Chomsky's approach for the fact that it refers almost exclusively to structure and ignores function. Halliday points out that early language has functional importance: smiling, crying and eye-contact. **Bruner** (1983) proposed an innate acquisition system LASS (*language acquisition support system*) which included social interaction, and applied his ideas to the study of autistic children (see evidence, above). **Vygotsky** (unit 6.2.1) also underlined the social importance of language.

Evaluation

- This does not contradict other theories, it is an addition.
- This model would predict that stone age cultures should have stone age languages, because language is a reflection of culture.
- It can't explain why blind children develop normal language despite limited social interactions (see unit 4.1.2).

④ *Interactionist theories.* **Piaget** (see unit 6.2.1) suggested that we do not need to explain language acquisition in terms of an innate, specialised processor but instead to see it as one outcome of a general intellectual ability.

- *General cognitive changes.* The fact the children of a certain age start producing two-word utterances may be because of a general cognitive maturity.
- *Interactions with the environment* facilitate linguistic and cognitive development.
- *Enrichment.* Children actively shape their perceptions using existing cognitive schemas. Thus, children acquire language through their assimilation of new words/concepts (top-down) and their accommodation of existing words/concepts (bottom-up) (*enrichment* or *input theory*).

    Evaluation. An extension of the Nativist position, stressing maturational aspects of language and thought, and their interdependence.

5.4.2 PRODUCTION AND COMPREHENSION OF LANGUAGE

Speech production

Speaking involves: thinking of what to say, selecting appropriate words, organising words grammatically, negotiating interpersonal contact and physically producing the words.

① *Speech errors.* Normal fluent speech may be understood by looking at errors.

- *Hesitations* indicate how speech is planned. **Maclay and Osgood** (1959) found that pauses at grammatical junctures tend to be filled with 'um' or 'er' whereas other pauses are silent. Such pauses help forward planning.
- *Spoonerisms,* or other phoneme/morpheme exchange errors. **Garrett** (1976) reported that 93% of the Spoonerisms that he observed occurred within the same clause, supporting the importance of the clause in speech production.

- *'Tip of the tongue'* phenomenon. **Brown and McNeill** (1966) read the definitions of unusual words to participants, who were able to get the initial letter correct 57% of the time while not being able to retrieve the actual word.

❷ *Conventions.* Speech takes place for interpersonal communication and must follow conventions, such as *turn-taking*. Infants learn this aspect of speech (see unit 5.4.1).

❸ *Speech units.* Intonation units tend to be about six words long, to contain a finite verb and the loudest section (or highest pitch) is near the end (**Gee**, 1986). The unit length (six words) may be related to STM (unit 5.3.1).

❹ *Spreading activation theory.* **Dell** (1986) proposed a series of processing stages:

- *Semantic* level: meaning is worked out.
- *Syntactic* level: outline of the utterance is produced, including the grammar.
- *Morphological* level: 'fleshing out', the root morpheme (e.g. 'jump') is adjusted by adding morphemes (e.g. 'jump-ing'). Morphemes are meaning units.
- *Phonological* level: phonemes (sound units) selected.

Processing takes place concurrently at all levels, though higher levels are always working slightly in advance of lower levels. A dictionary (*lexicon*), in the form of a connectionist network, spreads activation throughout the network when any one node is activated.

Evidence for. Speech errors occur because the wrong level has been activated, for example the *lexical bias effect* (errors tend to be actual words or morphemes). **Baars *et al.*** (1975) arranged for participants to repeat word pairs rapidly, errors were greater when the pair could be reformed into two new words (e.g. 'lewd, rip' can become 'rude, lip') rather than non-words ('luke, risk' would be 'ruke, lisk').

Evaluation

- The concept of spreading activation is powerful, generating testable propositions.
- The model can account for feedback, various kinds of brain damage and various speech errors. For example, Spoonerisms are failures at the phonological level, and 'tip of the tongue' phenomena can be understood in terms of spreading activation.
- Assumes that grammatical structure is worked out first and then words fitted in, however, for example, anticipation errors (a word spoken earlier in a sentence than it should be) suggest some sequential processing.

Writing

Writing involves different mechanical problems than speech.

❶ *Stages in the writing process.* **Hayes and Flower** (1986) proposed three main processes, which may or may not occur in sequence:

- *Planning*: producing ideas and a plan, guided by a goal.
- *Sentence generation*: turning the plan into writing. **Kaufer *et al.*** (1986) used *protocol analysis* to study the process of writing (a writer describes what they are doing while they write). They found that a writer typically produced many partial versions of a sentence before settling on the final, full version.
- *Reviewing*: evaluating specific words, phrases or overall structure. Expert writers spend longer doing this, making more changes especially to meaning.

Evaluation

- The model is based on only conscious activity, reported in protocol analysis.
- Useful for comparing more and less skilled writers.

❷ *Spelling.*

- Known words are located in a *graphemic output lexicon*.
- Unknown words are constructed using *phoneme-grapheme conversion*, based on regularities of spelling. A grapheme is a group of letters representing a sound.

Evidence for comes from studies of brain-damaged patients. **Shallice** (1981) studied PR who was able to spell and write after a stroke but had difficulty spelling words which resembled a correct word in sound (e.g. 'caught' instead of 'quart').

③ *Skilled writing.* **Bereiter and Scardamalia** (1987) distinguished two major strategies:
- *Knowledge telling strategy.* Unskilled writers (e.g. children) tend to write down everything they know, with some organisation.
- *Knowledge-transforming strategy.* Skilled writers possess *strategic knowledge* (knowledge about how to plan well-organised and coherent writing).

Language comprehension

Comprehension involves word recognition and semantic interpretation. It typically occurs very rapidly, and acts on parts of sentences (parsing) rather than waiting for the whole.

① *Schema theory* (Bartlett's study, unit 5.3.2). **Bransford and Johnson** (1972) found that both comprehensibility of a passage and subsequent recall were greater if participants were told the title ('Washing clothes') before rather than after reading the passage. The title generates schema which are helpful in interpreting the meaning of an otherwise somewhat meaningless text and this comprehension facilitates recall. **Ausubel** (1968) proposed that meaningful verbal learning was facilitated by presenting students with complex concepts (*advanced organisers*) *before* the material to be learned is presented.

② *Script theory.* **Schank and Abelson** (1977) explained comprehension in terms of schema and scripts (schema of appropriate behaviours). **Schank** (1975) developed a computer program called MARGIE to comprehend language consisting of three modules: a semantic parser which produces conceptual dependency diagrams, an inference mechanism which elaborates these diagrams using knowledge about the world, and a response generator, which uses the elaborated diagrams to produce paraphrases and answer questions.

③ *Construction-integration model.* **Kintsch** (1994) proposed a propositional model:
- Bottom-up processing: *a propositional net* (set of propositions) is generated from the text and entered in a short-term buffer.
- Top-down: *elaborated propositional net* is formed from STM propositions and related ones retrieved from LTM.
- *Integration process*: highly interconnected propositions create greatest activation across the net and are most likely to be selected.
- This scheme results in three representations: a *surface representation* (the original text), a *propositional representation* and *situational representation* (a mental model of the situation described in the text).

   Evaluation. The model makes very precise predictions. **Kintsch and Keenan** (1973) showed how processing time is affected by number of propositions. 'Romulus, the legendary founder of Rome, took the women of Sabine by force' has four propositions whereas 'Cleopatra's downfall lay in her foolish trust of the fickle political figures of the Roman world' has eight, and takes about four seconds longer to process.

④ *Transformational grammar.* **Chomsky** (see unit 5.4.1).

Speech comprehension

Listening involves identification of speech sounds (phonemes), prior to word recognition.

① *Bottom-up processes.* There are various problems to overcome:
- *Linearity.* One speech segment affects the following segment.
- *Non-invariance.* Phonemes are affected by the sounds before and after.
- *Segmentation.* Sounds are produced with no separations.
- *Differentiation.* Children have to learn to differentiate between native sounds, for example we can hear a difference between 'l' and 'r' but the Japanese cannot.
- *'Noise'.* The available information is often inadequate and people have to rely on other cues such as *lip reading*. **McGurk and MacDonald** (1976) played a videotape of someone saying 'ba' but dubbed to sound like 'ga'. Participants thought they heard 'da', mixing the lip reading with the sound they heard.

② *Top-down processes.* **Warren and Warren** (1970) played sentences with one sound missing '*eel'; participants heard 'wheel', 'meal' or 'peel' depending on the rest of the sentence. This *phonemic restoration effect* shows that expectations alter what we hear.

③ *Motor theory of speech perception.* **Liberman** *et al.* (1967) suggested that listeners articulate what they are hearing and this motor skill aids word recognition. This can't explain how infants with no speech have some comprehension.

④ *TRACE model.* **McClelland and Elman** (1986) proposed that a pattern of activation (trace) spreads through a system of nodes, those most activated are most likely to be selected. There are feature nodes, phoneme nodes and word nodes.

⑤ *Cohort model.* **Marslen-Wilson** (1990) proposed an interactive model:
- Bottom-up, the *word-initial cohort*: set of words which are consistent with the initial auditory stimulus, inclusion in the cohort is a matter of relative activation.
- Top-down: preceding or subsequent information enables the listener to eliminate words from this cohort in line with existing schema.
- *Recognition point*: all but one word has been eliminated.

Evidence for. **Marslen-Wilson and Tyler** (1980) found that participants were quicker at identifying target words if the context gave cues (normal sentence) than if it didn't (meaningless sentence). This supports an interactive rather than a serial model.

Reading

Reading is an automatic process (see unit 5.2.3), but the skills have to be learned.

① *Mechanics of reading.* Reading occurs in *saccades*, jumps separated by fixations of about 200 milliseconds or longer, depending on text difficulty. Generally people fixate on the first half of a word and may occasionally move backwards; each jump is equivalent to the *perceptual span*, about 10–20 characters. *Speed reading* is an attempt to expand the bottleneck by registering a whole line of text at one fixation.

② *Learning to read.* The task consists of:
- Learning the set of visual units (letters, graphemes) and corresponding sounds.
- Matching words to already known sounds, thus accessing their meaning.
- Maturational factors: readiness. **Gibson** *et al.* (1962) demonstrated that preschool children were less able to distinguish distinctive features of letter-like forms. **Bryant and Bradley** (1985) grouped pre-readers into those who were or were not able to categorise sounds. Four years later they tested reading ability and found high correlations between reading ability and earlier sound discrimination ability (see unit 9.4.2).

③ *Bottom-up and top-down*
- Bottom up: graphemes -> phonemes -> words -> lexicon (meaning).
- Top down: contextual cues -> meaning -> expectations -> influence word and letter perception. The *word superiority effect* (see unit 5.2.1) demonstrates top–down influences. **Carpenter and Dahneman** (1981) gave participants a passage about fishing; the last line was 'some of the best bass guitarists...'. People spend longer than normal on the word guitarists and backtrack, which shows the immediate effects of expectations.

Evaluation. An inexperienced reader relies more on bottom-up processing. Even proficient readers have to alternate between both strategies depending on, for example, their familiarity with the words and whether they are reading for gist. The fact that there are different processes means that different models are necessary.

④ *Interactive activation model.* **McClelland and Rumelhart** (1981) suggested that recognition at one level triggers expectations and inhibitions at other levels:
- *Feature.* When a feature is detected activation is sent to all letter units containing that feature, and other units are inhibited.
- *Letter.* When a letter is identified in a particular position, all word units which match are activated and all others are inhibited.
- *Word* recognition activates all relevant letter units and inhibits all other letter units.

Evaluation. This may be an oversimplification but is based on a popular concept. (See also the TRACE model of speech comprehension, above.)

⑤ *Triple-route model.* **Ellis and Young** (1988) proposed a model which could account for reading problems such as acquired dyslexia:

- Route 1: *Grapheme–phoneme conversion*: working out pronunciation from letters only. **Bub** *et al.* (1985) studied a surface dyslexic who could cope with regular words well even if they were rare, but could not pronounce irregular words.
- Route 2: *Lexicon plus semantic system*. A visual input lexicon is activated when a word is seen and the meaning is extracted from a semantic system. Phonological dyslexics can read real words but not non-words; using route 2 but not route 1.
- Route 3: *Lexicon only*. The semantic system is bypassed so that words can be read but not understood.

   Evaluation. A good account of reading in brain-damaged patients but normal speech may proceed along a single route.

5.4.3 MODELS OF HUMAN THOUGHT

Thinking is the mental processing of concepts. Intelligence is a measure of the quality of your thinking.

- *Concepts*: the internal representation.
- *Problem-solving*: thought directed towards discovering a solution for a problem.
- *Reasoning* or logical thinking: a kind of problem solving using consistent logic.
- *Decision-making*: making the best choice out of a set of alternatives.

Concepts

1. *Defining attributes*. A concept has a set of attributes (features) which are all necessary and distinct. **Collins and Quillan**'s (unit 5.3.3) hierarchical semantic network organises concepts into hierarchies on the basis of defining attributes.

2. *Characteristic attributes: prototypes*. Some concepts, such as 'bachelor', are clearly defined whereas others, such as 'bird', have ill-defined or *fuzzy* boundaries. **Rosch**'s (1975) *prototype model* suggested that there are classical concepts (which are not fuzzy) and probabilistic concepts based on typical features (prototypes). Concepts are hierarchically organised into superordinate, basic and subordinate levels; the basic level holds the most obvious aspect of any concept and is searched first for economy.

3. *Schemata and scripts*. Schema theory considers how concepts are related to each other in a more complex manner than a hierarchy, an interconnected network.

4. *Different forms*. **Bruner** suggested three modes: muscle memories (enactive), visual images (iconic) and abstractions (symbolic) (unit 6.2.1).

5. *Concept formation*. Some concepts are probably inborn, such as time and space, others have to be learned.

   - See differentiation and enrichment theories (at end of unit 5.1.2).
   - *Prototype formation*: **Reed** (1972) presented participants with a simplified set of faces, varying features such as nose length or eye spacing. When they were asked to classify the faces the most common strategy used was to abstract a prototype and compare each image against this.
   - *Hypothesis testing*. **Bruner** *et al.*, see below.

Problem-solving

1. *Convergent and divergent (creative) thinking*

   - *Convergent* = producing one correct solution to a problem by bringing information together, like deductive reasoning.
   - *Divergent* = creating one or more novel and unusual solutions to a problem which are appropriate in context and valued by others. There is no 'correct' solution.

   Wallas (1926) proposed four stages: (1) preparation: thinking, (2) incubation: sitting on it, (3) illumination: solution emerges; (4) verification: testing. Divergent thought requires more input at stage 4, whereas convergent thought requires more at stage 1.

2. *Cognitive style*. People show characteristic differences in their approach to problem-solving. **Hudson** (1963) found that science-oriented pupils tended to have a linear,

focused style of reasoning ('convergers') whereas arts students were more divergent, intuitive or impulsive ('divergers'). This may be a somewhat simplistic dichotomy, as people probably use more than one strategy. Training may encourage the use of a less favoured method (**deBono**'s, 1970, *lateral thinking*).

❸ *Mental set* is a readiness to respond in a particular manner. **Luchins** (1942) showed that, if participants became accustomed to a particular solution on various tasks (e.g. the water jar problem), they would continue to use the same method even when it no longer worked. **Duncker** (1945) demonstrated how people become 'fixed' (*functional fixedness*) on an interpretation. Participants were given candles, drawing pins and a box of matches and asked to mount the candle on the wall, their problem-solving was blocked because they thought in terms of the box as a container rather than as a platform. When they were given an empty box, they found the solution more easily. **Gick and Holyoak** (1980) showed how past experience can have a positive transfer effect. Using Duncker's radiation problem (how to destroy a tumour when x-rays kill *all* tissue), they found that if participants were first given a story which described an army converging on a fort they were much faster at solving the initial problem.

❹ *Trial-and-error learning.* Operant conditioning (unit 2.4.1) is a form of convergent learning through successive trials where errors act as negative reinforcement and success is positively reinforcing. **Thorndike** (1898) placed cats in a 'puzzle box' with some food outside. The cats needed to pull a string dangling from the ceiling to escape. By trying various solutions which were incorrect (negative reinforcement) they eventually found the correct one (positive reinforcement).

❺ *Insight learning.* A different approach is necessary for divergent problems. **Köhler** (1925) set chimpanzees various open-ended problems to solve. The animals might appear to give up, but later they would solve it in a flash, presumably having worked out the solution in their mind and planned their actions before starting.

❻ *Brainstorming.* An individual or group *uncritically* generates ideas in the initial phase, these are then evaluated and finally elaborated, again uncritically. This may not be efficient in terms of man hours but produces a greater range of ideas.

❼ *Means–end analysis.* **Newell and Simon** (1963) developed *problem-space theory*, which suggests that individuals select the shortest route between a current state and goal state using heuristic methods (methods which don't guarantee a solution; algorithms do). One example is *means–end analysis*:

- Note the *problem space* (distance between current and goal state).
- Create a *subgoal* to reduce this difference.
- Select an operator which will solve the *subgoal*.
- Recalculate the problem space and set a new *subgoal*.

Empirical evidence

- The *General Problem Solver* (GPS) was the computer program they wrote based on means–end analysis. *Protocol analysis* can be used to show that the model does demonstrate problem-solving behaviour. This involves recording a protocol (a record of what a person is thinking when engaged in a task) and comparing this with the computer trace (record of the computer's activity).
- If a person can structure a problem into various subgoals their overall performance should improve, **Egan and Greeno** (1974) gave participants five- and six-disc versions of the Tower of Hanoi. Those who had previous experience with three- and four-disc versions were better than a control group.
- If participants are given subgoals this should facilitate their problem-solving. **Simon and Reed** (1976) gave participants a five-missionaries and five-cannibals problem. It generally takes 30 moves to solve the problem but when participants were given a hint about different strategies this resulted in improved performance.

Evaluation

- The GPS was an early and influential computer program and theory.
- Means–end analysis works with well-defined goals but in everyday life people have to solve problems with unclear goals and many ambiguities.

Reasoning

① *Inductive reasoning.* General principles are inferred from specific cases, as in concept learning. **Bruner** *et al.* (1956) found that people used either a scanning strategy (a hypothesis is held until disproved, then another one is tried) or focusing strategy (focus on one feature and compare it with similar objects to see if features agree) when given a task of guessing which card (out of 81) an experimenter had selected. Computer programs which play chess either use the process of 'chunking' (setting subgoals) or they use number crunching methods which examine all the available possibilities (a scanning strategy).

② *Deductive reasoning.* Moving from the general to the specific, e.g. starting from a theory and predicting examples. An example of this is using syllogisms (a valid argument with three propositions, two are the premises and the third is the conclusion). **Wason** (1966) tested this with his four-card selection task (cards A, 4, D, 7; rule: 'If there is a vowel on one side of the card, then there is an even number on the other side'). People find it difficult to determine what card(s) need to be selected to test whether the rule is true or false. This may be due to difficulties in processing negative information: 'A and not (not B)' is harder though logically equivalent to 'A and B', because an intermediate step is required.

Griggs and Cox (1982) showed that people could cope much better with the same task presented in thematic form (cards: drinking a beer, drinking a coke, 16 years of age, 22 years of age; rule 'If a person is drinking beer, then the person must be over 19 years of age').

③ *Lack of logical thought*
- *Mindless behaviour.* **Dewey's** (1933) *'trouble' theory* of thinking suggests that most of the time we function on automatic pilot but, but any discrepancy calls for thought. **Langer** *et al.* (1978) demonstrated that people do function at a mindless level when complying (see unit 1.3.1).
- *Probability judgements*: when predicting heads or tails, there is a tendency in humans to expect tails after a run of heads, though the probabilities are the same on every trial (gambler's fallacy). **Edwards** (1961) asked participants to predict whether a mark would appear on the right or left. As the probability of the left side was increased so the selection of left also increased (a matching strategy). Animals are more likely to use a maximising strategy, to select the more common alternative most of the time, thereby increasing their success.
- *Inappropriate not illogical.* **Johnson-Laird** (1983) suggested that, just because reasoning fails, it doesn't mean that it is illogical. It may be because a person has used an inappropriate mental model.

Decision-making

① *Availability heuristic.* We make decisions based on the most 'available' information. **Tversky and Kahneman** (1973) gave participants a list of 19 well-known men and 20 even better-known women (this was reversed for another group). Participants, when asked how many men and women were in the list, greatly overestimated the number of women, presumably because the famous names were more available.

② *Representativeness heuristic.* When estimating probability a decision must be made about how representative a particular event is of the general population. **Kahneman and Tversky** (1972) asked participants to identify a random distribution, they chose 4,4,5,4,3 rather than 4,4,4,4,4 seeing the latter as too orderly to be random.

③ *Biases in statistical judgement.* People make subjective and incorrect judgements of probabilties (see 'Probability judgements' above).

④ *Group effects* are described in unit 1.3.3.

5.4.4 LANGUAGE AND THOUGHT

① *Language is thought.* **Watson** (1912) suggested that thinking occurs in the voice box. However, **Smith** *et al.* (1947) demonstrated that he could think even when paralysed by a drug. **Furth's** studies of the deaf (1966) show that people can be 'dumb' but still able to think and use language.

② *Strong position: language determines thinking* (linguistic determinism). **Whorf** (1956) and **Sapir** (1958) proposed the *Whorfian* or *Sapir-Whorf hypothesis*, that a person's thoughts are *determined* by the categories made available to them by their language. Orwell's concept of *Newspeak* (in *1984*) was a form of thought control.

Evidence for

- **Carroll and Casangrande** (1958) found that Navaho children were better at form recognition than American counterparts, and suggested that this was because their language stressed the importance of form. However, these differences may be due to experience as much as language.

    Evaluation. This extreme position is unlikely, as the evidence below suggests. The terms 'language' and 'thought' are relatively loosely defined which makes the hypothesis difficult to test.

③ *Weak position: language affects thinking.* Language may *alter* conceptualisation (*linguistic relativity hypothesis*), a position later taken by **Whorf**.

Evidence for

- *The Great Eskimo Vocabulary Hoax.* It has been suggested that many languages have a large vocabulary for certain concepts (e.g. the Eskimos and words for snow) which enables native speakers to make cognitive distinctions not available to speakers of other languages. However, **Pinker** (1994) points out that the Eskimos actually only have around 12 words for snow rather than the 50 or so that has been claimed, and that there are about the same number of 'snow words' in English (e.g. sleet, blizzard, powder). Even if Eskimos did have more words, it wouldn't be surprising because the more contact one has with a particular kind of thing the more one needs to represent finer distinctions. For example, people working in publishing have many words for printing fonts.

    Evaluation. It is the cognitive *need* to make distinctions which influences the vocabulary that a person develops rather than the other way round.

④ *Weakest position: language affects some cognitive processes.* Symbolic processes must be affected by the codes used to represent meaning.

- *Concept formation*: Vocabulary helps young children make discriminations; learning a new subject or skill generally involves learning a new vocabulary. At the very least language aids in concept formation. **Vygotsky** (1987) pointed out that the acquisition of a new word is the *beginning* of the development of a concept rather than the finish.
- *Memory*: Work on 'leading questions' show how language can alter perception. For example **Loftus** *et al.* (1978) showed how the use of 'a' or 'the' in a question changes the way people answer a question. 'Did you see the broken headlight?' assumes that there was a broken headlight whereas 'Did you see a broken headlight?' is more open-ended.
- *Perception.* **Carmichael** *et al.* (1932) gave two groups of participants different descriptions for the same set of drawings, e.g. a picture which looked like a thin crescent moon was described as a 'crescent moon' or 'the letter C'. Subsequent recall could be related to the labels.
- *Stereotypes* are perpetuated by the 'labels' people use to describe certain groups of people. **Hartland** (1991) claims there are 200 words for sexually promiscuous women but only 20 for men.
- *Restricted code.* **Bernstein** (1961) argued that only a certain kind of language ('elaborated code') allows users to articulate abstract concepts, and that children who use a 'restricted code' are unable to engage in these kinds of intellectual activity.

Labov (1970) pointed out that Bernstein's conclusions were due to a failure to recognise the subtleties of some forms of non-standard English and a confusion between social and linguistic deprivation.

⑤ *Is some thought independent of language?* Some concepts may exist independently of the language we use, and are based on innate discriminations (see 'Differentiation theory of perception, unit 5.1.2).

Evidence for

- *Perception of colour* is independent of language. **Rosch** (1978) tested the Dani (from New Guinea). They have only two colour words, equivalent to black and white. Dani participants were quicker at learning a new colour category based on 'fire-engine' red (which is closest to the pigment in the retina) than a category based on an 'off-red'. **Berlin and Kay** (1969) found that native speakers of different languages selected the same colours from a selection of 300 as the best example of each of their 'focal colours'.
- *Studies of the deaf* (**Furth**, 1966) have clearly established that many thought processes occur without benefit of language.
- *Mentalese* (**Pinker**, 1994) is the sensation of knowing what 'you meant to say'.

⑥ *The developmental view* (see unit 6.2.1).

- **Piaget**: cognitive changes precede and underlie linguistic advances. **Sinclair-de-Zwart** (1969) found that children who could not conserve also showed differences in their linguistic development: they used absolute rather than comparative terms such as 'big' rather than 'larger', and used a single term for different dimensions such as 'small' to mean 'short', 'thin', or 'few'. She tried to teach the non-conservers the verbal skills they were lacking but 90% of these children were still unable to conserve, supporting Piaget's view that cognitive maturity is a prerequisite for linguistic development.
- **Bruner**: the onset of language enables qualitatively different thinking and therefore thinking *depends* on language.
- **Vygotsky**: children who have mastered certain linguistic forms of expression are then stimulated to make cognitive advances. Thinking originates in the need to restructure a situation (*pre-linguistic thought*) whereas language starts with the need to communicate (*pre-intellectual language*). Language shapes thought when it takes on a thinking function.

Chapter roundup

5.1   Perceptual processes

5.1.1   *Theories of perception* describe behaviour in terms of bottom-up and/or top-down processes.

5.1.2   Perceptual *development* can be explained in terms of innate abilities which are modified by experience. Evidence comes from studies of human and animal neonates, and adult and cross-cultural studies.

5.1.3   Perceptions are *organised* in order to make sense of sensory data, this enables us to perceive depth, movement, patterns, constancies and visual illusions. Set is important.

5.1.4   *Individual* and *cultural* experience has a profound effect on perception.

5.2   Attention and performance limitations

5.2.1   Theories of *focused attention* use the information processing analogy of a filter at some point (early or late) in the system.

5.2.2   Theories of *divided attention* explain efficient processing in terms of central capacity, independent processors or a combined, hierarchical system.

5.2.3   *Automatic* actions are performed with little or no conscious control. This is due to practice and may be explained in terms of contention scheduling and memory retrieval.

5.2.4 *Performance deficits* include action slips, dual-task performance and attentional deficit hyperactivity disorder (ADHD).

5.3 Memory

5.3.1 There is good empirical evidence to support the *structuring* of memory into three distinct memory stores: SM, STM and LTM.

5.3.2 *Theories of memory* describe its structure (multiprocessor, working memory or PDP) or the processes (level of processing or schema).

5.3.3 Storage and recall depends on some method of *organisation*, this can be related to the structure of memory, to hierarchical or interconnected networks and to schema.

5.3.4 The activity of remembering can be observed in its breach – *forgetting*. Beware of confusing accessibility and availability; recognition is a better test of memory (and forgetting) than recall.

5.3.5 There are many *practical applications*, such as offering advice about eyewitness testimony, recall of medical information and mnemonics.

5.4 Language and thought

5.4.1 The ability to *learn words* appears to be present throughout life, whereas the capacity to develop grammatical language appears to be available only during a sensitive period in human development. It relies on social interaction and is related to function.

5.4.2 *Language production* can be studied in terms of speech errors, levels of processing in speech production (spreading activation theory) and stages in the writing process. *Language comprehension* involves bottom–up processes (detection of sounds and/or letters) and top–down processes (expectations about words and sentences).

5.4.3 *Thought* can be observed in concept formation, problem-solving, reasoning, and decision-making.

5.4.4 *Language and thought* can exist independently though they are interdependent much of the time: cognitive operations underlie linguistic development and language can affect cognitive processes.

ILLUSTRATIVE QUESTION

(a) Describe and evaluate **two** psychological explanations of forgetting from long-term memory. (14 marks)

(b) What practical advice, based on **either** or **both** of these explanations, could you offer someone preparing for an examination? (10 marks)

(AEB AS 1993)

Tutorial note

The question has been specifically directed at a limited area to prevent candidates presenting prepared answers. It is important to think about part (b) before deciding what particular explanations to use in part (a). For example, using repression in part (a) will severely limit your answer for part (b).

Part (a) requires both description and evaluation, which can be in terms of alternative explanations and criticisms of methodologies. Part (b) is description only but your answer should be psychologically informed rather than being a list of exam hints.

Suggested answer

(a) 'Forgetting' assumes that something was once stored in long-term memory and now either it has disappeared (a failure of availability), or that it is there, somewhere, but you can't 'bring it to mind' (a failure of accessibility). This essay will cover interference, an explanation in terms of lack of availability, and cue-dependent forgetting, which accounts for failures of accessibility.

Interference occurs when one set of information interferes with another and leads to a physical loss of a memory. This can apply to short-term and to long-term memory. Proactive interference is when an initially learned set interferes with later learning, retroactive interference is the reverse. Interference is typically tested by giving participants two lists of word-pairs (A-B and A-C). List 1 might have BEM-lawn whereas list 2 would have BEM-aisle (i.e. the same nonsense syllable paired with a word). Retroactive inhibition is shown by learning A-B, then A-C and testing A-B; proactive interference is tested by learning A-C, then A-B and recalling A-B. In both cases performance on A-B is decreased, though retroactive inhibition is stronger. **McGeoch and McDonald** (1931) showed that the more similar B and C items were the less the participant was able to subsequently remember.

Underwood (1957) noted that, if participants in the standard experiment are retested after 24 hours, recall of list 2 (A-C) diminishes but list 1 (A-B) remains stable. He explained this as proactive inhibition following the spontaneous recovery of items from list 1 acting proactively on list 2. But if interference led to a physical loss of memory, there could be no improvement therefore it must be inaccessible.

Ceraso (1967) found that recognition, as opposed to recall, is almost immune to interference. He tested recognition by giving participants list 1 and 2, then presenting them with a list of the nonsense syllables and a jumbled list of the other words. To test recall, he asked participants to list any of the words and scored this without regard to order. In both conditions, there were significant losses of memory. However, after 24 hours, recognition (accessibility) showed considerable spontaneous recovery, whereas availability remained stable.

Tulving and Psotka (1971) gave participants lists of 24 words belonging to one of six categories. When participants were asked to recall the lists, their performance was negatively related to the number of lists they were given, presumably due to retroactive interference. However, when the participants were given category names as cues, their performance stayed the same regardless of the number of subsequent lists. It might be that the presence of cues makes the task more like recognition than recall, and that it is not interference that causes forgetting, but changes in retrieval information. This interpretation is further supported by **Tulving** (1968), who asked participants to recall a list of words on several occasions, the words recalled each time were not the same. This suggests that there is more in memory than is accessible at any particular time. Therefore interference may be due to confused cues rather than a physical loss of a memory trace.

What makes for a good cue? **Morris, Bransford and Franks** (1977) asked participants to recall the contents of a number of sentences. If they were given recall cues which closely resembled the original item their recall was 4.7, with inappropriate cues it fell to 1.6. **Tulving** (1979) proposed the encoding specificity principle: the more similar a cue is to the target item, the better it will aid recall. **Thomson and Tulving** (1970) demonstrated this by showing that cues which are strongly associated (white paired with black) lead to better recall than weak associations (train-black). Tulving also claimed that cues should only be useful if they are encoded at the time of learning. However, **Jones** (1982) gave participants unrelated word pairs to learn (e.g. regal paired with beer). When their recall was tested, one group ('informed') were told that the cue, if reversed, gave a clue to its partner (e.g. regal=lager). The informed participants performed twice as well as uninformed participants, despite the fact that initially the cue (regal) was ineffective yet it was none the less there to be used if it later proved effective.

Cues do not have to be a significant word, they may also be the context or state in which something was learned. **Abernethy** (1940) demonstrated that participants who learned and were retested in the same room did better than those who weren't. **Godden and Baddeley** (1980) found that recognition is not affected by extrinsic context whereas recall is. This can be explained in terms of cues: recognition doesn't require cues whereas recall does. Police reconstructions of crimes are based on context-dependence. When a person revisits the scene of the crime their memory is jogged. A more common example is the smell of something like the sea may jog your memory for a particular incident at the seaside. There are alternative explanations for loss of accessibility, such as repressed forgetting, but cue-dependent forgetting undoubtedly explains most instances of recall failures.

Interference, as an explanation of forgetting, applies in a rather limited set of circumstances – when the two sets of data are very similar. Since this is relatively rare in everyday life, interference probably has limited application, whereas the opposite is true for cue-dependent forgetting. It can also be said that interference probably has little to do with semantic rather than episodic memory. Theories of loss of availability can't account for the behaviour of semantic memory.

(b) Some of the familiar methods for exam revision can be tied to avoiding interference or cue-dependent forgetting:

Interference

1   To avoid interference effects you should work for short spells with adequate breaks. Don't try to cram too much of the same thing in at once.
2   This is particularly true of the last 24 hours, when there will be little chance to recover from interference effects. You may think you've remembered an important chunk, but the evidence above suggests that spontaneous recovery may led to proactive interference so that the last part learned is forgotten.

Cue-dependent forgetting

1   The superiority of recognition to recall shows that, while you might have the distinct impression that much of what you learned has been forgotten, in fact it is there if you had the right cues. It is a common sensation to know that you know the answer but you can't quite recall it.
2   Cues should be embedded in the material as you are learning it. For example, the keyword method of inventing acoustic or imagery links enables one to remember otherwise meaningless associations.
3   The use of acronyms, acrostics or rhymes are examples of acoustic links. In these cases you store the keyword 'alongside' the data to be recalled.
4   The loci system works by forming strong visual links with everyday items; you 'place' the items to be remembered in, for example, a well-known street and later 'walk' down the street recalling them.
5   Extrinsic context may also act as a cue. If you can imagine the page the item was on in a book or the day that you revised the material, this may serve to jog your memory. In a sense this is a problem-solving approach to recall, since the cues are unavailable but you try to locate them by various strategies.
6   Organising notes is a means of establishing cues. For example, creating category headings, numbered lists or maintaining a personal glossary.

QUESTION BANK

Allow 35-40 minutes for each question.

Perceptual processes

1 . (a) What is meant by bottom-up perceptual processing? (4 marks)
    (b) Describe and critically assess **one** theory that explains perceptual processing in this way. (20 marks)

(AEB A 1996)

Points: Top-down processing can only be used in part (b) if it is explicitly offered as evaluation of bottom-up research.

2 (a) Using evidence from experimental studies, describe what psychologists have discovered about the development, in human infants, of:
   (i) pattern perception; (6 marks)
   (ii) depth perception. (6 marks)
   (b) Discuss **two** difficulties of investigating the development of perception in human infants. (8 marks)

(NEAB, 1991)

Points: In part (a) there are two strands, a description of development plus empirical evaluation, simply stating the evidence is not enough. Part (b) is straightforward but again remember to evaluate as well as describe.

3 'There is more to visual perception than meets the eye.'
Discuss the above statement in relation to theories of perceptual organisation.

(AEB A 1992)

Points: You must always address the quotation, and here this means comparing the extent to which the eye can physically explain perceptual organisation or the extent to which higher cognitive mechanisms are involved. You must restrict yourself to organisation and not perception in general.

Attention and performance limitations

4 Describe and evaluate experimental studies of selective attention.

(AEB A 1991)

Points: The question asks for experimental studies not theories, however the latter can be used to evaluate the former. You can use material on divided attention as a means of evaluation.

5 (a) Give **three** features of automatic processing and explain how one activity is likely to use automatic processing. (5 marks)
   (b) Discuss research evidence into automatic processing. (19 marks)

(AEB specimen)

Points: Make sure to fulfil the rubric (three features and one activity). In part (b) you are required to describe research (theory or empirical study) and also to evaluate it by, for example, criticising methodology, offering alternative accounts or suggesting applications.

Memory

6 Discuss psychological insights relating to the organisation of information in memory.

(AEB A 1993)

Points: Include models of memory as well as research specifically related to active organisation. Be sure to specifically address the issue of organisation rather than writing about 'types of memory'. A good answer should describe the appropriate models in terms of the way they explain organisation, and then evaluate these models.

7 (a) Describe briefly what is meant by 'levels of processing' in the study of learning. (5 marks)
   (b) Describe **one** experiment which was carried out to examine levels of processing. (5 marks)
   (c) Discuss the major differences between levels of processing and interference as alternative explanations of forgetting. (10 marks)

(NEAB A 1991)

Points: The word 'learning' in part (a) may be misleading, as the question is essentially on memory, which of course underlies learning. Part (c) focuses on forgetting rather than remembering. Answers related to memory in general are not relevant.

8 Discuss applications of psychological research on memory and describe the studies upon which these applications are based.

(AEB A 1992)

Points: Make sure you address this particular question (about practical applications) rather than writing an essay on memory and forgetting. Describe empirical research to support your points. Do not present a prepared answer but shape this to answer the specific question.

Language and thought

9 Critically consider the role of learning **and** experience in the development of language.

(AEB A 1993)

Points: You are challenged to reorganise the knowledge you have to answer this question. All biological evidence is relevant as a means of evaluating accounts of learning and experience (including social stimuli and function).

10 Describe and critically evaluate psychological insights into the comprehension of language.

(AEB A 1996)

Points: Candidates' answers are frequently triggered by a key word (in this case 'language') without properly reading the question. Beware of using theories of language acquisition or accounts of the relationship between language and thought, both of which are almost entirely irrelevant.

11 It has sometimes been asserted that the study of science encourages logical thinking.
   (a) Devise a study to test this hypothesis. Give details of the procedures and measures that you would use and your reasons for choosing them. (14 marks)
   (b) Discuss **one** strength and **one** weakness of the study you have devised. (6 marks)

(NEAB A 1992)

Points: The way the question is expressed tends to trigger recall of a particular study (Hudson's) but you should not restrict your experiment to a comparison of arts and science students. Be sure to operationalise the variables in your study.

12 Discuss the contribution of psychological research to our understanding of the relationship between language and thought.

(AEB AS 1996)

Points: Research refers to both theory and empirical study. It is likely that you will describe the relationship between language and thought using theories and evaluate these with empirical evidence.

CHAPTER 6

DEVELOPMENTAL PSYCHOLOGY

Units in this chapter:

Chapter overview

Development refers to the systematic changes that occur in an individual from conception to death, a lifelong process of change. At one time developmental psychology was almost entirely concerned with childhood but now has been extended to 'lifespan development'.

6.1 EARLY SOCIALISATION

6.1.1 EARLY SOCIAL DEVELOPMENT

- *Sociability* is the tendency to make social relationships, the infant is actively involved.
- *Bonding* is the formation of specific relationships. A bond is a tie.
- *Attachment* is the further development of early bonds. It is a mutual and intense emotional relationship between an infant and its caregiver(s).

Factors which determine attachments

1. *Feeding.* Until the 1950s thinking about attachment was dominated by Freudian and Behaviourist views.
   - Freud suggested that oral pleasure gained through feeding led to mother love.
   - Behaviourists argued that the feeder becomes a conditioned stimulus associated with satisfaction. The caregiver is also positively reinforced by a contented infant.
   - However, **Lorenz** (1953) showed that goslings became attached through mere exposure regardless of feeding (see unit 2.3.3).

2. *Physical contact.* Feeding is associated with close physical contact and social interaction. It may be these behaviours, rather than the feeding itself, which leads to attachment. **Harlow**'s research (see unit 2.3.3) demonstrated that physical contact was more important than feeding. **Anisfeld** *et al.* (1990) showed that babies were more securely attached to their mothers when they had experienced close physical contact in the form of a pouch-like baby-carrier.

❸ *Early contact: a critical period.* **Lorenz**'s work with goslings (unit 2.3.3) suggested that bonding is related to a critical period. **Klaus and Kennell** (1976) felt that the first 6–12 hours after birth were critical. They arranged for a group of mothers to have extra contact time with their newborn babies, including skin-to-skin contact, immediately after birth and to have an extra five hours daily. A year later these infants and mothers had stronger attachments. However, **Goldberg** (1983) reviewed a number of studies and concluded that the effects of early contact are neither large nor long-lasting.

Bowlby (below) suggested that children who did not have an attachment by the age of two would never recover. **Rutter** (below) felt that there may be a sensitive period, but recovery was still possible at any time.

❹ *Time.* Behaviourist theory also predicts that the person who spends most time with an infant should become the attachment figure. **Schaffer and Emerson** (1964) conducted a longitudinal and detailed study of 60 infants and found that in 39% of the cases the person who usually fed, bathed and changed the child was *not* the child's primary attachment object. **Fox** (1977) studied infants raised on Israeli kibbutzim, and observed their behaviour in the 'strange situation' (see below) with their mothers and their nurses (metapelets). The children sought comfort from their mothers indicating a stronger attachment despite spending shorter amounts of time with them than with the metapelets. This may be due to the fact that there is quite a high turnover rate of metapelets, but suggests that quality is more important than quantity.

❺ *Quality time: sensitivity and responsiveness* to infant's signals. **Ainsworth** *et al.* (1974) proposed that it is the quality not quantity of interaction that counts (the *caregiving hypothesis*). Anxious attachment results from mothers who respond less readily to an infant's needs. Secure attachment occurs when a mother is sensitive, sees things from an infant's viewpoint and is accepting. **Schaffer and Emerson** (1964) found that maternal responsiveness and total amount of stimulation were related to the infant's attachment.

❻ *Individual differences.* **Schaffer and Emerson** (1964) found evidence that some babies like cuddling while others don't. These differences were evident very early on and not related to how mothers handled their infants.

Other aspects of attachment

❶ *Stages of attachment*

Age (approx)	Attachment stage	Description
0–2 months	Asocial	Produce similar responses to social and asocial stimuli. Infant responds to voices and faces, shows recognition of main caregiver(s) by being more settled if held by that person and showing a broader smile when hearing that person's voice.
2–7 months	Indiscriminate	Preference for any human company, infant complains when put down. More likely to smile at familiar faces than strangers.
7–9 months	Specific	Infant protests when separated from one particular individual. Shows 'stranger anxiety' and develops a sense of object permanence.
9 + months	Multiple	Soon after main attachment formed, a wider circle of attachments to familiar people also develops.

❷ *Functions of attachment*
- It ensures the closeness of the caregiver for safety and food. It may be no accident that attachment bonds develop at the time when the infant becomes mobile.
- It provides an emotionally secure base from which to explore the world.
- It reduces distress (see unit 1.2.4).
- It promotes emotional and self-development (see unit 6.3.3).
- It acts as a model for later emotional relationships.

❸ *One or multiple attachments?*
- *Mother love.* **Mead** (1949) said that fathers are 'a biological necessity but a social accident'. There is evidence that the main caretaker need not be the mother. **Freud**

and Dann (1951) studied six orphans from German concentration camps, who had no relationships with adults. Their emotional survival is attributed to the attachment bonds they formed and maintained with each other.

- *Multiple attachments.* There are different *kinds* of attachment and each kind is important for healthy development. **Schaffer and Emerson** (1964) found that by 18 months very few infants (13%) were attached to only one person, some had five or more attachments. **Lamb** (1981) found that attachment figures may serve different functions rather than being in a hierarchy. Mothers may be preferred when the infant is upset or frightened, fathers are important for play. Many societies rely on multiple attachments, for example, **Ainsworth** (1967) studied the Ganda tribe of Uganda, where most infants were cared for by several adults and formed multiple attachments.
- *Monotropy.* **Bowlby** suggested that an infant needs one primary attachment which is stronger and offers a different kind of emotional support.

4 *Intensity of attachment.* **Schaffer and Emerson** (1964) found that intensely attached infants had mothers who responded quickly to their demands (high responsiveness) and who offered the child the most interaction. Infants who were weakly attached had mothers who failed to interact.

5 *Separation anxiety* is the distress an infant shows when left alone by their main caregiver. The period of *specific* attachments is defined by the onset of separation anxiety. The three typical stages are:

- *Protest.* Crying but able to be comforted, inwardly angry and fearful.
- *Despair.* Calmer, apathetic, no longer looking for caregiver, may seek self-comfort through, for example, thumb-sucking.
- *Detachment.* If the situation continues for weeks or months, the child may appear to be coping but is unresponsive, the return of caregiver may be ignored.

The degree of distress varies according to individual and situational differences. For example, the presence of other familiar persons or things will lessen anxiety, a securely attached child may become quite anxious due to changing family circumstances such as the arrival of a new baby.

6 *Attachment and cognitive maturity.* **Lester et al.** (1974) showed that a child's level of object permanence (see unit 6.2.1) was consistent with their separation anxiety, a measure of their attachment. They may co-occur because both are caused by the infant's developing cognitive schema, by 6 months the infant can recognise familiar objects and situations but equally can detect the unfamiliar and this causes distress. **Kagan** (1972) describes these as 'familiar faces in familiar places' schemes.

7 *Measuring attachment.* **Schaffer and Emerson** (1964) measured attachment by recording the infants' responses in seven everyday situations, such as when the infant was left in a pram outside a shop, or passed by while in their cot or chair.

Ainsworth (1978) developed the *Strange Situation*, a standardised means of assessing strength or quality of attachment, consisting of seven 3-minute episodes:

1 Parent and infant enter.	5 Parent leaves.
2 Stranger joins parent and infant.	6 Stranger returns.
3 Parent leaves.	7 Parent returns, stranger leaves.
4 Parent returns, stranger leaves.	

The key events are the parent's departure and return, and the child's behaviour in response, which has been classified as follows:

Type A, anxious-avoidant	No protest when parent leaves, ignores parent's return (10%).
Type B, securely attached	Mild protest on departure, on return seeks parent and is easily comforted (70%).
Type C, anxious-resistant	Seriously distressed on departure, when parent returns alternatively clings and pushes away (20%).

The percentages vary somewhat when tested in other cultures. For example, a German study found 40% of type A, and a Japanese study found 35% type C. However type B remains the majority group, such children have been found to be more socially outgoing, independent, co-operative, compliant and curious, and better able to cope with stress.

Theories of attachment

① *Psychodynamic approach.* An infant is born with innate drives towards sensory pleasure. Love has its origins in attachment to the person who satisfies the need for nourishment.

② *Behaviourist approach.* Hunger, pain and thirst are the basic biological drives which motivate an infant. An infant is attracted to those individuals who reinforce their social signals and who provide pleasant experiences. The caregiver is a conditioned reinforcer.

③ *Ethological approach.* The work of **Lorenz** and **Tinbergen** emphasised the survival value of innate behaviours and introduced several important concepts, such as critical or sensitive periods and imprinting (see unit 2.3.3).

④ *Bowlby's theory*
- *Maternal deprivation* (Freudian influence). **Bowlby** (1953) suggested that emotional care was as least as important as food and physical care. The lack of attachment leads to *maternal deprivation.*
- *Critical period* (ethological influence). **Bowlby** (1969) suggested that there is a critical period, up to the age of 2, during which children must form attachments. After this recovery should be rare. Attachment can be understood in terms of its adaptive and survival value (see unit 2.3.3).
- *Affectionless psychopathy.* **Bowlby** (1946) studied the records of 44 juvenile delinquents (thieves) and a control group of emotionally disturbed children. He found that some of the thieves had an affectionless character (lacked a sense of guilt or affection) and almost all of these had experienced prolonged maternal separations before the age of 2 whereas this was not true for most of the others. This suggests a link between affectionless psychopathy and early separation, though it should be remembered that this data was retrospectively collected and is correlational.
- *Monotropy.* **Bowlb**y first talked of a maternal bond, but later said this didn't have to be the mother.

⑤ *Rutter's criticisms of Bowlby.* **Rutter** (1981) made the following comments:
- Bowlby's views on the importance of deprivation have been amply confirmed by subsequent research.
- The single concept of maternal deprivation is misleading, it covers a range of experiences and outcomes which are quite different. For example, the problems associated with separation may be due to a history of family discord rather than bond disruption. **Rutter** *et al.* (1976) conducted a large scale study on the Isle of Wight and found that, in reasonable homes, separation did not lead to delinquency, and that if separation was due to illness, it was not associated with delinquency. Where there was stress associated with a separation, children were four times more likely to become delinquent. The study was correlational and did use retrospective data.
- A distinction should be made between the loss of attachment (deprivation) and the lack of it (privation), see unit 6.1.2.
- Experiences during the first few years do have special importance, however experiences at all ages are important.
- Individual differences should be taken into account. Many children are not damaged by deprivation.
- Other factors are important too, such as different types of parenting behaviour and the influence of school.

⑥ *Evaluation of Bowlby.* Evidence in unit 6.1.2 should be considered.
- The theory had an enormous impact.
- The concept of a critical period is probably too strong.
- Deprivation may not have permanent consequences, but privation does.
- Quality of attachment rather than quantity is important.

- A child may form multiple attachments.
- There are individual and cultural differences in the way attachments are formed (see unit 6.1.3).

6.1.2 ENRICHMENT AND DEPRIVATION

Enrichment

① *Perceptual development.* Institutionalised infants spend most of the time in their cribs receiving very limited emotional and cognitive stimulation. **White and Held** (1966) placed red and white mitts on institutionalised infants when they were aged less than one month, and also provided them with multicoloured sheets. After a period of several months this resulted in much earlier 'hand regard' (prolonged visual regard of the hands) than in a control group.

② *Cognitive development.* Programmes have been designed to give disadvantaged children preschool educational enrichment so they can start school on equal terms with other children and avoid a self-perpetuating cycle of failure.

- *Operation Head Start* (started in 1965) resulted in initial IQ gains but these turned out to be small and short-lived, and the costs were high. Follow-up studies such as **Lazar and Darlington** (1982) have found that participants were less likely to become pregnant, need welfare assistance, become delinquent, more likely to complete high school, to be employed after high school, and/or to continue in further education.
- *The Milwaukee Project.* **Heber** *et al.* (1972) worked with newborn infants and their low social class Black mothers who had IQs below 75. Half the group were 'controls' and received no extra treatment. The mothers in the experimental group were given help with job-related skills, parenting and housekeeping and their children were involved in a regular day-care programme from the age of 3 months. By the time the children entered school, the experimental group had a mean IQ of 124 whereas the control group's IQ was 94. By the age of 10 there was still a 10-point IQ difference.

③ *Linguistic development*

- *Reading.* **Bradley and Bryant** (1983) worked with a group of children whose original ability to discriminate sounds was very poor and spent two years teaching them sound categorisation skills. This led to significant improvement in reading.
- *Speech.* **Fowler** (1990) designed a programme for parents to use to develop language, involving games and play. They found significant gains, such as the use of pronouns five months earlier than normal.

④ *Emotional development*

- **Furman** *et al.* (1979) used a younger-peer therapy to help socially withdrawn preschool children. The children were given a series of play sessions with a partner who was either their age or 18 months younger. Both sets of children became more socially outgoing than a control group, and the ones playing with younger children did best of all.

Deprivation (the loss of attachment)

The absence of familiar figures leads to feelings of separation anxiety though individual differences in age, past experience and amount of self-control will moderate the effects of separation.

Empirical evidence related to *short-term* separations:

① *Day nurseries*

- *Emotional development.* **Kagan** *et al.* (1980) studied 33 infants over 2 years in a day-care centre and 67 control infants in their homes. They found no consistently large differences between the two groups of children on social, emotional or cognitive variables. There was large variability among all the children, but it was not related to the form of care.

- *Cognitive development.* **Tizard** (1979) found that the conversations between mother and child were more complex, had more exchanges and elicited more from the children than conversations between the child and their nursery school teachers. This is in part due to a teacher's lack of time and divided attention but also because they inevitably know the children less well.

❷ *Childminding*

- **Mayall and Petrie** (1983) observed and interviewed 66 pairs of mothers and minders in London. The children were under 2 years old. They found that the quality of care was very variable. Some children spent the day in a understimulated environment lacking love and attention, or had frequent, unsettling changes of minder. Some children had problems at home. They concluded that day care need not be disruptive but that it may be. The things which moderate the affects of childcare arrangements are (1) the quality of the care, (2) the stability of the arrangement, (3) the original attachment bond.
- **Bryant** *et al.* (1980) assessed 98 children, mothers and childminders through observation and questionnaire. They found that at least one third of the children were 'failing to thrive' and some were actually disturbed. Many minders felt that they did not have to form emotional bonds with the children nor did they have to stimulate them. In fact, minders rewarded quiet behaviour.

❸ *Hospitalisation*

- **Robertson and Robertson** (1968) made films of young children in brief separation: two boys being admitted to hospital and a residential nursery, and two girls who stayed with the Robertsons while their mother was in hospital. All the children received maternal care but the boys experienced a disruption of bonds whereas the girls had a substitute. The boys showed clear signs of acute distress, the girls were mildly anxious but adapted well. The Robertsons concluded that there was an important distinction between separation and bond disruption, only the latter causes distress. This research concerned a very small sample, the data was recorded unsystematically and the conditions were not equivalent.
- **Spitz and Wolf** (1946) found that apparently 'normal' children reacted to hospital separations by becoming quiet, apathetic and sad (*anaclitic depression*). The children recovered quickly when restored to their mother *if* the separation lasted less than three months. However, longer separations were rarely associated with complete recovery. It is possible that other factors associated with being in hospital were also distressing.
- **Douglas** (1975) followed all the children born in Great Britain during one week in 1946 (excluding illegitimate births and twins), testing them every 2 years over the next 26 years. He found strong evidence that a hospital admission of more than a week or repeated admission in a child under 4 was associated with an increased risk of behaviour disturbance and poor reading in adolescence.
- **Clarke and Clarke** (1976) reanalysed **Douglas'** data and found that the reason for this *apparent* association was because many of the children were in hospital because of problems associated with disadvantaged homes. Social rather than maternal deprivation was the main cause of subsequent delinquency.

Empirical evidence related to *long-term* separations:

❶ *Divorce.* **Amato** (1993) has identified five main reasons why divorce may lead to maladjustment. Children are affected differently depending on their coping resources.

- The absence of the non-custodial parent, a breaking of attachment bonds (Bowlby's view).
- The poor psychological adjustment of the custodial parent.
- Economic hardship.
- Interparental conflict (Rutter's view).
- Stressful life changes. **Cockett and Tripp** (1994) found that children from reordered families (divorced and remarried) were more likely to have health problems, need extra help at school, experience friendship difficulties and to suffer from low self-esteem. The more changes, the more long-term problems experienced.

② *Adoption.* Most adoptions take place early, before bonding begins, though the process of bonding may start even before birth, in the womb. All adopted children probably experience some sense of loss (deprivation), but rarely a *lack* of emotional care, in fact they often receive an excess of care. **Singer** *et al.* (1985) found the incidence of secure attachment to be equally high in adoptive children as non-adoptive ones.

③ *Death.* Parental death may be associated with feelings of helplessness and an increased risk of depression rather than delinquency (as is the case for separation and divorce). **Bifulco** *et al.* (1992, see unit 4.3.2) found a particularly high rate of depression among those whose mothers had died before the age of 6. This was not true where separation occurred before the age of 6. This suggests that there is a critical age, and that there is a difference between permanent deprivation (even where there are substitute attachments) and separation.

④ *Long-term effects of separation.* **Ainsworth** (1972) concluded from a review of research that when children have inadequate personal resources or when they may have to cope with too many potentially detrimental factors, they will be affected by emotional deprivation. Some children are more vulnerable than others because of their age, temperamental differences and/or other life experiences. However, most children are very resilient and many are not permanently damaged by separation.

Privation (the lack of attachment)

① *Institutional care*

- **Widdowson** (1951) studied a group of orphanage children who were malnourished. Dietary supplements didn't help but their weight improved when a harsh and unsympathetic supervisor was replaced. It may be that they were undeveloped because they lacked affection and emotional security (*deprivation dwarfism*). Stress causes certain hormones to be produced which affect physical health (see unit 3.4.3).

- **Goldfarb** (1943) followed two matched groups of infants, 15 remained in an institution while another 15 went to foster homes. When tested at age 12, the institutionalised group were backward in cognitive and social development, though even the fostered group were below average in some respects. However, the babies were not randomly assigned to the groups, so the reasons they were selected for fostering may have affected the outcome.

- **Skeels and Dye** (1939) observed how two apparently retarded children developed near normal IQs when transferred from their orphanage to a women's ward in an institution for the mentally retarded, the increased attention (attachments) must have helped. **Skodak and Skeels** (1949) tested this more rigorously by transferring 13 mentally retarded infants from their orphanage to an institution for the mentally retarded when they were less than 2. After 19 months in the new institution their mean IQ had increased from 64 to 92, whereas a control group who had stayed in the orphanage showed a decrease in IQ from 87 to 61 over the same period. When the children were assessed 20 years later it appeared that the differences between the groups remained (**Skeels**, 1966). One criticism should be considered: the children may have been responding to the researcher's expectations and it was this, rather than the increased stimulation, which led to their intellectual improvements.

- **Tizard and Rees** (1975), **Tizard and Hodges** (1978), **Hodges and Tizard** (1989) studied a group of children institutionalised before the age of 4 months. By the age of 4 years, 24 were adopted, 15 had returned home (often to single parents) and 26 remained in the institution. The children were tested at age 8 and 16: the adopted children were doing best and those who returned home were worst on measures of intellectual and social development. All the children showed some signs of emotional and attentional problems. This shows that some recovery is possible after the age of 4 and that a child's natural home may not necessarily be best.

- **Pringle and Bossio** (1960) studied children living in an institution. The most severely maladjusted (11 of them) had no lasting relationship with their family whereas those children described as the most stable (5 of them) had maintained contact. This suggests that privation leads to permanent emotional damage, whereas deprivation can be recovered from.

- **Kirk** (1958) found that institutionalised children only recover if they are given a continuing experience of enrichment, warmth and stimulation. If they were given enrichment before entering school, the effects soon wore off. However, when enrichment continued throughout their school life the changes were permanent.

Evaluation

- All of the studies involved small samples.
- Deprivation affects many aspects of development so it is difficult to say which is the primary cause of any maladjustment.

❷ *Children raised in isolation*

- *Genie* (**Curtiss**, 1977, see unit 5.4.1) was locked in a room until the age of 12. She was then cared for by a psychologist's family and engaged in much psychological research. Later she was fostered and abused again, at that point what language she had developed disappeared altogether. Her father thought she was retarded from birth.
- *Czechoslovakian twins* P.M. and J.M. (**Koluchova**, 1972, 1976, 1992), were isolated and undercared for by a stepmother until the age of 7. They were adopted by two loving sisters and by age 14 had near normal intellectual and social functioning.
- Also: Isabelle (**Mason**, 1942), Anna (**Davis**, 1947), sisters Mary and Louise (**Skuse**, 1984), and a Japanese brother and sister (**Fujinaga** *et al.*, 1992). All these children, when discovered, were extremely underdeveloped physically (deprivation dwarfism) and showed cognitive, social and emotional delays. If they were relatively young, they were able to recover reasonably well though never completely.

Evaluation. It is difficult to really draw any conclusions from these cases because:

- They are small samples.
- The data about their early childhood were collected retrospectively and were anecdotal.
- There is no way of knowing whether the children had at any time formed attachment bonds. If they *did* have attachments they would be deprived rather than privated.
- Any lack of development might be due innate backwardness.
- The accompanying cognitive deprivation affects emotional development.

❸ *Attachment disorder.* This is a recognised syndrome in the US with symptoms such as being unable to form relationships, showing little emotion and engaging in very aggressive and controlling behaviour. Children with this disorder have invariably been adopted after the age of 6 months, subsequently experiencing multiple foster homes or care institutions. This means that they have little or no early experience of attachments. When they are offered the chance to develop a relationship, it comes too late. Attachment disorder children appear to have no conscience, which may be due to the fact that they have been unable to identify with any parent figure (see unit 6.3.1).

6.1.3 SOCIAL AND CULTURAL VARIATIONS IN CHILDREARING

The version of normal development which is presented by psychologists is largely a Western one. Observed differences include:

❶ *Different historical practices.* Within our own culture different techniques are popular in different generations, often related to the 'scientific' wisdom of the time, for example scheduled feeding was prevalent in the 1950s whereas women today feed on demand. Parental discipline has also undergone dramatic changes.

❷ *Different social practices*

- *Breastfeeding* rates in this country are related to social class. **Jones** (1987) found that in lower social classes (III and IV) less than 40% of mothers breastfed whereas in higher classes the figure was greater than 60%. Breastfeeding has a significant effect on intelligence and health, as well as on emotional closeness.

- *Aggression.* **Newson and Newson** (1968) found social class differences in parental attitudes towards aggression; working-class parents actively encouraged their children to stand up for themselves while middle-class parents objected to such behaviour.

3 *Different cultural practices*

- *Distress.* **Konner** (1977) studied a culture in Botswana where children were not allowed to cry, the mothers breastfed the infants as soon as they were distressed.
- *Attachment.* **Ainsworth**'s study (see above) of the Ganda showed that multiple attachments were normal. **Fox**'s study of kibbutzim showed that children fared well with quality rather than quantity care from parents. Various studies have found cultural differences in the strange situation (see unit 6.1.2).
- *Deprivation.* **Kagan and Klein** (1975) studied an isolated group in Guatemala. In the first year of life the children are kept indoors and given little stimulation to protect them from the elements. They appear to suffer no ill effects in later life.
- *Gender development.* **Imperato-McGinley** *et al.* (1974) studied families in a remote village in the Caribbean (see unit 6.3.2) where a genetic condition meant that some girls became boys during puberty. They were able to accept this quite easily, which would not be true in Western society where gender is a far more critical part of an individual's self-concept.
- *Aggression.* **Mead**'s studies (see unit 1.4.4) related childrearing practices in different tribes to different kinds of aggressive behaviour.

4 *What do these differences tell us?*

- That psychologically healthy individuals can emerge from different rearing styles.
- That some styles may be associated with particular outcomes.
- That some behaviours may be universal.

5 *Evaluation of cross-cultural studies*

- It is difficult to identify any cause and effect.
- Studying other cultures and even other social groups involves an imposed etic (see unit 7.2.3).

6.2 COGNITIVE DEVELOPMENT

6.2.1 THEORIES OF COGNITIVE DEVELOPMENT

Piaget (1897–1980)

1 *The essence of the theory*

- *Biological* approach: cognitive development is mainly a consequence of maturation.
- *Structural* approach: intelligence is a matter of innate structures for acquiring and storing knowledge.
- There are *qualitative* differences between child and adult thinking.
- *Language* is an outcome of a generalised cognitive ability (see unit 5.4.1).

2 *The structure of the intellect.* Intelligence is adaptive.

- *Variant cognitive structures* develop with age:
  - *Schema* are cognitive representations of things or activities. A child is born with innate schema, reflex responses such as grasping schema. These schema integrate with each other, and new ones form in response to the environment.
  - *Operations* involve physical or symbolic manipulations.
- *Invariant cognitive structures*, the process of *adaptation* remains the same through life:
  - *Assimilation*: a new object or idea is understood in terms of existing schema.
  - *Accommodation*: schema are modified to fit new situations or information.

- *Equilibrium*. If existing schema are inadequate a state of disequilibrium occurs, driving the person to accommodate the schema, thus ensuring cognitive development.
- *Horizontal décalage* describes the fact that not all aspects of the same stage appear at the same time, for example the ability to conserve number and volume. Uneven cognitive performance is probably due to different learning experiences.

❸ *Stages in cognitive development*

Stage and age	Mode of thinking	Substages and characteristic behaviours
SENSORIMOTOR 0-2 years	Mainly focused on sensory and motor experiences. Beginnings of language and symbolic thought.	• Reflex activities (0–1 month), e.g. sucking. • Primary circular (repetitive) reactions (1–4 months). • Secondary circular reactions (4–8 months), e.g. kicking. • Co-ordination of secondary schemes (8–12 months): schemas used to solve problems, e.g. object permanence. • Tertiary circular reactions (12–18 months), experimenting with actions. • Symbolic problem solving (18 months +) infant no longer relies on physical representation of things.
PRE-OPERATIONAL (a) Pre-conceptual 2–4 years	Using symbols. Concepts not fully formed.	• Animism. • Egocentric thought. • Centration. • Inability to perform concrete operations such as conservation, reversibility.
(b) Intuitive 4–7 years	Reasoning doesn't use adult logic (syncretic).	• Moral realism (see unit 6.3.1).
CONCRETE OPERATIONS 7–11 years	More adult-like thought but still not abstract nor always using adult logic.	• Now can cope with conservation, centration, seriation, class inclusion, understanding numbers, reversibility. • Problem solving still tends to be random. • Moral relativity and empathy (see unit 6.3.1).
FORMAL OPERATIONS 11 years +	Formal logic and abstract thought.	• Systematic and organised deduction/induction. • Strong idealism. • Own values, beliefs and philosophies.

❹ *Empirical evidence*. Piaget's methods involved naturalistic observation and interviews, using a small sample, and often his own children. He spent more than 50 years amassing a detailed record of children's performance.

- *Object permanence*. Showed an infant a bright, attractive object, then hid it. At 4–5 months they will immediately forget it, by 10–12 months they will look for it. **Bower** (see below) found that younger children did have object permanence.
- *Unsystematic nature of thought*. Young children use *transductive reasoning*: if A has four legs and B has four legs, A must be B. For this reason a child may call all dogs 'Spot'. Another example of the unsystematic nature of their thought is the lack of distinction between *appearance and reality*. **DeVries** (1969) showed children a cat, and then hid the cat's head behind a screen while she strapped on a dog's head. The 3-year-olds thought it was a dog even though they saw the transformation, while the 6-year-olds were able to distinguish appearances from reality (see **Frank**, below, for criticism).
- *Egocentrism*. A young child finds it hard to take the perspective of another. In the *three mountains experiment* **Piaget and Inhelder** (1956) asked children aged 4–12 to say how a doll, placed in various positions, would view a model of a mountain range. The youngest children could only work from their own perspective, by age 9 they were sure of the doll's perspective. **Hughes** (see below) found they could cope better if the task made sense to them.
- *Centration* is focusing on the central part of a problem (inability to decentre). In *class-inclusion tasks* a pre-operational child cannot focus on the whole and the parts at the same time. If they are given 18 brown beads and 2 white beads (all of which are wooden), and asked 'are there more brown beads than wooden beads?', Piaget found

that the pre-operational child typically answered that there are more brown beads. **McGarrigle** (see below) found that a version with cows was easier to process.

- *Conservation* is the ability to understand that quantity is not changed even when a display is transformed. In the number conservation experiment, Piaget showed the child two identical rows of counters and asked whether they were both the same. He then made one row longer by moving the counters further apart and again asked whether they were the same. A child over 7 recognises that quantity cannot change and says 'yes'. Similar experiments were done with volume (water in a jar) and mass (balls of clay). **Rose and Blank** (see below) found that using two questions confuses younger children and **McGarrigle and Donaldson** (see below) found that a less artificial task led to earlier success.

- *Formal operational thinking.* Seriation involves making transitive inferences such as if A > B and B > C, then A must be > C; 'Edith is fairer than Susan. Edith is darker than Lily. Who is the darkest?' (from the Stanford-Binet Test). Children find this impossible during the concrete operations stage, unless it is presented in a concrete form, such as using dolls. **Bryant and Trabasso** (see below) found that practice can improve performance. **Piaget and Inhelder** (1956) tested *deductive reasoning* using the beaker problem. Children are given four beakers of colourless, odourless liquid and asked to find which combination turns yellow. They found that concrete thinkers try to solve the problem randomly whereas formal thinkers are systematic (see unit 5.4.3). **Shayer and Wylam** (1978) found that only 30% of 15–16 year olds had achieved formal operations.

- *Influence of thought on language.* **Sinclair-de-Zwart** (1969, see unit 5.4.4) produced evidence that the inability to conserve was related to linguistic development but that training in vocabulary did not increase the ability to conserve.

5 *Criticisms of the theory and the empirical evidence*

- *Age.* Other research has found that children develop certain cognitive structures earlier (or later) than Piaget claimed. **Bower** (1981) found that infants 5–6 months old showed surprise when an object that had been hidden behind a screen was no longer there when the screen was lifted. He also demonstrated that babies of 8 weeks tracked an object as it moved behind a screen by showing with their eyes where it should emerge. **Shayer and Wylam** (see above) found no formal operations in some older children.

- *Appropriateness of the task.* Piaget's tasks may have confused the children. In the object permanence task **Bower and Wishart** (1972) suggested that it was the way an object is made to disappear which influences the baby's response. If a baby is watched after the lights have been turned out (using infra-red cameras) they found that the baby continues to look for the object. In the three mountains task **Hughes** (1975) achieved better performance by hiding a doll from a toy policeman and **Borke** (1975) used the character Grover from Sesame Street driving along in his fire engine. **McGarrigle and Donaldson** (1974) used 'naughty teddy' to muddle the experimental displays 'accidentally' – many more 4–6-year-olds were then able to demonstrate conservation abilities, presumably because the question now made sense.

- *Form of questioning.* Children aim to please and so they respond to demand characteristics and/or experimenter bias. In the conservation experiment, **Rose and Blank** (1974) and **Samuel and Bryant** (1984) found that asking the question only once, after the transformation, had a significant effect, though there were still age differences. **Bruner and Kenney** (1966) suggest that the word 'more' may confuse the child. **Donaldson** (1978) suggested that the class-inclusion questions don't make sense; when children were asked 'Are there more black cows or more sleeping cows?' rather than 'Are there more black cows or more cows?' the percentage who answered correctly moved from 25 to 48%.

- *Other cognitive abilities.* **Bryant and Trabasso** (1971) showed that difficulty on transitive inference tasks may be due to memory failure rather than lack of ability. They trained children until they could perform a transitive task successfully, and found that they could then perform a more lengthy series of comparisons.

- *Practice.* If the development of cognitive structures is related to maturity then practice should not improve performance. **Danner and Day (1977)** coached students aged 10, 13 and 17 in three formal operations tasks. The effects were limited with the younger participants but very marked at 17 years, showing that training makes a difference but is still related to cognitive maturation. **Tait (1990)** compared the performance of blind and sighted children on tasks of conservation and found the blind children performed less well, emphasising the role of experience/practice. See also **Gibson** *et al.* in unit 9.4.2.

- *Effects of language.* **Frank (1966)** claimed that language can help overcome concrete thinking. He tested 4–6-year-olds on the volume conservation task with a screen in front of the beakers so the level was not visible. Almost all the older children coped, and half the 4-year-olds. When tested without the screen performance was improved over a pre-test experiment, which was attributed to the children's speech having been activated and thus overcoming domination by the iconic mode. They were also able to distinguish between appearance and reality. However, **Sinclair-de-Zwart** (see above) did not find that language training led to improved performance.

⑥ *Evaluation*

- Piaget's theory was the first comprehensive account of cognitive development.
- It changed the traditional view of the child as passive and stimulated an enormous amount of research.
- It had a large impact on education, particularly in primary schools (see unit 6.2.2).
- It underestimated children's early logical abilities and overestimated later stages.
- The influence of language, and social and emotional factors are largely overlooked.
- Piaget's evidence often lacked scientific rigour. The samples were small and open to experimenter bias.
- Critics tend to take the model too rigidly, and supporters suggest it should be viewed as a metaphor. The stages are not fact but a useful structure for understanding behaviour and generating research. *Neo–Piagetians* suggest that certain adjustments can be made to Piaget's theory to accommodate these criticisms (see Fischer, below).

Vygotsky (1896–1934)

① *The essence of the theory.* Vygotsky's work was first published in English in 1962. His books were banned during the Stalinist regime because they ran counter to the preferred theories of Pavlov.

- Cognitive development is the result of the child's *active construction* of their knowledge rather than passive conditioning.
- *Social and cultural influences*, especially language, are the driving force behind cognitive development.
- *Marxist theme*: the only way to bring about psychological change is by altering social conditions.

② *The structure of the intellect*

- *Elementary mental functions*: innate capacities such as attention and sensation.
- *Higher mental functions*. Cultural influences transform elementary functions into higher mental functions, such as problem-solving and thinking. Without culture an individual would not progress further than the elementary functions. Culture is transmitted via language and the help of persons with greater knowledge ('experts').
- *Zone of proximal development* (ZPD) is the distance between a child's current and potential abilities. The aim of instruction is to stimulate those functions which lie waiting in the ZPD.

3 *Stages in cognitive development*

Speech stage	Age	Function
Pre-intellectual, social speech	0–3	Language serves a social function, to control the behaviour of others, express simple thoughts and emotions. At the same time thought is pre-linguistic.
Egocentric	3–7	Language is used to control own behaviour but spoken out loud.
Inner speech	7+	Self-talk becomes silent and differs in form from social speech. Throughout life language serves these dual purposes, for thought and for social communication. Since social processes shape language, they also shape thought.

4 *Empirical evidence*
- **Shif** (Vygotsky, 1987) asked pupils to complete sentences which ended in 'because' or 'although' and found that they were better able to finish the sentences which dealt with scientific rather than everyday concepts. Vygotsky argued that this demonstrates a greater understanding of scientific concepts which is presumably because these are learned through instruction with expert guidance, whereas everyday concepts are assimilated through self-directed activity.
- **Freund** (1990) arranged for one group of children to play on their own with a doll's house, and another to play with their mothers. At the end the children who worked with experts (mothers) showed a dramatic improvement in their ability to perform a furniture sorting task.

5 *Evaluation*
- Vygotsky's approach has produced very little empirical support but lots of interest.
- The role of language and culture means that the approach offers practical applicability (see unit 6.2.2).

Bruner (1915–)

1 *The essence of the theory.* Bruner's contribution is based on a general interest in thought (see units 5.4.1 and 5.4.3). He was very taken with Vygotsky's views.

- *Thought* requires ways of representing the environment, which we do through action, image and word (modes of thinking).
- *Language* shapes and enables the development of thought.
- *Social frameworks* and experience influence cognitive development.
- This is an *information processing approach*, concentrating on how strategies for organising information change with age.

2 *The structure of the intellect*
- *Categories* are used to recognise and relate objects. A category is an abstraction of commonalties among events and experiences.
- *Hierarchies.* Categories are organised into a framework (*coding system*) with the more general (generic) at the top. Through such hierarchies we can explain remembering, discovering and learning (see units 5.3.3 and 5.4.3).
- *Modes of thinking* (enactive, iconic, symbolic) are 'recurrent themes'.
- *Skill acquisition.* Infants learn physical skills, such as grasping, during the enactive stage. These become automatic and act as modularised units which can be combined in different ways to build up a repertoire of new skilled behaviours and to allow attention to be freed for other things. As children grow older they also develop representational skills.

3 *Stages in cognitive development*

Mode	Age	Description and function
Enactive	0–1 years	Thinking is based entirely on physical actions. The infant learns by doing rather than through internal representation. This mode continues later in many physical activities.
Iconic	1–7 years	The use of mental images (icons) which may be based on sight, hearing, smell or touch.
Symbolic	7 +	Representation of the world through language, and other symbolic systems such as number and music.

④ *Empirical evidence*
- *Iconic and symbolic mode*. **Bruner and Kenney** (1966) arranged nine glasses on a 3x3 grid, in order of height and diameter. If the glasses were scrambled all the children were able to simply replace them (reproduction task). If the left and right glasses in the bottom row were swapped, 5-year-olds found it impossible to replace them all in the same manner (transposition task) because this requires use of the symbolic mode.
- *Effects of language*, see **Frank** (above).
- *Learning strategies* (scc 5.4.3, inductive reasoning). **Mosher** (1962) looked at the strategies used by children aged 6 to 12 in the game of 20 questions, to ascertain why a car went off the road. Older children used constraint-locating questions ('was it night-time?') whereas younger children asked direct hypothesis-testing questions ('did a bird hit the window?').
- *The role of tutoring*. Bruner followed Vygotsky in suggesting that expert instruction was important in stretching a child's capabilities. See evidence, above.

⑤ *Other information processing approaches.* Such approaches describe the intellect as a set of separate cognitive activities (perception, memory, attention, etc.) and development as the acquisition of related skills.

For example, **Fischer** (1980), also a neo-Piagetian, proposed that development proceeds through a series of skill structures called levels (*skill theory*). Specific skills at one level are built directly from specific skills at the preceeding level. There is gradual movement from one level to the next as the skills are gradually transformed. There are discrete stages in cognitive development which are tied to maturation but, at the same time, this process is continuous.

The advantage of this approach is that it allows for developmental differences across different domains of thinking. It also means that development could be measured in terms of skill level, for example the number of items which a child can recall.

⑥ *Evaluation*
- A more general approach to thought.
- Includes the influence of experience, language and social factors.
- Bruner's theory has had important educational implications (see unit 6.2.2).

6.2.2 PRACTICAL APPLICATIONS TO EDUCATION

'Education' in its widest sense includes not just teachers but parents, playleaders and toy manufacturers.

❶ *Piaget's theory*
- *The concept of readiness*. Children advance their knowledge because of biologically regulated cognitive changes. Outside influences should only have a minimal effect, and children should be offered stimuli which are moderately novel only when they are ready.
- *Self-discovery* and *self-motivation*. If you tell a child how to do something you prevent their complete understanding and remove their intrinsic sense of satisfaction.
- *Individualised*. Since each child matures at a different rate and has different schema, their learning programme should be unique.
- *Discovery learning*. Learning should be *child-centred and active*. The teacher should set tasks which are appropriate for pupils and intrinsically motivating. The teacher's role is not to impart knowledge but to ask questions or create situations which 'ask questions', thus creating disequilibrium and forcing the child to make accommodations.
- *Examples*. Has been most influential in nursery and primary education, but also Nuffield secondary science which relies on children making their own discoveries.

❷ *Vygotsky's theory*
- *Expert intervention* (by peers or adults) should be most effective when the expert is aware of the limits of the ZPD. Thus, the more sensitive an adult is to a child's competence and the more the adult exposes the child to processes necessary for successful problem-solving, the more the child should improve.

❸ *Bruner's theory*

- *Scaffolding.* **Woods, Bruner and Ross** (1976) described how an adult advances children's thinking by providing a framework (scaffolding) on which children can climb. The tutor has the task of engaging and maintaining children's interest, simplifying the task so as to reduce the number of steps required to reach the target, highlighting those that are relevant, and providing demonstrations for children to imitate. Such a technique demands special skills of the tutor in guiding rather than telling children what to do.
- *Discovery learning.* Children must organise new information for themselves by integrating it into existing hierarchies or adapting hierarchies to fit new situations. Learning is not a matter of mastering facts but inventing the structure for the facts.
- The *spiral curriculum* – the same principles are encountered at increasingly sophisticated levels.

❹ *Ausubel's theory*

- *Reception learning.* **Ausubel** (1963, 1977) argued that discovery learning is time-consuming and in many situations impossible. Meaningful verbal learning takes place by either relating new material to existing material (derivative subsumption) or extending previous knowledge (correlative subsumption).
- *Advance organisers* are sets of ideas given to the learner before the material to be learned. This provides a stable cognitive structure into which the new material can be subsumed (see unit 5.4.2).

❺ *Other theories* are discussed in unit 9.4.1

6.2.3 DEVELOPMENT OF MEASURED INTELLIGENCE

Intelligence is a hypothetical quality measured by intelligence tests (see unit 7.2.1). There are three factors which may affect intelligence test scores: genetic, environmental and test bias.

Genetic factors

❶ *Twin studies*

- Monozygotic (MZ) twins have more similar IQs than dizygotic (DZ) twins, which indicates a genetic component. **Bouchard and McGue** (1981) reviewed a number of studies and found an MZ correlation of .85 and DZ correlation of .58. **Pedersen** *et al.* (1992) reported on the Swedish Adoption/Twin Study of Ageing (SATSA); MZ twins reared apart or together had IQ correlations of about .79, DZ twins reared apart were .32 and together were .22. This suggests that about 80% of IQ is inherited.
- The similarity between MZ twins reared apart reflects a genetic component. **Newman** *et al.* (1928) found correlations for MZ twins of .67 reared apart and .91 when together. This shows that the genetic influence is greater.
- If MZ twins are reared apart they should nevertheless have very similar IQs. They are identical genetically but have had different environments. **Shields** (1962) gained access to a sample of 44 twins reared apart and together through an appeal on the BBC. The concordance for MZ twins reared apart was 0.77 and reared together was 0.76. This suggests little environmental influence. **Bouchard** *et al.* (1990) used data from over 100 twins in the Minnesota Study of Twins Reared Apart. They found that about 70% of IQ score is due to genetic variation.

Evaluation. **Kamin** (1974) criticised Shield's study and twin studies generally:

- The samples are relatively small.
- In reality the twins had often spent a substantial amount of time together. In Shields' study 14 sets of MZ twins were only separated after the age of 1 year and many were raised by relatives, often visiting each other.
- Those twins who were genuinely adopted might still have had similar environments because adoption agencies try to match backgrounds.
- Shields tested all the twins himself and has been accused of experimenter bias.

- If intelligence was entirely inherited, the MZ correlations should be 1.00, the fact that scores are lower shows a significant environmental component.
- A correlation is not evidence that one factor *caused* another. A third factor may been important. For example, identical twins may have a similar effect on people around them which creates expectations leading to self-fulfilling performance.
- The assumption that MZ twins are identical is wrong. **Allen *et al.*** (1976) found constitutional differences based on different birth and intrauterine experiences, and found that these could be related to different parental perceptions and expectations of the twins.

❷ *Familial studies.* **Bouchard and McGue** (1981) surveyed over 100 studies looking at familial correlations of IQ, and found that the closer the genetic link, the higher the correlation between IQ. For example, siblings reared together had a correlation of 0.45 and adopted siblings had a correlation of 0.31.

Evaluation

- This would seem to support the genetic position, but it could be taken equally as evidence for environment, as genetically related people usually also live in the same environment.
- Comparisons from one study to another involve grouping together many different tests.

❸ *Adoption studies.* Comparing a child and its natural parents.

- **Skodak and Skeels** (1949) followed 100 adopted children and their natural mothers. At the age of 4 the IQ correlation was 0.28 and at 13 it was 0.44. It appears that the effects of environment become less with age, the decline of environmental influence may be due to early enrichment and extra attention levelling out, and genetic factors showing through.
- **Horn** (1983) reported on the Texas Adoption Study which looked at about 300 families with adopted children. The biological mothers had all given the children up within one week of birth. The children at age 8 had a correlation of .25 with their biological mother (genetic link) and .15 with their adopted mother (environmental link). **Plomin** (1988) reported on the same children at age 10. They had a correlation of .02 with their adoptive siblings.

Evaluation

- There is usually a higher correlation between children and their biological rather than adoptive parents.
- Adoptions are often made to similar environments.

Environmental factors

❶ *Adoption studies.* Comparing a child and its adoptive parents.

- **Schiff *et al.*** (1978) found that children born to low SES parents who were subsequently adopted by high SES families, showed significant IQ gains when compared with siblings who had remained at home.
- **Scarr and Weinberg** (1977) found that on average adopted children have IQs that are 10 to 20 points higher than those of their natural parents. This may be because adoptive families tend to be 'better off' and adoptive children develop the higher end of their 'reaction range' (see unit 4.1.1)

Evaluation

- Adoptive families are generally smaller, wealthier and better educated than natural families. Both these factors would cause environmental factors to appear stronger.
- Early adopted children do better, favouring the idea that environment is important under suitable circumstances.

❷ *Social class*

- **Bernstein** (1961) introduced the notion of *restricted language* (code) as opposed to elaborated code. He argued that children from low SES groups learn a limited form of language which lacks, for example, abstract concepts. This affects their cognitive development and verbal intelligence. **Labov** (1970) rejected this idea and claimed that Bernstein was confusing social and linguistic deprivation, and had failed to recognise the subtleties of non-standard English.

- **Sameroff** *et al.* (1987 and 1993) conducted the *Rochester Longitudinal study*, which has followed over 200 children from a range of socioeconomic backgrounds since birth, keeping a record of IQ and life events. They found a clear negative (about .60) association between number of risk factors and IQ; risk factors include parental mental health, education, occupation, family support, stressful life events and family size. They also found that at age 4 high-risk children were 24 times as likely to have IQs below 85 than low-risk children. It was calculated that, on average, each risk factor reduced the child's IQ score by 4 points. When a child is not exposed to risk factors, genetic factors will be important in determining intelligence. When there are risk factors, these will be of more importance than the inherited ones.

Evaluation

- It is factors associated with low social class which cause low IQ, not social class *per se*.
- On the other hand, it is possible that low socio-economic parents are biologically less intelligent, those with more intelligence become better educated and are able to have higher living standards.

❸ *Family influence.* Parent–child interactions profoundly affect the development of IQ.

- Parental *expectations* influence a child's performance.
- *Stimulation*: studies of deprivation indicate how a *lack* of stimulation leads to IQ deficits (see unit 6.1.2). **Yarrow** (1963) found a correlation of .65 between IQ at 6 months and the amount of time the mother spent in social interaction with her child.
- *Birth order* is related to parental attention. **Zajonc and Markus** (1975) examined the IQ data of 40,000 Dutch males born in 1944. They found that IQ declines with family size and birth order. The reason is that, in larger families, each child has a smaller share of parental attention, less money and more physical deprivation. Children born first and only children receive a greater amount of parental time and have more resources directed at them (the *confluence model*).

❹ *Diet.* **Harrell** *et al.* (1955) gave low-income, expectant mothers supplementary diets. When their children were tested at 3 years they had higher IQs than those whose mothers had been given placebos. **Benton and Cook** (1991) demonstrated that IQ scores increased by 7.6 points when children were given vitamin supplements rather than a placebo.

❺ *Enrichment.* See Operation Head Start and the Milwaukee Project in unit 6.1.2.

Test bias

A child's IQ may be depressed or increased because of elements in the test itself.

❶ *Culture bias.* All tests are inevitably culture-biased because the items are drawn from the designer's experience and conception of intelligence, and the means of test validation are related to cultural ideals (see unit 7.2.1).

❷ *Motivation and test anxiety.* Lower-class children may have less desire to do well. **Zigler** *et al.* (1973) found that such children improved their test performance by 10 points if they had a play session with the tester beforehand to increase familiarity and decrease anxiety, whereas middle-class children only gained three IQ points.

6.3 SOCIAL BEHAVIOUR AND DIVERSITY IN DEVELOPMENT

6.3.1 THEORIES OF MORAL DEVELOPMENT

Learning and social learning explanations

Behaviourists and social learning theorists explain all behaviour in terms of: conditioning, reinforcement, rewards and punishment, and modelling (see unit 2.4.1).

1 *Effectiveness of punishment.* **Aronfreed** (1963) punished a group of young boys verbally for touching attractive toys either when they were in the act of reaching (group 1) or a few moments after (group 2). When later left alone with the toys, group 1 held out longer, suggesting a stronger conscience from forward conditioning.

2 *Counter-effectiveness of punishment.* Is punishment an effective method of learning right and wrong?

- It may produce hostility and a desire to rebel. **Glueck and Glueck** (1950) found that severe punishment was associated with delinquency in boys. **O'Leary** *et al.* (1974) found that the use of quiet rather than public reprimands in class was more effective with disruptive children.
- A person may get used to punishment, which means it has to continually be increased to be effective.
- The attention associated with punishment may be positively reinforcing. It may be as effective to ignore bad behaviour, which will then disappear through lack of reinforcement (the 'time out' method).
- The threat of punishment may be sufficient. This is contrary to Behaviourist theory because it involves a cognitive component.
- Punishment is useful in situations where an immediate effect is needed rather than in learning general moral principles, such as a child putting its hand near the fire. **Bower and Hilgard** (1981) consider that punishment must be prompt, intensive and clear if it is to be effective. It also helps if you show the person the right way to behave.

3 *Counter-effectiveness of rewards.* External rewards can destroy intrinsic motivation. **Lepper** *et al.* (1973) asked 55 preschool children to draw a picture, telling some of them that they would receive a certificate for good drawing. Two groups of children were given a certificate (the expected and unexpected groups). Some weeks later the children were again asked to draw a picture, they found that the no-certificate group were most willing to do a drawing, followed by those who had not expected the certificate. This supports the view that it is more valuable for children to be allowed to develop their own, internal sense of control.

4 *Parenting styles.* Is there an association between good moral development and behaviourist styles of parenting? **Hoffman** (1970) identified three major childrearing methods:

- *Love withdrawal.* Withholding attention, affection or approval when the child misbehaves, which creates anxiety over loss of love.
- *Power assertion.* Using superior power such as forceful comments, physical restraint, spanking or withdrawing privileges. May lead to fear, anger, resentment.
- *Induction.* Explain why a behaviour is wrong, emphasise how it affects others and suggest ways to make amends.

  The first two might be regarded as 'behaviourist styles'. Hoffman reviewed over 100 studies and concluded that there was a high correlation between more mature moral development and the use of induction, whereas the opposite was true for power assertion. Induction allows children to develop their own moral reasoning rather than to obey instructions mindlessly.

Evaluation. However, the data is correlational, and it could be that a morally less well-developed child needs more coercive forms of punishment whereas children who are already morally sophisticated can be reasoned with.

⑤ *Modelling.* Do people learn to behave more prosocially (morally) by imitating others? **Bryan and Test** (1967, see unit 1.4.1) showed that motorists are more helpful when they have seen someone else doing the same. In another study, when a model was seen placing money in a Salvation Army kettle, donations increased from other shoppers. **Beaman** *et al.* (1978) also showed how direct instruction increases prosocial behaviour (see unit 1.4.1).

⑥ *Evaluation*

- Some moral behaviour is obviously learned through reinforcement and modelling.
- It can explain how moral behaviour is related to particular situations rather than to principles (see 'Moral inconsistency', below) .
- Some moral behaviour will be the result of conscious decisions rather than conditioned responses.
- Behaviourist theory is based on the results of animal and laboratory experiments. It is wrong to assume that the same laws apply to everyday human behaviour.
- It does not account for the fact that children seem to pass through different stages of moral behaviour.

Psychodynamic explanations

Freud's view of moral development is part of his psychodynamic theory (see units 4.2.2 and 7.1.1).

❶ *The phallic stage and the superego*

- Around the age of 3 a child's sexual interest focuses on their genitalia and they feel desire for their opposite-sex parent (the *Oedipus complex*).
- This makes them see their same-sex parent as a rival. The child feels unconscious hostility, resulting in guilt. The child also feels anxiety and fear of punishment should his true desires be discovered.
- Resolution occurs through identification with the same-sex parent. Identification is the process of 'taking' on the attitudes and ideas of another person.
- Identification is also important for gender identity and attitudes towards authority.
- Unsatisfactory resolution results in problems such as amorality, homosexuality or rebelliousness.

❷ *The conscience* punishes you when you do something wrong. It is an internal representation of the 'punishing' parent and is composed of prohibitions imposed on you by your parents. The conscience appears at age 5 or 6 and is a source of 'guilt feelings'.

- **Freud** predicted an inverse relationship between guilt and wrongdoing, the more guilt a person experiences the less likely they are to do wrong. **MacKinnon** (1938) gave nearly 100 participants a test and left them alone with the answer book. Of those who cheated (about 50%) most said they did not feel guilty, which confirms the inverse relationship between guilt and wrongdoing.
- **Freud** explained the strong bonds between dominant parents and their children as the result of a threatening parent producing a greater fear of punishment, which leads to a stronger sense of identification.

❸ *The ego-ideal* rewards you when you behave in accordance with parental moral values. It is the source of feelings of pride and self-satisfaction, acting as the 'rewarding' parent.

❹ *Inconsistency of moral behaviour.* Freudian theory suggests that moral behaviour should be consistent because of the conscience, though there is the possibility of some inconsistency because of irrational behaviour by the id. **Hartshorne and May** (1928) found little consistency in moral behaviour. A child who cheated in one situation didn't in another. They also found that immoral behaviour was more governed by the probability of being caught than any principles of morality. **Gersen and Damon** (1978) showed that children don't distribute rewards as fairly as they said they would. In a pretend situation children gave an average of 18% of candy bars to themselves. In a real test a few months later, this rose to 29%.

⑤ *Erikson's theory of social development* (see units 6.3.3 and 6.4.1). Whereas Freud's theory is psychosexual, Erikson's is psychosocial. He de-emphasised the unconscious and emphasised the social world. Each stage of life is marked by a crisis, which must be confronted and resolved. Both parents influence the development of moral behaviour, which is a product of the superego (determining what is acceptable or not) and the ego (inhibiting undesirable impulses of the id). Since the ego is the rational component of the personality, morality must be related to cognitive development generally.

The early stages of development are:

Age	Life crisis	Activity	Favourable outcome	Unfavourable outcome	Important relationships
1	TRUST VS. MISTRUST	consistent, stable care	trust	suspicion, insecurity	maternal figure
2–3	AUTONOMY VS. SHAME	independence from parents	sense of autonomy and self-esteem	shame and self-doubt	parents
4–5	INITIATIVE VS. GUILT	exploration of environment	initiates activities	fear of punishment, guilt feelings	basic family
6–11	INDUSTRY VS. INFERIORITY	acquisition of knowledge	sense of competence and achievement	feelings of inadequacy and inferiority	family, neighbours, teachers

⑥ *Evaluation*

- The emphasis on the importance of early childhood had an enormous impact.
- The notion of the unconscious, irrational self has proved useful in explaining moral inconsistency.
- There is little empirical evidence to support psychodynamic theories.
- This view limits moral learning to the family, which may have been true in Freud's time, but it can't explain how children from one-parent families generally manage to develop a sense of morals.
- It assumes that morals are unconscious yet people make conscious moral decisions.

Cognitive-developmental explanations

Cognitive-developmental theories are characterised by:

- Innately determined stages of moral development.
- Each stage is defined by the kind of thought (cognition) used by a person to make moral judgements.
- An assumption that moral principles are universal and linked to moral behaviour.

① *Piaget's theory*

AGE (approximate)	0–5 years	5–8 +	9 +
STAGE	PREMORAL JUDGEMENT	MORAL REALISM *Heteronomous* morals (controlled by others).	MORAL SUBJECTIVISM / RELATIVITY *Autonomous* morals (controlled by oneself).
RULES	Rules not understood	Rules exist as 'things' (*realism*).	Rules mutually agreed and changeable (*relativism*).
MEANS OF EVALUATING ACTIONS:		Consequences.	Intentions.
PUNISHMENT		Make up for the damage done, to make *atonement*.	Punishment fits the crime, principle of *reciprocity*.
STAGE OF COGNITIVE DEVELOPMENT	Pre-operational, egocentric.	Intuitive, inability to conserve, later beginning concrete operations.	Concrete and formal operations.

② *Piaget's empirical evidence*

- *Realism vs. relativism.* **Piaget** (1932) played a game of marbles with a group of children and asked questions about the rules. He found that children under 3 used no rules at all, by the age of 5 rules were seen as inviolable and from some semi-mystical authority, and by the age of 10 children understood that people had invented the rules and they could be changed but only if all players agreed. **Linaza** (1984) found the same sequence of development in Spanish children, supporting the universal nature of such stages.
- *Intentions vs. consequences.* **Piaget** presented pairs of moral stories to children where one story had greater consequences but the intentions were good. He asked who was naughtiest and why. The heteronomous younger child could distinguish between intentional and unintentional actions but based their judgement on the severity of outcome. The autonomous older child used the motive/intention as the means for judgement. This is using internal as opposed to external responsibility as the basis for morality.
- *Other studies.* **Nelson** (1973) found that even 3-year-olds can make judgements about intentions if the information is made explicit. **Armsby** (1971) manipulated the stories so that there was a small amount of deliberate damage or a large amount of accidental damage. He found that younger children did take intention into account, but had difficulty weighing up the relative importance of value and intention.

Evaluation

- The game of marbles is a rather insignificant example of understanding rules and morals.
- The younger children may not have understood the moral stories and were only able to pick out the consequences. The stories confound intentions and consequences.
- The understanding of intention is more complex than Piaget suggested.

③ *Evaluation of Piaget's theory*

- Piaget's work introduced the idea of moral stages which are related to cognitive maturity.
- Piaget's empirical methods were not rigidly controlled and therefore his evidence may be influenced by experimenter bias.
- He probably underestimated children's moral sophistication in some situations.
- His account does not explain moral inconsistency.
- His account ignores emotional influences.

④ *Kohlberg's theory.* **Kohlberg** (1966) elaborated Piaget's theory and extended the scope right through to middle age. He attempted to account for moral reasoning rather than behaviour.

Level	Age	Stage
I Pre-conventional	6–13	1 Deference to authority, heteronomous. 2 Doing good to serve one's own interests, egocentric.
II Conventional	13–16	3 Care for the other, interpersonal conformity, 'good boy/girl'. 4 The primacy of social order, conscience, unquestioning acceptance of authority.
III Post-conventional or principled	16–20	5 Creation of social order, individual rights, questioning the law and authority to ensure justice. 6 Universal, ethical principles (later dropped because rarely, if ever exhibited except by e.g. Gandhi).

⑤ *Kohlberg's empirical evidence*

- *Moral dilemmas.* Kohlberg was more interested in why people made certain choices than what their choices were. He devised a set of dilemmas, such as Heinz and the druggist who wouldn't sell a drug to save Heinz's dying wife. **Kohlberg** (1963) tested a group of 10–16-year-old boys, and used their responses to construct the classification scheme. Each individual had 10 categorisations, one for each of the dilemmas. One category emerged overall as the more dominant for any individual, 10-year-olds mainly showed stage 2 reasoning, with some responses at stage 1 and 3. Sixteen-year-olds were mainly at stage 3. **Walker** *et al.* (1987) used 9 stages to allow for the fact that many children's reasoning falls between two stages, and found general agreement with Kohlberg. They found stage 2 reasoning dominates at age 10 and stage 3 at age 16. **Colby and Kohlberg** (1987) performed a more careful analysis of the original data and found only 15% reached stage 5 and there was no evidence whatsoever of stage 6 judgements.

- *Delinquents.* **Fodor** (1972) found that delinquents operate at a much lower level on the Kohlberg scales than non–delinquents.
- *Longitudinal study.* **Colby** *et al.* (1983) followed Kohlberg's initial participants over 20 years, ending up with 58 men. They were retested every 3 years. By the age of 36 participants were mainly reasoning at stage 4 (65% of their responses), stage 3 still accounted for about 30%, and stage 5 was 5%.
- *Cross-cultural support.* **Snarey** (1985) listed 27 different cross-cultural studies which found a progression from stages 1 to 4 at about the same ages. Very few studies found any stage 5 reasoning and where it occurred it was likely to be in urban areas.
- *Gender differences.* **Gilligan** (1982) suggested that Kohlberg's view of moral principles is limited to specific kinds of moral behaviour, in particular justice and fairness. He omitted the ethic of caring, something which is stronger in women. **Gilligan and Attanucci** (1988) asked a group of men and women to produce accounts of their own moral dilemmas. These were analysed and scored according to whether they emphasised the moral principle of care or of justice. Overall men favoured a justice orientation and women favoured a care orientation.

⑥ *Evaluation of Kohlberg's theory*

- The notion of 'dilemmas' recognises the fact that people behave differently in different situations (moral inconsistency).
- This may be the best available approach and has generated much empirical interest, despite the criticisms below.
- This is a theory of moral principles not behaviour. Kohlberg never claimed to predict behaviour, his interest was in moral reasoning.
- Stages 5 and 6 may be moral ideals, never achieved by some people.
- Gender bias. The theory is biased towards male morality (justice) as the participants were male.
- Culture bias. Kohlberg claimed that the moral stages are universal. In fact the stages reflect Western values of democracy and the assumption that such systems are more morally advanced than other social systems.
- Age bias. The dilemmas are biased towards older participants, some of them are irrelevant to children.
- The account ignores emotional influences.

Other perspectives

❶ *Biological perspective.* Some children may be born lacking a conscience and empathy, such as people suffering antisocial personality disorder (sociopaths). They tend to be underaroused in terms of activity in the autonomic nervous system and therefore less susceptible to conditioning (**Rosenhan and Seligman**, 1989).

❷ *Humanist perspective.* The route to learning moral behaviour is through warm family relationships which are conducive to emotional development and which lead a child to identify with appropriate prosocial models. **Rosenhan** (1970, see unit 1.4.1) found that the most altruistic people had warm relations with their parents and their parents thought and behaved altruistically.

6.3.2 THEORIES OF GENDER DEVELOPMENT

- A person's sex is the biological fact of being male or female.
- Gender is the maleness and femaleness of a person's behaviour.
- Gender role is the behaviour expected of an individual on the basis of their sex, masculinity or femininity.

The different approaches are not mutually exclusive, they each emphasise a different aspect of gender development.

① *The biological approach.* Genetic and hormonal factors cause gender-appropriate behaviours.

Evidence for

- *Hormones* control many sexual behaviours, such as ovulation and parenting behaviours.
- *Cross-cultural studies* have shown that some gender behaviours are universal, such as female interest in babies. **Mead** (1949) studied gender in a number of cultures and ultimately concluded that some behaviours were innately determined though many were related to cultural practices.
- The presence of *male hormones during prenatal development* leads to masculinisation of the brain. **Money and Ehrhardt** (1972) studied a group of girls with *androgenital syndrome*, their mothers had received male hormones during pregnancy to prevent miscarriage. As a result the girls developed male genitalia and, through childhood, their behaviour was described as tomboyish due to the prenatal androgens, though it may be that the girls were responding to the expectations of others (parents and teachers) who knew about their condition. **Imperato-McGinley** *et al.* (1974) studied the Batista family on a remote Caribbean island, where several children were born with female external genitalia but developed male genitalia at puberty and appeared to happily accept their new gender. The reason for this sudden change was an insensitivity to testosterone during development but in puberty there was enough to trigger further development. However, prenatally their brains were androgenised which may explain why they accepted their new role so readily.

Evidence against

- *Social influences.* **Goldwyn** (1979) described the case of Daphne Went, an XY individual with *testicular feminising syndrome* (TFS), an insensitivity to testosterone which results in female external genitalia. Mrs Went was content with her female role and adopted two children. It may be that her brain was also insensitive to the male hormones.

Evaluation

- Some gender differences are clearly biological, therefore the biological approach must be part of any account.
- Case histories show that genetic sex and gender need not correspond. Therefore biological explanations are not sufficient on their own.

② *Biosocial theory.* **Money and Ehrhardt** (1972) suggested that it is the interaction between biological and social factors which is important rather than biology directly. There is probably a critical or sensitive period, after which gender identity is fixed. They found that when pseudohermaphrodites were wrongly sexed at birth they rarely sought reassignment and it was generally successful only if done before the age of 2.

Evaluation

- This approach gives a fuller account.
- It is based on evidence from small samples of abnormal individuals.

③ *Psychoanalytic theory.* **Freud** suggested that sex-appropriate attitudes become internalised from identifying with the same sex parent. Satisfactory resolution of same and opposite sex parental conflicts occurs during the phallic stage (see unit 6.3.1). Freud said that women are sexually inferior, they have to make do with babies as a poor substitute for a penis. **Horney** (1924) suggested that the envy is not of the penis but of status, the penis is a symbol of men's superior status.

Evidence for

- **Hetherington** (1972) found that boys who lose a father after the age of 4 suffer little effect on their masculinity, whereas an early loss appears to result in gender role difficulties.

Evidence against

- One-parent or homosexual families should prevent normal gender development. However, **Hoeffer** (1981) found that children follow typical psychosexual development in such families.

Evaluation

- Freud was probably correct in identifying the age of 4 as a time of gender awareness.
- Freud was right in drawing attention to children's sexual awareness of their parents.

④ *Social Learning Theory.* Gender role identity is learned through reinforcement and modelling, a child is rewarded for sex-appropriate behaviour and punished for inappropriate behaviour. Behaviour is also learned indirectly through modelling of parents, stereotypes and media.

Evidence for

- *Parental reinforcement.* Even the earliest sex differences can be explained this way. **Smith and Lloyd** (1978) gave mothers a set of feminine-, masculine- and neutral-type toys. When a 6-month-old baby was dressed and named as a boy, the mothers encouraged more motor activity and gave masculine-type toys whereas this was not so when the baby appeared to be a girl.
- *Peer reinforcement.* **Lamp and Roopnarine** (1979) observed preschool children at play. Children generally reinforced peers for sex-appropriate play and were quick to criticise sex-inappropriate play. Children respond more readily to reinforcement by the same sex rather than opposite sex peers. This suggests that children already know what is sex-appropriate, their peers are just reinforcing that knowledge.
- *Television reinforcement.* **Williams** (1985) studied the effects of the arrival of TV to a town. He found that the children's sex role attitudes became more traditional and sex-stereotyped after two years of exposure to TV.
- *Stereotypes.* The existence of persistent stereotypes (a typical male is assertive, independent, good at maths; a typical female is dependent, relatively passive, good at verbal tasks) supports the claim that such beliefs are self-perpetuating. **Maccoby and Jacklin** (1974) undertook a massive review of more than 1,500 studies of gender differences and concluded that the differences observed were minimal and that most popular gender-role stereotypes are 'cultural myths'.
- *Cultural Relativism.* **Mead** (1935) initially concluded from her studies of three tribes in New Guinea, that gender was culturally determined. Later (1949) she changed her view to one of cultural relativism – some behaviours are innate and universal. In all three tribes, all the men were more aggressive in comparison with the women, though both sexes of the Arapesh were non-aggressive and both sexes of Mundugumour were aggressive.

Evidence against

- *Real gender differences.* **Jacklin and Maccoby** (1978) introduced unfamiliar 2½-year-olds to each other and dressed them in neutral clothing; they found that interactions were most lively and positive with same-sex pairs. This may well reflect an early incompatibility between girls and boys, partly based on biological differences such as boisterousness and partly due to learned preferences for toys and activities.
- *Variable reinforcement.* **Fagot** (1985) found evidence that teachers tend to reinforce 'feminine' behaviours in boys and girls such as quiet, sedentary activities, suggesting that children are exposed to a multiplicity of stereotypes and reinforcements.

Evaluation

- Reinforcements are not sufficiently consistent to explain all observed differences, but gender appropriate behaviours are clearly reinforced.
- This approach explains cultural differences and accounts for the influence of stereotypes.
- It overlooks biological (innate) factors.

⑤ *Cognitive-developmental theory.* **Kohlberg** (1966) argued that gender identity is a combination of social learning mediated by maturational and cognitive factors. The ability to form coherent, consistent thought (maturation) is necessary for the formation of gender concepts. The child actively organises its own identity.

Stage	Age	Characteristics
Gender identity	2–3½	The child can say its sex but doesn't understand that this is fixed.
Gender stability	3½–4½	Gender is now fixed and largely determined by external features such as clothing. Gender might change if you're wearing different clothes.
Gender consistency	4½–7	Gender conservation, child understands that gender is an unchanging quality.

Evidence for

- **Slaby and Frey** (1975) showed preschool children a film with men on one side and women on the other. Those children who had previously been rated as having gender consistency watched more same-sex models. This shows how they actively seek information which will help them develop gender-appropriate behaviour.

Evidence against

- **Maccoby** (1980) found that 3-year-olds learn many gender role stereotypes long before they attend to same-sex models.
- **Money and Ehrhardt** (above) claimed that gender reassignment was difficult after the age of 3.

Evaluation

- Combines a social learning approach with some aspects of biological development.
- Basic gender identity does appear between 2 and 5, in line with cognitive development.
- This view assumes that development proceeds in stages, and that gender identity is mediated by cognitive factors. This may not universally be true.

6 *Gender-schema theory.* **Martin and Halverson** (1981) suggested that once a child has a basic gender identity they are motivated to learn more about the sexes and incorporate this information into a gender schema. Like all schemas, this serves to organise relevant information and attitudes and will influence behaviour.

    Bem (1984) suggested that the traditional view that rigid sex-roles lead to psychological health may have outlived its usefulness. An androgynous approach is more flexible, allowing a person to select the best and most appropriate behaviours for themselves rather than being tied to a fixed gender schema. She measured masculinity and femininity (using the Bem Sex Role Inventory, BSRI) and found that androgynous individuals are more adaptable in different situations, have higher self-esteem and a greater sense of emotional well-being.

Evaluation

- Offers a middle ground between social learning and cognitive–developmental explanations.
- Explains how gender stereotypes persist, because people are more likely to remember information which is consistent with their schemas (see unit 1.1.3).
- Explains how gender behaviours occur before gender identity.
- Lacks mention of biological factors and assumes that all gender behaviour is mediated by cognitive factors.

6.3.3 THEORIES OF THE DEVELOPMENT OF THE SELF

1 *Social learning approach.* **Argyle** (1983) suggested that there are four main influences:

- *The reactions of others.* You see yourself as others see you. **Cooley** (1902) called this the '*looking-glass self*', social interaction provides self-knowledge and self-expectations. **Rosenthal and Jacobsen** (1968) demonstrated that pupils' IQs could be increased through the expectation from teachers that their IQs should be higher (*self-fulfilling prophecy*). **Guthrie** (1938) described a trick played on an unattractive girl by her classmates. They took turns asking her out, and soon she had actually become more attractive, presumably because her self-image changed and this led her to behave differently.

- *Comparison with others.* Many self-concepts are comparative terms, such as tall or clever, and therefore require the standards to be set by others.
- *Social roles.* Part of your self-concept is determined by your social role. **Goffman** (1959) suggested that life is a series of theatrical performances, each role is acted out in accordance with expectations about what is appropriate. **Kuhn** (1960) asked children to give answers to 'Who am I?'. In answers given by 7-year-olds, 25% related to social roles. This increased to 50% when 24-year-olds were asked.
- *Identification with models.* Both social learning and psychoanalytic theories suggest how models act as a means of developing a self-image. People with lower self-esteem are most ready to imitate others. Disabled children lack role models which may impair their self-development.

② *Cognitive-developmental approach.* A number of theorists have described four stages of self, which can be related to cognitive development generally.

- *Self-recognition.* A sense of bodily self, represented in early schema. This begins when the infant hears its own cry, or matches the action of its hand with the sensation. **Lewis and Brooks-Gunn** (1979) tested self-recognition by colouring an infants' nose with rouge. A child who responds by touching their own nose shows self-recognition. At 9–12 months, few children touched their noses, by 20 months 75% did. They also found that, by 18 months, most children can point to a photograph of themselves.
- *The categorical self.* The extension of self and a self-image, the child classifies themselves in terms of categories or social roles (see **Kuhn**, above). In early childhood the self-concept is physically based, and gender is particularly important (see unit 6.3.2). Ethnic awareness of self appears around the age of 4 or 5.
- *The psychological or private self.* Self-awareness of your own ability to deal with problems through reason and thought. Children of 3/4 can distinguish a thinking, psychological self from their physical self. Children of this age typically describe themselves in concrete terms but **Eder** (1990) also found that they can describe how they usually behave in certain situations which is evidence of a psychological self-concept. **Selman** (1980) used dilemmas to evaluate the development of private and public self. He found that by the age of 8 most children recognise the difference between their inner states and outward appearances. This is in agreement with the end of the egocentric self (unit 6.2.1).
- *The self in middle childhood and adolescence.* Self-descriptions gradually come to include inner qualities, a more abstract sense of self. In middle childhood traits are seen as enduring and inflexible, whereas by adolescence a trait may be viewed as specific to certain situations. For example the child may describe themselves as kind, the adolescent knows that they are only sometimes kind. The self-concept is under constant revision, but nowhere more critically than during adolescence (see unit 6.4.1).

③ *Social interaction: G.H. Mead's theory.* **Mead** (1934) considered that the self did not exist apart from the social context. Humans differ from most if not all animals in being able to perceive themselves (concept of self) and thus they are able to interact with themselves.

- 'I' is the subject of the interaction, the knower.
- 'Me' is the object, the being who is experiencing and who is socialised, the self as known.
- Development begins with a looking-glass self, 'me' defined by the reactions of significant others. Later, pretend play allows the child to develop the 'me' by testing various social contexts in which the child is the other person.

④ *Psychodynamic approach.* **Erikson** (1968) described the development of self over the lifespan (see units 6.3.2 and 6.4.1). Individuals define their selves in terms of the norms of their culture (see unit 7.1.1). This accords with **Noble**'s (1976) unit 7.2.3) view that Africans develop an extended sense of self.

⑤ *Humanist approach.* **Rogers** (see units 3.4.1 and 4.2.2) described self-actualisation as the key motive for human development.

⑥ *Situationalism.* **Mischel** (1968) has suggested that there is no such thing as a coherent self or personality. The self is a cognitive structure useful for organising the information you have about yourself, implicit personality theory (see unit 1.1.1) does this for the information you hold about others.

⑦ *The development of other self-concepts*
- *Self-esteem* is one's evaluation of oneself. It has a critical impact on performance. **Coopersmith** (1968) found that boys low in self-esteem were self-conscious, isolated, reluctant to join in activities and constantly underrated themselves. **Rogers** (1965) believed that high self-esteem develops out of unconditional positive regard from significant others. **Harter** (1983) found that it is not until the age of 10 that children have a sense of self-esteem, the under 7s do not fully understand the concept. Self-esteem is often lowered during adolescence, perhaps because of the adolescent's perception of physical appearance but also because of identity confusion.
- *Self-efficacy* is the belief in your own abilities, as distinct from the abilities themselves. Such beliefs generate expectancies, which in turn affect behaviour positively or negatively (self-fulfilling prophecy). **Collins** (1982) compared children who had a high or low sense of self-efficacy in terms of their performance on mathematical tasks. Those children with high self-efficacy, regardless of ability, solved more problems and, moreover, had better strategies for dealing with errors. Their beliefs were related to the amount of effort they made. **Weinberg** *et al.* (1979) gave participants an artificially raised sense of efficacy, which then led to improved performance. This was achieved by giving them false positive feedback.

6.4 ADOLESCENCE, ADULTHOOD AND OLD AGE

6.4.1 ADOLESCENCE

Adolescence is the transitional period from childhood to adulthood. In some societies there is no adolescence, there is simply a moment of change from boy to man usually marked by a rite of passage.

① *The biological approach.* There are major hormonal and physical changes requiring adjustments to self-image. The hypothalamus stimulates the pituitary to produce female or male hormones, and these lead to primary sexual changes (e.g. menstruation, enlargement of penis) and secondary sexual changes (e.g. pubic hair, body shape).

Jones and Bayley (1950) found that those who reached puberty earlier were seen as more attractive, self-confident, popular, and less attention-seeking and dependent by peers and adults. The effect was still apparent at age 17, and possibly even later. **Clausen** (1975) suggested that some advantages are because of size (for sports).

② *The psychodynamic approach.* **Freud's** psychosexual stages include a final *genital stage* which occurs at the onset of adolescence. There is an upsurge in sexual instincts and a drive towards independence. The personality is overhauled resulting in the development of new ego defence mechanisms:

- *Asceticism*: to deprive self of pleasurable experiences, particularly sexual.
- *Intellectualisation*: dealing with anxiety-provoking subjects through lengthy discussion.

If development is still fixed in early childhood, the individual can't reach maturity because their focus is still on their own body and satisfying body-related needs. They can't take on the larger responsibilities involving others.

❸ *The neo-Freudian approach: an identity crisis.* **Erikson** (1968, see units 6.3.1, 6.3.3 and 6.4.2) combined social and biological factors in his account of lifespan development. Erikson considered that the main task for the adolescent was to establish a new, enduring and unified sense of identity or self.

Age	Life crisis	Activity	Favourable outcome	Unfavourable outcome	Important relationships
12–18	IDENTITY VS ROLE CONFUSION	seeks coherent personality and vocation	strong personal identity	confusion	peers, ingroups and outgroups

Marcia (1980) extended some of Erikson's ideas into four non-sequential stages/outcomes:

- *Identity diffusion*, confusion, possible rebellion.
- *Identity foreclosure*, uncertainties avoided by committing self to safe, conventional goals without exploring alternatives, potentials not realised.
- *Identity moratorium*, decisions about identity put on hold.
- *Identity achievement*, individual emerges with firm goals, ideologies, commitments.

❹ *Cognitive-developmental view.* **Elkind and Bowen** (1979) proposed a kind of Piagetian egocentricism in adolescence, which has two facets. First, an 'imaginary audience', which is the belief that everyone is as concerned with our thoughts and behaviour as we are. Second, 'personal fable', which is the belief that we are special and will not die. This explains why many teenagers have a sense of invulnerability and engage in many high-risk activities such as drugs and driving fast on motorbikes.

There are parallels between the early adolescent and the preschool child: both are egocentric and both face the task of establishing a separate identity.

❺ *Recapitulation theory: a period of storm and stress.* **Hall** (1904) claimed that the adolescent had to experience the volatile history of the human race before reaching maturity. Many theorists, for example **Erikson**, have agreed with his view that adolescence is a troubled time, a time of teenage rebellion, drug use, delinquency, disenchantment and confusion.

Evidence for

- **Masterson** (1967) found that 65% of 12–18-year-olds showed evidence of anxiety.
- The National Children's Bureau study (**Fogelman**, 1976), which looked at a cohort of 11,000 16-year-olds, found that adolescence was a difficult time, particularly for parents who saw their children as solitary, irritable and fussy.

Evidence against. Reasons other than adolescence *per se* may lead to stress.

- **Rutter** *et al.* (1976) looked at behavioural and psychiatric disorder in their survey of adolescents on the Isle of Wight, and concluded that there was evidence of turmoil but many of the problems were mainly ongoing from childhood.
- *Cultural relativism.* **Mead** (1928) in her book 'Coming of Age in Samoa', suggested that turmoil may be due to growing up in an industrialised society. She observed that, in Samoa, sexuality is dealt with in an open, casual manner and therefore children are spared the guilt, anxiety and confusion which we experience.
- Adolescence is a *stressful time for parents* – perhaps the observed stress in adolescents is due to their parents' stress at this time of change, coping with a physically and psychologically different person and the conflicts of dependence and independence.
- *Person-environment fit.* **Eccles** *et al.* (1993) suggested that the reason many adolescents experience stress is due to the mismatch between their developing needs and the opportunities afforded to them by their social environments.

❻ *Coleman's focal theory.* **Coleman** (1980) disagreed with the view that adolescence was a time of storm and stress, or a period of identity crisis. He felt that the 'normal' adolescent focuses on one issue at a time, crises only occur when issues accumulate. **Coleman and Hendry** (1990) questioned 800 children aged 11–17 and found that different issues peaked at particular ages. For example, young boys are concerned about heterosexual relationships but later become concerned about conflicts with parents.

6.4.2 CHANGES IN ADULTHOOOD

1 *Erikson's eight ages of man.* **Erikson's** approach has been described in units 6.3.1 and 6.4.1. The remaining stages are shown below.

Age	Life crisis	Activity	Favourable outcome	Unfavourable outcome	Important relationships
20–40	Young adulthood INTIMACY VS. ISOLATION	deep and lasting relationships	ability to experience love and commitment	isolation	friends lovers
40–64	Middle adulthood GENERATIVITY VS. STAGNATION	being productive and creative for society	wider outlook	lack of growth, boredom and self-involvement	spouse children
65+	Late adulthood INTEGRITY VS. DESPAIR	review and evaluate life	sense of satisfaction, acceptance	regrets, fear of death	spouse children grandchildren

Empirical evidence

- **Hodgson and Fisher** (1979) found that most of the female undergraduates in their sample who were rated as identity achievers also had achieved intimacy, though half of those who were *not* identity achievers had also achieved intimacy. It may be that women achieve intimacy before identity.
- **Livson** (1981) used data from the Oakland Growth Study which began in 1934. She compared those who had originally been classed as traditionals or non-traditionals during adolescence. At age 40, the traditionals were resolving the issue of intimacy and by age 50 they were in the generativity stage. The non-traditional women appeared to be having a mid-life identity crisis at age 40, a throwback to adolescence. This did not hamper development because they went on to be the best adjusted at age 50.

Evaluation

- Erikson's theory has been very influential particularly because it introduced the idea of development throughout life.
- It is not easy to test empirically.
- The stages are meant to be universal but there are gender and culture differences. **Gilligan** (1982) pointed out that the model focuses exclusively on male patterns. **Lebra** (1976) described how both Japanese men and women focus on interdependence, collectivism, empathy and introspection rather than autonomy, equality, individuality and aggression.
- The scheme does not allow for individual differences (see **Livson** above).

2 *Levinson's seasons of a man's life.* **Levinson** (1986) offered an alternative to stage theory, he used the term 'seasons' because it doesn't imply progression but simply change. He based his scheme on biographical details collected through extensive interviews of 40 men aged 35-45. Periods of transition are stressful and necessary for healthy adjustment because they allow the individual to reassess what has gone before.

Age			
17–22	Early adulthood	EARLY ADULT TRANSITION	This is an exciting and stressful time, time to make life decisions, establish a home and family and select a career. The person's dream is formed.
23–8		Entering the adult world	
29–33		Age 30 transition	Some people experience self-doubt, a sense of life becoming more serious and time running out.
34–40		Settling down	Becoming one's own man (BOOM), looking for recognition and self-sufficiency.

Age			
41–45	Middle adulthood	MID-LIFE TRANSITION	May be a difficult period for those who have not realised their initial dreams. May coincide with the death of one's parents, maturing children, the menopause and other key changes.
46–50		Entering middle adulthood	A time to build on past decisions or start a new occupation.
51–55		Age 50 transition	Tension between attachment and separation.
56–60		Culmination of middle adulthood	Less inward looking, may take greater interest in family. Can be the most rewarding phase of life.
61–65		LATE ADULT TRANSITION	
65+	Late adulthood		An acceptance of the inevitability of physical decline, and of what life has been.

Empirical evidence

- **Valliant** (1978) followed a group of about 100 men from the time they were undergraduates (in 1940) to when they were in their later 40s, using physical and psychological assessments. Nearly all of those who were classed as 'best outcomes' at age 47 had married before the age of 30 and stayed married. Conversely, $3/4$ of those who were 'worst outcomes' had either married after age 30 or separated. The majority of the best marriages were formed between the ages of 23 and 29.
- **Roberts and Newton** (1987) found that women often established an occupation or marriage at a time beyond the early adult period.
- **Valiant** (above) also found few radical changes during the mid-life period, for some people it is the happiest time of their life, a time when they are reaching the peak of their career.
- **Livson** (above) found an interaction between lifestyle and personality which determines whether a person has a mid-life crisis, 'non-traditional' men and women often found it difficult.

Evaluation

- The scheme was originally gender-biased but data on women has been presented which fits this scheme.
- The empirical data is limited but is rich in detail.
- The data may suffer from a cohort effect, having problems or experiences particular to one generation.
- The mid-life crisis may not be universal. **Rutter and Rutter** (1992) reported that individuals who did not go through this crisis still remained psychologically healthy.

❸ *Gould's theory of the evolution of adult consciousness.* **Gould** (1980) extended Freud's theory to adulthood. To grow up you have to give up the fictions of childhood. **Gould** based his stage theory on the responses of over 500 white, middle-class people aged 16–50 years old.

Age	False assumption
18–21	'I will always belong to my parents and believe in their world.' Marriage at this age is an attempt to gain independence but may fail because such marriages are too dependent.
22–28	'Doing things my parents' way, with willpower and perseverance, will bring results. But if I become too frustrated, confused or tired or am simply unable to cope, they will step in and show me the right way.' This dependence on parents (or a loved one) prevents independence and ultimately leads to feelings of hostility.
28–34	'Life is simple and controllable. There are no significant coexisting contradictory forces within me.' One must recognise the contradictory pressures from within and without, and take a new perspective.
35–45	'There is no evil in me or death in the world. The sinister has been destroyed.' One must come to terms with mortality. Men have to recognise that success and hard work cannot protect them from dying, women may strike out on their own as a means of challenging man as the protector and coping with their own mortality.

Evaluation

- This is a culture-biased account, and age-limited.
- The data was collected by inexperienced students and may have been unreliable.

6.4.3 ADJUSTMENT TO OLD AGE

Changes in old age

① *Physical changes.* As a person gets older, their body and abilities become smaller, slower, weaker, lesser and fewer. For example, the bones become more brittle, brain cells are reduced, reflexes and reaction times are slower (**Bromley**, 1988). Other physical changes may not be related to ageing specifically but to disease states. **Williams** (1993) reported that, when healthy older participants are tested, 50% show signs of previously undetected heart disease. The remaining 50% are essentially no different from participants in their 20s.

② *Cognitive changes.* Does mental capacity decline? **Arlin** (1977) suggested a fifth stage of cognitive development: divergent thinking or problem-finding (rather than solving).

- *IQ.* **Wechsler** found that intelligence reaches a peak around the age of 30 when he was compiling the normative data for WAIS, his test of adult intelligence. **Burns** (1966) reported a longitudinal study where a set of people were tested at age 22 and again when they were 56, on average their IQs were higher. **Schultz** *et al.* (1980) found declines in fluid intelligence and spontaneous flexibility with age, but they found that some older participants were the best of all. Studies of IQ may suffer from the *cohort effect* if they compare one generation with another, older generations inevitably have lower IQs due to poorer diet. **Schaie** (1983) found, from a longitudinal study in Seattle, that cohort effects equal or exceed age differences.
- *Memory.* **Talland** (1968) found that participants aged 77 to 89 remembered less than half the number of items that a 20–5-year-old age group can recall on a short-term memory task, and also forgot more in the initial 90 seconds after presentation of a 3-letter word. **Kimmel** (1990) suggested that there may be dramatic declines shown in laboratory memory experiments and some everyday memory skills, but older people show highly competent memory skills in other areas, such as long-term recall or expert memory skills. Motivation is probably important.
- *Other cognitive tasks.* **Crossman and Szafran** (1956) established that older participants took longer on tasks involving discrimination when the number of alternatives increased. **McDonald** (1995) found that some older people could not cope with Piaget's three mountains task, requiring decentration. It may be that they could do the task but, when faced with a difficult situation they revert to a pre-concrete level of thought (see unit 6.2.1).
- *Wisdom.* In other cultures the old are revered for their wisdom. **Kimmel** (1990) distinguished between practical wisdom (in personally relevant situations) and philosophical wisdom (the meaning of life).

③ *Retirement.* See 'unemployment' in unit 6.4.4.

④ *Problems in assessing ability*

- *Health.* Some elderly have decreased abilities due to the effects of strokes and other progressive illnesses. **Birren** *et al.* (1963) examined a group of men aged 65–91: some had no obvious symptoms of disease but, on close medical examination, they in fact had certain mild diseases which would subtly affect performance.
- *Social deprivation.* Decline may be due to lack of stimulation rather than old age *per se*. Institutionalised elderly people may suffer similar ill-effects to children in orphanages. **Rubin** (1973) found that elderly people living in their own homes performed better on Piagetian tasks than those living in institutions.
- *Cohort effects.* Observed differences between older and younger participants may be due to generational differences.

Theories of old age

① *Social disengagement theory.* **Cumming and Henry** (1961) proposed that psychological well-being is promoted by a gradual withdrawal from personal contacts and world affairs. This was based on a 5-year study of nearly 300 individuals aged between 50 and 90. They observed that older people gradually lose contact with others, have fewer roles and are freed to play the roles they wish.

Evaluation

- **Bromley** (1988) suggested that this would lead to a policy of segregation for the elderly.
- **Havighurst** *et al.* (1968) followed up some of the original sample and found that some individuals remained active *and* content, in fact the most active were the happiest.

② *Activity theory.* **Havighurst** *et al.* (1968, above) proposed that continued or new interests and involvements maintain psychological health and long life. They felt it was important for the elderly to maintain a 'role count', the number of social roles they have to play. **Rubin**'s research (above) demonstrated how deprivation can lead to mental deterioration.

Evaluation

- There are inevitable individual differences. **Dyson** (1980) pointed out that social, physical or economic factors may dictate the amount of activity which is possible. Prescriptive theories, such as activity or disengagement, suggest what old people should be doing to promote well-being, whereas in fact there are the same individual differences as at any stage of life.

③ *Social exchange theory.* **Dowd** (1975) suggested that an individual 'agrees' to give up certain things (being a financially active member of society) in exchange for their increased leisure time and pension. This informal 'contract' contains expectations about how an older person will behave (see also 'Exchange theory', unit 1.2.1).

④ *Ages of man.* **Erikson** (1963, see unit 6.4.2) characterised the ageing years as a time of *integrity versus despair*. The individual reviews and evaluates their life, which results in either feeling satisfied and accepting the inevitability of death, or feeling regret and fearing death.

Evaluation

- This view describes old age as a continuing period of development.

6.4.4 LIFE EVENTS

Chronological age may not be a good predictor of behaviour, instead it may be better to look at the effect of common life events. **Holmes and Rahe** (1967, see unit 3.4.3) used the concept to describe the relationship between stress and health. **Coleman**'s Focal theory (unit 6.4.1) also predicts that it is the accumulation of problems that leads to stress.

① *Parenthood*

- Pregnancy scores 40 LCU (12th) on the Holmes and Rahe Scale, a new family member scores 39 LCU (14th) and a child leaving home scores 29 LCU (23rd).
- **Erikson**'s notion of generativity can include the production of children, though he put this stage at 40 plus.
- *Socialisation.* Parents socialise and are socialised by their children. The advent of children inevitably changes the parents' circle of friends and, mainly for women, changes their work or at least de-emphasises their career. It involves contact with schools and other institutions.
- *Stressful*: causes marital problems, possibly because people sometimes have children as a way of patching up their difficulties and also through conflicts over childrearing practices and jealousy. **Hultsch and Deutsch** (1981) found that 50–80% of adults described the birth of their first child as a moderate to severe crisis.

- *Self-image* is altered in the light of the new role. Becoming a parent also leads to a reassessment of your own parents.
- *Social class differences.* **Russell** (1974) found that middle-class parents were more dissatisfied than working-class parents. This may be because they start with higher ideals and the mother is more likely to have to give up a career.
- *Intervening variables.* Some women receive help from their mothers and their extended family; well-off families can afford nursery facilities. Otherwise much of the burden is usually placed on mothers. **Brown and Harris** (1978) found that women who don't work and have several children to look after at home are far more likely to become seriously depressed.
- *The empty nest.* Another side of parenthood is when it ends, often associated with mid-life crisis but it may also be a time of increased wealth and freedom. Most parents look forward to extending their parenting into grandparenthood.

② *Divorce*

- Divorce scores 73 LCU (2nd) on the Holmes and Rahe Scale, separation 65 LCU (3rd) and reconciliation 45 LCU (9th).
- *Health.* **Kiecolt-Glaser and Glaser** (1986) found poorer immune functions where persons were suffering marital disruption. **Carter and Glick** (1970) found increased rates of various illnesses, and suicide in women, among the divorced. **Cochrane** (1988) analysed data on admissions to UK mental hospitals and found the largest group was the divorced, with men being slightly more affected.
- *Loss.* **Clulow** (1990) argued that divorce is similar to death, both for the couple and their children. It involves grief, sorrow and anger.
- *Identity crisis.* Divorce involves reorganisation of routines and social circles.
- *Intervening variables.* Reactions vary depending on the length of the marriage, the age of the partners, the number and age of any children and who ended it, though it is always distressing for both partners.
- *Legal issues*: equitable distribution of possessions, including children. The process will be expensive and often creates considerable antagonism.
- *Limited period.* Divorce probably entails a few years of turmoil followed by recovery.
- *A stage theory.* **Bohannon** (1977) proposed the following stages

Emotional	The marriage ends with accompanying emotions.
Legal	The marriage is dissolved.
Economic	Financial arrangements are made.
Co-parental	Arrangements are made for the children.
Community	Relationships with friends and family are adjusted.
Psychic	Adjustment to being single and return of autonomy.

③ *Unemployment.* Some of the same factors which apply to unemployment also apply to retirement though the latter is more planned.

- Fired at work scores 47 LCU (8th) on the Holmes and Rahe Scale, change in financial state 38 LCU (16th), and there are at least 10 other associated changes on the scale.
- *Health and happiness.* **Warr** (1978) found that the unemployed had more psychological problems and poorer health than before they lost their jobs. They had increased depression, alcoholism and suicide. **Platt** (1986) found attempted suicides eight times more common among the unemployed, and most likely in the first month of unemployment.
- *Loss* of economic status, vocational identity, social contacts, sense of purpose and self-esteem, habitual daily routines. Leads to a sense of mourning, uselessness, insecurity.
- *Adjustments*: increased time with spouse, possibly moving house, loss of friends. More time for sleep, relaxation, family, friends.
- *Self-image*: new role, loss of income and status, change from active, economically productive member of society.
- *Age.* The older you are the more likely you are to remain unemployed and to have heavy family and financial responsibilities, which exacerbate distress. **Bromhall and**

Winefield (1990) found that men over 40 experienced poorer mental health and less life satisfaction than those unemployed for a similar length of time who were under 30.

- *Social class.* **Buss and Redburn** (1983) compared the reactions of steelworkers and managers to the closure of their factory. The managers remained better able to cope possibly because they had more savings but also because they felt their skills were transferable and they were more able to move.

- *Phases of unemployment.* **Argyle** (1989) reported that most studies suggest a series of regular reactions to unemployment:

  Shock, anger and incomprehension.
  Holiday period of optimistic job-searching.
  When the job search is unsuccessful, pessimism about money and the future sets in.
  Fatalism, apathy and no further job-seeking.

❹ *Bereavement*

- Death of spouse scores 100 LCU (1st) on the Holmes and Rahe Scale, the death of a close family member 63 LCU (5th), and of a close friend 37 LCU (17th).

- *Health.* **Hinton** (1967) found a higher incidence of death in recent widows than a sample of married women of the same age. **Parkes** (1987) found that 75% of widows sought medical advice within six months. However, **Mor** *et al.* (1986) suggested that this could be because illness was ignored in the period leading up to a spouse's death.

- *Symptoms.* **Clayton** *et al.* (1971) interviewed widows, whose symptoms were crying, lack of concentration, sleeping and poor memory. Abnormal grief may occur as a response to extreme circumstances. **Lindemann** (1944) described reactions after the Coconut Grove night-club fire: somatic distress, guilt, hostility, sense of unreality and preoccupation with the deceased.

- *Ostracism*: some people avoid the bereaved because they don't know how to cope and it may arouse their own fears.

- *Self-image*: change in relationships and resocialisation, ability to cope will change one's self-concept.

- *Individual differences.* Bereavement varies with person's own feelings about death and their emotional type, the type of death, the age of the deceased, relationship with the deceased (closeness, dependency, duration). Where interpersonal problems were unresolved the grieving is much harder.

- *Gender differences.* **Barrett** (1978) found that widowers had a lower morale, expressed greater dissatisfaction and required more help than widows.

- *Ways of coping*: cultural practices (e.g. funeral service), social supports (e.g. making immediate plans), reading books (helps to review the relationship and understand one's feelings). **Caserta and Lund** (1992) followed individuals for two years after the death of a spouse. Stress levels were lower and the ability to cope was higher than those expressed by a control group. This suggests that people's expectations are wrong, and that bereavement is not as difficult as they thought.

- *The bereavement process.* Mourning usually lasts between one and two years, which is reflected in the historical practice of wearing black for a year. **Bowlby** (1980) distinguished five phases of grief and mourning: (1) initial shock, denial, concentration on the deceased, (2) anger, (3) appeals for help, (4) despair, withdrawal, disorganisation, (5) resolution, reorganisation and new focus.

- *Parallels with the dying process.* **Kübler-Ross** (1969) interviewed over 200 dying patients and identified five processes (see next page) which characteristically occurred. She called them stages but there is probably no rigid progression or timing. The aim is to provide a framework for helping people through the dying process.

Denial	There's been an error. This is a healthy way of dealing with the initial shock.
Anger	'Why me?'. Denial is difficult to sustain, the dying person is angry at the healthy.
Bargaining	Make promises to church, charity, and so on, in the hope of an extension of the period of life.
Depression	Crying, deep sense of loss, need to express emotions.
Acceptance	If there's sufficient time to work through the previous feelings, the person often becomes emotionless and detached, welcoming quiet companionship.

⑤ *Evaluation of the life events approach*

- It emphasises crises as the main force in personality development.
- It de-emphasises individual differences.
- Social changes mean that descriptions need to be updated.

CHAPTER ROUNDUP

6.1 Early socialisation

6.1.1 *Early social development* includes sociability and the development of bonds and attachments. Attachments may be determined by feeding, contact, time or sensitivity. Bowlby's theory has been very influential.

6.1.2 *Enrichment and deprivation* affects social and cognitive development. Deprivation (separation) may not have long-term consequences but privation does.

6.1.3 *Social and cultural variations* in childrearing indicate that there is no single route to healthy development.

6.2 Cognitive development

6.2.1 *Theories of cognitive development* focus on innate invariant stages (Piaget), the importance of culture and experts (Vygotsky), a hierarchical acquisition of categories (Bruner). Neo-Piagetians (e.g. Fischer) described development as skill acquisition.

6.2.2 *Practical applications to education* include Piaget's discovery learning, Vygotsky's expert intervention, Bruner's scaffolding, and Ausubel's reception learning.

6.2.3 The *development of measured intelligence* is influenced by genetic and environmental influences, and test biases.

6.3 Social behaviour and diversity in development

6.3.1 *Moral development* can be explained by learning, social learning, psychodynamic and cognitive-developmental theories.

6.3.2 *Gender development* has been explained by biological, biosocial, psychodynamic, social learning, cognitive-developmental and gender-schema theories or approaches.

6.3.3 The *development of the self* can be understood in terms of social learning and cognitive-developmental explanations, and the theories of Mead, Erikson, and Mischel.

6.4 Adolescence, adulthood and old age

6.4.1 *Adolescence* is a time of biological changes, accompanied by identity crises (Erikson) or storm and stress (Hall). Other approaches include psychodynamic, cognitive-developmental and Focal theories.

6.4.2 *Changes in adulthood* have described by Erikson, Levinson and Gould.

6.4.3 *Adjustment to old age* involves coping with physical and cognitive changes, and retirement. Psychological health may be promoted by disengagement or activity, social exchange or ego integrity.

6.4.4 *Life events* include parenthood, divorce, unemployment and bereavement. These are stressful periods during lifespan development.

Illustrative question

(a) Explain what psychologists understand by the term 'attachment' in relation to the early socialisation of the child. (5 marks)

(b) Using appropriate evidence, discuss whether problems in forming attachments in infancy have an influence on the child's later development. (19 marks)

(AEB AS 1993)

Tutorial note

Part (a) requires a descriptive answer. One way to elaborate on your explanation is to look at how attachment can be measured. Part (b) is easily misread as a request for a prepared Bowlby essay. The question actually asks for a discussion about what happens when there are problems in forming attachments. You should try to address this and adapt your prepared answer to suit the circumstances. The use of the word 'infancy' means that reference to non-human animal studies is excluded unless it is made explicitly relevant.

Suggested answer

(a) Attachment is a mutual and intense emotional relationship between an infant and its caregiver(s). Early socialisation depends on this bond to promote closeness between an infant and its caregiver for security, food and stimulation, and to act as a model for later relationships. The amount of attachment which exists is inferred from separation anxiety, the distress that an infant displays when its prime caretaker leaves the room. This is tested in the strange situation.

In early development the infant has indiscriminate attachments, showing a preference for human company but is more likely to smile at familiar faces. At the age of 7–9 months the first specific attachments appear. The infant is more content when the attachment figure is near and can be better placated by that person, and they are less likely to feel afraid. Within a few months the infant develops a number of other attachments to other familiar people though there may remain a prime attachment. Each different person may offer a different kind of attachment.

(b) What happens when there are problems in forming attachments? The most well researched problem is that of separation which disrupts the attachment bonds. **Bowlby** (1953) suggested that emotional care was as least as important as food and physical care and that when young children were separated from their parents during an early critical period (less than 2 years old) this disrupted attachment bonds and had serious later consequences such as affectionless psychopathy. To support this **Bowlby** (1946) studied the records of 44 juvenile delinquents (thieves). He found that some of the thieves had an affectionless character (lacked a sense of guilt or affection). Of the thieves who were affectionless, most had experienced prolonged maternal separations before the age of 2. This was not true for most of the other thieves nor most of a control group. The data for this study was retrospectively collected so the results may not be reliable.

The **Robertsons** supported Bowlby's views and produced evidence to show the effects of disrupted bonds. They filmed four young children during periods of brief separation. Two boys being admitted to hospital and a residential nursery respectively, and two girls who stayed with the Robertsons while their mother was in hospital. All the children received maternal care but the boys experienced a disruption of bonds whereas the girls had a substitute. The boys showed signs of acute distress, the girls were mildly anxious but adapted well. The Robertsons concluded that there was an important distinction between separation and bond disruption, only the latter causes distress. This research concerned a very small sample, the data was recorded unsystematically and the conditions were not equivalent, therefore the evidence must be treated with caution.

Studies of children who were in hospital may support the view that separation affects attachment and later psychological adjustment. **Douglas** (1975) conducted a longitudnal study of all the children born in one week in 1946. He found strong evidence that a hospital admission of more than a week or repeated admission in a child under 4 was associated with an increased risk of behaviour disturbance and poor reading in adolescence. However, **Clarke and Clarke** (1976) reanalysed Douglas' data and found that the reason for this apparent association was because many of the children were in hospital because of problems associated with disadvantaged homes. Social rather than maternal deprivation was the main cause of delinquency.

Rutter (1981) also felt that it was a mistake to think that separation *per se* caused emotional disturbance. It may be due to a history of family discord rather than the final separation. **Rutter *et al.*** (1976) conducted a large-scale study on the Isle of Wight and found that, in good and fair homes, separation did not lead to delinquency, and that if separation was due to illness, it was not associated with delinquency. Where there was stress associated with a separation, children were four times more likely to become delinquent. This study again used retrospective data and was correlational so one cannot assume that stress caused anything only that it is associated with later behaviours.

There is other evidence that separation need not disrupt attachment. **Kagan *et al.*** (1980) studied the effects of day care and found no consistently large differences between a group of children attending day care from the age of 3-5 months for 2 years and a control group on social, emotional or cognitive variables. There was large variability among all the children, but it was not related to the form of care. **Fox** (1977) studied infants raised on Israeli kibbutzim, and found that they remained most attached to their mothers despite the fact that they spent more time with their metapelet. The fact that there is quite a high turnover rate of metapelets might explain the low attachment there, but there was still maternal attachment despite long and early separations.

Rutter (1981) also pointed out that the *loss* of attachments through separation may be have no long-term consequences but the *lack* of attachments (privation) results in permanent impairments. **Widdowson** (1951) studied a group of orphanage children who were malnourished. Dietary supplements didn't help but their weight improved when a harsh and unsympathetic supervisor was replaced. It may be that they were underdeveloped because they lacked affection and emotional security. This is called deprivation dwarfism and is seen in children raised in extreme isolation, for example Genie who was found at age 12. She had an early life of cognitive and emotional privation and was never able to recover. It is possible that she was brain damaged from birth. Other children in similar situations, such as the Koluchova twins, did recover probably because they were found earlier and went to live in a very supportive home.

Hodges and Tizard (1989) conducted a longitudinal study of children raised in an institution. The institution had a specific policy of staff not forming strong attachments with the children. Before the age of 4, 50 different caretakers had looked after the children. At this point 24 were adopted and 15 returned to often difficult homes. When the children were tested at age 8 and 16, the adopted children were doing best and those returned home worst on measures of intellectual and social development. Presumably the adopted children had experienced good attachments and their early experiences had not made recovery impossible. **Pringle and Bossio** (1960) also studied children living in an institution. They found that the children who appeared to be the most severely maladjusted had the least contact with their families. This suggests that a child who is rejected and *remains* unwanted is likely to become maladjusted, and supports the view that *privation* leads to permanent emotional damage, whereas *deprivation* can be recovered from.

Some children experience very early disruption to attachment bonds, such as those in neonatal special care. Many such infants have other physical problems, such as very low birth weight, so it is hard to know what leads to long-term ill effects. There is something called attachment disorder which occurs in children who spend their early life in institutions and have little or no early experience of attachment. They appear to be unable to form any later attachment.

The original question was 'What happens when there are problems in forming attachments?' **Ainsworth** (1972) felt that separation only had long-term consequences if there were other things wrong as well. On the other hand the evidence shows that privation does have permanent emotional and cognitive consequences.

Question bank

Allow 35–40 minutes for each question.

Early socialisation

1 Discuss the findings of psychological research into the effects on children of enrichment **and/or** deprivation.

(AEB A 1994)

Points: Remember that 'research' covers both theory and empirical study. Your answer should include psychological material which illustrates the effects of enrichment and/or deprivation on subsequent development, plus an evaluation of such material.

2 In the past developmental research has focused on white, European children. Discuss psychological evidence which indicates that this has produced culturally biased theories.

Points: Your discussion might involve examples from both sides of the ethnic divide: European and non-European, and a link between these and available theories. Evaluate your material using methodological criticisms.

Cognitive development

3 Outline **two** theories of cognitive development and evaluate these theories in terms of empirical evidence.

(AEB A 1992)

Points: In order to answer in the allowed time you must be selective in outlining the theories, don't simply write about ages and stages. The question specifically asks for evaluation in terms of empirical evidence.

4 Describe how any **one** theory of cognitive development can be applied to education.

(AEB A 1994)

Points: There is some room in this essay for a description of a theory of cognitive development but this should be focused on its application to education. The skill B element comes from applying the theory.

5 Discuss *ways* in which psychologists have investigated the interaction between environmental and genetic factors in determining intelligence test performance.

(AEB A 1995)

Points: Describe and evaluate empirical studies of environmental and genetic factors, and explain how these shed light on the interaction. Your evaluation should consider methodological criticisms.

Social behaviour and diversity in development

6 Describe and evaluate any **two** theories of moral development.

(AEB AS 1993)

Points: Select two theories on which you are well informed. If you select Piaget or Freud do not spend a great deal of time describing the general aspects of their theories, which would gain no marks. When evaluating a theory you might describe an alternative approach.

7 Evaluate, using psychological theories, the degree to which socialisation is important in the development of gender roles.

(AEB AS 1992)

Points: The question asks you to determine the extent that gender is socially, rather than biologically, determined. You are told to do this with theories of gender development. Reference to empirical studies will be necessary as a means of evaluation, and the studies themselves should be subjected to critical evaluation.

8 'The self that is most important is a reflection, largely from the minds of others' (Cooley, 1902). Discuss.

(AEB AS 1991)

Points: The quotation provides an opportunity to discuss social versus non-social determinants of self. A good answer should focus on the quotation rather than producing a standard prepared answer.

Adolescence, adulthood and old age

9 In the light of psychological theory and research, discuss the view that adolescence is inevitably a period of 'storm and stress'.

(AEB AS 1990)

Points: This is a question which frequently attracts anecdotal answers. You should present theories for and against this view and consider any methodological problems of the empirical studies cited.

10 'For people in middle age and onwards there are many opportunities for positive psychological development.' Use psychological studies to discuss this claim.

(AEB A 1991)

Points: A balanced essay should consider empirical studies looking at both positive growth and more passive disengagement. The question allows you to include both middle and old age and specifically refers to studies; you can use theories as a means of evaluation.

11 (a) Describe **one or more** major change in cognitive functioning which may be associated with old age. (10 marks).
   (b) Evaluate evidence of such change considering the extent to which it is inevitable. (14 marks)

(AEB AS 1993)

Points: Part (a) is skill A only, describe change(s) in old age but only those associated with cognitive functioning. In part (b) you should present skill B material, describing evidence of such change and evaluating this by considering individual differences.

12 Describe and assess research into the impact of critical life events in adulthood **and/or** senescence.

(AEB A 1996)

Points: You have a choice of the depth route (cover only a few life events but in considerable detail) or the breadth route (cover a large number of life events in less detail). Remember that 'research' includes both theory and empirical study.

CHAPTER 7

PERSPECTIVES IN PSYCHOLOGY

Units in this chapter:

Chapter overview

This chapter is eclectic, deriving knowledge from all parts of the syllabus, and presenting common threads: behaviourism and psychoanalysis, determinism and reductionism, controversy and ethics.

7.1 APPROACHES TO PSYCHOLOGY

7.1.1 MAJOR THEORETICAL ORIENTATIONS

The behaviourist approach

Behaviourists focus on objectively observable events and explain behaviour in terms of how it is learned through interactions with the environment (as opposed to innate factors); called *learning* or *conditioning theory*.

❶ *Key contributors*

- This approach has roots in nineteenth-century *empirical* philosophy (e.g. **Locke**).
- **Watson** (1913) coined the term 'behaviourism', suggesting that **Pavlov**'s *classical conditioning theory* could be used to explain all behaviour, an approach which was preferable to the *introspectionism* of the 19th century.
- **Thorndike** (1913) expanded learning theory to include *instrumental learning*.
- This was adapted by **Skinner** (1938) into the *operant conditioning* (see unit 2.4.1). Skinner's approach concentrated on the effects of behaviour rather than Pavlov's focus on the behaviours themselves, which allowed for a justifiable exclusion of mental events. Skinner's views represent *philosophical* or *radical behaviourism*, the position that there are private, less accessible activities (mental events) but these are not needed in the explanation of behaviour.
- *Neo-behaviourist* approaches are based on behaviourist principles but use *un*observable processes in their explanations, for example *social learning theory* (see unit 1.4.2) combines traditional learning theory with the concepts of identification (from psychoanalysis) and internal representation (from cognitive psychology).

② *Key concepts*: classical and operant conditioning, reflexes, positive and negative reinforcement, rewards, punishment, stimulus–response, shaping.

③ *Examples of behaviourist explanations.* Relationship formation (Byrne–Clore reinforcement-affect model, unit 1.2.1), aggression (social learning approach, unit 1.4.2), motivation (drive-reduction, unit 3.4.1), models of abnormality (behavioural models, unit 4.2.2), language acquisition (Skinner's theory, unit 5.4.1), moral, gender and self-development (units 6.3.1, 6.3.2 and 6.3.3).

④ *Applications*

- *Programmed learning* consists of breaking a topic down into *frames* or very small steps. A correct response acts as a reward and leads on to the next question. A programme may be *linear* (a list of frames) or *branching*, in which case the programme can 'respond' to mistakes by presenting the student with specific help (see unit 9.4.1).
- *Shaping verbal behaviour.* Autistic children can be taught to speak using progressive reinforcement. Initially the child is reinforced for any sound. Gradually, the rewards are given for vocalisations which become successively closer to words.
- *Behaviour therapies* (see unit 4.4.1).
- *Advertising* (see unit 7.2.1).
- *Biofeedback* (see unit 3.4.4) and *animal training* (pets and zoos).

⑤ *Positive points*

- Classic learning theory has had a major influence on all branches of psychology; *methodological behaviourism* is the view that all approaches use some behaviourist concepts to explain behaviour.
- Behaviourism has given rise to many practical applications.
- It is an empirical perspective which lends itself to scientific research. **Broadbent** (1961) argued that it is the best method for rational advance in psychology.

⑥ *Criticisms*

- A mechanistic perspective which ignores consciousness and subjective experience.
- Deterministic: behaviour is determined by the environment.
- Reductionist: reduces complex behaviour to stimulus–response links.
- It is largely based on work with animals. Behaviourists argue that the theory of evolution shows that human and non-human animals are quantitatively not qualitatively different and therefore such research is meaningful.
- The use of behaviourist principles to control others (as in some prisons and psychiatric institutions) is unethical. Both Watson and Skinner (see his book *Walden Two*) had a desire to use their principles to produce a better society.

The psychodynamic approach

The approach explains human development in terms of an interaction between unconscious, innate drives and early experience. Individual personality differences can be traced back to the way early conflicts were handled.

① *Key contributors*

- **Freud**'s theory is described in units 4.2.2 and 6.3.1.
- *Neo-Freudians*, such as **Erikson** and **Jung**, produced psychodynamic theories which placed less emphasis on biological forces and more on the influences of social and cultural factors. Erikson's work with adolescents and Sioux Indians led him to believe that many aspects of behaviour were culturally rather than biologically based.

② *Key concepts*: the structure of the personality (id, ego, superego), psychosexual stages (oral, anal, phallic, latent, genital), ego defence mechanisms (sublimation, repression, denial, displacement, projection), neurotic symptoms (Freudian slips), therapy (free association, rich interpretation, transference, dream analysis).

③ *Examples of psychodynamic explanations.* Prejudice (Scapegoat theory, unit 1.1.3), aggression (unit 1.4.3), sleep (dreams, unit 3.3.3), motivation (unit 3.4.1), models of abnormality (unit 4.2.2), psychopathology (units 4.3.2 and 4.3.3), early infant development (Bowlby, unit 6.1.1), moral and gender development (units 6.3.1 and 6.3.2), lifespan development (Erikson's theory, units 6.3.1, 6.4.1 and 6.4.2).

4 *Applications*: Psychotherapy and psychoanalysis (unit 4.4.1).

5 *Positive points*
- Freud's important contribution was to recognise childhood as a critical period of development, and to identify sexual (physical) and unconscious influences.
- The theory has been enormously influential within psychology.
- It has enduring appeal beyond psychology. **Hall and Lindzey** (1970) suggested that this is due to a fine literary style, a conception of man which is broad and deep and which combines the world of reality with make-believe.
- It is an idiographic approach.

6 *Criticisms*
- The theory lacks rigorous empirical support, especially regarding normal development. The 'evidence' comes largely from case studies of middle-class, European women many of whom were disturbed. The data was retrospectively collected and given subjective interpretation (experimenter bias).
- It reduces human activity to a basic set of structures, which are reifications.
- It is deterministic, suggesting that infant behaviour is determined by innate forces and adult behaviour is determined by childhood experiences.
- The original theory lays too much emphasis on innate biological forces.

The humanistic approach

Humanists reject determinist and reductionist approaches, preferring to emphasise individual uniqueness and subjective experience as well as a positive view of human nature, and the concepts of self and self-control (free will). Humanists believe that psychological theories should be humanly rather than statistically significant and that new research methods are needed to properly investigate human behaviour.

1 *Key contributors*
- **Maslow** (see unit 3.4.1) proposed a theory of motivation based on non-physiological as well as physiological needs.
- **Rogers** (see unit 4.2.2) described self-actualisation as the main force in personality development.

2 *Key concepts*: self-esteem, self-control, unconditional positive regard, subjective experience, new paradigm research (see unit 7.2.2).

3 *Examples of humanist explanations*. Motivation (Needs theories, unit 3.4.1), understanding of abnormal behaviour (unit 4.2.2), moral and self development (units 6.3.1 and 6.3.3).

4 *Applications*: client-centred therapy and counselling (unit 4.4.1).

5 *Positive points*. This approach has encouraged psychologists to accept the view that there is more to behaviour than objectively discoverable facts.

6 *Criticisms*. It is largely a vague, unscientific and untestable approach.

Comparing and contrasting all three approaches

	Behaviourist	Psychodynamic	Humanist
Behaviour	Mainly learned.	Innate forces and early experience.	Self-determined.
Prejudice	Learned norms and cognitive style (Adorno).	Repressed hostility projected onto outgroup.	Intergroup processes.
Aggression	Learned through reward, imitation.	Innate.	Self-controlled.
Motivation	Learned drives (drive-reduction).	Innate forces, repressed desires.	Desire for self-actualisation plus lower needs.
Explanations of abnormality	Conditioning.	Unresolved conflicts.	Difficulties with self-development.
Method of treating abnormal behaviour	Identify maladaptive behaviour and associations reformed (unlearning).	Search for deep meaning, insights from therapist.	Insights from client, leading to self-determined changes.
Moral and prosocial behaviour	Learned through reward and punishment.	Phallic phase, conflict with opposite sex parent.	Empathetic relations with significant others.
Psychology as a science	Yes.	Yes.	Human significance more important.
Importance of innate factors	Minimal relevance, e.g. reflexes.	Critical in understanding behaviour.	Important to understand some aspects of behaviour.
Free will or determined?	Shaped by the environment.	Driven by unconscious forces, irrational.	Each individual has the capacity to be free, rational and self-determining.
Reductionist	Yes.	Yes.	No.
Methods used to investigate human behaviour	Laboratory experiments, with animals. Nomothetic.	Case studies, idiographic.	Idiographic, subjective report. New paradigm psychology.

Other approaches: sociocultural (chapter 1), ethological (chapter 2), biological (chapter 3), information processing/cognitive (chapter 5), developmental (chapter 6).

7.1.2 DEBATES CONCERNING THE NATURE OF THE PERSON

Free will versus determinism

Behaviour is determined by internal or external forces, or individuals have an active role in determining their behaviour, i.e. they are free to choose.

Issues related to determinisim:

1 *The lawfulness of behaviour.* Absolute free will means that behaviour is completely random or not determined in any lawful way. However, even humanists believe that behaviour is governed by conscious decisions which have some regularity . **Heather** (1976) resolved this potential conflict by suggesting that much of behaviour is predictable though not inevitable, individuals are free to choose their behaviour but this is usually from a fairly limited repertoire. **James** (1890) suggested that *soft determinism* is a more realistic view than hard determinism, arguing that people act consistently within their character.

2 *Kinds of determinism*

- *Environmental determinism.* The behaviourist view is that we are controlled by external forces. **Skinner** said that freedom was an illusion, maintained because we are unaware of the environmental causes of behaviour (see criticisms of behaviourism, in unit 7.1.1).

- *Biological determinism.* Behaviour may be determined by internal (biological) factors. In this way all biological accounts are deterministic (chapter 3), as are some accounts of aggression (unit 1.4.2), abnormal behaviour (units 4.3.1, 4.3.2 and 4.3.3), language acquisition (unit 5.4.1) and gender development (unit 6.3.2). The psychodynamic approach is also determinist. **Freud** thought that freedom was an illusion, because the actual causes of our behaviour are unconscious and therefore hidden from us.
- *Genetic determinism.* Ethologists argue that we are born with innate characteristics which inevitably lead to certain behaviours, such as aggression (unit 1.4.2), altruism (units 1.4.1 and 2.3.1), maladaptive behaviour (units 4.3.1, 4.3.2, 4.3.3 and 4.3.4) and attachment (unit 6.1.1). The advantage of innately determined behaviour patterns is that they are adaptive and promote survival. This view of behaviour may be more applicable to animals where learning has less influence on behaviour.

3 *The assumptions of science* are that one thing determines another. The aim of scientific study is to investigate causes, which can then be used to predict future events. Is this determinist approach valuable? It can advance our understanding of human behaviour, for example research on helping behaviour (unit 1.4.1) or attention (unit 5.2.1). On the other hand, some psychologists feel that experimental research has little relevance to real life, for example research on social influences (units 1.3.1, 1.3.2 and 1.3.3) and new paradigm research (see unit 7.2.2).

4 *Moral responsibility.* When a person commits an antisocial act, it is possible to argue that the cause of their behaviour is due to biological (inherited) or social (TV) causes (see unit 1.4.3). We cannot hold individuals legally responsible for their actions if the causes were outside their control. Free will, on the other hand suggests that we each are morally responsible for our actions. **Sartre**, an existentialist philosopher, said that we are 'condemned to be free'; freedom is a burden because we must each be totally responsible for our behaviour and we must each respect each other's views. The law embodies this view.

Reductionism

Reductionism is any attempt to *reduce* a complex set of phenomena to some more basic components. Many psychological accounts which are determinist are also reductionist.

1 *Kinds of reductionism*

- *Environmental reductionism.* Reducing behaviour to the effect of environmental stimuli, as in behaviourist explanations.
- *Physiological reductionism.* Explaining behaviour in terms of physiological mechanisms (chapter 3, and unit 1.4.2 on aggression).
- *Evolutionary reductionism.* Explaining behaviour in terms of evolutionary principles (chapter 2).
- *Machine reductionism.* Explaining behaviour in information processing terms (chapter 5). Interconnectionist networks have been described by **Penrose** (1990) as holist as opposed to reductionist in so far as the network behaves differently from the individual parts.
- *Experimental reductionism* is the use of controlled laboratory studies to gain understanding of similar behaviours in the natural environment.

2 *Arguments in favour*

- Reductionism may be a necessary part of understanding how things work.
- Reductionist arguments are easier to test empirically, and easier to discuss.
- Reductionist explanations are appropriate, the problem is that experiments have yet to identify all the facts.

3 *Arguments against*

- Reductionist explanations often take attention away from other levels of explanation and mean that we fail to usefully understand behaviour.
- They are necessary but not sufficient. **Legge** (1975) used the example of a person signing their name, to illustrate how reductionist explanations fail to provide a

complete account of behaviour. *Gestalt* psychologists believed that the sum of the parts may not equal the whole (*holism*). Humanists also focus on the whole.

❹ *Levels of explanation.* **Rose** (1976) suggested that the controversy over reductionism is due to a semantic confusion. If psychologists attempt to 'explain away' psychological phenomena using reductionist concepts, the result is unsatisfactory. However, if one accepts that there is a *hierarchy of levels of explanation*, then it is possible to see that reductionist explanations are one *universe of discourse* and contribute to explaining behaviour. Rose proposed that physical explanations are at the bottom, moving through chemical, anatomical-biochemical, physiological, psychological (mentalistic), social psychological and, finally, sociological explanations.

❺ *Alternatives to reductionism*: Gestalt psychology, humanism, interconnectionist networks.

7.2 CONTROVERSIES IN PSYCHOLOGY

7.2.1 'CONTROVERSIAL' APPLICATIONS OF PSYCHOLOGICAL RESEARCH

The use of psychological research in advertising

❶ *Motivation.* A need for an item must be created. In the case of pre-existing needs, such as for bread, the motive to buy a particular *brand* is important (e.g. through price, quality). Where there is no pre-existing need, it must be created, as in the case of children's toys. See psychological theories of motivation (unit 3.4.1).

❷ *Attitude formation.* Motivation is related to having positive attitudes.

- *Conditioning*: higher-order classical conditioning and operant conditioning (unit 2.4). Advertisers typically pair an attractive person or item (unconditioned stimulus) with their product (conditioned stimulus) to produce a positive attitude towards their product (conditioned response). **Staats and Staats** (see unit 1.1.3) demonstrated how attitudes are learned through conditioning, however behaviour is not always related to attitudes (see **LaPiere** in unit 1.1.3).
- *Liking* is increased through exposure and increased familiarity. **Zajonc** described this as the 'mere exposure effect' (see unit 1.2.2). However, too much familiarity may decrease liking. **Belch** (1982) found that experimental participants who saw an advertisement more frequently were less likely to recall the details, or to respond positively, than those who saw it once.
- *Confirmatory bias.* People prefer information which is consistent with their stereotypes (see unit 1.1.3). This may explain why advertisers continue to use outdated stereotypes (**Manstead and McCullough**, in unit 1.4.3).
- *Post-decisional dissonance.* Post-purchasing information is sought to support the decision already made. **Brehm** (1956) found that housewives were more likely to rate certain household items highly *after* they had purchased them than before.
- *Reactance.* People may resist attempts to change their attitudes (see unit 1.3.1).

❸ *Memorability.* Advertising information must be remembered and recalled at the appropriate moment.

- *Mnemonic devices* (unit 5.3.5). Imagery, repetition and meaning improve memorability. **Belch** (above) found that repetition may have an inverse effect.
- *Jingles.* **Yalch** (1991) found that jingles increased cued recall but not recognition because the verbal material is not well processed. However, cued recall is probably more typical of real life where consumers are presented with in-store reminders (product names) and the jingle is then brought to mind.

- *Positive attitudes*. **Matthur and Chattopadhyay** (1991) found that viewers who watched a 'happy' TV programme had better recall of advertisements which had been shown during the programme than those who watched a more sombre programme.
- *Inconsistent information*. **Heckler and Childers** (1992) found that information which was both unexpected and irrelevant to an advertisement was better recalled. Incongruent information disturbs cognitive balance and leads to greater attention.

④ *Consumer behaviour*. Psychologists analyse consumer demand and preferences, advising advertisers on effective strategies to increase sales and evaluating the success of an advertising campaign.

⑤ *Ethical considerations*. Psychologists have a professional obligation to consider the applications of their research findings (see unit 7.3.3).

The use of psychological research in propaganda and warfare

Propaganda is an organised programme of selected information. It is psychological warfare. It may be altruistic (e.g. a new vaccination programme) or exploitative and dishonest.

① *Attitude change and persuasive communications*. The *Yale model of communication* (unit 9.3.4) proposes how attitudes may be changed. However, a person may superficially *comply* with a set of attitudes but remain unpersuaded. Theories of behavioural rather than attitude change include a person's desire to change (*health belief model*, unit 9.3.4).

② *Coercive persuasion or brainwashing*. Some methods of attitude change may employ measures which decrease an individual's ability to resist. **Schein** (1956) studied Korean POWs, summarising the process as three basic phases:

- *Unfreeze* or disrupt person's current attitudes and beliefs, through physical deprivation, social isolation and disorientation.
- *Replace* with new attitudes, using direct and indirect instruction, and by forcing certain behaviours (forced compliance), which starts as outward conformity but leads to corresponding changes in privately held attitudes.
- *Refreeze* new attitudes by giving rewards, asking for public statements of belief, initiation rites and awarding group membership leading to personal identification.

③ *Warfare* is waged through the use of propaganda. Psychological knowledge may be used in other ways to understand *why* people fight, see for example human aggression (unit 1.4.2) and prejudice (unit 1.1.3). It can also explain some techniques or outcomes of war, for example stress (post-traumatic stress disorder, unit 4.3.3), interrogation techniques using, for example, sensory deprivation, and the design of machinery with human factors in mind (ergonomics).

④ *Ethical considerations* must relate the means to the ends (see unit 7.3.1).

The use of psychological research in psychometric testing

A psychometric test is an objective and standardised measure of a small but carefully chosen sample of some aspect of human psychological ability.

① *Design of psychometric tests*. A 'good test' must have:

- *Reliability* (repeatability).
  - Internal: all test items should measure the same thing, demonstrated by using the *split-half technique* (original test items are randomly assigned to two halves).
  - External: the test should produce the same score when repeated, demonstrated by *test-retest* (same test is given to the same people on different occasions), but this may suffer from a practice effect. Instead equivalent, alternate or parallel forms can be used.
- Validity (soundness). Does the test measure what it claims to measure?
  - Internal : (1) *face* validity: do the test items look valid?, (2) *content* validity: a systematic examination of test content to see if it covers a representative sample of the intended behaviour.

- External: (1) *criterion* validity: high correlation between test scores and some independent, non-test criterion such as teacher's ratings or future performance – concurrent and predictive validity respectively, (2) *construct* validity: relationship between the test and an underlying construct.

- *Standardisation.* To interpret a test score there needs to be information about 'normal' performance and standard deviations from this. This can be achieved by:
  - *Norm referencing*: establishing norms for a target population.
  - *Criterion referencing*: establishing objective criteria of what is expected.
  - *Standardised conditions* of testing are also important to ensure equivalence.

- *Discriminatory power.* If everyone does well (*ceiling effect*) or poorly (*floor effect*) the test is not providing useful information in distinguishing between candidates.

❷ *Intelligence tests* aim to assess a person's intellectual *capacity* rather than what they can actually *do* (measured by ability tests). Intelligence quotient (IQ) is a test score adjusted for age.

- *Written (group) tests*, e.g. British Ability Scales and AH6.
- *Oral (individual) tests*, used especially with children, e.g. Stanford–Binet, and the Wechsler scales for children (WISC) and adults (WAIS).
- *Verbal scales* test verbal performance, e.g. 'Choose the word which is opposite in meaning to the word in capital letters: PARTISAN: A, commoner; B, neutral; C, unifier; D, ascetic; E, pacifier' (from the Scholastic Aptitude Test).
- *Non-verbal or performance scales* for children, and non-literate testees, and non-verbal aspects of intelligence, e.g. Raven's progressive matrices or the Wechsler performance scale (part of WISC).
- *Creative thinking*, e.g. ask for unusual uses for ordinary objects, such as a brick.
- *The uses of intelligence tests*: personnel selection (unit 9.2.2), educational placement (e.g. the 11+), evaluating enrichment programmes in terms of IQ gains (e.g. Operation Headstart, unit 6.1.2), psychological research (e.g. collecting evidence of innate gender differences, unit 6.3.2).

❸ *Issues surrounding the use of intelligence tests*

- *Individual differences.* Test performance may be depressed by anxiety and poor conditions. Some people do worse than others.
- *Theoretical biases.* All tests are designed from some theoretical vantage point, this leads to both *designer* and *culture bias*. **Jensen** (1969) sparked off a controversy when he suggested that Black people have innately lower IQs. This may be due to test culture bias – we might expect White people to do poorly on **Dove**'s (1968) *Dove Counterbalance General Intelligence Test*.
- *The effects of learning.* It is impossible to separate *potential* from the ways we have learned to use it. Therefore all tests are inevitably culture-biased.
- The *illusion of reality*. A numerical value has a profound effect, giving the illusion that we are measuring something real like foot size.
- *Narrow conception of intelligent behaviour.* The motivation to succeed, task persistence and ability to evaluate performance are all important.
- *A political tool.* Testing is part of the social process of discrimination, legitimising classification (*labelling*) while masquerading as being objective and scientific.

❹ *Personality tests* measure motivational, emotional, interpersonal and attitudinal characteristics, as distinct from abilities.

- *Nomothetic: self-report personality inventories*: pencil-and-paper tests suitable for group use based on traits and factor analysis, e.g. Cattell's 16 Personality factor, Eysenck's Personality Inventory and Questionnaire (EPI, EPQ), and the Minnesota Multiphasic Personality Inventory (MMPI).
- *Idiographic: phenomenological techniques* are more concerned with the whole person and subjective perceptions, e.g. repertory grid (**Kelly**), Q-sort, semantic differential technique and the Rorschach ink blot test.
- *Measures of interest* e.g. Kuder Vocational Preference Record, IPAT Music Preference Test of Personality.

- *The uses of personality tests*: personnel selection (unit 9.2.2), career choice (interest inventories) and diagnosis of abnormal behaviour (unit 4.2.1).

⑤ *Issues surrounding the use of personality tests*
- *Theoretical bias.* Tests are biased by the personality theory which generated them.
- *Social desirability bias.* Individuals tend to answer questions so that they appear in a better light.
- *Important decisions are made* about, for example, a career or psychotherapy.
- *Assumption that personality is consistent.* **Mischel** (1968) suggested that any observed regularities in behaviour do not result from enduring personality traits, but are due to situational regularities – we find ourselves in similar situations and have learned what behaviours are appropriate in particular situations. If this is true, personality tests *cannot* predict behaviour.

7.2.2 PSYCHOLOGY AS A SCIENCE

① *What is a science?* The objective collection of facts and the organisation of these facts into theories.
- The *scientific method* consists of a cycle:
  - Inductive phase: observation, generalisation, theory.
  - Deductive phase: hypothesis-formation, method, data collection, theory adjusted.
- The *laboratory experiment* (see unit 8.1.1) is the best but not only means of hypothesis testing (for example, naturalistic observations use the scientific method). The key concepts are objectivity, control, manipulation, replication and falsification (**Popper** suggested that it is never possible to *prove* a hypothesis; there it can only be falsified).

Criticisms
- Science may be an impossible ideal, no investigator is truly objective and no observations are unaffected by the process of being observed. **Heisenberg**'s *uncertainty principle* suggests that even in physics there is a limit to certainty because of imperfect measuring instruments and the influences of the observer.
- *Social representation theory* (unit 1.1.1) suggests that people's beliefs or schema evolve through interpersonal communication. Science is not a timeless concept but a feature of a particular group of people at a particular time in history. Their beliefs are subject to the same group pressures as other groups (see unit 1.3.3).

② *Is psychology a science?*
- *Yes.* Psychologists apply the scientific method and conduct well-controlled, repeatable scientific experiments. They use the results of such experiments to develop theories which then generate new hypotheses.
- *No.* The problems of bias in science are especially problematic in psychology where the object of study is active and intelligent. Experimental artefacts, such as experimenter bias, demand characteristics and sample bias (see units 1.3.1 and 1.8.2) mean that it may be impossible to conduct objective and repeatable research.
- *Pre-science?* **Kuhn** (1970) suggested that psychology has not yet evolved into a science because there is no single paradigm or perspective which encompasses all of human behaviour research. **Palermo** (1971) argued that, far from being a pre-science, psychology has already undergone several paradigm shifts, such as structuralism (introspection), behaviourism and information processing. *New paradigm research* is another shift (see below). Kuhn's conception was that science develops through pre-science, to science to revolution; Palermo's account would place psychology in the revolution phase.

③ *Are the goals of science appropriate to the study of human behaviour?* Even if one accepted that psychology was scientific, we must ask what relevance this approach has to the understanding of human behaviour.
- The scientific approach is both *determinist* and *reductionist* (see unit 7.1.2). This means that scientific experiments may not have *ecological validity*.

241

- All scientific research is based on *restricted samples*, in psychology these are culturally and socially biased (see unit 7.2.3).
- *Humanists* feel that objective data can tell us little about subjective experience; new paradigm research (**Reason and Rowan**, 1981) is an attempt to make orthodox research meaningful in everyday terms. This is similar to *ethnogenics* (**Harré and Secord**, 1972), an approach influenced by the derived etic approach (see unit 7.2.3).

7.2.3 BIASES IN THEORY AND RESEARCH

Cultural diversity

Culture has been defined as the '[hu]man-made part of the environment' (**Segall** *et al.*, 1990). It is a product of socialisation, a means of distinguishing one group from another and of establishing personal identity within the group (see 'social identity theory', unit 1.1.1).

1 *Cross-cultural research.* Psychologists study different cultures for two main reasons:

- *Discovering innate, universal behaviours.* For example, research related to perceptual development (unit 5.1.2), language and thought (unit 5.4.4), and gender development (unit 6.3.2).
- *Developing theories which apply to all humans*, not just those in the Western world. For example, cross-cultural studies of attraction (unit 1.2.3), obedience (unit 1.3.1), childrearing (unit 6.1.3) and moral development (unit 6.3.1).

Problems with cross-cultural research

- Outsiders may not understand the language or may misinterpret an action.
- An outsider's own cultural biases produce expectations which alter what they 'see'.
- Outsiders use methods derived from an alien culture (see 'Emics and etics', below).
- Outsiders may have a hostile reception which will bias their observations.
- Observations are made of a sample and may not be typical of the whole culture being studied. It is also wrong to imagine a culture as being a homogenous group of people; differences within a culture may be as large as those between cultures.

2 *Eurocentric and ethnocentric perspectives.* Our view of behaviour is inevitably blinkered by our historical and cultural vantage point, and by the restricted sample of participants used in psychological research (middle-class, White, European, male undergraduates). Examples include: research into interpersonal relationships (unit 1.2.2), helping behaviour (unit 1.4.1), stress (unit 3.4.3) and attention (unit 5.2.1).

   Nobles (1976) equated the domination of Western psychology with nineteenth-century colonialism, because it is a tool of oppression and domination. This can be seen in the Western view of Black intelligence (see unit 7.2.1) and the self-concept. The Western world view of self emphasises individuality, independence, survival of the fittest and control over nature; whereas Africans value co-operation, similarity, survival of the tribe and oneness with nature. This latter view leads to an 'extended' sense of self, one which is not limited to the individual but instead is defined in terms of 'we'.

3 *Emics and etics*

- *'Emics'* are cultural specifics, as in 'phonemics', the study of universal sounds as they contribute to meaning in a particular language.
- *'Etics'* are universals of behaviour, as in 'phonetics', the study of universal sounds independent of meaning.
- *Imposed etic.* A technique or theory which is rooted in the researcher's own culture and used to study other cultures. Examples include: intelligence tests (unit 7.2.1), theories of moral development (unit 6.3.1), the treatment of abnormal behaviour (unit 4.4.1) and androcentric theories (below). **Berry** (1969) has suggested that a *derived etic*, as used in ethnographic anthropology, can resolve the problem. It is a series of emic studies in several different cultures using local people and focusing on culture-specific phenomena.

Gender bias

Gender is one means of defining a sub-cultural group, therefore some of the material on cultural diversity applies to gender biases.

❶ *Gender differences.* There are real differences between the sexes: obvious physical differences and well-documented psychological ones, such as intellectual and moral differences (unit 6.3.1). **Maccoby** (1980) argued that the differences within each gender are at least as large as the differences between genders.

Some *psychological* differences have a physical basis, for example the tendency for young boys to be more active is due to the fact that they have higher metabolic rates. Other psychological differences may be the result of:

- *Socialisation.* Girls are led to have lower self-expectations. Boys and girls learn appropriate masculine and feminine behaviours.
- *Androcentric research* (see below) and a *publishing bias.* Articles which do *not* find sex differences are less likely to be published.

❷ *Androcentric (masculinist) research.* Theories which are derived from research using male participants and then presented as a theory of *human* behaviour. This often results in female behaviour being seen as abnormal.

- Theories of psychopathology (units 4.2.3).
- **Kohlberg**'s theory of moral development (unit 6.3.1).
- **Erikson**'s theory of self-development (units 6.3.1, 6.3.2, 6.4.1 and 6.4.2).

❸ *Alpha-biased theories* describe real and enduring gender differences which can be positive, negative or neutral.

- *Evolutionary theory* (unit 2.4.1) is alpha biased, it tends to emphasise gender differences and explain these in terms of adaptiveness.
- **Gilligan** suggested that females have a different moral sense (unit 6.3.1).
- **Freud**'s theory suggests that males are morally superior (unit 6.3.1).

❹ *Beta-biased theories* ignore or minimise gender differences, usually because they are based on research which uses only male or female participants and *assumes* that what is true for one sex is true for all humankind.

- All male participants: **Sherif** and **Tajfel**'s studies of prejudice (unit 1.1.3), **Asch**, **Milgram**, and **Zimbardo**'s studies of social influence (unit 1.3.1), **Brown** *et al.* and **Patterson** *et al.*'s studies of aggressiveness (unit 1.4.2), **Rahe** *et al.* and **Friedman and Rosenman**'s studies of stress (unit 3.4.3).
- Mainly or all female participants: **Freud**'s patients (unit 7.1.1), **Hofling** *et al.*'s study of obedience (unit 1.3.1), **Lerner and Lichtman** and **Darley and Latané**'s studies of helping behaviour (unit 1.4.1), **Felipe and Sommer**'s study of proxemics (unit 9.5.1).

❺ *Feminist psychology* has proposed a paradigm shift in the study of human behaviour. The traditional approach in psychology is to emphasise internal, individual causes. Feminist psychologists argue that this approach perpetuates myths about gender differences because it involves an imposed etic (see above) and is self-fulfilling. The alternative is to focus on the social context and subjective interpretation.

Bem (1993) proposed an *encultured lens theory*: women are disadvantaged by androcentrism, gender polarisation and biological essentialism. She argued that explanations of behaviour often rely on male interpretations, this means that female behaviour is often pictured as abnormal, as in the case of pre-menstrual disorders. This is a similar argument to **Laing**'s existential view of schizophrenia (see unit 4.3.1) – we can only understand the schizophrenic if we understand his/her subjective experiences.

Feminist psychologists propose a new psychology which focuses on the individual and on social context.

7.3 ETHICAL ISSUES IN PSYCHOLOGY

7.3.1 ETHICAL ISSUES IN HUMAN RESEARCH

Ethics is that which is deemed acceptable in human behaviour in pursuit of certain goals or aims. It is not simply a question of 'right' but of balance between ends and means. Ethical guidelines for psychologists are produced by the British Psychological Society (BPS) and the American Psychological Association (APA).

① *Designing research.* An investigator should weigh anticipated costs and benefits, aim to leave things as they were prior to any research, and aim to only perform positive manipulations. Any research likely to involve deception, stress, involuntary participation or invasion of privacy should be checked with colleagues and should be used only when it is the sole option. *Natural experiments* avoid the problems of intervention but are rare and involve specialised samples.

In some situations it might be unethical to withhold treatments from a control group (e.g. testing a new educational method or psychotherapy).

② *Deception and informed consent.* The single blind technique (e.g. using confederates, describing a study falsely) enables collection of unbiased data. Informed consent inevitably leads to participant expectations and will alter results.

It is not possible to gain informed consent in some situations, such as with certain participants (children or the mentally ill, e.g. **Little Albert** unit 4.3.3), in field experiments (e.g. **Piliavin** *et al.*, unit 1.4.1), in studies involving naturalistic observation and retrospective case studies (e.g. **Kitty Genovese**, unit 1.4.1). At least in laboratory experiments, informed consent can be obtained during debriefing.

③ *Overcoming ethical objections to deception*

- *Presumptive consent.* Seeking approval from the general public prior to an experiment, as in **Milgram**'s experiment (unit 1.3.1).
- *Prior general consent.* Seeking prior approval from participants. **Gamson** *et al.* (1982, unit 1.3.1) asked their volunteers if they would participate in research on: brand recognition of commercial products, product safety, topics in which you will be misled about the purpose until afterwards, or group standards. When the participants had agreed to being involved in all of the studies, they were told that only the last kind was in progress currently; they had agreed to be deceived.
- *Participants don't mind.* Milgram's participants said afterwards that they did not object to the deception. **Christiansen** (1988) reports that participants don't seem to object to deception as long as it is not extreme.
- *Role play* can be used but may not avoid participant distress (e.g. **Zimbardo**'s study, unit 1.3.1).
- *Questionnaires.* Situations can be described in detail and participants asked to say how they would behave. However, social desirability bias may affect responses and there is a lack of relationship between attitudes and behaviour (unit 1.1.3).

④ *The right to withdraw.* A participant may give their informed consent because they do not fully understand what the research will involve. Once involved they may understand better and should have the right to withdraw. This may affect the research; **Gardner** (1978, see unit 9.5.1) produced a different set of results when he gave participants the right to withdraw and thus, unintentionally, gave them the sense of control.

Some participants may feel they cannot withdraw because they have made a 'deal' with the investigator, either accepting payment (e.g. **Newcomb**'s students were given rent-free accommodation in return for their participation, unit 1.2.2) or agreeing to participate as part of course requirements (e.g. **Navon**, unit 5.1.1).

⑤ *Conducting the research: protection of participants.* If participants experience any *distress* the research should stop immediately. All investigators should maintain the highest standards of *safety*. Distress includes feeling embarrassed, being angered (e.g. **Schachter and Singer**, unit 3.4.2), feeling you may have harmed someone else (e.g. **Darley and Latané**, unit 1.4.1) or being made to feel inferior (e.g. **Rosenthal and Jacobsen**, unit 6.3.3). **Genie**'s mother (unit 5.4.1) objected to the extensive testing of her daughter, saying it was stressful, and she sued the psychologists responsible.

6 *Debriefing.* Participants should be told the full details and outcome of the research as soon as possible. This gives the investigator a chance to find out if any deception worked.

7 *Confidentiality and privacy* must be assured, especially with respect to any published data and computer-held documents (Data Protection Act).

8 *After the research.* All investigators should report their findings honestly (e.g. **Burt**'s twin studies, 1955), and should provide a detailed record so others can use their data.

9 *Ethical objections with hindsight.* It is easy to be critical once research is completed.

- *The ends are unanticipated.* Knowledge is often gained unintentionally, 'understanding grows because we examine situations in which the end is not known' (**Milgram**, 1974).
- *The means are unanticipated.* The results of many psychology studies seem obvious in retrospect, but during planning no major ill effects were anticipated. **Milgram** claimed this was true in his experiment.
- *Distasteful outcomes.* **Aronson** (1992) suggested that the acceptability of any research procedure may be related to our unconscious dislike of the obtained results; for example in Milgram's experiment we transfer our dislike of the finding to a criticism of the methodology (see unit 1.3.1).

7.3.2 THE USE OF NON-HUMAN ANIMALS IN RESEARCH

Investigations with animals include laboratory experiments and naturalistic observations.

1 *Are non-human animals preferable as research participants?*

- It depends on the kind of behaviour being studied. In some situations animal research would have no relevance (e. g. reading) or minimal relevance (e.g. stress).
- Non-human animals are cheaper, less susceptible to experimenter bias and demand characteristics, and easier to study because their behaviour is less complex.
- One can study instinctive behaviour in animals because the effects of learning are often minimal whereas in humans, innate behaviours are masked by experience.
- Animals can be conditioned more successfully.
- Many animals reproduce more quickly so that successive generations can be followed (e.g. **Calhoun**'s study of overcrowding, unit 9.5.1).
- Their use poses *fewer* ethical problems, in fact there are some procedures which would be impossible with human participants.
- They cannot report what they are thinking.

2 *Is non-human animal research relevant to human behaviour?*

Yes

- Some aspects of behaviour are unquestionably the same, for example, studying the behaviour of nerves.
- Behaviourists argue that different species differ quantitatively because they have all evolved from common ancestors and share the same 'building blocks' of behaviour.
- Even if the results are not directly applicable, the comparisons which can be made are at least useful, as in the case of evolutionary theories and comparative studies.
- The results of non-human animal studies may point the way to possibly fruitful research with humans (e.g. **Lorenz**'s study of imprinting, unit 2.3.3).

No

- Humanists argue that humans are qualitatively different from animals, because of certain (probably) unique features, such as consciousness and language.
- Simply because structures are the same doesn't mean they perform the same function (e.g. research on the brain and emotion, unit 3.4.2).

- The fact that humans rely on cultural transmission more than non-human animals means that the same rules do not apply. **Koestler** (1970) coined the term *ratomorphism* to describe generalisations which are made from non-human animals.
- There is the danger of *anthropomorphism* – imputing human feelings to animals.

③ *What is ethical in terms of the use of non-human animal participants?*

- Benefits may be measured in human terms , for example **Harlow**'s work with monkeys had important consequences in child institutions (see unit 2.3.3).
- Non-human animal research may contribute directly to improving the life of animals, as in protecting the environments of endangered species.
- Suffering needs to be assessed without being anthropomorphic. Do rats have the same feelings as primates? What about plant life? Suffering is related to consciousness (see unit 3.3.1).
- Even research which involves a very low level of suffering, such as genetic engineering and selective breeding, raises ethical questions about humans interfering with nature.
- It is often only with hindsight that we are truly able to judge the value of *or* the suffering involved in an experiment (e.g. **Harlow**'s research).

④ *The facts about non-human animal research.* **Coile and Miller** (1984) examined a body of American psychological articles and found that only 7% had been primarily concerned with animals, the rest were based on human participants. The **Animals Act** (1986) has laid down strict guidelines for animal research and such research usually requires a licence from the Home Office. In America, all work except that involving rats, mice and birds must be licensed by the government. In addition the British Psychological Society (1985) strongly advises psychologists to:

- Avoid, or at least minimise, discomfort to living animals.
- Discuss any such research with a Home Office inspector.
- Be familiar with the unique requirements of the species they are studying.
- Minimise the number of participants used.
- Consider the relative costs and benefits, and alternatives – such as using naturalistic observation rather than experimental manipulation, or *in vitro* techniques, though this is more appropriate to medical research.

7.3.3 ETHICAL RESPONSIBILITIES OF PSYCHOLOGISTS

Scientists have a moral obligation with regard to the usefulness and ethics of their research and its ultimate applications. A professional person belongs to a self-governing group, with the right and duty to stop 'unprofessional' members from practising.

① *Responsibilities towards individuals*

- *The psychological researcher* has a duty to treat both human and non-human participants ethically, as discussed earlier in this unit.
- *Responsibilities as a practitioner.* Practising psychologists, such as psychotherapists or educational psychologists, can be agents of change. They may also be responsible for collecting data about people, such as conducting questionnaires or administering psychometric tests. They must consider: informed consent, deception, protection against harm or distress, privacy and confidentiality.
- *Social control.* There is a wider issue, beyond the *treatment* of 'disturbed' patients. Psychologists also decide *who* needs treatment. **Heather** (1976) suggested that the classification of abnormality is not absolute, it is relative to a culturally determined set of morals (see unit 4.2.1).

② *Responsibilities towards society*

- *How research results are used.* Moral responsibility includes concern over how research results are used, e.g. those from studies of obedience.
- *Social manipulation.* Psychological research may be used politically as 'scientific proof' for a new policy or reform. For example, when a government wishes to promote family values psychological evidence can be used to demonstrate that single-parent families are psychologically unhealthy.

- *Responsibilities regarding other psychologists.* One of the BPS guidelines concerning ethical principles in research states that psychologists have a duty to monitor the work of their peers and students. This includes reporting any dishonest conduct or malpractice. Psychologists also have a duty to publish the full details of any research and to give other psychologists access to their data.
- *Obligation to conduct meaningful and honest research* which can 'better' people's lives, such as the reduction of prejudice (unit 1.1.3) or aggression (unit 1.4.2).

3 *Socially sensitive research.* Research which has direct social consequences creates particular problems because it is often concerns issues where there is little agreement, much bias and serious implications.

- *'Alternative' sexuality.* **Hamer** *et al.* (1993) found evidence of a 'gay gene' by looking at the genes of homosexual brothers. If this is true, it could lead some people to test unborn children. Researchers who find evidence against the pathological model may have a favourable bias towards alternative sexuality, for example **Kitzinger and Coyle** (1995).
- *Race-related research.* This kind of research inevitably involves the use of an 'imposed etic' (unit 7.2.3). **Jensen**'s (1969) research concluded that Black Americans were intellectually and innately inferior, this would have important implications for education. Other race-related psychological research may be more positive, such as attempts to understand why some people are more prejudiced than others and how to reduce such prejudice (unit 1.1.4).

Chapter roundup

7.1   Approaches to psychology

7.1.1 *Behaviourism* is the view that all behaviour is learned; the *psychodynamic* approach describes how biological factors interact with early experience to create personality; *humanists* believe that subjective experience is the best means of representing human behaviour even though it may not be fully accurate.

7.1.2 *Free will* and *determinism* represent two ends of a continuum, neither extreme are tenable positions and pose difficulties for scientific research and the law. *Reductionist* explanations are necessary but not sufficient in understanding human behaviour. A combination (different universes of discourse) is preferable.

7.2   Controversies in psychology

7.2.1 Psychological research is used in many *controversial applications*, which can be evaluated in terms of means and ends.

7.2.2 Psychology is a *science* to the extent that it uses scientific methods, but this is challenged by issues of bias and appropriateness.

7.2.3 Many psychological theories have *culture and gender biases*: they are eurocentric, ethnocentric, androcentric and alpha- or beta-biased. Derived etics and feminist perspectives offer new approaches.

7.3   Ethical issues in psychology

7.3.1 Research with *human* participants should involve informed consent, the right to withdraw, the limited use of deception, no harm to participants, respect of confidentiality and privacy, and thorough debriefing.

7.3.2 Research with *non-human animals* should be evaluated in terms of whether it is preferable, relevant and/or ethical. Actual practice should also be considered.

7.3.3 Psychologists have *responsibilities* as researchers and practitioners to behave in an honest and humane manner, and produce meaningful work. Areas of socially sensitive research are especially critical.

Illustrative question

Is psychology a science? Critically discuss this question. (24 marks)

Tutorial note

Weaker candidates tend to confuse the concept of 'science' or the 'scientific method' with 'scientific experiments'. Your answer should demonstrate an understanding of all three. You can then consider the extent to which psychology does or does not fit into the requirements of a science. A good essay should present a balance between the arguments for *and* against the position that psychology is a science. Further critical evaluation might be in terms of the desirability of the scientific approach. It is good to use specific examples to demonstrate your knowledge and understanding.

Suggested answer

Is psychology a science? In order to answer this question we first must determine what a 'science' is and then see if that definition fits psychology. In addition we can ask whether the scientific approach is desirable in psychology.

A science is a field of study where knowledge is gained through objective observation and experiment. In contrast, philosophers use rational argument to prove their theories. **Malim *et al.*** (1992) state there are four goals of any science. These are: to describe events as objectively as possible, to use such descriptions to predict future events and propose hypotheses, to gain greater knowledge through hypothesis testing and finally, to give us greater control of the world around us through understanding cause and effect.

The scientific method is the means by which scientists develop theories and collect data. A scientist proposes a theory on the basis of a collection of facts. Such facts are the result of objective observation. A theory can then lead to generalisations being made about behaviour which generate expectations or hypotheses about other related phenomena. The scientist tests his hypothesis by setting up a controlled experiment, where he manipulates an independent variable (IV) and observes changes in the dependent variable (DV). The experimental results are used to support or refine the theory.

The key features of the scientific method are objectivity, control and replication. The scientific experiment is the best means of achieving this, though there are other methods, such as naturalistic observation and interviews. In a scientific experiment all variables are objectively defined and observed. They are controlled so that we can be sure that any change in the DV is due to the IV rather than other extraneous variable. A good experiment should also be repeatable because otherwise the result might just be a freak accident.

If psychologists want to claim that psychology is a science then they must demonstrate that they share the same method and goals of science.

Psychologists do many experiments and aim to fulfil the rigours of the scientific method. Behaviourists and cognitive psychologists especially like to use laboratory settings. For example, memory experiments where participants are given a list of words to learn, followed by an interference task, and then a recall task. Some participants might be given cues to help recall whilst a control group received no help. Behaviourists conduct experiments with animals, such as **Pavlov**'s well-known experiments with dogs whereby he demonstrated classical conditioning and **Skinner**'s experiments with pigeons.

The problem with such experiments is that it is not always possible to generalise from them to real human experience. In the case of memory experiments, they lack real-life validity and only tell us about a particular kind of memory (episodic). Animal experiments may also lack generalisability. Behaviourists think there is only a quantitative difference between animals and humans and therefore generalisations can be made, but not all psychologists agree with this saying that language, learning and consciousness make humans qualitatively different.

Critics of experimental psychology point out that experiments with live participants, especially humans, are not objective. Experimenters influence the behaviour of their participants because of their expectations. This is called the experimenter bias and was demonstrated by **Rosenthal and Jacobsen** (1968) in a classic experiment where some children's IQs increased as a result of their teachers being given higher expectations for them. The experimenter effect can be overcome by using double blind techniques but even when neither experimenter nor participant knows the aim of the experiment they still have expectations and this may affect the results.

Experimental psychologists defend their viewpoint with the argument that *all* scientific experiments are affected by experimenter bias. For example, in physics today it is recognised that we cannot observe anything without changing it. This is part of **Heisenberg**'s uncertainty principle, which also states that there are no certainties in the universe.

There are alternatives to the scientific *experiment* which are still considered to be scientific methods. They are less powerful because it is less possible to demonstrate cause and effect, but they have more real-life validity. For example, ethologists conduct controlled observation studies in naturalistic environments. By using several observers they can decrease subjectivity and claim to discover objective facts.

Early psychologists, such as **Wundt**, used introspection as a method of scientific enquiry. It was a highly disciplined technique where students were trained to be able to report their conscious experience. The Behaviourists rejected this approach on the grounds of its inherent subjectivity and they also rejected consciousness as an unnecessary concept. More recently psychologists have returned to introspection as the only means of exploring some aspects of human behaviour, such as the study of imagery and problem-solving. For example, **Newell and Simon**'s work on the general problem-solver is based on reports of what individuals do when they solve problems.

It seems that all research methods can be considered as scientific because they strive to be as objective as possible, and even traditional sciences are not as objective as was once thought. All methods share the goals of science as described above by **Malim et al.** (1992).

However, we should evaluate the question 'Is psychology a science?' by asking whether such an approach is *desirable* in psychology. The scientific approach to psychology is implicitly reductionist and mechanistic: reductionist because it attempts to identify constituent elements of behaviour – even Wundt's research was considered reductionist – and mechanistic because it aims to identify cause and effect relationships. Some psychologists, most notably the humanists, regard these as undesirable goals for psychology. **Cohen** (1958) called it 'ratomorphic robotic psychology'.

Humanists such as **Maslow** and **Rogers** regard the scientific approach as potentially dehumanising, though they do not reject it. Instead they suggest that subjective and objective approaches should be integrated, and the experiential aspect of human behaviour should be recognised. They put forward a phenomenological approach which aims to explain behaviour from the point of view of the perceiver rather than an objective observer. **Harré and Secord** (1993) proposed a new approach called ethogenics or new paradigm research which will integrate everyday psychology with traditional research methods, aiming to produce facts which are significant in human rather than statistical terms.

A second issue with respect to the desirability of the scientific approach is the matter of control. This is one of the goals of science but there are important ethical considerations in relation to the control of human behaviour which is based on psychological research. For example **Skinner** proposed in his novel 'Walden Two', that principles of behaviourism could be applied to social engineering so that an ideal world could be created. Such social control might be desirable in some ways but is not very ethical.

In conclusion, psychology clearly can be considered as a science, especially in the light of changing perceptions of science generally. The question remains as to whether it is the only valid approach or whether it is desirable.

Question bank

Allow 35–40 minutes for each question.

Approaches to psychology

1 (a) At playgroup one morning a 4-year-old girl pushes a smaller younger girl off a tricycle and rides away on it. Give reasons from **each** of the following perspectives for the older child's behaviour:
     (i)   behavioural perspective;
     (ii) cognitive perspective;
     (iii) psychoanalytic perspective. (12 marks)
   (b) Critically evaluate an eclectic approach to the understanding of human behaviour. (8 marks)

(NEAB June 1995)

Points: AEB candidates might substitute 'humanistic' for 'cognitive'. When discussing each perspective make sure you clearly link the key features of that perspective to your explanation. In part (b) do not just use another perspective but a strictly eclectic one.

2 Discuss the issue of freedom versus determinism in a psychological context.

(AEB A 1990)

Points: Define your terms carefully and give examples from your psychological studies. A good answer will include the implications of both views.

3 (a) What is meant by reductionism in psychology? (4 marks)
   (b) Outline reductionist explanations of behaviour from **two** different areas of psychology. (10 marks)
   (c) Assess the appropriateness of reductionist explanations of behaviour. (10 marks)

(AEB A 1994)

Points: Take care to answer parts of the question appropriately and not reuse the same material. Part (a) is a definition and should include examples. Part (b) is a description of only two explanations which must be selected from different areas of your studies. Part (c) is an evaluation (positive and negative) of any reductionist explanations in terms of their appropriateness, in other words you should look at the usefulness of such explanations as well as criticising them.

Controversies in psychology

4 Describe and evaluate the use of psychological research in **either** advertising **or** psychometric testing.

Points: Remember that 'research' includes both theories and empirical studies. For everything you describe, offer some evaluation in terms of, for example, applicability, contradictory evidence and methodology.

5 Describe and evaluate the role of scientific method in any major approach to psychology.

(AEB A 1995)

Points: Your answer should describe such methods and evaluate them by giving examples. You must limit yourself to examples from one approach only, though comparisons could be made to other areas of the syllabus. You should present well-informed arguments about scientific methods not just experiments.

6 Discuss any **two** psychological theories in terms of their culture bias.

Points: Describe and evaluate theories which have some culture bias and offer an informed discussion of both positive and negative points.

Ethical issues in psychology

7 Discuss the ethics of psychological practices that involve behaviour change in humans.

(AEB A 1996)

Points: You can describe behavioural change with respect to experiments and the treatment of abnormal behaviour. Ensure that your discussion is directed at human behaviour only.

8 Discuss the use of animals in psychological research and consider the ethical issues raised by such research.

(AEB A 1992)

Points: Beware of emotive, ill-informed arguments. Do not simply list animal experiments and remember that there are other kinds of research with animals which do not involve harm but raise ethical questions.

RESEARCH METHODS IN PSYCHOLOGY

Units in this chapter

8.1 *The nature of psychological enquiry*
8.2 *The design and implementation of investigations*
8.3 *Data analysis*

Chapter overview

Psychologists strive to uncover 'facts' about human behaviour using formal research methods. They aim to base their theories on empirical evidence rather than appealing to common sense. Throughout this book, reference is made to the empirical 'facts' generated by research. It is important to understand how these facts have been gathered, and the related practical and ethical considerations, in order to be able to evaluate properly the evidence psychologists use.

8.1 THE NATURE OF PSYCHOLOGICAL ENQUIRY

8.1.1 EXPERIMENTAL METHODS

Laboratory experiments

In an experiment the relationship between two things is investigated by deliberately producing a change in the independent variable (IV) and recording what effect this has on the dependent variable (DV).

❶ *Uses*

- To determine a causal relationship between two variables.

❷ *Advantages*

- Extraneous variables can be well controlled.
- It can be replicated.
- Examples: **Milgram** (unit 1.3.1) and **Ainsworth** (unit 6.1.1)

3 *Disadvantages*

- It is an artificial situation, therefore the results may not generalise to real life.
- Total control is in reality never possible. The results may be affected by, for example: experimenter bias, demand characteristics, volunteer bias, sample bias (see section 8.2). There may be extraneous variables beyond control or unknown to the experimenter.
- Some classes of participants, such as children, react poorly under experimental conditions.

4 *Ethical considerations*

- Informed consent and lack of deception aren't always possible (see unit 7.3.1).
- Participants should not be subjected to stressful or negative manipulations.

Field experiments

Experiments conducted in more natural surroundings, where the participants are unaware that they are participating in a psychology experiment. The IV is still manipulated.

1 *Uses*

- To gain more real-life validity.
- Examples: **Piliavin** *et al.* (unit 1.4.1) and **Hofling** *et al.* (unit 1.3.1).

2 *Advantages*

- The technique avoids experimenter bias and demand characteristics because the participants are unaware of the experiment.

3 *Disadvantages*

- Inevitably extraneous variables are harder to control.
- Some design problems remain, such as sample bias and some demand characteristics.
- It is more time-consuming and expensive than laboratory experiments.

4 *Ethical considerations*

- It is not possible to gain consent or give debriefing.
- Participants may be distressed by the experience.

8.1.2 QUASI- AND NON-EXPERIMENTAL METHODS

Natural experiments

If conditions vary naturally, the effects of an IV can be observed without any intervention by the experimenter. It is still an experiment in the sense that a cause and effect are being identified, but not a 'true' experiment since the IV is not manipulated.

1 *Uses*

- Where conditions vary naturally.
- The only way to study cause and effect where there are ethical objections to manipulating the variables.
- Examples: **Williams** (unit 1.4.3 and 6.3.2) and **Shields** (unit 6.2.3).

2 *Advantages*

- As for field experiments.

3 *Disadvantages*

- Participants may be aware of being studied and show improvements just because of this (the Hawthorne effect).
- Inevitable loss of control over extraneous variables.
- Such conditions are not always possible to find.

4 *Ethical considerations*

- It may involve withholding treatment from one group, as when a new educational programme is being tested.

Investigations using correlational analysis

A numerical value is calculated to represent the degree to which two sets of data are correlated. The reason for the relationship can only be supposed. The terms IV and DV are not used, the variables are called covariables. Perfect positive correlation is +1.00. With large sample sizes a value as little as ±30 can be significant positive or negative correlation.

❶ *Uses*

- Where experimental manipulation would be unethical or impossible.
- It indicates a trend and is a good starting point for later experimental studies where cause might then be investigated.
- Examples: **Rahe** *et al.* (unit 3.4.3) and **Bouchard and McGue** (unit 6.2.3).

❷ *Advantages*

- Provides useful information about variables which can be statistically tested.

❸ *Disadvantages*

- It establishes a relationship only, not a cause and effect.
- The relationship may be due to other extraneous variables. For example, height and IQ are linked because diet influences both.
- Correlations only deal with linear relationships. There are many other kinds of relationships, such as the curvilinear association in the **Yerkes-Dodson** effect (see unit 3.4.3). These may be overlooked by simply calculating the correlation coefficient.

❹ *Ethical considerations*

- Causal inferences shouldn't be made.

Naturalistic observation

Behaviour is observed in the natural environment. All variables are free to vary and interference is kept to a minimum. No IV is manipulated but nevertheless a hypothesis may be tested.

❶ *Uses*

- When behaviour is studied for the first time, observation is needed to establish possible relationships.
- It is good for working with young children, wild animals and uncooperative participants.
- It offers a way to study behaviour where there are ethical objections to manipulating variables.
- Examples: **von Frisch** (unit 2.4.3) and **Mead** (unit 6.3.2).

❷ *Advantages*

- It gives a more realistic picture of spontaneous behaviour. It has high ecological validity.
- If the observer(s) remain undetected, the method avoids most experimental effects, such as experimenter bias, demand characteristics and evaluation apprehension.

❸ *Disadvantages*

- It is not possible to infer cause and effect.
- It is difficult to replicate and therefore you cannot be certain that the result was not a 'one off'.
- It is not possible to control extraneous variables.
- Observer bias: the observer sees what he 'wants' to see.
- Observer reliability: there are likely to be differences between different observers (low inter-observer reliability) or the same observer on different occasions.
- Where participants know they are being watched (disclosed observations) they may behave unnaturally. Even non-participant observers, by their mere presence, can alter a situation.

❹ *Ethical considerations*

- Undisclosed observations preclude the right to informed consent.
- Disclosed observations may affect the individuals observed.

Case studies

A case study is a detailed account of a single individual, small group, institution or event. It might contain data about personal history, background, test results and the record of interviews.

❶ Uses

- When a behaviour is rare.
- To provide insights from an unusual perspective.
- Examples: **Gregory and Wallace** (unit 5.1.2) and **Operation Head Start** (unit 6.1.2).

❷ Advantages

- Gives in-depth picture producing rich data.
- Relates to real life.

❸ Disadvantages

- Usually involves recall of earlier history and therefore is unreliable.
- Close relationship between experimenter and participant introduces bias.
- Cause and effect are difficult to establish.
- Not rigorous methodology, often unstructured and unreplicable.
- Limited sample, lacks generalisability.
- Time-consuming and expensive.

❹ Ethical considerations

- Confidentiality and privacy must be protected. Individuals should not be named.

Interviews

Interviews can be highly structured or little more than an informal 'chat'. **Piaget**'s 'clinical method' involved a group of predetermined questions which were then expanded in response to the child's answers. This maximises the amount of data gathered but increases bias.

❶ Uses

- Provides information about a person's thoughts which are not otherwise accessible.
- Examples: **Rosenhan** (unit 1.4.1) and **Piaget** (unit 6.2.1).

❷ Advantages

- Rich data can be obtained.
- Interviews may be held for practical reasons, such as saving the time and money necessary for more elaborate measures.

❸ Disadvantages

- It requires well-trained interviewers.
- Interviews may not be comparable because different interviewers ask different questions (low inter-interviewer reliability). Reliability may also be affected by the same interviewer behaving differently on different occasions.
- The interviewer's expectations may influence the interviewee's performance (halo effects, confirmatory bias, attribution errors, racial/sexual/ageist prejudices).
- People often don't actually know what they think and therefore respond to suggestion and response biases.
- The interviewee's expectations may affect the interviewer's performance.
- The method relies on self-report, which is open to problems such as social desirability bias.

❹ Ethical considerations

- Deception may be necessary.
- Questions may relate to sensitive issues.
- Confidentiality and privacy must be respected.

Content analysis

An observational technique which examines behaviour indirectly by using, for example, books, diaries or TV programmes and counting the frequency of particular behaviours, such as gender-related words.

❶ *Uses*

- Detailed analysis of written or verbal material.

❷ *Advantages*

- Relates to real life, ecological validity.
- Can easily be replicated.

❸ *Disadvantages*

- Likely to be a subjective bias in scoring.
- The method fails to take account of interrelationships.

8.2 THE DESIGN AND IMPLEMENTATION OF INVESTIGATIONS

Aims and hypotheses

Research aims are the stated intentions of what question(s) are planned to be answered.
A *hypothesis* is a formal, unambiguous statement of what you predict.

- The *null hypothesis* (H_0) is a statement of 'no difference' between the populations being studied.
- The *alternate hypothesis* (H_1) makes a prediction about the effect of the IV on the DV, or about the difference between the samples as a result of the IV.
- *One-tailed hypothesis* predicts the direction of the effect.
- *Two-tailed hypothesis* anticipates a difference but not the direction.

Experimental designs

❶ *Repeated measures* (test-retest). The same participant is tested before and after the experimental treatment, therefore *all* participants are exposed to the IV and tested on the DV.

Advantages

- Good control for irrelevant participant variables.
- Related measures statistics are more sensitive.
- Needs fewer participants.

Disadvantages

- Order effects can affect final performance.
- Participants may guess the purpose of the experiment after the first test.

❷ *Matched participants.* Participant variables are controlled by matching pairs of participants on key attributes. One partner is exposed to the IV, and both are compared in terms of their performance on the DV.

Advantages

- No order effects or other problems of repeated measures design.
- Participant variables partly controlled.
- Can use related design statistics which are more powerful.

Disadvantages

- Matching is difficult, time-consuming and may waste participants.
- Matching is inevitably inexact.

❸ *Independent groups.* Comparison is made between two unrelated groups of participants. The participants are in groups not pairs. One group receives the experimental treatment, the other doesn't. Their performance on the DV is compared.

Advantages
- Used where repeated measures are not possible.
- No order effects and other problems of repeated measures.

Disadvantages
- Lacks control of other participant variables.
- Needs more participants.
- Statistical measures for independent measures are less powerful.

Selecting participants (sampling)

Sample. Part of a population selected such that it is considered to be representative of the population as a whole.

Sampling population. Population from which the sample is actually drawn, which in itself may be unrepresentative. For example selecting a sample from one school.

Target population. The total number of cases about which a specific statement can be made.

Sampling techniques:
- *Random sample.* Every member of the population has an equal chance of being selected, therefore it is an unbiased sample. This can be achieved with random number tables or numbers drawn from a hat.
- *Systematic or quasi-random sample.* For example, every 10th case. There is no bias in selection, however every person does not stand an equal chance of being selected (therefore quasi-random).
- *Opportunity or accidental sample.* Selecting participants because they are available, for example asking people in the street. It is sometimes mistakenly regarded as random whereas it is invariably biased.
- *Volunteer or self-selected sample.* Participants who become part of an experiment because they volunteer when asked. The results are likely to suffer from a volunteer bias because such participants are usually more highly motivated and perform better than randomly selected participants.
- *Stratified sample.* The population is divided in distinct sections or strata in relation to factors considered relevant, for example social class. The researcher then randomly selects a pre-set number of individuals from each strata.
- *Quota sample.* Also uses stratified methods but the sample is not randomly determined, the researcher seeks; for example, any five individuals satisfying each criteria.

Categorising behaviour

Observational studies require methods of categorising behaviour to ensure consistency and reduce time in situations where it is limited.

❶ *Methods of recording data*
- *Grid* of behavioural categories. Tick occurrences of target behaviours.
- *Rating* of behaviour, score each individual in terms of degree, such as amount of interest shown.
- *Codes*: a system of symbols or abbreviations is developed as a shorthand.
- *Diaries*: participants and/or observers keep a diary of events, either at the time or at the end of the day. May be necessary to limit awareness of being observed.
- *Sketches*: showing who or what is where.
- *Categories*: preassigned categories of behaviour derived from earlier research, for example *ethograms*.

❷ *Sampling techniques*
- *Event sampling*: a list of behaviours is drawn up and a frequency count kept of their occurrence.
- *Time sampling*: observations are made at regular intervals, such as once a minute.
- *Point sampling*: the observer concentrates on one individual until sufficient record has been made of their behaviour, then moves on to another participant.

Variables

In any research there are two kinds of variables:

❶ *Experimental variables*, the ones we are studying.

- *The independent variable* (IV) is the one which is specifically manipulated so that we can observe its effect on the *dependent variable* (DV). The DV is usually the one we are measuring or assessing.
- *Operational definition* is necessary in order to make a variable measurable and unambiguous. The definition is based on a set of operations or objective components. For example hunger might be defined in terms of the number of hours since a participant last ate or a rating scale of how hungry they feel.
- Variables can be measured on different *scales of measurement*:
  - *Nominal*, named categories, for example Winter, Spring, Summer, Autumn.
  - *Ordinal*, ordered, for example hot, warm, cool, cold.
  - *Interval*, intervals of equal size, for example the Fahrenheit scale.
  - *Ratio*, an interval scale with a true zero point, for example the absolute zero scale.

❷ *Extraneous variables* are any variables which may affect the DV (aside from the IV) and therefore prejudice the results. These may be random or systematic (see below).

Minimising the effects of situational variables

If extraneous variables are random then one can assume that the effects will be equally spread across all conditions. If extraneous variables vary systematically it should be possible to eliminate or balance them (*systematic elimination*):

- *Standardised procedures* are used to ensure that conditions are equivalent for all participants, this includes the use of *standardised instructions*.
- *Counterbalancing*. Give half the participants condition A first while the other half get condition B first. This prevents order effects which could improve (e.g. practice) or depress (e.g. boredom) performance.
- *Equivalent measures*. When a participant is retested, the test must be given in two equivalent forms to prevent advantages gained through practice.
- *Random allocation*. Any bias in placing participants in experimental or control groups can be overcome by randomly determining the group they are placed in.
- *Randomisation*. All test stimuli should be presented in random order to prevent bias (e.g. order effects).

Relationship between researchers and participants

❶ *Examples of the influence of researchers on participants*

- *Experimenter effect or bias*. An experimenter has expectations about the outcome of an experiment and may indirectly and unconsciously communicate these to the participant (human or animal). This affects the participants' behaviour. **Rosenthal and Jacobsen** (1968, see unit 6.3.3) provided empirical support for this self-fulfilling prophecy. This is different from the *experimental effect*, which is the effect of the experimental treatment.
- *Hawthorne effect*. A person's performance may improve, not because of the experimental treatment, but because they are receiving unaccustomed attention. Such attention increases self-esteem and leads to improved performance. The effect is named for the Hawthorne electrical factory where it was first observed by **Mayo** (1933).
- *The Greenspoon effect*. Participants are subtly reinforced by the experimenter's comments. **Greenspoon** (1955) was able to alter participants' responses by using subtle reinforcement of 'right' or 'wrong' answers. He said 'mm-hmm' whenever the participant said a plural word or 'huh-uh' after other responses. This led to increased or decreased production of plural words in random word generation.
- *Demand characteristics*. Those features of an experimental setting that 'invite' the participant to behave in particular ways. They bias a participant's behaviour. One

example is the participant's attempts (not necessarily conscious) to guess what the experiment is about, and do (or not do) what is expected of them. **Orne** (1962) tested this by telling participants they were participants in an experiment investigating sensory deprivation. In fact they were not deprived at all, yet they displayed the classic symptoms, in other words they did what they were expected to do.

② *Reasons why participants are likely to be influenced*

- *The experiment as a social situation.* Participants prefer to behave in a socially acceptable manner. This is true even when performing anonymously or when answering questions on paper.
- *An active participant.* **Orne** (1962) argued that the picture of the participant as automaton is a foolish ideal. Participants actively search for clues about how to behave.
- *Evaluation apprehension.* A participant is aware of being 'tested' and wants to appear normal and create a good impression. In order to overcome anxiety and uncertainty, the participant tries to guess what the experimenter really wants.
- *The experimenter's expectations.* There are pressures on a researcher to produce useful results. Even in double-blind situations the experimenter is not 'expectation free'.

③ *Ways of overcoming researcher and participant reactivity*

- *Single-blind technique.* Participants are not informed of the aim of the experiment until after it is finished. This attempts to control participant bias.
- *Double-blind technique.* Neither participant nor experimenter are aware of the 'crucial' aspects of the experiment. This aims to avoid both participant and experimenter bias.
- *Placebos* are a control for the effects of expectations because participants think they are receiving the experimental treatment when they are not. They receive a 'treatment' which appears the same as the real thing but does not have its critical effects.
- *Undisclosed observation.* In a field or natural experiment, the participant has no expectations because they are unaware of being part of an experiment.
- *Standardised instructions.* Helps to prevent experimenter bias.

Other research techniques

- *Pilot study.* A smaller, preliminary study which makes it possible to check out standardised procedures and general design before investing time and money in the major study. Any problems can be adjusted.
- *Confederate or stooge.* A person who appears in an experiment as a participant but who is instructed by the researcher to act in certain ways to influence the real participants, unbeknownst to the real participants.

Generalisability

All research data is used to make generalisations about humans or animals. There are some important qualifications to consider when doing this:

- *Sampling bias.* True random sampling is rare. A lot of experiments use volunteers drawn from psychology departments.
- *Biased data.* Some distortion is inevitable due to uncontrolled extraneous variables and experimenter bias.
- *Publishing bias.* Research whose findings are positive or in agreement with current thinking is more likely to be published.
- *Validity.* Does the research actually measure what it sets out to measure? Methods for determining validity are listed in unit 7.2.1.
- *Reliability.* A true test of any research result is replication. Psychology never finds 100% agreement between similar studies because:
  - It is difficult to *repeat* standardised procedures exactly.
  - *Test reliability* (see 7.2.1). The stimulus material may be inconsistent.
  - *Interobserver reliability.* In any research involving more than one researcher, there may have been a significant difference in researcher behaviours.

8.3 DATA ANALYSIS

8.3.1 QUANTITATIVE ANALYSIS OF DATA

Descriptive statistical techniques

❶ *Measures of central tendency* are ways of giving the most typical or central value.
- *Mean* ($\overline{X}$ or arithmetic mean). Add up all the values and divide by N. Use with symmetrical distributions and/or no extreme values.
- *Median*. The middle or central value in an ordered list. Use with skewed data and/or data with extremes.
- *Mode*. The modal group is the most common. Bimodal means two modes. Use with bimodal distributions and/or nominal data.

❷ *Measures of dispersion*
- *Variation ratio* is the proportion of non-modal scores to the total number of scores. Use with modal data.
- *Range*. The distance between lowest and highest value. Quick to calculate but affected by extreme values. Use with symmetrical distributions.
- *The interquartile range*. Place all values in order, find mid-point (Q2), then halve again to get Q1 and Q3, giving four equal groups. Reasonably simple and less affected by extremes than the range.
- *Standard deviation* (s). The difference between each value and the mean is calculated, and then the mean of these differences is worked out. This is the most accurate measure because it takes the distance between all values into account.
- *Variance* (s^2). The standard deviation squared.

❸ *Measures of distribution*
- Methods which can be used with *any kind* of measurement: tables, bar and pie charts, pictograms.
- Methods suitable for *ordinal and interval data* only: histogram (area of the bars must be proportional to the frequencies represented), frequency polygon (mid-point of each bar joined to show continuous change), line graph, curved line graph, ogive (cumulative frequency).
- Methods for *correlational data*: scattergram, each pair of values is plotted against each other to show if a consistent trend is present. The correlation may be positive (trend from bottom left to top right), negative (trend from top left to bottom right) or none (even spread).
- *The normal distribution* is a bell-shaped, symmetrical and unimodal curve. The mean, median and mode all have the same value. Many different variables are normally distributed, such as height, intelligence and the life of light bulb. It is the theoretically expected distribution when a sample is drawn from an infinite population in which all events are equally likely to occur and the variables are continuous: 68% of a population will be 1 standard deviation from the mean, 95% will be 2 standard deviations from the mean.

Inferential statistical techniques

Inferential statistical tests involve inferences being drawn from sample data to a population as a whole.
- *Two sample tests of difference* consider whether the two samples come from the same population.
- *Two sample tests of correlation* determine the extent to which both variables covary systematically.

| | Tests of difference | | Tests of correlation |
	Related measures	Independent measures	
Nominal data	SIGN TEST	CHI-SQUARED TEST	CHI-SQUARED TEST
Ordinal, interval or ratio data	WILCOXON MATCHED PAIRS SIGNED RANKS TEST	MANN-WHITNEY U TEST	SPEARMAN'S RHO (RANK ORDER TEST OF CORRELATION)

8.3.2 QUALITATIVE ANALYSIS OF DATA

1 *Interviews.* **Foster and Parker** (1995) suggest the following possibilities:

- *'Giving voice'*. Re-present what the interviewee has said using selective quotations and describing the key details.
- *Grounded theory.* Make explicit what is implicit in the text. Derive categories which represent the text and provide a means of analysis. This approach is grounded in the interview text.
- *Thematic analysis.* Organising the interview material in relation to specific original research questions or themes.
- *Discourse analysis* aims to reveal how the text is organised by identifying a number of competing themes or discourses.

2 *Case studies* may employ various means of investigation, such as questionnaires, interviews, observation, role playing or documentary analysis.

- Produce *a rich record* ('giving voice') of the individual, small group, institution or event.
- Produce *interpretations*: grounded theory, thematic and/or discourse analysis.

3 *Observation*

- Analyse data from time, event and point sampling using descriptive and inferential statistics (i.e. quantitative analysis).
- Produce a *detailed record* of observed behaviour ('giving voice').
- Produce *interpretations* (as above) which may lead to further quantitative analysis.

8.3.3 INTERPRETATION OF RESULTS

Statistical significance

Statistical significance is the conclusion that a set of results are unlikely to have occurred by chance alone. This leads us to reject the null hypothesis (H_0) and accept the alternative version (H_1) that the results were due to the experimental treatment. This may be erroneous in the case when they were caused by extraneous factors

A test of significance yields a probability (p) of whether the results were due to chance, $p \leq 0.01$ means that the probability is less than 1 in 100 (1%) that the results could have occurred by chance if the null hypothesis is true. This level of probability leads us to feel that this isn't very likely, therefore we would reject H_0 and accept H_1.

Level	Probability	Significance	When used
1% level	($p \leq 0.01$)	highly significant, stringent (reject H_0, accept H_1)	Used in research affecting human health where we would want to take few chances.
5% level	($p \leq 0.05$)	significant (reject H_0, accept H_1)	Acceptable level for psychology research.
10% level	($p \leq 0.10$)	marginal, low or lenient (accept H_0)	May indicate need for better methodology.

Ecological and experimental validity

Both ecological and experimental validity affect the extent to which any findings can be applied to real-life human behaviour.

- *Ecological validity* is the extent to which a research result can generalise beyond the setting in which it was gathered.
- *Experimental validity* is the extent to which an experimental result is 'true'. Experimental reliability and the use of controlled procedures are important in determining experimental validity.
- The more you control an experimental situation, the less ecological validity it has.
- The more a study has ecological validity, the more likely that extraneous variables will affect the results and reduce the experimental validity of the research.

Chapter roundup

8.1   The nature of psychological enquiry

8.1.1 *Experimental methods* involve deliberate manipulation of an independent variable to observe the effect on a dependent variable. The laboratory is the best place to do this but field experiments have greater ecological validity.

8.1.2 *Quasi- and non-experimental methods* include natural experiments, investigations using correlational analysis, naturalistic observation, case studies, interviews and content analysis.

8.2   The design and implementation of investigations

The steps involved in good research design and implementation:

- Decide on the *aims* of the study, based on current theory.
- Write an unambiguous *hypothesis*.
- Select an *appropriate design*.
- Select the *sample*.
- Decide how to *categorise behaviour*.
- Define *variables*.
- Minimise the effects of *situational variables*.
- Minimise the effects of the *relationship between researchers and participants*.
- Consider *generalisability* (reliability and validity).

8.3   Data analysis

8.3.1 *Quantitative analysis of data* includes measures of central tendency, dispersion and distribution, and inferential statistical tests.

8.3.2 *Qualitative analysis of data* from interviews, case studies and observations includes 'giving voice' (rich record), grounded theory, and thematic and discourse analyses.

8.3.3 *Interpretation of results* depends on understanding statistical significance and ecological validity.

Illustrative question

From AEB, 1992

A group of researchers decided to investigate whether there was an association between people's age and their ability to tell the difference between music played to them on record, cassette and compact disc. They placed an advertisement in a newspaper asking for volunteers who would be interested in participating in the study. There were 218 respondents. For the purpose of the study the researchers divided respondents into two age groups: those under the age of 40 and those aged 40 and over. Having first carried out a pilot study, the researchers began testing the discriminative listening skills of the two age groups. The procedure that the researchers used was as follows: participants were asked to which type of music they would prefer to listen in this investigation: rock, jazz or classical. One of the researchers then played each participant a single recording of their preferred type of music three times: once from a record, once from a cassette and once from a compact disc. The order of presentation of the three formats was randomised for each participant. After hearing the three presentations each participant was asked to identify which of the presentations was from a record, which was from a cassette and which was from a compact disc. Participants' responses were recorded as being correct (all three formats correctly identified) or incorrect (less than three formats correctly identified). The researchers analysed these data using a chi-squared test. The results were as follows:

Table 1: *Number of participants who were correct/incorrect*

Age of participants	Correct	Incorrect
Under 40 years	85	35
Over 40 years	55	43

The chi-squared analysis produced a value of 4.47.

The relevant line (df=1) of the statistical table for chi-squared interpretation was:

Table 2

Significance level	0.1	0.05	0.01	0
Chi-squared value	2.71	3.84	6.64	10.83

(From AEB A 1992)

(a) State an appropriate null hypothesis for the above study. (1 mark)

Illustrative answer: There is no significant association (difference) between the conditions (the age of the participants and their ability to discriminate between the media used), any relationship which occurs will be due to chance.

(b) What is an independent variable? (1 mark)

Illustrative answer: The one which is deliberately manipulated/controlled by the experimenter to create a difference between the experimental and control conditions.

(c) What is a dependent variable? (1 mark)

Illustrative answer: The variable which is measured in order to assess the effect of the IV.

(d) What was the dependent variable in the above study? (1 mark)

Illustrative answer: The participant's identification of the media (record/cassette/CD).

(e) Identify the target population in the above study. (1 mark)

Illustrative answer: The total readership of the newspaper for that particular issue.

(f) Identify the sample in the above study. (1 mark)

Illustrative answer: The people who responded to the advertisement, a self-selected sample of 218 people.

(g) What is meant by the term 'pilot study'? (1 mark)

Illustrative answer: A preliminary, usually smaller-scale study prior to the main study.

(h) Give two reasons why a pilot study was used here. (2 marks)

Illustrative answer: For example to try out standardised instructions and procedures, becoming familiar with the techniques to be used, testing scoring procedures, determining whether any changes need to be made.

(i) Identify one possible uncontrolled variable in the study and describe the effect it may have had. (3 marks)

Tutorial note: 1 mark for naming the possible effect plus 1 mark for explaining how this would be important, another mark if this description is detailed.

Illustrative answer: For example, the fact that the sample were volunteers, no means of assessing hearing ability, no control of participants' familiarity with the different media, no control for variations in the music played to each participant. In each case the main problem is that such effects would be systematic rather than randomly distributed between the age groups, for example older persons might well have poorer hearing or have a preference for classical rather than rock music.

(j) Describe how you would have dealt with this uncontrolled variable. (3 marks)

Tutorial note: The answer to this is entirely dependent on the previous answer; 1 mark for a common-sense solution, full marks for an answer which shows an awareness of 'good practice'.

Illustrative answer: For example, give all participants a hearing test and eliminate any whose hearing is worse than the set standard to ensure equivalence between groups.

(k) Give two reasons why a chi-squared test was used to analyse the results of the above study. (2 marks)

Illustrative answer: For example, nominal data, independent samples (not related), association required, the expected frequencies were high enough (any two).

(l) What is meant in Table 2 by the phrase 'significance level'? (2 marks)

Illustrative answer: The probability that the results can be attributed to chance factors or random error rather than the IV. ('The level of probability' would be given 1 mark)

(m) Explain whether the null hypothesis would be retained or rejected. (3 marks)

Illustrative answer: The null hypothesis would be rejected at the 5% level (1 mark) because the observed value of chi-squared is 4.47 (1 mark) which is greater than the critical value of 3.84. (1 mark) (An alternative answer is to accept the null hypothesis at the 1% level because the critical value for this is 6.64.)

[NB two questions omitted because no longer on the syllabus]

Question bank

Allow 15 minutes for each question.

1 (a) Give **two** ways in which the laboratory experiment and the natural experiment could be considered different. (2 marks)
  (b) State **two** limitations of conclusions that might be drawn from natural experiments. (2 marks)
  (c) What is meant by *naturalistic observation*? (1 mark)
  (d) Briefly outline the main factors that a researcher must consider when choosing to use the naturalistic observation technique. (3 marks)

(AEB specimen)

Points: Use the marks for each question to guide you in the detail required for the answer. The questions are fairly specific about what is required ('state two' or 'briefly outline').

2 A team of psychologists decides to investigate human responses to emergency situations. They feel that the most suitable means of doing this will be a field study where each member of the team observes what people do when a pedestrian drops all her books.
(a) Write down an unambiguous hypothesis for this research. (1 mark)
(b) The dependent variable is the behaviour exhibited by members of the public. How might this variable be operationalised? (2 marks).
(c) Describe one extraneous variable and how it might be controlled. (2 marks)
(d) Explain how you might maximise reliability in this study. (3 marks)

Points: In part (b) you would receive 1 mark only for saying 'help collect books', for full marks you need to provide some further details such as a time factor.

3 A psychologist wished to find out whether intelligence increases during adolescence. The psychologist sampled 200 12-year-olds, with equal numbers of males and females. Each male and female was given a standardised intelligence test. The same adolescents were retested at ages 14, 16 and 18 years. The psychologist recorded the raw score from the intelligence test for each adolescent. The mean scores for the adolescents at the different ages are shown in the table below.

Table 1 *Mean scores for adolescents at different ages.*

Age in Years	12	14	16	18
Mean Test Score	108	120	136	137

A number of statistical tests were carried out and significant differences were found between test scores of the 12- and 14-year-old age groups. No significant difference was found between the 16- and 18-year-old age groups.

(NEAB module PS02 Summer 1996)

(a) State the null hypothesis for this study. (2 marks)
(b) What are the raw data in this study? (1 mark)
(c) (i) What statistical test might the psychologist have used to investigate the difference between intelligence test scores at the ages of 12- and 14-year-olds? Justify your answer. (4 marks)
  (ii) What level of significance should the psychologist use? Justify your answer. (3 marks)
  (iii) Having calculated a value for the test identified in (c) (i) above, how would the psychologist determine whether or not a significant difference exists? (2 marks)
(d) Name and briefly describe a test of intelligence that might have been used in this study. (4 marks)
(e) (i) The psychologist decided to use a different, but equivalent form, of the intelligence test at each age. Why do you think the psychologist did this? (2 marks)
  (ii) How might you show that different forms of an intelligence test are equivalent? (2 marks)
(f) Identify **three** variables the psychologist might need to control when **selecting** the sample of 200 12-year-olds. Explain your choice. (6 marks)
(g) The study carried out is a longitudinal study. Discuss **one** advantage and **one** disadvantage of this type of research method. (4 marks)

Points: It is important to attempt an answer for each part of the question, even if you are not sure of the correct response, because otherwise valuable marks are lost.

APPLIED AND CONTEMPORARY PSYCHOLOGY

Units in this chapter

Chapter overview

Applied psychology is the use of psychological research in everyday settings, for the benefit of humankind. Such information may be derived specifically for certain applications (as in the Applied Psychology Unit at Cambridge or a market research company) or may be drawn from academic research. Everyday uses of psychological data appear throughout this book. However, there are some specialist applications which are examined in this chapter.

9.1 CONTEMPORARY TOPICS IN PSYCHOLOGY

9.1.1 SUBSTANCE USE AND ABUSE

The main characteristics are:

- Improper use of substances over a prolonged period (misuse).
- Impaired psychosocial functioning (abuse).
- Psychological or physiological adaptation to the drug (addiction).

Why are some substances addictive?

❶ *Characteristics of physical dependence*

- *Tolerance or habituation.* The body increasingly adapts to the substance and needs larger doses to achieve the same effect. These increases eventually level off.
- *Withdrawal.* When the substance is discontinued the person may experience symptoms such as anxiety, craving, hallucinations, nausea and headache.

② *Characteristics of psychological dependence*
- *Reinforcing*. **Solomon** (1977) described the addictive cycle: a substance has a pleasurable effect and also has reinforcing properties of tolerance (positive) and withdrawal (negative).
- Many *activities* being centred around it.

Why do people become abusers?

① *Biological*. The body's response to stress and pain is to produce endorphins, naturally occurring opiates. Therefore the effects of opiates can be biologically explained in terms of tension-reduction. **Banyard** (1996) suggested that another biological explanation may centre on dopamine pathways in the brain, but that addiction is such a personal experience that biological explanations are unlikely to be very helpful.

② *Genetic predisposition*. Alcohol dependence is four times more likely in children whose parents are alcoholic (**Sarafino**, 1990). This is true even when the children have been adopted. **Schuckit** (1985) found that genetically prone problem drinkers may lack the ability to experience the effects of drinking at lower blood concentrations and therefore have less negative feedback.

③ *The addictive personality*. The majority of people who try potentially addictive substances do not go on to become dependent. Dependence has been linked with low social conformity, rebellion and impulsiveness. The problem with any research is that it inevitably draws on existing users, making it difficult to distinguish between factors which may be effects of use from those which may have caused it.

④ *Social and environmental factors*
- *Poor environmental conditions*. Tension and poverty are associated with drugs.
- *Family*. Use tends to run in families, which may be due to modelling.
- *Desirable social image*. **McKennell and Bynner** (1969) found that smoking is associated with being attractive and tough.
- *Context*. Abusers come to associate drug use with certain situations and emotions. **Wikler** (1948) observed that drug-dependent patients experienced withdrawal symptoms if another patient described the settings associated with drug use.
- *Compensation for lack of social stimulation*. **Alexander** *et al.* (1978) kept a group of rats in isolated conditions while a second group had roomy, social conditions. Both were given morphine solution to drink. After they had habituated to the morphine only the isolated rats continued to prefer the morphine solution to water.

Treatments

① *Self-help groups* such as Alcoholics Anonymous, provide social support and an opportunity to make a public statement of intention. This is important in attitude change (see unit 9.3.4). Such techniques are hard to assess because of the anonymity.

② *Psychotherapy*. Group therapy is more cost-effective.

③ *Therapeutic communities* offer expert guidance and close supervision.

④ *Substitution therapy* such as nicotine gum or replacing heroin with methadone, a longer-lasting, oral drug with no euphoric effects. The effectiveness may be due to several factors: the lack of euphoria may break the addiction cycle, and contextual dependency is lessened because methadone is oral and given by doctors. **Callahan** (1980) found methadone therapy was successful as long as addicts were prevented from continuing with other substance abuses.

⑤ *Abstinence-oriented therapy*. Detoxification or quitting 'cold turkey' requires social support and medical supervision. There tends to be a high drop-out rate.

⑥ *Aversion therapy* (see unit 6.4.1). Negative affect is paired with the abused substance to recondition the patient. For example, smoking a lot of cigarettes to cause sickness, using electric shocks, or imagining negative scenes.

⑦ *Self-management strategies*. Methods without the benefit of formal treatment. According to the US Surgeon General, 95% of smokers quit on their own. **Glasgow** *et al.* (1985) found that people stop smoking by using oral substitutes, or rewards for quitting and punishments for backsliding.

⑧ *Cognitive strategies*, such as attribution retraining (see unit 1.1.2) and other therapies (see unit 4.4.1).

⑨ *Models of behavioural change* (see unit 9.3.4).

Prevention

❶ *Availability.* **Townsend** (1993) found that cigarette consumption fell as the price rose, and vice versa.

❷ *Legislation and policing.* Outlawing drugs may prevent some usage but it means that the sources are not regulated thus allowing poor quality substances, spread of diseases like AIDS and association with crime.

❸ *Health promotion campaigns.* **McGuire** (1964) suggested that you can prepare people to resist temptation by giving them a set of strong counterarguments, in the same way that inoculations provide us with antibodies. **McAlister** *et al.* (1980) found that this type of programme used in a high school reduced the likelihood of smoking by half.

9.1.2 PARANORMAL PHENOMENA

Paranormal or *psi-phenomena* are those activities which cannot be explained using known laws and principles. 'Psi' is the hypothetical force underlying such phenomena. *Extrasensory perception* (ESP) includes telepathy, clairvoyance and precognition; perceptions occurring outside any known sensory system.

Empirical studies of paranormal phenomena

❶ *Telepathy.* Information is passed from another person via unknown senses.

Experimental support using forced- or restricted-choice techniques.

- *Zener cards* (**Rhine**, 1934). These have 5 symbols repeated on 25 cards. The experimenter looks at each card and the participant reports what they think the experimenter is seeing. Rhine reported results considerably beyond chance. **Soal and Bateman** (1954) produced highly significant results with a man called Basil Shackleton. It may be better to do research with selected individuals who are known to have paranormal capabilities.
- The *Ganzfeld technique* (**Honorton**, 1974). A receiver is placed in total isolation, ping-pong ball halves taped over their eyes and white noise played through headphones. The sender is also isolated and concentrates on a picture randomly selected from four others. The receiver tries to identify the image. **Honorton** (1985) analysed 28 studies using the Ganzfeld technique and found that 38% of the time participants were able to identify the correct picture. A chance level would be 25%.

Evidence against

- **Marwick** (1978) reanalysed Soal's data and found some numbers had been added (fraud). When these were removed, the results were at chance level.
- Other researchers failed to replicate **Rhine**'s work. Rhine suggested this was due to negative experimenter effects because other investigators were goats (see below).
- **Hyman** (1985) criticised the Ganzfeld work saying the experimental procedures were not rigorous enough and there were problems with the statistical analysis. When he reanalysed the same 28 studies he found that less than half of them had significant results, which might be because some experimenters are sheep and others are goats. **Honorton** (1985) also did a meta-analysis and came up with different results to Hyman, supporting his original conclusions. **Honorton** *et al.* (1990) designed a fully automated project (no experimenter bias) which produced significant results.

❷ *Clairvoyance.* Information comes from distant or hidden objects or events.

- *Remote viewing (free-response methods)* involves an experimenter going to a remote location, then the participant reports any images which arise. Afterwards a judge tries to match images with a set of possible target locations. **Targ and Puthoff** (1977) reported higher than chance findings but **Marks and Kammann** (1980) couldn't replicate this and suggested that the transcripts contained clues about previous targets and this increased the likelihood of a match.

③ *Precognition.* Information comes from the future.

- *Premonition studies.* **Fairley** (in **Blakemore and Hart-Davis**, 1995) studied over 1,000 premonitions and found that many were surprisingly accurate, though they often lacked sufficient detail to be of any use in averting disasters. Some individuals were particularly accurate but not when they were tested more rigorously in a laboratory.

  Evaluation. It is likely that people have many premonitions but it is only those which are confirmed by subsequent events which are remembered.

④ *Psychokinesis* (PK). A person influences a physical event without direct intervention.

- *Macro-PK* (moving objects). **Weil** (1974) was at first convinced by Uri Keller's ability to bend spoons until James Randi, a magician, demonstrated the same feats and showed Weil how they were done. Weil concluded that what we perceive is not the same as what is real; our beliefs and perceptions alter what we perceive.

- *Micro-PK* (changing probabilistic or microscopic systems). **Rhine** (1947) used a dice-throwing machine to try to demonstrate the power of the mind over random events, with some success. **Schmidt** (1970) devised the equivalent of an electronic coin-tossing task. He asked participants to watch a circle of nine lamps. Whenever a lamp lit up, they had to try to make it move either clockwise or anti-clockwise. The lamps used a strontium-90 radioactive source emitting particles at random intervals so that movement was caused by microscopic changes. Some participants appeared able to influence the subatomic processes. **Schmidt** (1976) was also successful with another task, where a radioactive source generated random numbers which were converted into clicks on an audio-tape. Participants were able to influence the clicks, for example making them preponderantly strong or weak, even when the tapes had been made some time in advance.

  Evaluation. Other PK researchers have not replicated Schmidt's findings.

Explanations of paranormal phenomena

① *They are real* and represent a special state of consciousness, at a preconscious level. It may be that such phenomena are not susceptible to scientific research and we need to discover other techniques to prove their validity.

② *Participant and experimenter bias.* Experimental results are not due to real phenomena, belief is a critical factor in performance. **Schmeidler and McConnell** (1958) found that believers in psi-phenomena (sheep) consistently scored higher than non-believers (goats). Non-believers often scored significantly below chance (*psi-missing*). Experimenters will influence participants positively or negatively depending on whether they are sheep or goats respectively. It is difficult to say which might come first, belief or experience, but in either case the self-fulfilling prophecy would predict this cycle will be self-perpetuating.

③ *Cognitive illusions.* **Blackmore** (1992) has explained psi-phenomena as a form of cognitive illusion – we are used to things having explanations and seek to provide one. At least 'sheep' do, 'goats' accept that some things are simply random coincidences and are not caused by anything. **Brugger** *et al.* (1990) found that goats were better at generating random numbers than sheep (they gave more consecutive repetitions of the same digit), i.e. they cope with random occurrences better.

④ *Publication bias.* There is a tendency for positive paranormal research to be published whereas studies which report no significance are rejected. This misrepresents the actual research which has taken place and produces a bias in favour of the existence of psi-phenomena. However, **Honorton and Ferrari** (1989) looked at over 300 forced-choice studies, and found a small but significant effect. They say this couldn't be due to selective reporting because, they calculated, there would have to be 46 unpublished studies to reduce the significance effect.

9.2 PSYCHOLOGY AND ORGANISATIONS

9.2.1 MOTIVATION AND JOB SATISFACTION

Motivation in the workplace

Motivation is the force that energises, directs and sustains behaviour (see unit 3.4.1).

❶ *Extrinsic motivation.* Doing work for external rewards. **Taylor** (1916) proposed the Theory of Scientific Management. He believed that money was the prime motivator (as well as suggesting that jobs and people must be designed to fit each other).

Evaluation

- This presumes that workers are rational. **Warr** (1982) found that approximately 30% of people would continue working even if it were not financially necessary.
- Extrinsic motivation may decrease intrinsic motivation (see unit 6.3.1), so pay might even decrease productivity.

❷ *Needs theories: intrinsic motivation.* Doing work for its own sake. Examples include the Protestant work ethic, voluntary work.

- *Levels of need.* **Maslow** (see unit 3.4.1) proposed that workers first need to satisfy lower levels of need such as food and security (both obtained with money), and then they can address higher, intrinsic needs such as esteem and self-actualisation.
- *ERG theory.* **Alderfer** (1972) suggested three types of needs: existence needs (physiological and safety), relatedness needs (social interactions) and growth needs (individual development and achievement of potential). These are not necessarily hierarchical.
- *Achievement.* **McClelland** (1961) suggested that people vary in terms of their desire for achievement, power and affiliation. This may be related to occupational choice in the first place. People high in the need to achieve (nAch) choose risky, entrepreneurial professions. This theory may be male biased. **McClelland and Boyatzis** (1982) found that people in managerial positions did have a high need for power, and that those with a high need for affiliation do best in teamwork situations

Evaluation

- These theories suggest that jobs need to fit people rather than vice versa.
- This approach may ultimately be too expensive.

❸ *Reinforcement theory.* The behavioural model of operant conditioning (see unit 2.4.1) suggests that organisations should reward and thus increase desirable behaviours (such as high productivity or ideas) and punish, and thus reduce, undesirable behaviours (lateness and absenteeism), as a means of motivating the workforce.

Evaluation. Conditioning theory is based on work with animals and may not satisfactorily explain human behaviour. It is a reductionist and deterministic account of human behaviour.

❹ *Job design theories.* People may want to work more if their job is well-designed, enlarged or reorganised. For example:

- *Job characteristics*: **Hackman and Oldham** (1976) proposed three dimensions for satisfaction: the job should have meaning and variety (job characteristics), individuals should be given greater sense of responsibility (autonomy) and they should have feedback about the results of their work.
- *Job enrichment.* A motivational programme which redesigns jobs so that workers have a greater role in the planning, doing and evaluating of their jobs. **Janson** (1971) found that typists improved their production rates when they were asked to correct their own mistakes, this is less true for manual workers.

Evaluation. The failure of such programmes may be due to poor implementation.

❺ *Equity theories.* Equity can be achieved by (1) everyone being paid equally; (2) those who are skilled or in higher levels of an organisation being paid more; (3) those who do boring unpopular jobs being paid more because others have intrinsic rewards.

- **Adams** (1965) suggested that workers are motivated to reduce perceived inequities between work inputs (experience, education, effort) and outputs (pay, fringe benefits, status, interest).
- **Vroom** (1964) proposed *VIE theory*: valence (desirability of outcome), instrumentality (likelihood of receiving the benefit) and expectancy (relationship between effort and achievement). Workers weigh the expected costs and benefits before they are motivated to take action.

    Evaluation. This again assumes that people behave rationally. **Argyle** (1989) reported that there are good correlations between instrumentality and productivity, but generally research indicates that workers don't seek rewards in a simple, rational way, such as both theories suggest.

⑥ *Goal-setting theory.* **Locke** (1968) investigated the specific parameters which might motivate workers to achieve certain goals. Goals should be specific, quantified, achievable and set by workers. Pressure to achieve them should not be too great.

- *Incentive schemes*, such as individual piecework, workers are paid in relation to productivity rates rather than time. **Guzzo** *et al.* (1985) found that incentives were more successful than other strategies in a meta-analysis of 13 studies.
- *Group piecework* encourages co-operation and reduces conflicts. However, piecework makes increased quantity but not quality.

Evaluation

- The model assumes that goals are simple and not conflicting, which may not be true.
- It is hard to study the effect of incentives alone since they are usually accompanied by a number of other changes.
- **Hollenbeck** *et al.* (1989) didn't find that students performed better when they set their own goals, except if they were high achievers.

⑦ *Organisational commitment.* Loyalty to the organisation can increase motivation, for example through employee ownership, profit-sharing, benefits and social activities. In the *Japanese organisational style* motivation is aroused by a sense of responsibility to the employer and work group and a total commitment to productivity rather than job satisfaction. This is linked with a cultural tradition of duty and the family.

Job satisfaction

Satisfaction leads to personal well-being and dissatisfaction decreases the desire to work.

① *Causes of satisfaction*

- *The job.* Boredom can be reduced and satisfaction increased when jobs are rotated, modified or enriched, as described above.
- *Fit* between the worker and their job. **Carlson** (1966) found that workers who had a large mismatch between their abilities and the requirements of the job, didn't get satisfaction from the job. This may be because satisfaction only comes from doing something that you feel is appropriate to your self-image.
- *Pay* is more often a matter of dissatisfaction. Satisfaction may be more dependent on relative than absolute pay. Workers may gain greater satisfaction from performance-related bonuses or profit-sharing schemes.
- *Benefits.* Schemes to benefit the employee aside from direct pay, such as medical insurance, pension schemes, childcare.
- *Work relationships.* Smaller workgroups experience more satisfaction. Satisfaction decreases in conditions where opportunities for interaction are reduced such as a noisy factory. Social interactions provide emotional support.
- *Work environment.* Clean, quiet conditions are more pleasant for work.
- *Industrial democracy.* Increased participation tends to lead to greater satisfaction, though **Wall and Lischeron** (1977) found this was not true for all workers, for example nurses had a low desire to take part in decisions.
- *Organisational structure*, such as size, fewer levels of hierarchy, participation, constructive supervision, praise, encouragement and pleasant social atmosphere.

- *Individual differences.* The fit between the person (personality, knowledge, skills) and the job.
- *Leadership style* (see 1.3.2).
- Also: job security, organisational communication, status, promotion prospects.

② *Effects of job satisfaction.* It is difficult to ascertain whether certain features are actually causes or effects of job satisfaction. **Hayward** (1966) reported a low correlation between satisfaction and performance, indicating that performance is influenced by a wealth of factors.

- *Productivity.* **Petty** *et al.* (1984) found correlations between job satisfaction and productivity of 0.31 for higher levels of workers and 0.15 for lower ones.
- *Physical and mental health.* **Cooper and Marshall** (1976) suggested that certain aspects of work, such as performing boring tasks and conflicts with other personnel, may be intervening variables which decrease both job satisfaction and health.
- *Life satisfaction.* Work is still a major part of most people's lives and self-concept.
- *Voluntary absenteeism.* It is hard to assess absenteeism at the managerial level because the hours of work are variable.
- *Involuntary staff turnover.* Probably less a function of job satisfaction than of organisational commitment.

③ *Theories of job satisfaction*

- *Two-factor theory of satisfaction and dissatisfaction.* **Herzberg** (1966) interviewed 200 professionals and found that motivators (e.g. responsibility, recognition and achievement) lead to satisfaction, whereas hygienes (e.g. benefits, pay levels, working conditions), if absent, lead to dissatisfaction. Both need to be OK.
- *Vitamin model.* **Warr** (1987) suggested that there are some attributes which produce consistently positive effects (like vitamin C or money) and there are other factors which are toxic when excess (like vitamin A or interpersonal contact). We need minimum daily amounts of good vitamins and limited amounts of the toxic ones.
- *Need-satisfaction.* A congruence between needs and rewards leads to satisfaction. **Hackman and Oldham** (1976) found that not everyone wants a demanding job.
- *Social information processing.* **Salancik and Pfeffer** (1977) suggested that certain social perceptions (e.g. comparisons with others, affiliation with co-workers, group norms and organisational climate) led to satisfaction. **Thomas and Griffin** (1983) manipulated social cues and found that job satisfaction increased as predicted.

9.2.2 PERSONNEL SELECTION

The cost to the organisation of employing the wrong person in a job is high, therefore much energy is devoted to personnel selection – finding the right person for the right job.

① *Job analysis.* The systematic study of the tasks involved in and the qualities needed to perform a job. Job analysis includes wage evaluation and performance criteria for assessment. One tool for writing a job description is the Position Analysis Questionnaire (PAQ, **McCormick** *et al.*, 1969), a structured questionnaire to analyse jobs in terms of 187 elements arranged in six categories: information input, mental processes, work output, relationship with other persons, job context and other characteristics.

② *Finding potential applicants* through newspaper advertisements, employment agencies, walk-ins (applicant-initiated). The effectiveness of each varies with the level of the job and being able to reach the 'right' potential applicants (employer-initiated).

③ *Screening applicants.* Collecting appropriate information to determine suitability.

- *Application forms*: standard forms or open-ended. Lower-level positions require less information and the form can be more specific. Weighted forms enable a score to be calculated for each applicant. Research indicates which factors are good predictors of job success and these are given more weight.
- *References and curriculum vitae* are invariably skewed in a positive direction.
- *Peer assessment.* When recruitment is within the organisation, peers can rate or nominate each other.

④ *Selecting the employee.* Generally involves face-to-face methods.

- *Psychometric testing* (a signs approach). IQ, personality and aptitude tests (see unit 7.2.1).
- *Situational exercises* (a samples approach). Applicants are asked to perform tasks that approximate to actual work, such as role playing a management task or leaderless group discussion. **Argyle** (1989) claimed that this technique is good for selecting higher-level workers, with a good correlation with later job performance (validity).
- *Interviews* tend to have low validity because they are conducted haphazardly by inexperienced interviewers with inevitable biases (halo effects, attribution errors, too lenient/severe, racial/sexual/ageist prejudices). Interviewers often do much of the talking and ask different questions of each candidate, which makes it difficult to compare applicants. Interviewees are often nervous and may succeed because they are good at self-presentation and/or intelligent rather than being in possession of job-related skills. The interview method can be improved by: structuring the interview, using a method of scoring/rating the applicant, asking questions which are job related, training the interviewers, using a panel of interviewers who discuss judgements.
- *Multiple 'hurdles'.* At each stage some applicants are rejected, using a combination of tests and interviews, as well as involving different personnel in assessment.

⑤ *Making the decision*

- *Clinical approach.* Subjective judgements which are generally prone to error though better when handled by experienced decision-makers.
- *Statistical decision-making models.* Each piece of information is weighted in relation to its value in predicting future job performance.
- *Assessment centres.* In a large organisation it may be feasible to have an expert department. The costs of such procedures are offset by their greater effectiveness.
- *Legal burden.* In the US the employer has a duty to show that their screening and selection methods are valid indicators of future performance. Any hiring of disproportionate numbers of a 'protected group' (based on the numbers who applied) may be investigated.

9.3 PSYCHOLOGY AND HEALTH

9.3.1 MODELS OF HEALTH PSYCHOLOGY

① *The biomedical model.* When health fails it is a matter of diagnosing the symptoms and applying a treatment. The key features of this model are:

- *Reductionism.* Illness can be reduced to simple processes.
- *Single factor causes.* Each illness has *a* cause rather than a range of contributory factors.
- *Mind–body distinction.* The approach has its roots in Cartesian dualism. Descartes proposed that the mind and body were two separate systems.
- *Illness not health* is the only thing which matters. Therefore prevention is unnecessary.

Evaluation

- This model was more appropriate in the past when most illness was due to single micro-organisms, such as influenza or TB. In recent years, the more common illnesses are heart disease and cancer which are 'caused' by a range of factors and treatment is diffuse.
- The increase in the cost of health care means that greater attention has been given to prevention.
- The concept of health has been broadened to encompass more than just 'not being ill'.

② *The biopsychosocial model.* **Engel** (1980) proposed that psychological and social factors should be considered as well as biological ones.

- A *systems approach* because it is concerned with the interactions between systems from the micro-level (body chemicals) to the macro-level (a person's culture and family). Other systems include the immune system and psychological systems (cognition, emotion).
- A *lifespan approach* because it emphasises how people and illness develop over time.
- A *humanistic and holistic approach* because it focuses on the whole person.

Evaluation. This model acknowledges that illness is multi-causal in origin and that mind and body cannot be separated.

9.3.2 PAIN

The role of pain

- To warn an individual that damage is occurring and a response is necessary.
- To promote learning to avoid harmful situations in the future.
- Some pain serves no useful purpose, chronic pain becomes a problem in itself.

Sensation and perception of pain

1 *Damage with no pain*

- *Congenital analgesia.* Some individuals are born without the ability to feel pain. **Melzack and Wall** (1988) described Miss C. who showed no physiological response to any pain stimuli. She had many health problems as a result.
- *Episodic analgesia.* The sensation of pain does not occur immediately after injury, as when an injured athlete only feels pain when the contest is over. **Melzack *et al.*** (1982) found this was true for 37% of people arriving in US accident departments.

2 *Pain with no damage*

- *Phantom limb pain.* Some amputees report severe pain in the area of the amputated limb even years later (**Melzack**, 1973).
- *Headache and migraine* are not related to any tissue damage nor an apparent cause.
- *Causalgia.* Sensation of severe burning pain in a region of previous injury.

3 *Pain in proportion to damage.* Small scratches which are not life threatening may hurt more than large wounds. Kidney stones are excruciating but not dangerous.

4 *Referred pain.* Pain originating from internal organs is perceived as coming from elsewhere because the internal organs share the same neural pathways with other body parts, the brain misattributes the source. For example, appendicitis is felt in the upper-middle abdomen, whereas the appendix is on the lower right.

5 *The effect of emotion on pain.* Tension acts like a volume control on pain. **Beecher** (1956) found that only 33% of soldiers in battle in the Second World War required morphine, whereas civilians with similar wounds required much higher doses.

6 *Placebo effect.* Placebos may produce endorphins through the expectation of pain relief, mimicking the body's natural response to pain. **Levine *et al.*** (1978) gave volunteers receiving dental surgery a placebo injection either two hours before or two hours after an injection of naloxone, a drug which blocks the production of endorphins. Pain increased when participants received naloxone suggesting that, prior to injection, there were endorphins present which were responsible for pain relief.

Theories of pain

1 *Specificity theory.* There is a separate sensory system for perceiving pain, with specialised receptors and pathways. A stimulus causes the release of *algogenic* substances which activate nerve endings. These transmit messages to the neuronal synapse in the dorsal horns of the spinal cord where *substance P* is released, and then second-order neurons transmit messages to the pain centres in the brain.

Evaluation

- This describes the straightforward relationship between tissue damage and pain, but not the psychological influences which are apparent in the evidence above.

- There is no evidence to support a 'pain area' in the brain.
- Stimulation of nerve endings produces a variety of sensations.

② *Pattern theories.* There is no separate system for pain, pain is felt following any kind of excessive stimulation. **Crue and Carregal** (1975) suggested that the temporal and spatial discharge of peripheral nerve fibres represented codes which led to different sensations.

Evaluation

- Again this cannot account for psychological factors.
- There is evidence of specialised receptor cells: *nociceptive cells* which respond only to pain, cells which respond to intense stimuli (pain and touch), and cells which respond only to touch.

③ *Gate control theory.* **Melzack and Wall** (1982) proposed the existence of a gate which is located at the neuronal synapse in the spinal cord. When the gate is open signals are relayed to the brain. The more 'closed' the gate, the less pain is experienced. Three factors are involved:

- *Activity in pain fibres.* The stronger the stimulus, the more active the pain fibres.
- *Activity in other peripheral fibres* concerned with mild stimuli cause activity in A–beta fibres which tends to close the gate and decrease the sensation of pain. This explains why gentle rubbing may reduce pain.
- *Messages that descend from the brain.* Some higher cognitive activity, such as anxiety, may have a general effect on closing the gate through endorphin action. Other mental activity may affect specific parts of the body. This aspect explains how hypnotism may affect the sensation of pain (see unit 3.3.4).

Conditions which open the gate:

- Physical: amount of activity in nerve fibres (specificity theory).
- Psychological: increased tension, thinking about the pain, boredom.

Conditions which close the gate:

- Physical: counterstimulation, medication.
- Psychological: relaxation, distraction, involvement in other activities.

Evaluation

- This account combines physiological and psychological factors.
- It explains many aspects of pain experience, such as why you may not feel any pain when you hit your finger with a hammer while working.
- It has stimulated a great deal of research, much but not all of it supportive.

④ *Cognitive models* particularly try to explain the behaviour of chronic pain sufferers.

- *'Fear of pain' model.* **Lethem** *et al.* (1983) suggested that people are either avoidant or confrontational in response to pain. Avoidant responses lead to an avoidance spiral: the more you don't do something the greater the avoidance response. A person who injures their leg and finds exercise difficult may give up exercise, in which case the next time they try to exercise the pain will be worse and their inactivity will be reinforced. Another person might be determined to persist and therefore their pain will decrease, positively reinforcing their actions.
- *Beliefs about pain.* **Philips and Jahanshahi** (1986) suggested that beliefs rather than the actual pain can best predict an individual's future behaviour. **Kent** (1985) found that anxious dental patients estimated pain as more severe three months after treatment than they had immediately after treatment.

Controlling pain

① *Chemicals* such as peripherally acting analgesics (e.g. aspirin), centrally acting analgesics (e.g. morphine), local anaesthetics (e.g. novacaine) and depressants (e.g. sedatives). Such methods are used extensively but they are not useful for chronic pain because of addiction problems and side-effects.

② *Physical therapies* aim to:
- *Decrease tension* which usually exaggerates pain, for example relaxation, massage.
- *Increase suppleness*, for example exercise or hot compress.
- *Counterstimulate*, for example TENS (transcutaneous electrical nerve stimulation), used by women in labour, leads to release of endorphins. **Goldstein** (1980) suggested that listening to exciting music can reduce pain in this way.
- *Remove the source*, as in surgery.

③ *Cognitive methods* aim to alter the way the person views the pain in terms of cognitions (beliefs, expectations).
- *Increasing sense of control.* **Wernick** (1983) worked with severe burn patients and found that enhancing their sense of control led to their spontaneous decision to reduce medication. **Girodo and Wood** (1979) trained participants to cope with the cold pressor task by making positive self-statements ('I can cope'). One group of participants additionally were given explanations as to why this method works (enhancing their sense of personal control) and they experienced less pain.
- *Attention diversion* works for brief episodes, for example looking at a nice picture or singing a song. **Turk** *et al.* (1983) reported that this is successful if it fully engages the person and when the pain is mild or moderate. **Cogan** *et al.* (1987) found that participants tolerated 50% more pain when in a laughter group (listening to a recording of Lily Tomlin) or relaxation group than in a narrative condition (a educational lecture) or control group.
- *Pain redefinition*, for example 'it hurts but it's good for you'. **Basler and Rehfisch** (1990) trained patients with chronic pain to reinterpret their pain experience, avoid negative thinking and use distraction at key times. These patients reported less pain and visited the doctor less than a control group.

④ *Insight therapies* aim to change how the whole person feels as well as thinks. A chronic pain sufferer often becomes depressed, embedded in the sick role (see unit 4.1.2). Counselling (unit 4.4.1) or group therapy may help.

⑤ *Behaviour therapy* (see unit 4.4.1). Setting goals and using operant conditioning to reverse the initial, non-adaptive learning between pain and aversive stimulus. Works best when pain behaviours are ignored and health behaviour is rewarded, otherwise attention only serves to reinforce pain behaviours. Biofeedback is also an example (see unit 3.4.4).

⑥ *Hypnosis* is related to relaxation and endorphin blocking (see unit 3.3.4).

9.3.3 PSYCHOLOGICAL ASPECTS OF ILLNESS

The patient–practitioner relationship

① *Kinds of relationship.* Szasz and Hollander (1956) suggested:
- *Activity–passivity*. An active doctor treats a passive patient. This works well when the patient is truly passive but otherwise implies an authority structure. Authority may create stress with disastrous consequences. **Jarvinaan** (1955) found that patients in coronary intensive care units were most likely to relapse or have a fatal heart attack 10 minutes before doctors were due to start their rounds.
- *Guidance–co-operation*. An expert doctor expects a willing patient to follow advice, which implies that a patient has a duty to doctor rather than vice versa. This relationship works for acute illness.
- *Mutual participation*: preferred by patients but rare. **Geersten** *et al.* (1973) found that patients were more willing to follow the advice of doctors who had a more personal approach.

② *The contribution of the relationship to healing.* Patients respond to social treatment as well as medical treatment. Faith in the doctor may have some curative effect, in the same way that expectations influence all our behaviour (see unit 6.3.3). Positive relationships may help patient–practioner contact in other ways, for example **DiMatteo** *et al.* (1986) found that patients were more likely to keep appointments with doctors who were rated as more sensitive to others' emotions.

③ *Communication*
- *Encoding* (conveying what you mean). The doctor has to translate expert, technical knowledge into lay terms. Patients may ask for information but really they want reassurance. **Linn and DiMatteo** (1983) found that patients preferred to have a reassuring communication than a humorous one. Patients have simple models of illness, and find it difficult to comprehend that there is no simple answer. **Boyd** *et al.* (1974) found that 60% of patients appeared to have misunderstood their doctor's instructions when interviewed immediately after leaving the consultation.
- *Decoding* (understanding what the other person means). Doctors should use some open-ended questions. **Stone** (1979) found that patients preferred doctors with an attentive listening style. This helps uncover useful information which may aid diagnosis. Non-verbal behaviours also give indications of what is wrong or what the patient is feeling. **Hays and DiMatteo** (1984) found that patients regulate the distance between themselves and the doctor as a function of their fear and distrust.

④ *Individual differences*
- *In doctors.* **Byrne and Long** (1974) analysed 2,500 medical consultations in many different countries and classed doctors as doctor-centred (brief, closed questions focusing on the initial problem mentioned) or patient-centred (open-ended questions and involvement of the patient in decision-making).
- *In patients.* The relationship may break down when a patient is overly critical, ignores what the doctor is saying, insists on tests or diagnoses which the doctor thinks are unnecessary or wrong, or makes sexually suggestive remarks.

⑤ *Teaching doctors better 'bedside manner'.* **Orth** *et al.* (1987) found that they could improve blood pressure in hypertensive patients by training doctors better in their ability to elicit and explain symptoms.
- *Non-verbal behaviours.* Doctors should avoid non-verbal leakage (see unit 3.4.2) which might indicate prejudices. **Milmoe** *et al.* (1967) found a negative correlation between the amount of anger in a doctor's voice and his/her success at referring alcoholics for treatment. **Duck** (1992) listed touch, open-arm position, eye contact, smiles and nods as correlated with increased positive impressions from the patient.
- *Non-medical needs* should be anticipated and dealt with. **Lau** *et al.* (1982) found that patients were more satisfied when their doctor specifically addressed psychosocial aspects of their illness rather than just medical ones.
- *Improve communication.* Doctors should use an informal, chatty style as in normal conversation.

Reasons for failure to comply with medical requests

① *Learning theory* suggests that the reason is that punishment is usually delayed (e.g. lung cancer).

② *Failure to remember* or misunderstanding information, for example, what the doctor advises or the correct dosage. **Ley** (1988) estimated that patients forget 44% of what they are told. This can be alleviated by the use of written information and community care by nurses (see research by **Ley** in unit 5.3.5).

③ *Unpleasant side-effects.* A person may consciously or unconsciously avoid or quit a treatment because of the side-effects.

④ *The seriousness of the illness.* A more serious illness may make it more likely that someone will take advice. On the other hand, a person may repress advice as a means of coping.

⑤ *Patient–practitioner relationship* (see above). A practitioner may fail to communicate information helpfully. Doctors often assume that their advice will be followed but patients take active decisions.

⑥ *Personal beliefs.* The particular orientation of a practitioner may not agree with the individual's own attitudes. For example, Scientologists refuse any medical intervention on principle. Some people support homeopathic methods or common-sense approaches.

⑦ *Individual differences.* Some patients (women and older people) are more compliant.

⑧ *Lifestyle.* Compliance is reduced when treatment interferes with a patient's lifestyle (see unit 9.3.4).

⑨ *Overcoming failure.* **Banyard** (1996) suggested that these problems may be overcome by:

- *Feedback*, reports of health improvement encourage further compliance.
- *Self-monitoring*, patients should record their own diet or blood glucose levels.
- *Tailoring the regime*, treatment should fit the habits and lifestyle of the patient.
- *Prompts and reminders*, ways of remembering when to take medicine.
- *Contingency contract*, making a contract between patient and health worker setting out goals and rewards.
- *Modelling*, imitating the behaviour of other successful patients.

The role of psychological factors in physical illness

Models of health behaviour (see unit 9.3.4) can be used to explain the actions taken by people with chronic illnesses.

① *Diabetes*

- *Frequency.* Diabetes affects about 5% of the population with most cases appearing after childhood.
- *Cause.* It occurs when the pancreas stops producing sufficient insulin. This results in too much glucose in the blood which ultimately will cause death. The kind of diabetes that appears in childhood is usually of the insulin-dependent kind. It is possible that complete loss of insulin production may be caused by virus infections of pancreas cells which, in susceptible individuals, leads to a loss of these cells. Less severe forms of diabetes may occur when genetically vulnerable individuals overeat.
- *Treatment.* Daily injections of insulin, glucose monitoring and a carefully regulated diet are necessary in insulin-dependent diabetes. In non-insulin-dependent diabetes, the pancreas is usually still able to produce some insulin and it is therefore possible regulate the condition through dietary control.
- *Psychological factors.* Diabetes requires major changes to a person's lifestyle and considerable psychological readjustment. There are often problems with non-compliance due to, for example, a denial reaction to the disease and embarrassment about testing and injecting. **Wing** *et al.* (1986) found that 80% administered their injections unhygenically, 77% tested their urine inaccurately and 75% did not eat the proscribed diet. See also 'Coping with disability', unit 4.1.2.

② *Asthma*

- *Frequency.* About 1 in 7 children are affected, especially boys, and 1 in 20 adults. In most cases asthma appears before the age of 5 and the symptoms will disappear by the time the child reaches adulthood.
- *Cause*: an allergic reaction to, for example, pollen, dust, soap powders, and specific foods. The tendency to develop asthma appears to be passed on by a cluster of genes that are associated with eczema and hay fever; all of which are allergic reactions. Attacks may be aggravated by infections, weather, exercise, pollution, smoking (active or passive) or psychosocial factors such as stress.
- *Symptoms*: difficulty with breathing, which can be very frightening and is, in fact, life threatening. In the UK 2,000 asthmatics die every year.
- *Treatment* involves learning behavioural techniques and counselling to help the patient understand what causes the problem and how to relax during an attack. Sufferers are also given inhalers which dilate the bronchia and help breathing, or are given inhaled steroids which reduce the inflammation in the lungs.
- *Psychological factors*, such as stress and expectations, influence the severity of attacks. Psychological techniques are useful in coping with attacks.

③ *Coronary heart disease and cancer.* See studies by **Friedman and Rosenhan** and **Morris** *et al.*, unit 3.4.3.

9.3.4 LIFESTYLES AND HEALTH

Aspects of lifestyles

Lifestyle is the pattern of behaviours which are associated with a person's habits, home, job, socioeconomic class and culture.

① *Smoking* is associated with chronic heart disease (CHD), cancer, stroke, and generally more infections particularly respiratory ones. It may affect non-smokers as well through passive smoking. **Russell** *et al.* (1986) found that the nicotine concentrations in the urine of non-smokers was 0.7% that of smokers, and therefore estimated that 1,000 non-smokers may die per year in the UK of smoking-related diseases. This affects people who frequent smoky environments and also the children of smokers, who are more likely to have increased respiratory infections.

② *Alcohol.* Prolonged use may lead to cancer, liver cirrhosis, brain damage (Korsakoff's syndrome), and foetal alcohol syndrome in the foetuses of pregnant women. Excessive bouts of drinking are related to injuries which are both accidental (e.g. drunk driving) and non-accidental (e.g. wife beating). **Smith and Kraus** (1988) found that accidents of various types, such as unintentionally firing a gun or a boating mishap, are related to drinking. **Press** (1987) recorded that over 50% of fatal car accidents involve drunk driving.

There is the possibility that moderate drinking may be beneficial or related to healthy lifestyles. For example, **Friedman and Kimball** (1986) found a positive correlation between moderate drinking and lower illness rates.

③ *Substance abuse* (see unit 9.1.1) is associated with accidents, foetal harm, overdoses, and illness because of shared needles (e.g. AIDS and hepatitis).

④ *Stress* is related to illness (see unit 3.4.3) and accidental injury. A person's job or living conditions may create stress.

⑤ *Diet.* In the last 30 years much attention has been paid to the association of certain dietary risk factors and outcomes. For example, knowledge about:
- Cholesterol and hardened arteries, has led people to eat foods low in saturated fats.
- Salt and hypertension, has led Americans to reduce their salt intake drastically to the point where they were not getting enough salt.
- Carbohydrate and excess weight is associated with CHD. An obsession with dieting has led to other problems such as bulimia (see unit 4.3.4).
- Fibre and colon cancer.

⑥ *Exercise.* **Paffenbarger** *et al.* (1986) followed nearly 17,000 Harvard graduates for a period of 12 years and found that mortality rates were significantly lower among those who were physically active, regardless of hypertension, smoking or weight.

⑦ *Unhealthy living* is related to poor health, such as infrequent medical checks, unsafe practices (e.g. driving too fast and without seatbelt), risk-taking (e.g. dangerous sports) and exposure to the sun. **Belloc and Breslow** (1965) measured illness (in terms of lack of work absence) and good health practices (in terms of amount of daily sleep, eating breakfast, little eating between meals, being near correct weight, never smoking, little alcohol intake and regular physical exercise). They found a clear positive correlation.

⑧ *Social relations.* Friends reduce illness (see unit 3.4.3) and marriage has been related to better health (see unit 1.2.4).

Models of health behaviour

① *Reasoned action theory.* **Ajzen and Fishbein** (1980) suggested that a behavioural intention is determined by (1) perceived facts and (2) social norms. For example, smoking behaviour might be determined by 'smoking causes cancer' (a perceived fact) and 'my parents smoke' (a social norm) therefore 'I won't be so foolish' (an intention) which leads to refusing a cigarette.

Evaluation
- This suggests a direct link between thoughts and behaviour, however empirical evidence doesn't support this (see unit 1.1.3).

- The model is limited to the effect of attitudes and social norms on behaviour.
- The model assumes that people behave rationally whereas this is not always true (see unit 5.4.3).
- **Ajzen** (1988) modified this model to produce *the theory of planned behaviour*, this includes the influence of perceived control.

➋ *Health belief model.* **Becker and Rosenstock** (1984) suggested that a person's behaviour can be predicted from three groups of sociocognitive factors:

- *Perceived threat* of disease X. We evaluate the perceived seriousness of the disease and our own perceived susceptibility. Cues to action (e.g. article in newspaper, reminder from dentist) will finally influence if we act.
- *Perceived benefits and barriers*, such as financial or situational ones.
- *Personal variables.* Demographic (age, sex, race) and sociopsychological factors (personality, class) influence both of the above.

   Abraham *et al.* (1992) found that perceived costs were the most important factor in Scottish teenagers' decision to use condoms, as opposed to perceived seriousness, susceptibility and effectiveness. A review of studies by **Haynes** *et al.* (1979) found a link between compliance and perceived vulnerability, severity of illness and costs/benefits. More evidence is included in the illustrative essay at the end of the chapter.

Evaluation

- This model has been used with some success and has been useful in generating research and designing questionnaires.
- It is difficult to measure some of the variables in the model such as perceived susceptibility.
- This model again assumes that human thought is always rational and that intentions and behaviour are linked.
- The model suggests that health campaigns should concentrate on perceived costs.

Changing health behaviour

➊ *Learning theory and cognitive-behavioural strategies*

- Offering financial incentives.
- Teaching self-control. **Farquhar** *et al.* (1977) assessed a programme to reduce cardiovascular disease through changes in smoking, diet and exercise over a 3-year period. Participants who received face-to-face instruction in self-control plus a mass media campaign did better and the effects were longer lasting than those who only heard the propaganda.

➋ *Self-efficacy theory.* **Bandura** (1977) proposed that the belief in your own competence (self-efficacy) will influence the effort you put into, for example, changing your lifestyle. Judgements of self-efficacy may be derived from:

- Observations of own achievement.
- Observations of the performance of others encourage one to try oneself.
- Emotional state, feelings of anxiety lead to low self-efficacy.

   Wulfert and Wan (1993) found that the best predictor of condom use among college students was whether they felt it didn't interfere with good sex, i.e. high self-efficacy. This suggests that just knowing the health risks is not enough to change behaviour.

➌ *Appeals to fear.* **Sutton** (1982) reviewed 35 studies and found that increases in fear were consistently associated with changes in intention or behaviour in the direction of the fear-arousing message.

   However, **Jepson and Chaiken** (1990) found that emotional tension interfered with the ability to systematically process information. **Janis and Feshbach** (1953) gave participants one of three talks about tooth decay: (1) strong fear appeal, emphasising painful consequences, (2) moderate fear appeal, describing the dangers less dramatically and (3) minimal fear appeal which discussed cavities but not the consequences. Participants in group (1) were most worried but ultimately showed the least change in their behaviour.

④ *The Yale model of communication.* **Hovland** *et al.* (1953) proposed that persuasive messages have certain key features (see also 'Advertising', unit 7.2.1):

- The *source* of the message should be credible.
- The *argument* should be one-sided unless the audience is not sympathetic to the message, in which case a two-sided message is best.
- *Conclusions* should be stated rather than being left to the individual to work out.
- The *message* should be short, clear and direct. It should be vivid and not full of technical terms.
- The person should *actively* participate in receiving the message if possible.

⑤ *The spiral model of behavioural change.* **Prochaska** *et al.* (1992) proposed a model which explained both professionally- and personally motivated changes in health behaviour:

- *Precontemplation.* The person is unaware of a problem.
- *Contemplation.* The person is thinking about doing something in relation to the problem.
- *Preparation.* The person has decided to take action and may have begun to make some minimal changes.
- *Action.* The person has made changes to their behaviour or environment for a significant period of time (ranging between one day to six months).
- *Maintenance.* Continued action for more than six months.

The model is a spiral because people are usually not successful at the first attempt so they have to repeat these steps several times, each time getting further towards action and maintenance. **Prochaska** *et al.* suggested that smokers usually have to make three or four attempts before they reach the maintenance stage.

Evaluation. This model incorporates behaviour as well as attitudes.

9.4 PSYCHOLOGY AND EDUCATION

9.4.1 PROMOTING EFFECTIVE LEARNING

Learning styles

① *Tracking.* Dividing the class into ability or interest groups, and setting appropriate work.

② *Programmed instruction.* Any auto-instructional device which allows the learner to work at their own pace without the help of a teacher. May be computer- or book-based.

- *Linear programs* are based on operant conditioning principles (see unit 2.4.1), a correct response is reinforcing. The material is broken down into frames and the student is asked to make a response. They are given prompts to ensure correct responses and positive feedback. Feedback is immediate which is important for reinforcement. **Kaess and Zeaman** (1960) showed that positive feedback is more effective than negative feedback.
- *Branching programs* use longer frames and multiple choice answers. The route through the program is determined by the student's answers; when errors are made the learner is sent to a sequence of remedial frames and then back to the main branch.

Evaluation. Programmed instruction offers active participation and immediate feedback. These same principles can be applied to teaching.

③ *Individual differences.* **Dunn and Griggs** (1988) pointed out that some students, for example, work best in the mornings and prefer highly structured regimes. If you have a profile of each learner you could tailor the classroom to individual learning style. This is possible on a limited scale.

Attribute-treatment interaction (ATI) involves matching certain personal attributes to teaching styles. For example, highly structured methods have been shown to benefit low ability or anxious students (**LeFrançois**, 1991).

④ *Mastery learning.* **Bloom** (1976) suggested that aptitude should be regarded as a function of speed: there are fast and slow learners rather than more or less able pupils. If work is adapted to each individual's pace, they will ultimately all achieve a similar standard, i.e. given optimal conditions all students achieve mastery of the same material.

- *Formative evaluation.* Learning requires constant evaluation to guide the instruction process.
- *Corrective procedures* are used in conjunction with formative evaluation, such as individualised and peer tutoring, alternative teaching materials and reteaching.
- *Mastery of previously identified objectives* is the ultimate aim rather than summative, end-of-course assessments.
- *Class progression.* The whole class progresses together from one unit to the next. The faster students are given extra enriched work while waiting.
- *No students fail*, everyone gets either an 'A' or an 'I' to mean incomplete.

Evaluation

- This approach increases motivation because of the inherent expectation that all learners will succeed if they work hard enough.
- It provides successful experiences for all learners.

⑤ *Personalised system of instruction* (PSI). **Keller** (1968) further elaborated mastery learning largely for use with college students. A course is broken down into small units, students may take as much time over each unit as necessary and, when they are ready, take a short unit quiz. Immediate feedback tells them whether to proceed to the next unit or revise the previous unit. At the end of the course there is an examination.

   Evaluation. **Bangert** *et al.* (1983) reviewed 51 studies of individualised learning and concluded that success was modest but, considering the effort involved, not significantly better than other methods. The learning experience may be more rewarding.

⑥ *Discovery learning* (see unit 6.2.2).

Teaching styles

A teaching style is an identifiable and related group of teaching activities. A teacher's style is derived from their personality, personal philosophy, books and teacher training.

① *Teacher-centred approaches* (formal, didactic, authoritarian, direct, traditional).

- *Description.* The emphasis is on the group, on assessment, on staying in your seat, on a body of facts conveyed by an expert.
- *Use of extrinsic rewards.* Praise, gold stars, good grades. **Brophy** (1981) suggested that praise should be informative, creditable and not too frequent. Extrinsic rewards may be counterproductive (see unit 6.3.1, **Lepper** *et al.*)
- *Use of punishment.* May be counterproductive in motivating students (see unit 6.3.1). Pupils may habituate, or wish to rebel. Some see it as dehumanising and mechanistic, like training animals. The same principles of conditioning may not be appropriate for humans.
- *Use of assessment and feedback.* It is more likely to be summative, pupils are motivated by the threat of terminal assessment. It is more likely to be extrinsic (supplied by others).
- *Use of power relationships to motivate pupils.* This may alienate some pupils.

② *Pupil-centred approaches* (discovery, indirect, democratic, informal, progressive).

- *Description.* The approach is centred on the pupil's needs and readiness, on group work, on student freedom and self-directed activity, not on assessment.
- *Use of intrinsic rewards.* **Piaget** (see unit 6.2.2) suggested that if students motivate themselves, this makes learning more effective. **Maslow** (see unit 3.4.1) suggested that self-actualisation drives people forward to learn. **White** (see unit 3.4.1) suggested that people have a competence motive so they don't need extrinsic rewards.
- *Use of some punishment.* It is more likely to be authoritative (or inductive) rather than authoritarian (see unit 6.3.1), using reason rather than power.
- *Use of assessment and feedback.* The student should be self-motivated without assessment. Any assessment which is used is more likely to be formative, pupils will be motivated by continual feedback, and intrinsic assessment (i.e. self-assessment).

③ *Comparing effectiveness.* **Flanders** (1970) concluded that most classrooms (two-thirds) arc tcachcr-dirccted.

- Some styles are better in some situations.
- There are many overlaps between the two approaches, e.g. use of praise.
- There are individual differences, some people are better motivated by the teacher-centred approach because they lack self-direction. Others may enter a self-fulfilling cyclc. **Holt** (1964) claimed that traditional teaching methods resulted in some children learning to fail.
- Each approach is related to different aims: the teacher-centred approach emphasises curriculum content whereas the pupil-centred approach is concerned with personal development and self-direction as well as knowledge. **Bennett** (1976) found that formal methods were related to higher academic achievement. **Horwitz** (1976) found that informal methods were associated with higher self-concepts, greater creativity and co-operation.

9.4.2 THE ACHIEVEMENT OF READING

The process of reading is discussed in unit 5.4.2.

Methods of teaching reading

① *The phonic method.* Children are taught phonemes rather than letter 'names' which encourages them to 'sound out' words. There was a vogue in the 1970s for the initial teaching alphabet (ITA) which consisted of a letter for every phoneme. Children used special books and later had to change over to traditional symbols and spelling.

② *The whole word method* ('Look and Say'). At one time this was the universal method and still has to be used for words not susceptible to sounding out, such as ' yacht'. It may be a good starting place. As reading skills progress words are recognised by their overall shape (word templates).

③ *Book schemes.* There are many structured reading programmes available. Once children have progressed enough they can use 'real' books.

Assessment of reading ability

Assessment is through reading tests. They provide a reading age (RA), which can be compared with chronological age to give an indication of progress. A diagnosis of dyslexia is made when there is a developmental lag out of proportion to a child's IQ (see unit 4.1.3).

① *Word lists*, such as the Burt Word Reading Test. Children are asked to read a set of 50 words which become progressively more difficult. RA is derived from the point that they have reached when they have made their fifth mistake. The words are unrelated and sometimes obscure, making the task an artificial one. *Word attack skills* can be assessed by observing how children cope with unfamiliar words.

② *Cloze (gap-fill) procedure*, such as the Macmillan Group Reading Test. Children are given paragraphs with a few missing words for them to fill in. The paragraphs and words become progressively more difficult. The task is more realistic than a word list and can be administered to a group.

③ *Diagnostic tests*, such as the Neale Analysis of Reading Ability. The child reads a set of graded passages aloud. The test provides information about accuracy, comprehension and speed. The test provides the means to analyse mistakes for deciding future strategies. Children must be fairly fluent readers to do this test.

Subskills of reading

① *Visual.* Children must learn to discriminate letter shapes. **Gibson** *et al.* (1962) asked children to identify a letter-like stimulus out of 12 transformations of the same shape. They found that children under 5 perceived the transformations as all being the same, whereas older children could detect the distinctive features – a skill necessary for reading. Since the children all had different visual experiences, the age difference appears to be related to maturational rather than experiential factors.

When learning to read the most common confusions arise between b, h and d, and m and w. This may because children take time to learn that letters, unlike other objects, are not the same when they are reversed.

❷ *Linguistic ability.* By the age of 5 their word idiosyncrasies are few and they have a reasonable understanding of grammar (see unit 5.4.1).

❸ *Auditory.* Children need to develop a sensitivity to sounds. **Bryant and Bradley** (1985) tested 400 pre-readers on their ability to categorise sounds, by asking them to detect the odd one out (e.g. bun, hut, gun). Four years later they tested reading ability and found high correlations between reading ability and earlier sound discrimination. They also found correlations between IQ and reading but these weren't as large, showing that sound sensitivity is an important factor.

Rhyming and alliteration train sound discrimination, as in children's nursery rhymes.

9.4.3 BEHAVIOUR MODIFICATION

Corrective strategies

The principles of behaviour modification (see unit 4.4.1) underlie the strategies that many teachers use.

❶ *Token economy* (see unit 4.4.1). **O'Leary and Becker** (1967) worked with a group of 9-year-old emotionally disturbed children for a year. Each student received a daily score for achieving certain target behaviours such as 'face the front' or 'desk clear'. These scores could be exchanged for small toys. The teachers gave additional reinforcement in the form of praise. Deviant behaviour was much reduced at the end of the year.

Evaluation
- Token systems take time to establish and present problems in selecting suitable reinforcers.
- **Kazdin and Bootzin** (1972) found that tokens were not effective for all students.

❷ *The Premack principle.* **Premack** (1965) suggested that a behaviour that occurs frequently should be used to reinforce less frequent behaviour. We often reward ourselves in this way, for example watching TV after doing two hours of homework. School children who have not behaved inappropriately (or behaved appropriately) might be allowed to engage in a reinforcing activity, such as painting. This is similar to a token economy but easier to organise.

❸ *Reinforcement.* **Michael** (1967) proposed seven principles which are critical if a teacher is to control behaviour through consequences:
- The consequences should be defined in terms of their effect on the learner. A student might draw up a *reinforcement menu* which lists all those activities which would be reinforcing.
- The effects of reinforcement should be automatic.
- Reinforcement should be closely related to terminal behaviour.
- Reinforcement should be consistent.
- Consequences should follow behaviour very closely.
- Reinforcement needs to be potent because a large amount is necessary for behavioural change.
- The learning situation should consist of clear steps each of which can be reinforced.

❹ *Punishment*
- *Physical punishment* contravenes current views on individual rights.
- *Verbal punishment.* Teachers most often have to discipline children for minor misdemeanours such as lateness or talking. Reprimands are commonly used. **Van Houten and Doleys** (1983) reviewed a number of studies and concluded that reprimands which identified the undesirable behaviour and elaborated on why it was wrong were more effective than reprimands which simply expressed disapproval. **Van**

Houten *et al.* (1982) found that reprimands delivered at a distance of 1 metre were more effective than those delivered from 7 metres. Close contact may permit reinforcement using non-verbal gestures.

Evaluation

- Some situations require immediate intervention and don't lend themselves to rational discussion. The punishment of specific behaviours can be highly informative.
- A punishing agent provides a model of aggressiveness and teaches the child that power assertion is the way to resolve disputes.

⑤ *Time-out methods* (see unit 4.4.1) stop inappropriate behaviours being reinforced through attention. The child may be asked to sit at the back of the class or outside the classroom.

⑥ *Reasoning* is an alternative to behavioural methods. **Walters and Grusec** (1977) argued that techniques which arouse empathy for others are more effective than reasoning which focuses on personal consequences. Younger children need more specific reasons for requests but past school age children become progressively more able to deal with abstract requests. **Hoffman** (see unit 6.3.1) found that an induction style of parenting was the most effective way to discipline children.

Evaluation. This approach enables children to learn empathy and prosocial behaviours which could not be taught through punishment.

Preventative strategies

① *Good interpersonal relations.* It helps to know everyone's names and to know key details about individual pupils. This reflects the amount that the teacher cares. Humour and 'with-it-ness' also help. **Kounin** (1970) watched videotapes of teachers and concluded that good classroom management was related to teachers being aware of what was going on in their classrooms, he called this 'with-it-ness'. **Copeland** (1987) called this teacher vigilance and attentiveness, and found that teachers high in this quality had pupils who remained on-task and were less disruptive (on-task behaviours include doing what the teacher says and getting on with work).

② *Setting rules.* It helps both teachers and students to know the limits. **Doyle** (1968) observed that successful classroom managers were the ones who spent time at the beginning of the year establishing procedures and routines. It helps if these rules are democratic.

③ *Legitimate praise.* Students respond best to praise when it is deserved. **Brophy** (1981) suggested that effective praise should not be too frequent, it should be contingent on specific behaviours, it should be credible and informative. It should not be random, nor be given for mere participation rather than quality of performance.

④ *The learning environment.* Desks can be arranged in a non-traditional manner and the teacher may decorate the room with posters and plants. Some schools have open plan classrooms which affects teaching styles and teacher–pupil interactions. **Whedall** *et al.* (1981) found that less able children performed more on-task behaviours when seated in rows. This wasn't true for the more able pupils.

9.5 PSYCHOLOGY AND THE ENVIRONMENT

9.5.1 ENVIRONMENTAL EFFECTS ON BEHAVIOUR

① *Noise* may be most stressful when unpredictable and uncontrollable.

- **Cohen** (1980) found that prolonged exposure to noise is correlated with increases in physical illnesses, higher mortality rates, mental illness and interpersonal conflict. This may be because more psychic energy is expended in the course of adapting.
- **Cohen** *et al.* (1973) tested children on auditory discrimination and reading ability. Those children living on the lower floor of high rise buildings (where the noise is greatest) performed less well than the children from the highest floors. They concluded that exposure to loud, unpredictable noise was responsible.
- **Glass** *et al.* (1969) found that participants made fewer errors on a clerical task when the background noise was predictable. **Gardner** (1978) replicated this study but didn't get the same results and thought this might be because participants had signed a consent agreement which also gave them a sense of control. When only half of the participants were given consent forms he demonstrated that it was control which cancelled out the effects of unpredictability.

② *Air pollution*, such as from car exhaust and cigarette smoke. **Rotton** *et al.* (1979) found that increased amounts of air pollution resulted in people feeling less happy. **Russell** *et al.* (see unit 9.3.4) found that passive smoking increases the likelihood of cancer in non-smokers.

③ *Climate and weather*

- *Hot weather.* **Cunningham** (1979) found that people are less likely to agree to be interviewed when the weather is hot. **Baron and Ransberger** (see unit 1.4.2) found a curvilinear relationship between heat and aggression (similar to the **Yerkes-Dodson** law, see unit 3.4.3). **Anderson and Anderson** (1984) found a positive correlation between aggressive crime and temperature over a two-year period. There was a marked increase above 88° F.
- *Ion levels* (atmospheric electricity), as associated with thunderstorms, are related to increases in suicides, industrial accidents and some types of crime. **Baron** *et al.* (1985) increased the levels of negative ions in a laboratory and found that type A individuals (see unit 3.4.3) behaved more aggressively, suggesting that the effect was to increase general activation levels. **Baron** (1987) found that negative ions had negative effects on certain cognitive activities, such as proof-reading, memory span and decision-making.
- *Seasonal affective disorder* (see unit 3.3.2) is a depressive illness associated with winter.

④ *Crowding and density.* Density is the objective or physical measure, crowding is the subjective or psychological response (crowd behaviour is different again, see unit 1.3.3).

- *Social pathology hypothesis.* **Calhoun** (1962) varied the population densities of rat communities and found that crowding led to pathological behaviour ('behavioural sink'). There was plenty of food and water, but presumably the lack of space led to stress. He found increased levels of aggression, physical illness, cannibalism and abnormal reproductive behaviours (hyperactive and hypersexual males, females who didn't build nests for young or nourish them, 95% of the young died before reaching maturity). This suggests an innate mechanism to prevent overpopulation. **Freedman** (1977) found a high correlation between symptoms of social pathology (such as admissions to mental hospitals) and urban density. However, a correlation doesn't mean that the link is causal, migration (see below) may explain why city dwellers are less psychologically healthy.
- *Density-intensity hypothesis.* Increased density leads to more sensory stimulation, physiological arousal and stress (see 'Arousal-aggression hypothesis', unit 1.4.2). The arousal may be attributed to something else, such as excitement as at a football match,

in which case crowding is not felt. **Worchel and Yohai** (1979) played a 'subliminal noise' (there was no noise) to five-person groups to test the effect on performance. When the groups sat closely together and were told that the noise would be stressful the participants did not feel as crowded as those who expected relaxing effects or sat spaced apart. They attributed the 'stress' to the sound rather than the density.

- *Interference*. If the crowd does not interfere with personal goals, a sense of crowding is diminished.
- *Cultural differences*. Asians in Hong Kong have lower levels of pathology than Westerners living less densely in, for example, Los Angeles.
- *Social versus spatial density*. **Baum and Valins** (1977) suggested that there is a difference between the number of people present in a constant space (social density) and a ratio of available space and number of people (spatial density). Social density causes more negative responses. **Baron** *et al.* (1976) found that where three people occupied the same size dormitory as two people (social density) they liked their room-mates less, felt less satisfied with living conditions, and did less well at college. **Ehrlich and Freedman** (1971) gave groups of people various games to play. The smaller the room, the more competitive the participants, indicating that spatial density also leads to aggression.

5 *Personal space* (proxemics) is a means of organising social behaviour to control density and crowding. There is a balance between too much contact, leading to stress and aggression, and too little contact, leading to a sense of isolation. **Hall** (1966) suggested that personal space can be divided into four zones:

- *Intimate* distance (0 to 0.5 m.) for close contact: lovers, family or fighting.
- *Personal* distance (0.5 to 1 m.) for everyday interactions between familiar people.
- *Social* distance (1 to 4m.) for impersonal transactions, as in business.
- *Public* distance (over 4 m.) for formal settings, such as addressing an audience.

These norms act as a channel for non-verbal communication. You communicate your relationship to others in terms of personal distance. Any intrusion is felt as a threat.

The degree of comfort or discomfort you feel varies with:

- *Personal characteristics* such as age, sex, culture, personality.
- *Characteristics of the other person* such as non-verbal behaviours, similarity, sex.
- *Interpersonal relations* such as status, degree of friendship, family and culture.
- *Situational factors* such as being inside or outside, size of room, task.

Middlemist *et al.* (1976) observed that men had more difficulty urinating in a public toilet when another user (confederate) stood in the next urinal, thus invading his personal space. **Storms and Thomas** (1977) interviewed participants from a distance of either 6 or 30 inches. If the interviewer behaved in an unfriendly fashion, the close contact situation was interpreted as invasion whereas when behaviour was friendly the participant evaluated the interviewer positively. **Felipe and Sommer** (1966) observed the reaction of students in a library. If a confederate invaded their personal space most of the students built some kind of physical barrier or signalled with body posture, some actually left and one asked for more space. There was little effect if the confederate sat at a normal distance (shoulder distance about 60 cm.).

6 *Territories*. **Altman** (1975) distinguished three other types of territory:

- *Primary* territories. Private places with a sense of ownership rather than something you use a lot, such as a named car parking space.
- *Secondary* territories. Available to many but not all people, established through regular use, moderate control can be exerted, such as the place where you sit in class which is a territory only available to your classmates.
- *Public* territories. Available to everyone, yours only while you use it, such as a telephone box.

Territories have social importance:

- Extension of your personal and group *identity*.
- Establishing and maintaining *privacy*. Lack of privacy leads to anxiety. Buildings are designed to protect this (see below).

- *Reducing aggression* through, for example, the 'owner wins' strategy (see units 2.1.1 and 2.1.2) and settled territories. **Sundstrom and Altman** (1974) studied the behaviour of delinquent boys in their institutional home. At first, the two most dominant boys controlled the most desirable areas; disruptive and aggressive behaviour was at a minimum. When these boys were transferred and replaced by two new members, fighting and disruptive behaviour increased dramatically until, after a few weeks, territories became re-established.
- *Reproduction*. Many people feel a need to have a home before they start a family.

  Territories can be defended using signs, such as furnishings in a room or a fence around a garden, or threatening behaviour. See also 'Defensible space', below.

7 *Urban living*. Cities are not only associated with higher levels of stress, but also with pathological behaviours such as crime and mental illness. Why?

- *Population size*. **Perry and Simpson** (1987) monitored the growth of Raleigh, North Carolina over a decade. They found that as the population increased, murder rates and rates for aggravated assault decreased whereas rape incidences increased. **Whyte** (1989) found that an individual is more likely to be the victim of a criminal offence in the parking lot of a suburban shopping mall than in the middle of a large city. This suggests that it is not the number of people which is important, but other features of the urban environment.
- *The physical environment*. Many inner city areas are derelict, have inadequate public services and are smelly, polluted, noisy and dirty. **Amato and McInnes** (1983) compared interpersonal behaviours (eye contact, smiling, speaking) in a shopping mall (pleasant and arousing) with a downtown construction site (unpleasant and arousing) and found that people were more friendly in the pleasant environment.
- *The psychological environment* such as multiracial problems, racial tensions, contrasts between rich and poor, overstimulation and crowding (see above).
- *Migration*. Young people move to the city seeking 'better lives', those city dwellers with adequate resources move out, leaving behind those who are aged or deprived. **Linsky and Straus** (1986) suggested that such movement entails the loss of stable interpersonal relationships and normative guidelines, which in turn leads to maladaptive social behaviour (see also 'Drift', unit 4.2.3).
- *Coping*. City dwellers learn to cope by filtering out irrelevant stimuli (ignoring the presence of others) and seeking oases (city parks)

8 *Architecture, urban planning and interior design* can minimise undesirable environmental effects.

- *Housing projects*. **Yancey** (1971) documented the breakdown of the Pruitt-Igoe housing project (see question number 5 in the question bank at the end of this chapter). **Newman** (1972) compared the Van Dyke project (14-storey buildings separated by open spaces, isolated stairwells) and the Brownsville project (6-storey X-shaped buildings with some 3-storey wings, entrances used by only a small number of families and anyone entering was overlooked by a number of windows). More maintenance jobs were required at the Van Dyke project and there was more crime. The data is correlational but Newman suggested that defensible spaces will foster positive attitudes: boundaries should be established both inside and outside the buildings and residents must be able to watch over these secondary territories.
- *Institutional environments*. **Baum and Valins** (1977) found that students in traditional dorms (long corridor with bedrooms, toilets and kitchens off it) felt crowded and lacking in privacy compared with students in suite-style dorms (a few bedrooms clustered round a central, communal area) which provide secondary, defensible spaces. Open-plan arrangements in, for example, nursing homes, encourage interaction but neglect the fact that residents need somewhere of their own. Football stadiums are equipped with seats to reduce aggression.
- *Urban environments*. The provision of open spaces and floral displays are means of making the environment more pleasant. It also helps to move traffic away from city centres to eliminate noise, dirt and pollution, and to vary the landscape with buildings of different shapes and textures.

- *Interior design.* The arrangement of furniture can communicate power (an official behind a desk) or co-operation (a round table for committee use). The decor of a room influences mood: the police conduct interrogations in a bare room, a man woos a woman in a candlelit restaurant; red is exciting and blue is leisurely. **Argyle** (1988) reported that children tested in blue, yellow, yellow-green and orange rooms scored 12 points more on an IQ test than those tested in white, black or brown rooms. **Kwallek and Lewis** (1990) found that participants made more proof-reading errors in a red office than in a white office.

9 *Environmental disaster.* Natural and man-made disasters have short- and long-term consequences (see 'Post traumatic stress syndrome', unit 4.3.3).

- *Natural disasters* such as hurricanes and earthquakes cause enormous personal and financial problems. They may be harder to cope with now, when people have come to expect more control over their lives.
- *Technical catastrophes* such as the accident at the Chernobyl nuclear power station or the Zebrugge ferry disaster. The problem of designing accident-free systems is a concern for psychologists (see unit 5.2.4). Increased levels of chlorofluorocarbons (CFCs) are thought to have caused holes in the earth's ozone layer, leading to global warming.
- *Toxic exposure*, such as to pollutants, radiation or the sun's rays.

Chapter roundup

9.1 Contemporary topics in psychology

9.1.1 *Substance use and abuse* can be understood in terms of physical and psychological dependence, individual differences in becoming abusers and in responding to treatment. Methods of prevention are important.

9.1.2 *Paranormal or psi-phenomena* include telepathy, clairvoyance, precognition and psychokinesis. These may be real or we can explain observed effects in terms of participant/experimenter bias, cognitive illusions and publication bias.

9.2 Psychology and organisations

9.2.1 Worker *motivation* may be due to intrinsic or extrinsic factors. Theories include reinforcement, job design, equity and goal-setting, plus organisational commitment. *Job satisfaction* is related to motivation, and can be considered in terms of causes, effects and theories (two-factor, vitamin, need-satisfaction, serial information processing).

9.2.2 *Personnel selection* proceeds through various stages: job analysis, finding, screening, and selecting a suitable worker.

9.3 Psychology and health

9.3.1 *Models of health* include the biomedical and biopsychosocial models.

9.3.2 The sensation of *pain* has physical and psychological elements. Explanations include specificity, pattern and gate control theories. Control may be achieved through chemical, physical, cognitive, insight, or behavioural methods as well as hypnosis.

9.3.3 *Psychological aspects of illness* include patient–practitioner relationships, an analysis of why patients do not comply with medical requests and the role of psychological factors in physical illness.

9.3.4 *Lifestyles* can be illness risks, such as smoking, alcohol, substance abuse, stress, diet, exercise, unhealthy living and social relations. Such behaviour can be explained through models of health behaviour (theories of reasoned action and health belief) and models of changing health behaviour (self-efficacy, appeals to fear, the Yale model and the spiral model).

9.4 Psychology and education

9.4.1 *Learning can be promoted* through learning styles (using tracking, programmed instruction, different learning styles, mastery learning or a personalised system of instruction) and teaching styles (teacher- versus pupil–centred education).

9.4.2 *Reading* is learned using phonic or whole word methods, and is related to visual, linguistic and auditory skills. Tests include word recognition, cloze procedure and diagnostic measures.

9.4.3 *Behaviour modification* may be achieved through corrective strategies, such as token economy, the Premack principle, reinforcement, punishment, time–out methods and reasoning, or preventative strategies, such as good interpersonal relations, setting rules, use of legitimate praise and designing the learning environment.

9.5   Psychology and the environment

9.5.1 *Behaviour is influenced by environmental factors* such as: noise, pollution, climate and weather, crowding and density, personal space, territory, urban living, architecture, urban planning, interior design and environmental disasters.

Illustrative question

Dr Feelgood

Did you know:

- breast cancer is one of the leading causes of cancer deaths and of all deaths among women. In Britain 1 in 12 and in America 1 in 10 women is likely to have breast cancer at some time in their lives, especially after the age of 50;
- in 1995 15,000 British women will have died of breast cancer;
- testicular cancer is the leading cause of cancer deaths and the second leading cause of all deaths among American men between the ages of 15 and 35;
- both breast and testicular cancer are effectively treated, and have very high cure rates if treated early;
- only a quarter or a third of individuals practice BSE or TSE.

Psychologists are interested in the role of health beliefs in people's practice and non-practice of health, illness and sick role behaviours such as BSE and TSE. What determines health-related behaviour?

(a) Describe models or theories of health behaviour. (8 marks)

    [*HINT: you could use the example above or one of your own choice to illustrate the models or theories.*]

(b) Evaluate these models or theories of health behaviour. (10 marks)

    [*HINT: you may wish to consider how much research evidence is gained by psychologists; whether the research evidence supports the models; whether the models have ecological validity; theoretical strengths and weaknesses of the models.*]

(c) Based on the evidence presented above, suggest a campaign aimed at promoting the practice of BSE and TSE. (6 marks)

(OCEAC A 1996)

Tutorial note

Marks are awarded for detail, accuracy and use of psychological terminology. You should try to convey your understanding of the material and, where possible to place your answer in a wider context, that is, to make generalisations and relate the research to other areas of psychology that you have studied.

    In part (a) you are given a hint about using examples as a means of *describing* theories of health behaviour, leave evaluation to the next part of the question. Use psychological terminology accurately and appropriately. In part (b) you should offer a balanced evaluation of these models, being both critically positive and negative. In part (c) you should demonstrate your ability by being able to apply the knowledge that you have in an effective manner.

Suggested answer

(a) If a health worker wanted to understand why so few individuals engaged in BSE or TSE they might refer to models of health behaviour. Such models explain the conditions under which people choose to engage in behaviour which promotes health.

One model is the Theory of Reasoned Action proposed by **Ajzen and Fishbein** (1980). They suggested that a behavioural intention is determined by (1) perceived facts and (2) social norms. BSE should occur when a woman knows that self-examination can reduce the risk of cancer and knows that breast cancer is a high risk (perceived facts). If the woman is also aware that BSE is commonly practised by her friends (social norms) then she should be encouraged to do it herself.

Another model is **Becker and Rosenstock**'s (1984) Health Belief Model. They proposed that a person's behaviour can be predicted from three groups of sociocognitive factors. A sociocognitive factor is a combination social influences and the way a person thinks about something (cognitive).

The three factors are perceived threats, perceived costs/benefits and personal variables. The threat (cognitive) comes from an evaluation of the seriousness of the disease and your own susceptibility. In the case of breast cancer, a woman should be aware of how possible it is to treat the disease and how often it is fatal. She might consider all the factors which make it more likely that she could get breast cancer, such as having close relatives who got it and not having breastfed. Seriousness and susceptibility interact with 'cues to action'. These are things like programmes on the TV, a visit to the doctor or knowledge of a friend who got breast cancer.

The second factor is an evaluation of the benefits versus the barriers. A perceived benefit might be early detection of breast cancer, and a barrier could be forgetting to do it or the anxiety which it arouses. If a person practises BSE they may detect cancer and therefore, in the short term, it might be preferable to avoid it.

The final factor is social, a younger woman or one from a lower socioeconomic class or one whose personal inclination is to ignore problems (personality) will be less likely to act.

Taken together all these factors influence the likelihood that the woman will act, i.e. examine her breasts regularly.

(b) Both models suggest that there is a direct link between actions and behaviour, however empirical studies have found a lack of association. For example, **DeFleur and Westie** (1958) asked students whether they would be photographed with Black colleagues. When they were later asked to have a photograph taken, 30% behaved differently from the attitude they had expressed. **Bagozzi** (1981) showed that, when people said they would give blood, they didn't always do it when later given the opportunity. The people who were most likely to be consistent were those who had previously given blood. Nevertheless there was some relationship between attitudes and behaviour, people who said they wouldn't, didn't.

A different model, the spiral model of behavioural change described by **Prochaska et al.** (1992), described health behaviour in terms of behaviour as well as cognitions. In this model a person starts unaware of the problem, awareness leads to thinking about doing something, followed by preparation for action, action and then maintenance. It is a spiral model in that people are usually not successful at the first attempt so they have to repeat these steps several times, each time getting further towards action and maintenance.

A further criticism of both theories is that they assume that people behave rationally, whereas there is good evidence that they don't, and that people don't think about things in a detailed manner. Much of the time we function on a kind of autopilot. **Langer et al.** (1978) showed that people happily complied to requests from a stooge to jump a photocopier queue even if the stooge supplied no reason.

Both models also ignore the person's past experience. Bagozzi's study showed that previous behaviour can be a significant factor.

On the positive side, both models suggest that beliefs influence health behaviour and this is clearly true.

The health belief model has been useful in designing questionnaires and generating research. **Stillman** (1977) designed a scale of perceived benefits/barriers and susceptibility to breast cancer, and found significant correlations between the scale and the practice of BSE. **Calnan** (1984) found that the sociocognitive factors were among the best predictors of whether women would attend a class on BSE or a clinic offering mammography.

This model also has useful predictions for altering behaviour. For example it suggests that health campaigns should concentrate on perceived costs.

(c) I would suggest that a campaign to increase BSE and TSE should concentrate on:

1 Facts – communicating the facts of cancer to people especially those in target age ranges. This would include information on the likely outcomes of the disease, the benefits of taking preventative measures, and the effectiveness of preventative measures and/or methods of treatment.

2 Helping people make a realistic assessment of their susceptibility. **Weinstein** (1982) showed that people tend to be optimistic about the likelihood that they will suffer from chronic illnesses; they think that other people are more likely to get the disease.

3 Provide cues to action, such as posters and, if there is sufficient money, TV advertisements. It might help to encourage people to discuss breast cancer with their friends to arouse social norms.

4 Offer suggestions about overcoming possible barriers, such as forgetting to do the breast examination or the anxiety that might be felt.

Question bank

Allow 25–30 minutes for NEAB module questions, 35–40 minutes for NEAB end-of-course papers and 50–55 minutes for OCEAC ones.

Contemporary topics in psychology

1 (a) Discuss, with reference to empirical studies, **two** explanations offered by psychologists as to why people engage in substance abuse. (10 marks).
 (b) Using **one** example of substance abuse, compare the effectiveness of any **two** treatments used by psychologists. (10 marks)

(NEAB module 3 Spring 1995)

Points: Ensure that you follow the rubric of the question: give two explanations, one example and two treatments. If you provide more than this you will not gain extra credit and will waste valuable examination time. If you present less than required, you lose marks – even weak knowledge will be worth some credit. Ensure that you use empirical support and critically evaluate these plus any arguments you present.

Psychology and organisations

2 (a) Explain what is meant by work motivation. (4 marks)
 (b) Describe **one** empirical study in which motivation in a work setting has been investigated. (6 marks)
 (c) Jim is a trainee solicitor preparing to take his final examinations in a few weeks time. He admits that he has lost interest in his course and cannot seem to motivate himself. What advice would you give Jim in order to increase his motivation?

Justify your answer with reference to theory and research in psychology. (10 marks)

(d) Discuss approaches used by psychologists to measure job satisfaction. (10 marks)

(NEAB paper 2 1996)

Points: In part (a) your definition should refer specifically to work. In part (b) you could describe Mayo's study (see the 'Hawthorne effect', unit 8.2.1). In part (c), for full marks, you should refer to at least two theories and relate your answer to the problem cited.

Psychology and health

3 Vivienne has regular, and very painful, headaches. She has consulted her GP who has referred her to a pain management clinic. The clinic has decided on a treatment programme based upon the application of the *gate control theory* of pain management.

(a) Outline the main features of the gate control theory of pain. (4 marks)

(b) (i) Describe a treatment based upon gate control theory that the clinic might suggest to help Vivienne manage her headaches. (2 marks)

(ii) Explain how the treatment you described might be justified in terms of the gate control theory. (2 marks)

(c) Discuss **three** factors which may affect the extent to which people may comply with medical advice. Support your answer by reference to appropriate empirical evidence. (12 marks)

(NEAB module 8 Summer 1995)

Points: Use the mark scheme to guide you in the length and depth of answer required in each part. In part (a) you should outline the theory and relate it to the perception of pain. In part (c) ensure you do include three and only three factors and that you cite empirical evidence.

Psychology and education

4 (a) What is meant by *promoting effective learning*? (6 marks)

(b) Explain how teachers may plan and prepare for effective learning. (10 marks)

(c) Discuss the difficulties that teachers have when they attempt to promote effective learning. (14 marks)

(NEAB paper 2 Summer 1996)

Points: In part (a) use examples to support your explanation. In part (b) a good answer will describe two/three methods in detail or four/five methods in less depth. In part (c) you might cover three difficulties in depth or a good array in less detail.

Psychology and the environment

5 *Pruitt-Wigan?*

The Pruitt-Igoe project was built in inner city in St. Louis, United States, in 1954. In this project 12,000 persons were relocated into 43 buildings 11-storeys high, containing 2,762 apartments. The design was praised. However, within a few years it was a shambles; broken glass, tin cans and abandoned cars covered the playground and car parks. Some buildings had broken windows, others were boarded up. Inside was the smell and stench of urine, trash and garbage. The elevator was in disrepair. Plumbing and electrical fixtures had been pulled out of the apartment and hallway walls. Residents reported that they had no friends; that gangs had formed and rape, vandalism and robbery were common. By 1970, 27 of the 43 buildings were vacant. Soon afterwards it was totally demolished. (Bell, P.A. *et al.*, *Environmental Psychology*, pp. 350–1 (Harcourt Brace Jovanovich, 1990))

Architectural designs such as the Pruitt-Igoe project read like 'how-not-to' guides for designing public housing. Many design changes have been made since then and forty years later new designs are being proposed. The following headline is from the *Wigan Reporter*, Friday 17 February 1995:

Housing estate lay-out fights crime

A new housing estate will soon be built incorporating a clever layout of paths and roads engineered specifically to try to combat crime. Police believe that the pioneering crime-beating 91-home design is a strong candidate for the national 'Secured by design' architectural award.

(a) Describe psychological studies on architecture and housing design. (8 marks) [*HINT: you could base your answer on reasons for the failure of the Pruitt-Igoe project.*]

(b) Evaluate psychological evidence on architecture and housing design. (10 marks) [*HINT: you may wish to consider comparing social with physical explanations; the ethics of urban renewal; comparing theories of gentrification; how psychologists gained their evidence (e.g. the 'single variable' versus the 'urban/rural' approach).*]

(c) Based on your knowledge of public architecture and housing design, suggest what features the Wigan housing estate is likely to include to make it a potential award winner. (6 marks)

(OCEAC A 1996)

Points: In part (a) your studies should be accurately described and placed in the wider context. In part (b) you should use a number of criteria, which are wide-ranging and detailed. You should make generalisations and mention strengths and weaknesses. In part (c) marks are available for the application of a wide range of effective ideas.

TEST RUN

In this section:

Test Your Knowledge Quiz

Test Your Knowledge Quiz Answers

Progress Analysis

Mock Exam

Mock Exam Suggested Answers

■ This section should be tackled towards the end of your revision programme, when you have covered all your syllabus topics, and attempted the practice questions at the end of the relevant chapters.

■ The Test Your Knowledge Quiz contains short-answer questions on a wide range of syllabus topics. You should attempt it without reference to the text.

■ Check your answers against the Test Your Knowledge Quiz Answers. If you are not sure why you got an answer wrong, go back to the relevant unit in the text: you will find the reference next to our answer.

■ Enter your marks in the Progress Analysis chart. The notes below will suggest a further revision strategy, based on your performance in the quiz. Only when you have done the extra work suggested should you go on to the final test.

■ The Mock Exam is set out like real exam papers. These contain a wide spread of topics and question styles, as used by the examination boards. You should attempt the papers under examination conditions, in the time allowed, and without reference to the text.

■ Compare your answers to our Mock Exam Suggested Answers. We have provided tutorial notes to each question showing what must be included for a good answer, and pitfalls to avoid.

TEST YOUR KNOWLEDGE QUIZ

For each sentence below, write down the appropriate psychological terms, concept, theory or name. *Only answer the units which you have studied.*

1.1.1   A theory which describes how your self-image is determined by the various social groups you belong to.

1.1.2   People tend to overemphasise dispositional rather than situational factors.

1.1.3   An explanation which suggests that prejudice arises from direct competition between groups over scarce and valued resources.

1.1.4   A method proposed to foster mutual interdependence in the classroom.

1.2.1   The theory that interpersonal relationships are based on costs and rewards.

1.2.2   The theory that the same factors which led to initial attraction in interpersonal relationships also lead to its breakdown.

1.2.3   Relationships which are governed largely by equality of affect rather than exchange.

1.2.4   The term, related to self-development, for seeing ourselves as others see us.

1.3.1   The loss of social inhibitions through anonymity.

1.3.2   The theory that leadership effectiveness is related to the favourability of the situation for the leader.

1.3.3   Well learned, simple motor tasks.

1.4.1   The presence of others leads to a decreased likelihood of help being offered.

1.4.2   The theory that learning occurs through both direct and indirect reinforcement.

1.4.3   Watching television is harmful because it prevents children engaging in other activities.

1.4.4   The observer who recorded aggressive behaviour among the tribes of New Guinea.

2.1.1   The evolutionary force by which one individual is favoured over another.

2.1.2   The distribution of individuals when all individuals are free to use a resource.

2.1.3   The evolution of marking patterns based on universal indicators of poisonous prey.

2.2.1   The theory that sexual displays are universal indicators of genetic resistance to disease.

2.2.2   The theory that males are likely to care for young when they cannot be sure that the offspring are theirs.

2.2.3   The system where one female mates with many males.

2.2.4   The conflict of interest in mammalian parents and young over when to stop feeding milk.

2.3.1   Reproductive success as measured by the success of close genetic relatives rather than individual success.

2.3.2   A model which describes behaviour in terms of a balance between costs and benefits.

2.3.3   A period when an individual is optimally receptive to acquiring certain behaviours.

2.3.4   A signalling display originating in conflicting motivations such as approach-avoidance.

2.4.1   The occurrence of a conditioned response to a stimulus which is similar to the original stimulus.

2.4.2   A substance found in some animals which may help in direction finding using magnetic information.

2.4.3   The researcher who trained and enculturated Kanzi and Panbanisha.

2.4.4   Humans may negatively imprint on intimate associates during a critical period of early childhood.

3.1.1   The part of the brain which integrates ANS activity.

3.1.2   A state of dynamic equilibrium.

3.1.3   The junction between nerve cells.

3.1.4   When the brain is unable to resynthesise transmitter substances fast enough, the opposite effect is felt.

3.2.1   Removing large portions of the brain to discover the effect on behaviour.

3.2.2   The area of the brain associated with speaking and understanding.

3.2.3   The theory which suggests that there are three pairs of colour receptors, each working in opposition.

3.3.1   The characteristic activity of the aroused brain.

3.3.2   The area of the brain thought to generate circadian rhythms.

3.3.3   The type of sleep during which individuals experience increased eye movement and heart rate but also body paralysis.

3.3.4   A theory which explains hypnosis as the result of consciousness being divided into separate streams.

3.4.1   The theory that fulfilling needs is reinforcing and leads to learning.

3.4.2   The hormone most closely associated with emotional experiences.

3.4.3   The model which describes the internal processes following prolonged stress.

3.4.4   The class of drugs used to relieve stress.

4.1.1   The label given to cases of retardation where no clear cause exists and is assumed to be due to a combination of innately low intelligence plus an environmental deficit.

4.1.2   The condition which results from brain cell death in the motor cortex.

4.1.3   A diet free of additives which aims to alleviate the symptoms of ADHD.

4.1.3   A form of autism where the child's intellect remains normal or even superior.

4.2.1   The diagnosis scheme used in Great Britain.

4.2.2   The model of abnormal behaviour which suggests that such behaviour is due to organic states.

4.2.2   Rogers' concept of the key to a successful client–patient relationship.

4.2.3   A form of schizophrenia due to an acute stress reaction from the pressures of disadvantaged social living conditions.

4.3.1   The model which suggests that mental illness is the result of an interaction between biological and environmental factors.

4.3.2   The theory that affective disorder may be due to fluctuations in serotonin and noradrenalin.

4.3.3   The suggestion that we have an innate predisposition to develop certain fears.

4.3.4   The condition characterised by compulsive eating and purging.

4.4.1   A form of therapy where a patient learns deep relaxation and constructs a hierarchy of increasingly threatening situations.

4.4.1   Patients tend to exaggerate their unhappiness at the beginning of therapy and do the reverse at the end.

4.4.2   A legal verdict which makes no judgement about the sanity of the defendant but may result in imprisonment in a mental hospital.

5.1.1   Stimulus patterns which are produced as we move around the environment.

5.1.2   The researchers who designed the visual cliff experiment.

5.1.3   The tendency to perceive things on the basis of prior expectation.

5.2.1   The model of selective attention that all information receives a limited amount of processing before selection takes place.

5.2.2   The theory of divided attention that there are separate processors responsible for different tasks, each with individual capacities.

5.2.3   Processes which do not require attention and are difficult to modify once learned.

5.2.4	Examples of attentional failure due to absent-mindedness.
5.3.1	Participants in memory experiments recall words from the beginning and end of a list better.
5.3.2	Knowledge about personal events and people.
5.3.3	The model of memory which allows for spreading activation and negative links.
5.3.4	Forgetting caused by a failure of availability and competing information.
5.4.1	The hypothetical innate device which enables all humans to acquire language.
5.4.2	A model which combines top-down and bottom-up processes in the comprehension of speech.
5.4.3	A heuristic problem-solving method proposed by Newell and Simon which creates subgoals as a method of reducing the problem space.
5.4.4	The hypothesis that language affects thinking.
6.1.1	The principle that an infant needs one primary attachment figure.
6.1.2	A project aimed at giving preschool children enrichment so they can start school on equal terms with other children.
6.1.3	The researcher who studied the Ganda tribe of Uganda.
6.2.1	The process by which new schema are modified to fit new situations or information.
6.2.1	The distance between a child's current and potential abilities.
6.2.2	The child will only acquire knowledge when they are biologically mature.
6.2.3	Children from low socioeconomic groups use a limited form of language which lacks, for example, abstract concepts.
6.3.1	A style of parenting which involves explaining why a behaviour is wrong and how it affects others.
6.3.1	That part of the personality which rewards you when you behave in accordance with parental moral values.
6.3.2	A condition where genetic males develop as females due to an insensitivity to testosterone.
6.3.3	The self which is concerned with social roles.
6.4.1	The stage of identity crisis where decisions about identity are put on hold.
6.4.2	Erikson's crisis of middle age.
6.4.3	The theory that psychological well-being in old age is promoted by a gradual withdrawal from personal contacts.
6.4.4	The most stressful life event.
7.1.1	The view that private, mental events may exist but are not needed in the explanation of behaviour.
7.1.2	The view that our behaviour is determined by external forces.
7.1.2	Explaining all behaviour using information-processing concepts.
7.2.1	A means by which a psychometric test can be shown to measure what it claims to measure using external factors.
7.2.2	The theory that there is a limit to certainty because of imperfect measuring instruments and the influence of the observer.
7.2.3	A technique or theory which is rooted in the researcher's own culture and used to study other cultures.
7.3.1	Seeking approval from the general public about the ethics of a piece of research prior to an experiment.
7.3.2	Imputing human feelings to animals.
7.3.3	Research which has direct social consequences.
8.1.1	Research where the effect of a deliberate change in one variable is observed on another.

8.1.2   A correlation which is not linear.

8.2.1   Selecting participants because they are available.

8.2.1   Those features of an experimental setting which invite a participant to behave in certain ways.

8.3.1   The distance between the highest and lowest value in a group of scores.

8.3.2   Organising original interview material in relation to specific original research questions or themes.

9.1.1   The body increasingly adapts to chemical substances with repeated use.

9.1.2   A forced-choice technique used to investigate paranormal phenomena where a person is placed in isolation and tries to name a picture being observed by someone else.

9.2.1   A group of theories which suggest that worker motivation can be improved by reorganising the tasks that have to be done.

9.2.1   Herzberg suggested that satisfaction comes from motivators. What leads to dissatisfaction?

9.2.2   The systematic study of tasks involved in, and the qualities needed to perform, a job.

9.3.1   The micro-level of the biopsychosocial approach.

9.3.2   The theory that there is a separate system for detecting and registering pain.

9.3.3   The kind of doctor–patient relationship where the doctor regards him/herself as the expert and expects the patient to follow advice willingly.

9.3.4   The theory that health behaviour can be predicted by a combination of perceived facts and social norms.

9.3.4   The concept that belief in your own competence will influence the effort you put into changing your behaviour.

9.4.1   A form of programmed instruction where the learner who makes an error is sent to a sequence of remedial frames to help them understand, and then returned to the main program.

9.4.1   A style of learning/teaching which emphasises learning speed rather than ability.

9.4.2   A method of testing reading where the pupil is given paragraphs with missing words to be filled in.

9.4.3   A form of behaviour modification where a person is given a reward in the form of a preferred activity to reinforce less frequent or non-preferred behaviour.

9.5.1   Territories which are available to everyone and yours only while you use it.

TEST YOUR KNOWLEDGE QUIZ ANSWERS

1.1.1 Social identity theory.

1.1.2 Fundamental attribution error.

1.1.3 Realistic conflict theory.

1.1.4 Jigsaw method.

1.2.1 Social exchange theory.

1.2.2 Fatal attraction theory.

1.2.3 Communal relationships.

1.2.4 The looking-glass self.

1.3.1 Deindividuation.

1.3.2 Contingency theory.

1.3.3 Dominant responses.

1.4.1 The bystander effect.

1.4.2 Social learning theory.

1.4.3 Displacement effect.

1.4.4 Mead.

2.1.1 Selective pressure.

2.1.2 Ideal free distribution.

2.1.3 Mullerian mimicry.

2.2.1 Handicapping theory.

2.2.2 Paternity certainty hypothesis.

2.2.3 Polynandry.

2.2.4 Weaning conflict.

2.3.1 Inclusive fitness.

2.3.2 Optimality model.

2.3.3 Sensitive period.

2.3.4 Displacement activity.

2.4.1 Generalisation.

2.4.2 Magnetite.

2.4.3 Savage-Rumbaugh.

2.4.4 Westermarck effect.

3.1.1 Hypothalamus.

3.1.2 Homeostasis.

3.1.3 Synapse.

3.1.4 Rebound effect.

3.2.1 Ablation.

3.2.2 Broca's area.

3.2.3 Opponent-process theory.

3.3.1 Beta waves.

3.3.2 Suprachiasmatic nucleus (SCN).

3.3.3 Rapid eye movement (REM).

3.3.4 Neo-dissociation theory.

3.4.1 Drive-reduction theory.

3.4.2 Adrenalin.

3.4.3 General adaptation syndrome (GAS).

3.4.4 Anxiolytic drugs, e.g. Valium.

4.1.1 Cultural-familial retardation.

4.1.2 Cerebral palsy.

4.1.3 Feingold diet.

4.1.3 Asperger's syndrome.

4.2.1 ICD-10.

4.2.2 The medical model.

4.2.2 Unconditional positive regard.

4.2.3 West Indian psychosis.

4.3.1 Diathesis-stress model.

4.3.2 Permissive amine theory of mood disorder.

4.3.3 Biological preparedness.

4.3.4 Bulimia nervosa.

4.4.1 Systematic desensitisation (SD).

4.4.1 The hello–goodbye effect.

4.4.2 Guilty but mentally ill (GBMI) verdict.

5.1.1 Optic flow patterns.

5.1.2 Gibson and Walk.

5.1.3 Perceptual set.

5.2.1 Late selection model.

5.2.2 Modular theory.

5.2.3 Automatic processes.

5.2.4 Action slips.

5.3.1 Serial position effect.

5.3.2 Episodic memory.

5.3.3 Interconnected semantic network.

5.3.4 Interference.

5.4.1 Language acquisition device or system (LAD or LAS).

5.4.2 The Cohort model.

5.4.3 Means–end analysis.

5.4.4 Linguistic relativity hypothesis.

6.1.1 Monotropy.

6.1.2 Operation Head Start or Milwaukee Project.

6.1.3 Ainsworth.

6.2.1 Accommodation.

6.2.1 Zone of proximal development (ZPD)

6.2.2 Readiness.

6.2.3 Restricted code.

6.3.1 Induction.

6.3.1 Ego ideal.

6.3.2 Testicular feminising syndrome.

6.3.3 The categorical self.

6.4.1 Identity moratorium.

6.4.2 Generativity versus stagnation.

6.4.3 Social disengagement theory.

6.4.4 Death of a spouse.

7.1.1 Radical behaviourism.

7.1.2 Environmental determinism.

7.1.2 Machine reductionism.

7.2.1 Construct or criterion validity.

7.2.2 Heisenberg's uncertainty principle.

7.2.3 Imposed etic.

7.3.1 Presumptive consent.

7.3.2 Anthropomorphism.

7.3.3 Socially sensitive research.

8.1.1 An experiment.

8.1.2 A curvilinear relationship.

8.2.1 An opportunity or accidental sample.

8.2.1 Demand characteristics.

8.3.1 Range.

8.3.2 Thematic analysis.

9.1.1 Tolerance.

9.1.2 The Ganzfeld technique.

9.2.1 Job design theories.

9.2.1 Hygienes.

9.2.2 Job analysis.

9.3.1 Body chemicals.

9.3.2 Specificity theory.

9.3.3 Guidance–co-operation.

9.3.4 Reasoned action theory.

9.3.4 Self-efficacy.

9.4.1 Branching programs.

9.4.1 Mastery learning.

9.4.2 Cloze procedure.

9.4.3 The Premack principle.

9.5.1 Public territories.

PROGRESS ANALYSIS

Place a tick next to those questions you got right, and a cross next to those which were wrong. Leave unanswered questions blank.

Question ✓	Question ✓	Question ✓	Question ✓	Question ✓	Question ✓	Question ✓	Question ✓
1.1.1	2.1.1	3.1.1	4.1.1	5.1.1	6.1.1	7.1.1	9.1.1
1.1.2	2.1.2	3.1.2	4.1.2	5.1.2	6.1.2	7.1.2	9.1.2
1.1.3	2.1.3	3.1.3	4.1.3	5.1.3	6.1.3	7.1.2	9.2.1
1.1.4	2.2.1	3.1.4	4.1.3	5.2.1	6.2.1	7.2.1	9.2.1
1.2.1	2.2.2	3.2.1	4.2.1	5.2.2	6.2.1	7.2.2	9.2.2
1.2.2	2.2.3	3.2.2	4.2.2	5.2.3	6.2.2	7.2.3	9.3.1
1.2.3	2.2.4	3.2.3	4.2.2	5.2.4	6.2.3	7.3.1	9.3.2
1.2.4	2.3.1	3.3.1	4.2.3	5.3.1	6.3.1	7.3.2	9.3.2
1.3.1	2.3.2	3.3.2	4.3.1	5.3.2	6.3.1	7.3.3	9.3.4
1.3.2	2.3.3	3.3.3	4.3.2	5.3.3	6.3.2	8.1.1	9.3.4
1.3.3	2.3.4	3.3.4	4.3.3	5.3.4	6.3.3	8.1.2	9.4.1
1.4.1	2.4.1	3.4.1	4.3.4	5.4.1	6.4.1	8.2.1	9.4.1
1.4.2	2.4.2	3.4.2	4.4.1	5.4.2	6.4.2	8.2.1	9.4.2
1.4.3	2.4.3	3.4.3	4.4.1	5.4.3	6.4.3	8.3.1	9.4.3
1.4.4	2.4.4	3.4.4	4.4.2	5.4.4	6.4.4	8.3.2	9.5.1

My total mark is: _____ (A) out of _____ (B). This is _____ % (A/B × 100).

If you scored 1–25%

You need to do some more work. The Mock Exam is intended as a test of exam technique. It will be wasted if your basic syllabus coverage is insufficient. Make a realistic assessment of your understanding of each chapter. This will give you a further revision plan to work from. You will need to attempt the Test Your Knowledge Quiz one more time before you are ready to go on to the Mock Exam.

If you scored 26–50%

You need to do a little more work. The Mock Exam is intended as a test of exam technique. It will not be really useful until you have filled in the gaps in your knowledge. If you have time, go through the unit list at the beginning of each chapter and revise all those that look unfamiliar. If you don't think you have time to do this, look through the questions at the end of each chapter, and the notes on points to include. You should then attempt the Test Your Knowledge Quiz again.

If you scored 51–75%

You are just about ready to attempt the Mock Exam. First, however, you should look through the questions at the end of each chapter, and the notes on points to include. This will be a good guide to which syllabus areas are still unfamiliar. If you do not think you have time to do this, go over those chapters whose reference is given in the Quiz answers for the questions you got wrong. You should then be ready to go on to the Mock Exam.

If you scored 76–100%

Congratulations. You have sufficient grasp of the syllabus topics to get real value out of attempting the Mock Exam under exam conditions. First, however, you should go back to the specific chapter referred to in the Test Your Knowledge Quiz answers for each question you got wrong. Reassure yourself that there is no real gap in your knowledge.

If you are following the terminal route:

Paper 2: do modules 4 and 5.

Time allowed: 3 hours. Answer **four** questions from at least three sections.

Paper 3: do modules 6 and 7.

Time allowed: 3 hours. Answer **one** question from the first three sections and all the questions from last section.

Otherwise choose the appropriate modules below.

MODULE 4

Time allowed: 1¹/₂ hours. Answer **one** question from each section.

Section A: social psychology

1 Describe and evaluate psychological insights into the origins of prejudice. (AEB A 1993)

2 Describe and evaluate **two** theories of interpersonal relationships. (AEB module 4 Spring 1997)

3 Discuss some of the problems involved in the experimental study of conformity and/or obedience. (AEB AS 1994)

4 Describe and evaluate recommendations for the reduction of aggressive behaviour derived from social psychological research. (AEB A 1996)

Section B: comparative psychology

5 (a) Consider **two** ways in which non-human animals compete for resources.

(12 marks)

(b) Critically assess how animals might benefit from these forms of competition. (AEB module 4 Spring 1997)

(12 marks)

6 (a) Consider the nature of parent–offspring conflict. (12 marks)

(b) Assess the implications of this conflict. (AEB module 4 Spring 1997) (12 marks)

7 Discuss imprinting in non-human animals. (AEB A 1996)

8 Describe attempts to teach 'language' to non-human animals and consider the extent to which these attempts have been successful. (AEB A 1992)

MODULE 5

Time allowed: 1¹/₂ hours. Answer **one** question from each section.

Section A: bio-psychology

1 Describe and evaluate research into the effects of any **two** drugs on behaviour. (AEB module 5 Spring 1997)

2 'There is no question that the study of specialisation of function of the two cerebral hemispheres is one of the most productive and important lines of research in neuropsychology.'

Discuss this statement in relation to split brain studies. (AEB module 5 specimen)

3 Discuss the extent to which psychological research has been useful in furthering our understanding of sleep states. (AEB AS 1992)

4 Consider the influence of learning **and** experience on stress. (AEB A 1996)

Section B: atypical development and abnormal behaviour

5   Describe and evaluate research into any **two** emotional and behavioural problems in childhood (e.g. attention-deficit hyperactivity disorder; autism; developmental dyslexia). (AEB module 5 Spring 1997)

6   (a) Describe any **one** system of classification used in the diagnosis of abnormal behaviour.   (12 marks)
     (b) From a psychological viewpoint, assess some of the problems in classifying abnormal behaviour. (AEB module 5 specimen)   (12 marks)

7   A mother, describing the effect on the family of having a schizophrenic son, said, 'It's as though we were hit by lightning'.
     (a) Describe **two** possible consequences for the family of having a son suffering from schizophrenia.   (6 marks)
     (b) Discuss research which has shown how family and other environmental factors may contribute to the onset of schizophrenic breakdown. Support your answer with reference to theory and empirical evidence. (NEAB module PS04 Summer 1996)   (14 marks)

8   'The improvement claimed by psychotherapists after treatment (is) no more or less extensive than that found without any treatment at all ... Considerable improvement occurs ... simply with the passage of time' (H.J. Eysenck, 1957). Discuss. (AEB A 1993)

MODULE 6

Time allowed: 1½ hours. Answer **one** question from each section.

Section A: cognitive psychology

1   (a) Outline **two** differences between *bottom-up* and *top-down* models of perception.   (6 marks)
     (b) Discuss **two** explanations cognitive psychologists have given for perceptual illusions. (NEAB module PS07 Summer 1996)   (14 marks)

2   Describe and evaluate research related to divided attention.

3   Use psychological evidence to discuss explanations of forgetting in humans. (AEB A 1991)

4   Compare and contrast theories of language. (AEB A 1990)

Section B: developmental psychology

5   Describe and evaluate research into factors which influence the development of attachments in humans during their first few years of life. (AEB AS 1996)

6   (a) Describe any **one** theory of cognitive development.   (12 marks)
     (b) Analyse applications of this theory to education. (AEB specimen module 6)
                                                                                       (12 marks)

7   Critically consider the view that the self **develops** as a result of socialisation processes. (AEB A 1993)

8   Describe and critically evaluate any **one** theory of personality change in adulthood (for example, Erikson or Levinson). (AEB module 6 Spring 1997)

MODULE 7

Time allowed: 1½ hours

Answer one question from **Section A**. Answer **all** the questions from **Section B**.

Section A: perspectives

1   Describe and evaluate the contributions of either the psychoanalytic approach or the behaviourist approach to the understanding of behaviour. (AEB A 1993)

2 Discuss applications of psychometric tests including the controversies surrounding their use. (AEB module 7 Spring 1997)

3 Use evidence to discuss ethical problems in psychological research. (AEB A 1988)

Section B: research methods in psychology

4 (a) Explain the phrase a *correlational study*. (2 marks)
  (b) Describe **two** different kinds of correlation. (2 marks)
  (c) Describe a situation where the use of the correlational technique would be appropriate and explain why. (4 marks)
  (d) State **two** disadvantages of using the correlational·technique. (4 marks)

5 A student designed a laboratory experiment which used repeated measures design to investigate whether words presented together with a pictorial image are better remembered than words presented without a pictorial image. Forty words – 20 for each experimental condition – were each printed onto cards. Words were matched for their frequency of occurrence and were all five-letter nouns. Words were [5] presented to an opportunity sample of participants. In condition **A**, words were presented without a pictorial image, and in condition **B** with a pictorial image. The presentation of the sets of cards was counterbalanced. Data were analysed using the Wilcoxon Matched Pairs Signed Ranks Test. The student concluded that the null hypothesis could be rejected ($p<0.05$). However, in discussing the results the [10] student expressed concern about the ecological validity of the experiment.
  (a) Explain the purpose of counterbalancing in this experiment (line 8). (2 marks)
  (b) Explain how the presentation of the card sets could have been counterbalanced in this experiment. (2 marks)
  (c) Name **one** alternative experimental design that could have been used for this experiment and suggest **one** disadvantage of this alternative design. (2 marks)
  (d) Explain the sentence 'The student concluded that the null hypothesis could be rejected ($p<0.05$)' (line 10). (2 marks)
  (e) Suggest **two** reasons why the Wilcoxon Matched Pairs Signed Ranks Test was considered to be an appropriate test to analyse the data obtained. (2 marks)
  (f) Explain the term *ecological validity* (line 11). (2 marks)
  (g) Identify **one** reason why the student might have expressed concern about the ecological validity of this experiment. (AEB module 8 Spring 1997) (1 mark)

MOCK EXAM SUGGESTED ANSWERS

MODULE 4

Section A: social psychology

1 'Insights' are perceptions which increase understanding. Therefore you might include psychologically informed theories and/or studies in your answer. Ensure that you stick with *origins* and do not include ideas on how to reduce prejudice except if you use this material specifically to evaluate any theory.

2 You should attempt this question only if you are sufficiently familiar with *two* appropriate theories, otherwise you immediately lose many of the marks. You might use other theories as a means of evaluating the two main theories. Your theories might be relevant to any aspect of relationships: formation, maintenance or breakdown.

3 Note that the question specifically asks you to discuss the *problems* which occur when studying conformity and/or obedience *experimentally*. *Descriptions* of such experiments will count for a very limited number of marks.

4   This question focuses exclusively on the *reduction* of aggression and on *social psychological* research. This means that any material related to the causes of aggression will be irrelevant unless it is specifically tied to a recommendation about reduction. Any research which is not social psychological will receive no credit unless it is used specifically to evaluate the social psychological recommendations made.

Section B: comparative psychology

5   Part (a) is skill A only. You should describe two methods of competition for resources. Reserve your evaluation for part (b) and do this in terms of the benefits offered to the animals from the methods described in part (a). Make sure you attempt to describe **two** methods, otherwise you will immediately lose half the marks for the question.

6   This question is again divided into skill A (description) and skill B (evaluation) in parts (a) and (b) of the question respectively. In the first part you should describe the various ways that parent–offspring conflict occurs. You might take the 'depth' route and describe one or two ways but in considerable detail, using examples. Or take the 'breadth' route and cover more but in less detail. In the second part, evaluation must be achieved through looking at the implications of the conflict for both parent and offspring.

7   Note that the question concerns *non-human* animals, and therefore material on human imprinting will not be relevant. A good answer might look at examples of imprinting, different types of imprinting, the claims made for imprinting, the functional significance of imprinting and the consequences of misdirected imprinting. Your essay should be well balanced, providing arguments for and against the material offered.

8   The question first asks for straightforward descriptions of efforts to teach 'language' to non-human animals. You might try to consider a variety of different animals and techniques. When considering the successfulness of these attempts you should try to establish a working definition of 'language' and consider the extent to which non-human animals have demonstrated this. Offer both positive and negative critical arguments.

MODULE 5

Section A: biopsychology

1   Remember that the term 'research' covers both theory and empirical evidence. You must limit yourself to *two* drugs (not classes of drugs) which would be best selected for being as different as possible. Describe what is known about the effects of the drugs and offer critical considerations of any theories or studies.

2   When a quotation appears in any question you must be sure to address it specifically in your answer. The statement here refers to lateralisation and localisation, which should be described and evaluated with reference to *split-brain* studies. You could evaluate these studies by considering research with patients who don't have split-brains (do these support the conclusions of split-brain studies?) and criticisms of experimental work.

3   The question allows you to describe both theories and empirical research related to sleep states. Your evaluation can be in terms of the extent to which such research adequately explains sleep, and could include methodological or ethical criticisms.

4   Many candidates will use this question to present a prepared essay on stress. This should be adapted to the special features of the question, that is, to consider how both *learning* and *experience* contribute to stress. You can also include methods of coping with stress, and you might try to differentiate between learning and experience.

Section B: atypical development and abnormal behaviour

5   'Research' includes theories and empirical studies. These can be described and/or used for evaluation. Critical consideration can be made of methodology, ethics and the usefulness of the theories. You must present *two* problems which are related to childhood, otherwise you lose half of the marks for the question. Nothing is gained, and time is wasted, by describing more than this unless the problems are specifically used as a means of evaluation. You do not have to use the examples given.

6   Part (a) is skill A only, a description of DSM or ICD. This should be fairly detailed and might include information about the overall objectives and methodology. All evaluation should be left to part (b) which specifically asks for a psychologically informed assessment of the *problems* of classifying abnormal behaviour (skill B). A good answer will consider the issues of reliability and validity in the context of classification (not, for example, psychometric testing). There are other issues, such as labelling, the treatment resulting from classification and ethical considerations.

7   In part (a) you should describe *two* consequences for the *family*. Your comments should be detailed and reflect an accurate understanding of schizophrenia. In part (b) you must use empirical evidence and theory to describe and evaluate the influence of environmental factors. Other explanations of schizophrenia can be used as a means of evaluation.

8   The main issue presented by the quotation is about the effectiveness of treatment and the possibility of spontaneous remission. Answers which discuss treatments will be largely irrelevant. A good answer should specifically address the quotation and display familiarity with psychological concepts and research. It should be well balanced, using arguments for and against the statement made by Eysenck.

MODULE 6

Section A: cognitive psychology

1   In part (a) you should describe *two* (only) differences between the named models of perception. A good response would name the differences and explain how this is so. In part (b) you should present description and evaluation of psychological explanations of perceptual illusions. You can take the 'depth' route and present only a few but give these in considerable detail, with examples and critical consideration of experimental methods and theoretical relevance. The 'breadth' route might consider more explanations and a range of different kinds of illusion.

2   The question specifically refers to divided attention, therefore selective attention will be of only minimal relevance by way of comparison. Research can include empirical evidence and theories, which should both be described and used to evaluate each other. Any research can also be evaluated in terms of methodology. Your answer should contain a good balance of description and evaluation.

3   Material on memory will be of minimal relevance. Your answer should contain accurate descriptions of psychological studies which help to explain forgetting. These can be evaluated in terms of the theories they generate and methodological criticisms.

4   A theory of language could be any account which explains an aspect of language. It is most likely that you will select theories which account for the acquisition of language since these offer good scope for comparing and contrasting. You could alternatively consider theories on the relationship between language and thought. You should offer descriptions of your chosen theories and then suggest in what ways they are similar and different. You might do this in series or in parallel.

Section B: developmental psychology

5 This question is not about maternal deprivation, although this will form part of your discussion. The focus of the essay should be on the various elements which influence early attachment. Your answer should describe such factors and evaluate them using empirical evidence and theories.

6 In part (a) you should select only *one* theory and limit yourself strictly to a *description* of the theory. This description should be detailed and accurate, examples may help to amplify your outline. Do not simply present an 'ages and stages' account of development but include other elements such as the structure of the intellect. Evaluation in part (b) is in terms of the application of this theory to education. You can consider education in its widest sense, including parents and toy manufacture.

7 You should only attempt this question if you are familiar with theories of self-development and not use material from other units which has only marginal relevance. The essay should describe how the self develops through social processes and evaluate this using empirical evidence and other, contrasting accounts of self-development.

8 You should select one theory, which does not have to be the same as the examples given and describe this theory in detail. The critical evaluation can be achieved using empirical evidence and other, alternative accounts of adulthood. Note that the question refers specifically to *personality change* and therefore reference to other changes might be only of minimal value in terms of evaluation.

MODULE 7

Section A: perspectives

1 You must focus on the *contributions* of your chosen approach, rather than describing the approach itself. Your answer should therefore describe any contributions and evaluate the value of these using empirical evidence. Ideally you should cover a number of contributions in some detail, though you may take a breadth or depth route. You certainly should mention more than one contribution.

2 The question is directed at the applications of psychometric tests. In order to discuss this you might, for example, briefly describe such tests, consider in more detail how such tests are used, outline issues related to test design, and evaluate their use by considering alternatives to testing. The question specifically requests that you also critically assess the *controversies* surrounding their use as a means of evaluating psychometric tests.

3 The question is a general one related to ethics, with no restrictions about non-human animal material. You should describe and evaluate any ethical problems, including issues of responsibility, but must use evidence to support your arguments. You might consider a few problems in some depth or a greater number of problems more superficially.

Section B: research methods in psychology

4 Use the mark scheme to guide you in the depth of response required. Check that you have included all you know as it is easy to overlook key information.

5 Ensure that you give an answer for each question, even if you are uncertain. Never give two answers in the hope that the examiner will credit the correct one. Read the stimulus passage carefully.

INDEX